Shahrazad relating a story to the Sultan

THE HARVARD CLASSICS
EDITED BY CHARLES W ELIOT LLD

STORIES FROM THE THOUSAND AND ONE NIGHTS
(THE ARABIAN NIGHTS' ENTERTAINMENTS)

TRANSLATED BY
EDWARD WILLIAM LANE

REVISED BY
STANLEY LANE-POOLE

WITH INTRODUCTION AND NOTES

VOLUME 16

P F COLLIER & SON COMPANY
NEW YORK

Designed, Printed, and Bound at
The Collier Press, New York

CONTENTS

1

2 **CONTENTS**

INTRODUCTORY NOTE

"THE THOUSAND AND ONE NIGHTS" *is one of the great story-books of the world. It was introduced to European readers by the French scholar Galland, who discovered the Arabic original and translated it into French in the first decade of the eighteenth century; but its earlier history is still involved in obscurity. There existed as early as the tenth century of our era a Persian collection of a thousand tales, enclosed in a framework which is practically the one used in the present collection, telling of a King who was in the habit of killing his wives after the first night, and who was led to abandon this practise by the cleverness of the Wezir's daughter, who nightly told him a tale which she left unfinished at dawn, so that his curiosity led him to spare her till the tale should be completed. Whether more than the framework of the Arabian collection was borrowed from this Persian work is uncertain. The tales in the collection of Galland and in more complete editions discovered since his time are chiefly Persian, Indian, and Arabian in source, and in ultimate origin come from all the ends of the earth. No two manuscripts have precisely the same contents, and some of the most famous of the tales here printed are probably not properly to be regarded as belonging to the collection, but owe their association with the others to their having been included by Galland. Thus "'Ali Baba and the Forty Thieves" is found in no Oriental version of the "Nights," and "'Ala-ed-Din and the Wonderful Lamp" was long supposed to be in the same situation, though within recent years it has turned up in two manuscripts.*

Both the place and the date of the original compilation are still matters of dispute among scholars. From such evidences as the detailed nature of the references to Cairo and the prevailing Mohammedan background, Lane argued that it must have been put together in Egypt; but this opinion is by no means universally accepted. As to date, estimates vary by several centuries. Burton, who believed in a strong Persian element, thought that some of the oldest tales, such as that of "Sindibad," might be as old as the eighth century of our era; some thirteen he dated tenth century, and the latest in the sixteenth. There is a fair amount of agreement on the thirteenth century as the date of arrangement in the

3

*present framework, though they were probably not committed to
writing till some two centuries later.*

*Of a collection of fables, fairy-stories, and anecdotes of his-
torical personages such as this, there can, of course, be no question of a single author. Both before and after they were placed
in the mouth of Shahrazad, they were handed down by oral recitation, the usual form of story-telling among the Arabs. As in
the case of our own popular ballads, whatever marks of individual
authorship any one story may originally have borne, would be
obliterated in the course of generations of tradition by word of
mouth. Of the personality of an original editor or compiler, even,
we have no trace. Long after writing had to some extent fixed
their forms, the oral repetition went on; and some of them could
be heard in Mohammedan countries almost down to our own
times.*

*In the two hundred years of their currency in the West, the
stories of the "Nights" have engrafted themselves upon European
culture. They have made the fairy-land of the Oriental imagination and the mode of life of the medieval Arab, his manners and
his morals, familiar to young and old; and allusions to their inci-
dents and personages are wrought into the language and literature
of all the modern civilized peoples. Their mark is found upon
music and painting as well as on letters and the common speech,
as is witnessed by such diverse results of their inspiration as the
music of Rimsky-Korsakoff, the illustrations of Parrish, and
the marvelous idealization of their background and atmosphere
in Tennyson's "Recollections of the Arabian Nights," "Barmecide
Feast," "Open Sesame," "Old Lamps for New," "Solomon's
Seal," "The Old Man of the Sea," "The Slave of the Lamp,"
"The Valley of Diamonds," "The Roc's Egg," Haroun al-Raschid
and his "Garden of Delight,"—these and many more phrases and
allusions of every-day occurrence suggest how pervasive has been
the influence of this wonder-book of the mysterious East.*

*The translation by E. W. Lane used here has been the stand-
ard English version for general reading for eighty years. The
translations of "'Ali Baba" and "'Ala-ed-Din" are by S. Lane-
Poole and for permission to use the latter we are indebted to
Messrs. G. P. Putnam's Sons.*

INTRODUCTION

In the name of God, the Compassionate, the Merciful.

PRAISE be to God, the Beneficent King, the Creator of the universe, who hath raised the heavens without pillars, and spread out the earth as a bed; and blessing and peace be on the lord of apostles, our lord and our master Mohammad, and his Family; blessing and peace, enduring and constant, unto the day of judgment.

To proceed:—The lives of former generations are a lesson to posterity; that a man may review the remarkable events which have happened to others, and be admonished; and may consider the history of people of preceding ages, and of all that hath befallen them, and be restrained. Extolled be the perfection of Him who hath thus ordained the history of former generations to be a lesson to those which follow. Such are the Tales of a Thousand and One Nights, with their romantic stories and their fables.

It is related (but God alone is all-knowing, as well as all-wise, and almighty, and all-bountiful), that there was, in ancient times, a King of the countries of India and China, possessing numerous troops, and guards, and servants, and domestic dependents; and he had two sons; one of whom was a man of mature age; and the other, a youth. Both of these princes were brave horsemen; but especially the elder, who inherited the kingdom of his father, and governed his subjects with such justice that the inhabitants of his country and whole empire loved him. He was called King Shahriyar: his younger brother was named Shah-Zeman,[1] and was King of Samarkand. The administration of their governments was conducted with rectitude, each of them ruling over his subjects with justice during a period of twenty years with the utmost enjoyment and happiness. After this

[1] [Shahriyar, "Friend of the City;" Shah-Zeman, "King of the Age."]

5

period, the elder King felt a strong desire to see his brother, and ordered his Wezir[2] to repair to him and bring him.

Having taken the advice of the Wezir on this subject, he immediately gave orders to prepare handsome presents, such as horses adorned with gold and costly jewels, and memluks,[3] and beautiful virgins, and expensive stuffs. He then wrote a letter to his brother, expressive of his great desire to see him; and having sealed it, and given it to the Wezir, together with the presents above mentioned, he ordered the minister to strain his nerves, and tuck up his skirts, and use all expedition in returning. The Wezir answered, without delay, I hear and obey; and forthwith prepared for the journey: he packed his baggage, removed the burdens, and made ready all his provisions within three days; and on the fourth day, he took leave of the King Shahriyar, and went forth towards the deserts and wastes. He proceeded night and day; and each of the kings under the authority of King Shahriyar by whose residence he passed came forth to meet him, with costly presents, and gifts of gold and silver, and entertained him three days; after which, on the fourth day, he accompanied him one day's journey, and took leave of him. Thus he continued on his way until he drew near to the city of Samarkand, when he sent forward a messenger to inform King Shah-Zeman of his approach. The messenger entered the city, inquired the way to the palace, and, introducing himself to the King, kissed the ground before him, and acquainted him with the approach of his brother's Wezir; upon which Shah-Zeman ordered the chief officers of his court, and the great men of his kingdom, to go forth a day's journey to meet him; and they did so; and when they met him, they welcomed him, and walked by his stirrups until they returned to the city. The Wezir then presented himself before the King Shah-Zeman, greeted him with a prayer for the divine assistance in his favour, kissed the ground before him, and informed him of his brother's desire to see him; after which he handed to him the letter. The King took it, read it, and understood its contents; and answered by expressing his readiness to obey the commands of his brother. But, said he (addressing the Wezir), I will not go until I have entertained thee three days. Accordingly, he lodged him in a

---

[2] [In Persian and Turkish, Vezir; popular, Vizier.]
[3] Male white slaves.

palace befitting his rank, accommodated his troops in tents, and appointed them all things requisite in the way of food and drink: and so they remained three days. On the fourth day, he equipped himself for the journey, made ready his baggage, and collected together costly presents suitable to his brother's dignity.

These preparations being completed, he sent forth his tents and camels and mules and servants and guards, appointed his Wezir to be governor of the country during his absence, and set out towards his brother's dominions. At midnight, however, he remembered that he had left in his palace an article which he should have brought with him; and having returned to the palace to fetch it, he there beheld his wife sleeping in his bed, and attended by a male negro slave, who had fallen asleep by her side.

On beholding this scene, the world became black before his eyes; and he said within himself, If this is the case when I have not departed from the city, what will be the conduct of this vile woman while I am sojourning with my brother? He then drew his sword, and slew them both in the bed: after which he immediately returned, gave orders for departure, and journeyed to his brother's capital.

Shahriyar, rejoicing at the tidings of his approach, went forth to meet him, saluted him, and welcomed him with the utmost delight. He then ordered that the city should be decorated on the occasion, and sat down to entertain his brother with cheerful conversation: but the mind of King Shah-Zeman was distracted by reflections upon the conduct of his wife; excessive grief took possession of him; and his countenance became sallow; and his frame emaciated. His brother observed his altered condition, and, imagining that it was occasioned by his absence from his dominions, abstained from troubling him or asking respecting the cause, until after the lapse of some days, when at length he said to him, O my brother, I perceive that thy body is emaciated, and thy countenance is become sallow. He answered, O brother, I have an internal sore:—and he informed him not of the conduct of his wife which he had witnessed. Shahriyar then said, I wish that thou wouldest go out with me on a hunting excursion; perhaps thy mind might so be diverted:—but he declined; and Shahriyar went alone to the chase.

Now there were some windows in the King's palace commanding a view of his garden; and while his brother was looking out from one of these, a door of the palace was opened, and there came forth from it twenty females and twenty male black slaves; and the King's wife, who was distinguished by extraordinary beauty and elegance, accompanied them to a fountain, where they all disrobed themselves, and sat down together. The King's wife then called out, O Mes'ud! and immediately a black slave came to her, and embraced her; she doing the like. So also did the other slaves and the women; and all of them continued revelling together until the close of the day. When Shah-Zeman beheld this spectacle, he said within himself, By Allah! my affliction is lighter than this! His vexation and grief were alleviated, and he no longer abstained from sufficient food and drink.

When his brother returned from his excursion, and they had saluted each other, and King Shahriyar observed his brother Shah-Zeman, that his colour had returned, that his face had recovered the flush of health, and that he ate with appetite, after his late abstinence, he was surprised, and said, O my brother, when I saw thee last, thy countenance was sallow, and now thy colour hath returned to thee: acquaint me with thy state.—As to the change of my natural complexion, answered Shah-Zeman, I will inform thee of its cause; but excuse my explaining to thee the return of my colour.—First, said Shahriyar, relate to me the cause of the change of thy proper complexion, and of thy weakness: let me hear it.—Know then, O my brother, he answered, that when thou sentest thy Wezir to me to invite me to thy presence, I prepared myself for the journey, and when I had gone forth from the city, I remembered that I had left behind me the jewel that I have given thee; I therefore returned to my palace for it, and there I found my wife sleeping in my bed, and attended by a black male slave; and I killed them both, and came to thee: but my mind was occupied by reflections upon this affair, and this was the cause of the change of my complexion, and of my weakness: now, as to the return of my colour, excuse my informing thee of its cause.—But when his brother heard these words, he said, I conjure thee by Allah that thou acquaint me with the cause of the return of thy colour:— so he repeated to him all that he had seen. I would see this, said

Shahriyar, with my own eye.—Then, said Shah-Zeman, give out that thou art going again to the chase, and conceal thyself here with me, and thou shalt witness this conduct, and obtain ocular proof of it.

Shahriyar, upon this, immediately announced that it was his intention to make another excursion. The troops went out of the city with the tents, and the King followed them; and after he had reposed awhile in the camp, he said to his servants, Let no one come in to me:—and he disguised himself, and returned to his brother in the palace, and sat in one of the windows overlooking the garden; and when he had been there a short time, the women and their mistress entered the garden with the black slaves, and did as his brother had described, continuing so until the hour of the afternoon-prayer.

When King Shahriyar beheld this occurrence, reason fled from his head, and he said to his brother, Shah-Zeman, Arise, and let us travel whither we please, and renounce the regal state, until we see whether such a calamity as this have befallen any other person like unto us; and if not, our death will be preferable to our life. His brother agreed to his proposal, and they went out from a private door of the palace, and journeyed continually, days and nights, until they arrived at a tree in the midst of a meadow, by a spring of water, on the shore of the sea. They drank of this spring, and sat down to rest; and when the day had a little advanced, the sea became troubled before them, and there arose from it a black pillar, ascending towards the sky, and approaching the meadow. Struck with fear at the sight, they climbed up into the tree, which was lofty; and thence they gazed to see what this might be: and behold, it was a Jinni[4] of gigantic stature, broad-fronted and bulky, bearing on his head a chest.

---

[4] Sing. of Jinn (Genii), being created of fire. The species of Jinn is said to have been created some thousands of years before Adam. According to a tradition from the Prophet, this species consists of five orders or classes; namely, Jann (who are the least powerful of all), Jinn, Sheytans (or Devils), 'Efrits, and Marids. The last, it is added, are the most powerful; and the Jann are transformed Jinn; like as certain apes and swine were transformed men. The terms Jinn and Jann, however, are generally used indiscriminately, as names of the whole species (including the other orders above mentioned), whether good or bad; the former term is the more common. [Iblis is Satan, their King.] " Sheytan " is commonly used to signify any evil Jinn. An 'Efrit is a powerful evil Jinni: a Marid, an evil Jinni of the most powerful class. The Jinn (but generally speaking, evil ones) are called by the Persians Divs; the most powerful evil Jinn, Narahs (which signifies " males," though they are said to be males and females); the good Jinn, Peris, though this term is commonly applied to females.

He landed, and came to the tree into which the two Kings had climbed, and, having seated himself beneath it, opened the chest, and took out of it another box, which he also opened; and there came forth from it a young woman, fair and beautiful, like the shining sun. When the Jinni cast his eyes upon her, he said, O lady of noble race, whom I carried off on thy wedding-night, I have a desire to sleep a little: and he placed his head upon her knee, and slept. The damsel then raised her head towards the tree, and saw there the two Kings; upon which she removed the head of the Jinni from her knee, and, having placed it on the ground, stood under the tree, and made signs to the two Kings, as though she would say, Come down, and fear not this 'Efrit. They answered her, We conjure thee by Allah that thou excuse us in this matter. But she said, I conjure you by the same that ye come down; and if ye do not, I will rouse this 'Efrit, and he shall put you to a cruel death. So, being afraid, they came down to her; and, after they had remained with her as long as she required, she took from her pocket a purse, and drew out from this a string, upon which were ninety-eight seal-rings; and she said to them, Know ye what are these? They answered, We know not.—The owners of these rings, said she, have, all of them, been admitted to converse with me, like as ye have, unknown to this foolish 'Efrit; therefore, give me your two rings, ye brothers. So they gave her their two rings from their fingers; and then she said to them, This 'Efrit carried me off on my wedding-night, and put me in the box, and placed the box in the chest, and affixed to the chest seven locks, and deposited me, thus imprisoned, in the bottom of the roaring sea, beneath the dashing waves; not knowing that, when one of our sex desires to accomplish any object, nothing can prevent her. In accordance with this, says one of the poets:

Never trust in women; nor rely upon their vows;
For their pleasure and displeasure depend upon their passions.
They offer a false affection; for perfidy lurks within their clothing.
By the tale of Yusuf be admonished, and guard against their
    stratagems.
Dost thou not consider that Iblis ejected Adam by means of
    woman?

And another poet says:—

Abstain from censure; for it will strengthen the censured, and
  increase desire into violent passion.
If I suffer such passion, my case is but the same as that of many a
  man before me:
For greatly indeed to be wondered at is he who hath kept himself
  safe from women's artifice.

When the two Kings heard these words from her lips they
were struck with the utmost astonishment, and said, one to
the other, If this is an 'Efrit, and a greater calamity hath happened unto him than that which hath befallen us, this is a circumstance that should console us:—and immediately they departed, and returned to the city.

As soon as they had entered the palace, Shahriyar caused his
wife to be beheaded, and in like manner the women and black
slaves; and thenceforth he made it his regular custom, every
time that he took a virgin to his bed, to kill her at the expiration of the night. Thus he continued to do during a period of
three years; and the people raised an outcry against him, and
fled with their daughters, and there remained not a virgin in
the city of a sufficient age for marriage. Such was the case
when the King ordered the Wezir to bring him a virgin according to his custom; and the Wezir went forth and searched, and
found none; and he went back to his house enraged and vexed,
fearing what the King might do to him.

Now the Wezir had two daughters; the elder of whom was
named Shahrazad; and the younger, Dunyzad. The former had
read various books of histories, and the lives of preceding kings,
and stories of past generations: it is asserted that she had collected together a thousand books of histories, relating to preceding generations and kings, and works of the poets: and she
said to her father on this occasion, Why do I see thee thus
changed, and oppressed with solicitude and sorrows? It has
been said by one of the poets:—

Tell him who is oppressed with anxiety, that anxiety will not last:
As happiness passeth away, so passeth away anxiety.

When the Wezir heard these words from his daughter, he related to her all that had happened to him with regard to
the King: upon which she said, By Allah, O my father, give me
in marriage to this King: either I shall die, and be a ransom

for one of the daughters of the Muslims, or I shall live, and
be the cause of their deliverance from him. I conjure thee
by Allah, exclaimed he, that thou expose not thyself to such
peril:—but she said, It must be so. Then, said he, I fear for
thee that the same will befall thee that happened in the case
of the Ass and the Bull and the husbandman.—And what, she
asked, was that, O my father?

Know, O my daughter, said the Wezir, that there was a certain
merchant, who possessed wealth and cattle, and had a wife
and children; and God, whose name be exalted, had also endowed him with the knowledge of the languages of beasts and
birds. The abode of this merchant was in the country; and
he had, in his house, an ass and a bull. When the bull came
to the place where the ass was tied, he found it swept and
sprinkled; in his manger were sifted barley and sifted cut
straw, and the ass was lying at his ease; his master being
accustomed only to ride him occasionally, when business required,
and soon to return: and it happened, one day, that the merchant
overheard the bull saying to the ass, May thy food benefit thee!
I am oppressed with fatigue, while thou art enjoying repose:
thou eatest sifted barley, and men serve thee; and it is only
occasionally that thy master rides thee, and returns; while I am
continually employed in ploughing, and turning the mill.—The
ass answered, When thou goest out to the field, and they place
the yoke upon thy neck, lie down, and do not rise again, even
if they beat thee; or, if thou rise, lie down a second time; and
when they take thee back, and place the beans before thee, eat
them not, as though thou wert sick: abstain from eating and
drinking a day or two days, or three; and so shalt thou find
rest from trouble and labour.—Accordingly, when the driver
came to the bull with his fodder, he ate scarcely any of it; and
on the morrow, when the driver came again to take him to
plough, he found him apparently quite infirm: so the merchant
said, Take the ass, and make him draw the plough in his stead
all the day. The man did so; and when the ass returned at
the close of the day, the bull thanked him for the favour he had
conferred upon him by relieving him of his trouble on that
day; but the ass returned him no answer, for he repented most
grievously. On the next day, the ploughman came again, and
took the ass, and ploughed with him till evening; and the ass

returned with his neck flayed by the yoke, and reduced to an extreme state of weakness; and the bull looked upon him, and thanked and praised him. The ass exclaimed, I was living at ease, and nought but my meddling hath injured me! Then said he to the bull, Know that I am one who would give thee good advice: I heard our master say, If the bull rise not from his place, take him to the butcher, that he may kill him, and make a nat'⁵ of his skin:—I am therefore in fear for thee, and so I have given thee advice; and peace be on thee!—When the bull heard these words of the ass, he thanked him, and said, To-morrow I will go with alacrity:—so he ate the whole of his fodder, and even licked the manger.—Their master, meanwhile, was listening to their conversation.

On the following morning, the merchant and his wife went to the bull's crib, and sat down there; and the driver came, and took out the bull; and when the bull saw his master, he shook his tail, and showed his alacrity by sounds and actions, bounding about in such a manner that the merchant laughed until he fell backwards. His wife, in surprise, asked him, At what dost thou laugh? He answered, At a thing that I have heard and seen; but I cannot reveal it; for if I did, I should die. She said, Thou must inform me of the cause of thy laughter, even if thou die.—I cannot reveal it, said he: the fear of death prevents me.—Thou laughedst only at *me,* she said; and she ceased not to urge and importune him until he was quite overcome and distracted. So he called together his children, and sent for the Kadi and witnesses, that he might make his will, and reveal the secret to her, and die: for he loved her excessively, since she was the daughter of his paternal uncle, and the mother of his children, and he had lived with her to the age of a hundred and twenty years. Having assembled her family and his neighbours, he related to them his story, and told them that as soon as he revealed his secret he must die; upon which every one present said to her, We conjure thee by Allah that thou give up this affair, and let not thy husband, and the father of thy children, die. But she said, I will not desist until he tell me, though he die for it. So they ceased to solicit her; and the merchant left them, and went to the

---

⁵ Nat': a large round piece of leather which, spread upon the ground, serves as a table for dinner, etc.

stable to perform the ablution, and then to return, and tell them the secret, and die.

Now he had a cock, with fifty hens under him, and he had also a dog; and he heard the dog call to the cock, and reproach him, saying, Art thou happy when our master is going to die? The cock asked, How so?—and the dog related to him the story; upon which the cock exclaimed, By Allah! our master has little sense: *I* have *fifty* wives; and I please this, and provoke that; while *he* has but one *one* wife, and cannot manage this affair with her: why does he not take some twigs of the mulberry-tree, and enter her chamber, and beat her until she dies or repents? She would never, after that, ask him a question respecting anything. —And when the merchant heard the words of the cock, as he addressed the dog, he recovered his reason, and made up his mind to beat her.—Now, said the Wezir to his daughter Shahrazad, perhaps I may do to thee as the merchant did to his wife. She asked, And what did he? He answered, He entered her chamber after he had cut off some twigs of the mulberry-tree, and hidden them there; and then said to her, Come into the chamber, that I may tell thee the secret while no one sees me, and then die:—and when she had entered, he locked the chamber-door upon her, and beat her until she became almost senseless and cried out, I repent:—and she kissed his hands and his feet, and repented, and went out with him; and all the company, and her own family, rejoiced; and they lived together in the happiest manner until death.

When the Wezir's daughter heard the words of her father, she said to him, It must be as I have requested. So he arrayed her, and went to the King Shahriyar. Now she had given directions to her younger sister saying to her, When I have gone to the King, I will send to request thee to come; and when thou comest to me, and seest a convenient time, do thou say to me, O my sister, relate to me some strange story to beguile our waking hour:—and I will relate to thee a story that shall, if it be the will of God, be the means of procuring deliverance.

Her father, the Wezir, then took her to the King, who, when he saw him, was rejoiced, and said, Hast thou brought me what I desired? He answered Yes. When the King, therefore, introduced himself to her, she wept; and he said to her, What aileth thee? She answered, O King, I have a young sister, and

I wish to take leave of her. So the King sent to her; and she came to her sister, and embraced her, and sat near the foot of the bed; and after she had waited for a proper opportunity, she said, By Allah! O my sister, relate to us a story to beguile the waking hour of our night. Most willingly, answered Shahrazad, if this virtuous King permit me. And the King, hearing these words, and being restless, was pleased with the idea of listening to the story; and thus, on the first night of the thousand and one, Shahrazad commenced her recitations.

STORIES FROM
THE THOUSAND AND ONE
NIGHTS

[*Nights 1—3*]

THE STORY OF THE MERCHANT AND THE JINNI

IT has been related to me, O happy King, said Shahrazad,
that there was a certain merchant who had great wealth,
and traded extensively with surrounding countries; and
one day he mounted his horse, and journeyed to a neighbouring country to collect what was due to him, and, the heat
oppressing him, he sat under a tree, in a garden, and put
his hand into his saddle-bag, and ate a morsel of bread and
a date which were among his provisions. Having eaten the
date, he threw aside the stone, and immediately there appeared before him an 'Efrit, of enormous height, who, holding a drawn sword in his hand, approached him, and said,
Rise, that I may kill thee, as thou hast killed my son. The
merchant asked him, How have I killed thy son? He answered, When thou atest the date, and threwest aside the
stone, it struck my son upon the chest, and, as fate had
decreed against him, he instantly died.

The merchant, on hearing these words, exclaimed, Verily
to God we belong, and verily to Him we must return! There
is no strength nor power but in God, the High, the Great!
If I killed him, I did it not intentionally, but without knowing it; and I trust in thee that thou wilt pardon me.—The
Jinni answered, Thy death is indispensable, as thou hast
killed my son:—and so saying, he dragged him, and threw
him on the ground, and raised his arm to strike him with the
sword. The merchant, upon this, wept bitterly, and said to

17

the Jinni, I commit my affair unto God, for no one can
avoid what He hath decreed:—and he continued his lamentation, repeating the following verses:—

Time consists of two days; this, bright; and that, gloomy; and life,
  of two moieties; this, safe; and that, fearful.
Say to him who hath taunted us on account of misfortunes, Doth
  fortune oppose any but the eminent?
Dost thou observe that corpses float upon the sea, while the
  precious pearls remain in its furthest depths?
When the hands of time play with us, misfortune is imparted to us
  by its protracted kiss.
In the heaven are stars that cannot be numbered; but none is
  eclipsed save the sun and the moon.
How many green and dry trees are on the earth; but none is
  assailed with stones save that which beareth fruit!
Thou thoughtest well of the days when they went well with thee,
  and fearedst not the evil that destiny was bringing.

—When he had finished reciting these verses, the Jinni said
to him, Spare thy words, for thy death is unavoidable.

Then said the merchant, Know, O 'Efrit, that I have debts
to pay, and I have much property, and children, and a wife,
and I have pledges also in my possession: let me, therefore,
go back to my house, and give to every one his due, and
then I will return to thee: I bind myself by a vow and
covenant that I will return to thee, and thou shalt do what
thou wilt; and God is witness of what I say.—Upon this, the
Jinni accepted his covenant, and liberated him; granting him
a respite until the expiration of the year.

The merchant, therefore, returned to his town, accomplished all that was upon his mind to do, paid every one
what he owed him, and informed his wife and children of
the event which had befallen him; upon hearing which, they
and all his family and women wept. He appointed a
guardian over his children, and remained with his family
until the end of the year; when he took his grave-clothes
under his arm, bade farewell to his household and neighbours, and all his relations, and went forth, in spite of
himself; his family raising cries of lamentation, and
shrieking.

He proceeded until he arrived at the garden before mentioned; and it was the first day of the new year; and as he

sat, weeping for the calamity which he expected soon to befall him, a sheykh, advanced in years, approached him, leading a gazelle with a chain attached to its neck. This sheykh saluted the merchant, wishing him a long life, and said to him, What is the reason of thy sitting alone in this place, seeing that it is a resort of the Jinn? The merchant therefore informed him of what had befallen him with the 'Efrit, and of the cause of his sitting there; at which the sheykh, the owner of the gazelle, was astonished, and said, By Allah, O my brother, thy faithfulness is great, and thy story is wonderful! if it were engraved upon the intellect, it would be a lesson to him who would be admonished!— And he sat down by his side, and said, By Allah, O my brother, I will not quit this place until I see what will happen unto thee with this 'Efrit. So he sat down, and conversed with him. And the merchant became almost senseless; fear entered him, and terror, and violent grief, and excessive anxiety. And as the owner of the gazelle sat by his side, lo, a second sheykh approached them, with two black hounds, and inquired of them, after saluting them, the reason of their sitting in that place, seeing that it was a resort of the Jann: and they told him the story from beginning to end. And he had hardly sat down when there approached them a third sheykh, with a dapple mule; and he asked them the same question, which was answered in the same manner.

Immediately after, the dust was agitated, and became an enormous revolving pillar, approaching them from the midst of the desert; and this dust subsided, and behold, the Jinni, with a drawn sword in his hand; his eyes casting forth sparks of fire. He came to them, and dragged from them the merchant, and said to him, Rise, that I may kill thee, as thou killedst my son, the vital spirit of my heart. And the merchant wailed and wept; and the three sheykhs also manifested their sorrow by weeping and crying aloud and wailing: but the first sheykh, who was the owner of the gazelle, recovering his self-possession, kissed the hand of the 'Efrit, and said to him, O thou Jinni, and crown of the kings of the Jann, if I relate to thee the story of myself and this gazelle, and thou find it to be wonderful, and more so than the adventure of this merchant, wilt thou give up to me a third of thy claim to his blood? He answered, Yes, O sheykh; if thou relate to me the story, and I find it to be as thou hast said, I will give up to thee a third of my claim to his blood.

THE STORY OF THE FIRST SHEYKH AND THE GAZELLE

THEN said the sheykh, Know, O 'Efrit, that this gazelle is the daughter of my paternal uncle, and she is of my flesh and my blood. I took her as my wife when she was young, and lived with her about thirty years; but I was not blessed with a child by her; so I took to me a concubine slave, and by her I was blessed with a male child, like the rising full moon, with beautiful eyes, and delicately-shaped eyebrows, and perfectly-formed limbs; and he grew up by little and little until he attained the age of fifteen years. At this period, I unexpectedly had occasion to journey to a certain city, and went thither with a great stock of merchandise.

Now my cousin, this gazelle, had studied enchantment and divination from her early years; and during my absence, she transformed the youth above mentioned into a calf; and his mother, into a cow; and committed them to the care of the herdsman: and when I returned, after a long time, from my journey, I asked after my son and his mother, and she said, Thy slave is dead, and thy son hath fled, and I know not whither he is gone. After hearing this, I remained for the space of a year with mourning heart and weeping eye, until the Festival of the Sacrifice;[1] when I sent to the herdsman, and ordered him to choose for me a fat cow; and he brought me one, and it was my concubine, whom this gazelle had enchanted. I tucked up my skirts and sleeves, and took the knife in my hand, and prepared myself to slaughter her; upon which she moaned and cried so violently that I left her, and ordered the herdsman to kill and skin her: and he did so, but found in her neither fat nor flesh, nor anything but skin and bone; and I repented of slaughtering her, when repentance was of no avail. I therefore gave her to the herdsman, and said to him, Bring me a fat

[1] The Grest Festival, commencing on the 10th of Dhu-l-Hijjeh, when the pilgrims, halting on their return from mount 'Arafat to Mekkeh, in the valley of Minè, perform their sacrifice.

calf: and he brought me my son, who was transformed into a calf. And when the calf saw me, he broke his rope, and came to me, and fawned upon me, and wailed and cried, so that I was moved with pity for him; and I said to the herdsman, Bring me a cow, and let this—

Here Shahrazad perceived the light of morning, and discontinued the recitation with which she had been allowed thus far to proceed. Her sister said to her, How excellent is thy story! and how pretty! and how pleasant! and how sweet!—but she answered, What is this in comparison with that which I will relate to thee in the next night, if I live, and the King spare me! And the King said, By Allah, I will not kill her until I hear the remainder of her story. Thus they pleasantly passed the night until the morning, when the King went forth to his hall of judgment, and the Wezir went thither with the grave-clothes under his arm: and the King gave judgment, and invested and displaced, until the close of the day, without informing the Wezir of that which had happened; and the minister was greatly astonished. The court was then dissolved; and the King returned to the privacy of his palace.

[On the second and each succeeding night, Shahrazad continued so to interest King Shahriyar by her stories as to induce him to defer putting her to death, in expectation that her fund of amusing tales would soon be exhausted; and as this is expressed in the original work in nearly the same words at the close of every night, such repetitions will in the present translation be omitted.]

When the sheykh, continued Shahrazad, observed the tears of the calf, his heart sympathized with him, and he said to the herdsman, Let this calf remain with the cattle.—Meanwhile, the Jinni wondered at this strange story; and the owner of the gazelle thus proceeded.

O lord of the kings of the Jann, while this happened, my cousin, this gazelle, looked on, and said, Slaughter this calf; for he is fat: but I could not do it; so I ordered the herdsman to take him back; and he took him and went away. And as I was sitting, on the following day, he came to me, and said, O my master, I have to tell thee something that thou wilt be rejoiced to hear; and a reward is due to me for bringing good news. I answered, Well:—and he said, O merchant, I have a daughter who learned enchantment in her youth from an old woman in our family; and yesterday, when thou gavest me the calf, I took him to her, and she looked at him, and covered her face, and wept, and then laughed, and said, O my father, hath my condition become so degraded in thy opinion that thou bringest before me strange men?—Where, said I, are any strange men? and wherefore didst thou weep and laugh? She answered, This calf that is with thee is the son of our master, the merchant, and the wife of our master hath enchanted both him and his mother; and this was the reason of my laughter; but as to the reason of my weeping, it was on account of his mother, because his father had slaughtered her.—And I was excessively astonished at this; and scarcely was I certain that the light of morning had appeared when I hastened to inform thee.

When I heard, O Jinni, the words of the herdsmen, I went forth with him, intoxicated without wine, from the excessive joy and happiness that I received, and arrived at his house, where his daughter welcomed me, and kissed my hand; and the calf came to me, and fawned upon me. And I said to the herdsman's daughter, Is that true which thou hast said respecting this calf? She answered, Yes, O my master; he is verily thy son, and the vital spirit of thy heart.—O maiden, said I, if thou wilt restore him, all the cattle and other property of mine that thy father hath under his care shall be thine. Upon this, she smiled, and said, O my master, I have no desire for the property unless on two conditions: the first is, that thou shalt marry me to him; and the second, that I shall enchant her who enchanted him, and so restrain her; otherwise, I shall not be secure from her artifice. On hearing, O Jinni, these her words, I said, And thou shalt have all the property that is under the care of thy father besides; and as to my cousin, even her blood shall be lawful to thee. So, when she heard this, she took a cup, and filled it with water, and repeated a spell over it, and sprinkled with it the calf, saying to him, If God created thee a calf, remain in this form, and be not changed; but if thou be enchanted, return to thy original

form, by permission of God, whose name be exalted!—
upon which he shook, and became a man; and I threw
myself upon him, and said, I conjure thee by Allah that
thou relate to me all that my cousin did to thee and to thy
mother. So he related to me all that had happened to them
both; and I said to him, O my son, God hath given thee one
to liberate thee, and to avenge thee:—and I married to
him, O Jinni, the herdsman's daughter; after which, she
transformed my cousin into this gazelle. And as I happened
to pass this way, I saw this merchant, and asked him what
had happened to him; and when he had informed me, I sat
down to see the result.—This is my story. The Jinni said,
This is a wonderful tale; and I give up to thee a third of
my claim to his blood.

The second sheykh, the owner of the two hounds, then
advanced, and said to the Jinni, If I relate to thee the story
of myself and these hounds, and thou find it to be in like
manner wonderful, wilt thou remit to me, also, a third of
thy claim to the blood of this merchant? The Jinni
answered, Yes.

THE STORY OF THE SECOND SHEYKH
AND THE TWO BLACK HOUNDS

THEN said the sheykh, Know, O lord of the kings of the
Jann, that these two hounds are my brothers. My father
died, and left to us three thousand pieces of gold;[2] and
I opened a shop to sell and buy. But one of my brothers
made a journey, with a stock of merchandise, and was
absent from us for the space of a year with the caravans;
after which, he returned destitute. I said to him, Did I not
advise thee to abstain from travelling? But he wept, and
said, O my brother, God, to whom be ascribed all might
and glory, decreed this event; and there is no longer any
profit in these words: I have nothing left. So I took him up
into the shop, and then went with him to the bath, and
clad him in a costly suit of my own clothing; after which,
we sat down together to eat; and I said to him, O my
brother, I will calculate the gain of my shop during the year,

[2] Dinar, about half-a-guinea.

and divide it, exclusive of the principal, between me and thee. Accordingly, I made the calculations, and found my gain to amount to two thousand pieces of gold; and I praised God, to whom be ascribed all might and glory, and rejoiced exceedingly, and divided the gain in two equal parts between myself and him.—My other brother then set forth on a journey; and after a year, returned in the like condition; and I did unto him as I had done to the former.

After this, when we had lived together for some time, my brothers again wished to travel, and were desirous that I should accompany them; but I would not. What, said I, have ye gained in your travels, that I should expect to gain? They importuned me; but I would not comply with their request; and we remained selling and buying in our shops a whole year. Still, however, they persevered in proposing that we should travel, and I still refused, until after the lapse of six entire years, when at last I consented, and said to them, O my brothers, let us calculate what property we possess. We did so, and found it to be six thousand pieces of gold: and I then said to them, We will bury half of it in the earth, that it may be of service to us if any misfortune befall us, in which case each of us shall take a thousand pieces, with which to traffic. Excellent is thy advice, said they. So I took the money and divided it into two equal portions, and buried three thousand pieces of gold; and of the other half, I gave to each of them a thousand pieces. We then prepared merchandise, and hired a ship, and embarked our goods, and proceeded on our voyage for the space of a whole month, at the expiration of which we arrived at a city, where we sold our merchandise; and for every piece of gold we gained ten.

And when we were about to set sail again, we found, on the shore of the sea, a maiden clad in tattered garments, who kissed my hand, and said to me, O my master, art thou possessed of charity and kindness? If so, I will requite thee for them. I answered, Yes, I have those qualities, though thou requite me not. Then said she, O my master, accept me as thy wife, and take me to thy country; for I give myself to thee: act kindly towards me; for I am one who requires to be treated with kindness and charity, and

who will requite thee for so doing; and let not my present
condition at all deceive thee. When I heard these words,
my heart was moved with tenderness towards her, in order
to the accomplishment of a purpose of God, to whom be
ascribed all might and glory; and I took her, and clothed
her, and furnished for her a place in the ship in a handsome
manner, and regarded her with kind and respectful attention.

We then set sail; and I became most cordially attached
to my wife, so that, on her account, I neglected the society
of my brothers, who, in consequence, became jealous of me,
and likewise envied me my wealth, and the abundance of
my merchandise; casting the eyes of covetousness upon the
whole of the property. They therefore consulted together
to kill me, and take my wealth; saying, Let us kill our
brother, and all the property shall be ours:—and the devil
made these actions to seem fair in their eyes; so they came
to me while I was sleeping by the side of my wife, and took
both of us up, and threw us into the sea. But as soon as
my wife awoke, she shook herself, and became transformed
into a Jinniyeh. She immediately bore me away, and placed
me upon an island, and, for a while, disappeared. In the
morning, however, she returned, and said to me, I am thy
wife, who carried thee, and rescued thee from death, by
permission of God, whose name be exalted. Know that I
am a Jinniyeh: I saw thee, and my heart loved thee for
the sake of God; for I am a believer in God and his
Apostle, God bless and save him! I came to thee in the
condition in which thou sawest me, and thou didst marry
me; and see, I have rescued thee from drowning. But I
am incensed against thy brothers, and I must kill them.—
When I heard her tale, I was astonished, and thanked her
for what she had done;—But, said I, as to the destruction
of my brothers, it is not what I desire. I then related to
her all that had happened between myself and them from
first to last; and when she had heard it, she said, I will, this
next night, fly to them, and sink their ship, and destroy
them. But I said, I conjure thee by Allah that thou do it
not; for the author of the proverb saith, O thou benefactor
of him who hath done evil, the action that he hath done is
sufficient for him:—besides, they are at all events my

brothers. She still, however, said, They must be killed;—
and I continued to propitiate her towards them: and at last
she lifted me up, and soared through the air, and placed me
on the roof of my house.

Having opened the doors, I dug up what I had hidden
in the earth; and after I had saluted my neighbours, and
bought merchandise, I opened my shop. And in the following night, when I entered my house, I found these two
dogs tied up in it; and as soon as they saw me, they came
to me, and wept, and clung to me; but I knew not what had
happened until immediately my wife appeared before me,
and said, These are thy brothers. And who, said I, hath
done this unto them? She answered, I sent to my sister,
and she did it; and they shall not be restored until after the
lapse of ten years. And I was now on my way to her, that
she might restore them, as they have been in this state ten
years, when I saw this man, and, being informed of what had
befallen him, I determined not to quit the place until I should
have seen what would happen between thee and him.—This
is my story.—Verily, said the Jinni, it is a wonderful tale;
and I give up to thee a third of the claim that I had to his
blood on account of his offence.

Upon this, the third sheykh, the owner of the mule, said
to the Jinni, As to me, break not my heart if I relate to thee
nothing more than this:—

The Story of the Third Sheykh and the Mule

The mule that thou seest was my wife: she became
enamoured of a black slave; and when I discovered her
with him, she took a mug of water, and, having uttered a
spell over it, sprinkled me, and transformed me into a dog.
In this state, I ran to the shop of a butcher, whose daughter
saw me, and being skilled in enchantment, restored me to
my original form, and instructed me to enchant my wife in
the manner thou beholdest.—And now I hope that thou wilt
remit to me also a third of the merchant's offence. Divinely
was he gifted who said,

Sow good, even on an unworthy soil; for it will not be lost
    wherever it is sown.

When the sheykh had thus finished his story, the Jinni shook with delight, and remitted the remaining third of his claim to the merchant's blood. The merchant then approached the sheykhs, and thanked them, and they congratulated him on his safety; and each went his way.

But this, said Shahrazad, is not more wonderful than the story of the fisherman. The King asked her, And what is the story of the fisherman? And she related it as follows:—

THE STORY OF THE FISHERMAN

THERE was a certain fisherman, advanced in age, who had a wife and three children; and though he was in indigent circumstances, it was his custom to cast his net, every day, no more than four times. One day he went forth at the hour of noon to the shore of the sea, and put down his basket, and cast his net, and waited until it was motionless in the water, when he drew together its strings, and found it to be heavy: he pulled, but could not draw it up: so he took the end of the cord, and knocked a stake into the shore, and tied the cord to it. He then stripped himself, and dived round the net, and continued to pull until he drew it out: whereupon he rejoiced, and put on his clothes; but when he came to examine the net, he found in it the carcass of an ass. At the sight of this he mourned, and exclaimed, There is no strength nor power but in God, the High, the Great! This is a strange piece of fortune!— And he repeated the following verse:—

O thou who occupiest thyself in the darkness of night, and in peril!
Spare thy trouble; for the support of Providence is not obtained
    by toil!

He then disencumbered his net of the dead ass, and wrung it out; after which he spread it, and descended into the sea, and—exclaiming, In the name of God!—cast it again, and waited till it had sunk and was still, when he pulled it, and found it more heavy and more difficult to raise than on the former occasion. He therefore concluded that it was full of fish: so he tied it, and stripped, and plunged and dived, and pulled until he raised it, and drew it upon the shore; when he found in it only a large jar, full of sand and mud; on

28

seeing which, he was troubled in his heart, and repeated the
following words of the poet:—

O angry fate, forbear! or, if thou wilt not forbear, relent!
Neither favour from fortune do I gain, nor profit from the work of
my hands.
I came forth to seek my sustenance, but have found it to be
exhausted.
How many of the ignorant are in splendor! and how many of
the wise, in obscurity!

So saying, he threw aside the jar, and wrung out and
cleansed his net; and, begging the forgiveness of God for his
impatience, returned to the sea the third time, and threw
the net, and waited till it had sunk and was motionless: he
then drew it out, and found in it a quantity of broken jars
and pots.

Upon this, he raised his head towards heaven, and said,
O God, Thou knowest that I cast not my net more than four
times; and I have now cast it three times! Then—exclaiming, In the name of God!—he cast the net again into the
sea, and waited till it was still; when he attempted to draw
it up, but could not, for it clung to the bottom. And he exclaimed, There is no strength nor power but in God!—and
he stripped himself again, and dived round the net, and
pulled until he raised it upon the shore; when he opened it,
and found in it a bottle of brass, filled with something, and
having its mouth closed with a stopper of lead, bearing the
impression of the seal of our lord Suleyman.[1] At the sight
of this, the fisherman was rejoiced, and said, This I will
sell in the copper-market; for it is worth ten pieces of gold.
He then shook it, and found it to be heavy, and said, I

---

[1] No man ever obtained such absolute power over the Jinn as Suleyman
Ibn-Da'ud (Solomon, the Son of David). This he did by virtue of a most
wonderful talisman, which is said to have come down to him from heaven.
It was a seal-ring, upon which was engraved " the most great name " of
God; and partly composed of brass, and partly of iron. With the brass he
stamped his written commands to the good Jinn; with the iron [which they
greatly dread], those to the evil Jinn, or Devils. Over both orders he
had unlimited power; as well as over the birds and the winds, and, as is
generally said, the wild beasts. His Wezir, Asaf the son of Barkhiya, is
also said to have been acquainted with " the most great name," by uttering which the greatest miracles may be performed; even that of raising the
dead. By virtue of this name, engraved on his ring, Suleyman compelled
the Jinn to assist in building the Temple of Jerusalem, and in various other
works. Many of the evil Jinn he converted to the true faith; and many
others of this class, who remained obstinate in infidelity, he confined in
prisons.

must open it, and see what is in i., and store it in my bag; and then I will sell the bottle in the copper-market. So he took out a knife, and picked at the lead until he extracted it from the bottle. He then laid the bottle on the ground, and shook it, that its contents might pour out; but there came forth from it nothing but smoke, which ascended towards the sky, and spread over the face of the earth; at which he wondered excessively. And after a little while, the smoke collected together, and was condensed, and then became agitated, and was converted into an 'Efrit, whose head was in the clouds, while his feet rested upon the ground: his head was like a dome: his hands were like winnowing forks; and his legs, like masts: his mouth resembled a cavern: his teeth were like stones; his nostrils, like trumpets; and his eyes, like lamps; and he had dishevelled and dust-coloured hair.

When the fisherman beheld this 'Efrit, the muscles of his sides quivered, his teeth were locked together, his spittle dried up, and he saw not his way. The 'Efrit, as soon as he perceived him, exclaimed, There is no deity but God; Suleyman is the Prophet of God. O Prophet of God, slay me not; for I will never again oppose thee in word, or rebel against thee in deed!—O Marid, said the fisherman, dost thou say, Suleyman is the Prophet of God? Suleyman hath been dead a thousand and eight hundred years; and we are now in the end of time. What is thy history, and what is thy tale, and what was the cause of thy entering this bottle? When the Marid heard these words of the fisherman, he said, There is no deity but God! Receive news, O fisherman!—Of what, said the fisherman, dost thou give me news? He answered, Of thy being instantly put to a most cruel death. The fisherman exclaimed, Thou deservest, for this news, O master of the 'Efrits, the withdrawal of protection from thee, O thou remote![2] Wherefore wouldst thou kill me? and what requires thy killing me, when I have liberated thee from the bottle, and rescued thee from the bottom of the sea, and brought thee up upon the dry land?—The 'Efrit answered, Choose what kind of death thou wilt die, and in what manner thou shalt be killed.—What is my offence, said the fisherman,

[2] [Implying a malediction, but excepting bystanders.]

that this should be my recompense from thee? The 'Efrit replied, Hear my story, O fisherman.—Tell it then, said the fisherman, and be short in thy words; for my soul hath sunk down to my feet.

Know then, said he, that I am one of the heretical Jinn: I rebelled against Suleyman the son of Da'ud; I and Sakhr the Jinni; and he sent to me his Wezir, Asaf the son of Barkhiya, who came upon me forcibly, and took me to him in bonds, and placed me before him: and when Suleyman saw me, he offered up a prayer for protection against me, and exhorted me to embrace the faith, and to submit to his authority; but I refused; upon which he called for this bottle, and confined me in it, and closed it upon me with the leaden stopper, which he stamped with the Most Great Name: he then gave orders to the Jinn, who carried me away, and threw me into the midst of the sea. There I remained a hundred years; and I said in my heart, Whosoever shall liber-ate me, I shall enrich him for ever:—but the hundred years passed over me, and no one liberated me: and I entered upon another hundred years; and I said, Whosoever shall liber-ate me, I will open to him the treasures of the earth;—but no one did so: and four hundred years more passed over me, and I said, Whosoever shall liberate me, I will perform for him three wants:—but still no one liberated me. I then fell into a violent rage, and said within myself, Whosoever shall liberate me now, I will kill him; and only suffer him to choose in what manner he will die. And lo, now thou hast liberated me, and I have given thee thy choice of the manner in which thou wilt die.

When the fisherman had heard the story of the 'Efrit, he exclaimed, O Allah! that I should not have liberated thee but in such a time as this! Then said he to the 'Efrit, Pardon me, and kill me not, and so may God pardon thee; and destroy me not, lest God give power over thee to one who will destroy thee. The Marid answered, I must positively kill thee; there-fore choose by what manner of death thou wilt die. The fisherman then felt assured of his death; but he again im-plored the 'Efrit, saying, Pardon me by way of gratitude for my liberating thee.—Why, answered the 'Efrit, I am not going to kill thee but for that very reason, because thou

hast liberated me.—O Sheykh of the 'Efrits, said the fisherman, do I act kindly towards thee, and dost thou recompense
me with baseness? But the proverb lieth not that saith,—

We did good to them, and they returned us the contrary; and such,
    by my life, is the conduct of the wicked.
Thus he who acteth kindly to the undeserving is recompensed in
    the same manner as the aider of Umm-'Amir.[3]

The 'Efrit, when he heard these words, answered by saying, Covet not life, for thy death is unavoidable. Then said
the fisherman within himself, This is a Jinni, and I am a man;
and God hath given me sound reason; therefore, I will now
plot his destruction with my art and reason, like as he hath
plotted with his cunning and perfidy. So he said to the
'Efrit, Hast thou determined to kill me? He answered, Yes.
Then said he, By the Most Great Name engraved upon the
seal of Suleyman, I will ask thee one question; and wilt thou
answer it to me truly? On hearing the mention of the Most
Great Name, the 'Efrit was agitated, and trembled, and replied, Yes; ask, and be brief. The fisherman then said,
How wast thou in this bottle? It will not contain thy hand
or thy foot; how then can it contain thy whole body?—Dost
thou not believe that I was in it? said the 'Efrit. The fisherman answered, I will never believe thee until I see thee in
it. Upon this, the 'Efrit shook, and became converted into
smoke, which rose to the sky and then became condensed,
and entered the bottle by little and little, until it was all
enclosed; when the fisherman hastily snatched the sealed leaden
stopper; and, having replaced it in the mouth of the bottle,
called out to the 'Efrit, and said, Choose in what manner
of death thou wilt die. I will assuredly throw thee here into
the sea, and build me a house on this spot; and whosoever
shall come here, I will prevent his fishing in this place, and
will say to him, Here is an 'Efrit, who to any person that
liberates him, will propose various kinds of death, and then
give him his choice of one of them. On hearing these words
of the fisherman, the 'Efrit endeavoured to escape; but could
not, finding himself restrained by the impression of the seal
of Suleyman, and thus imprisoned by the fisherman as the
vilest and filthiest and least of 'Efrits. The fisherman then

[3] The hyena.

took the bottle to the brink of the sea. The 'Efrit exclaimed, Nay! nay!—to which the fisherman answered, Yea, without fail! yea, without fail! The Marid then addressing him with a soft voice and humble manner, said, What dost thou intend to do with me, O fisherman? He answered, I will throw thee into the sea; and if thou hast been there a thousand and eight hundred years, I will make thee to remain there until the hour of judgment. Did I not say to thee, Spare me, and so may God spare thee; and destroy me not, lest God destroy thee? But thou didst reject my petition, and wouldst nothing but treachery; therefore God hath caused thee to fall into my hand, and I have betrayed thee.—Open to me, said the 'Efrit, that I may confer benefits upon thee. The fisherman replied, Thou liest, thou accursed! I and thou are like the Wezir of King Yunan and the sage Duban.—What, said the 'Efrit, was the case of the Wezir Yunan and the sage Duban, and what is their story? The fisherman answered as follows:—

THE STORY OF KING YUNAN AND THE SAGE DUBAN

KNOW, O 'Efrit, that there was, in former times, in the country of the Persians, a monarch who was called King Yunan, possessing great treasures and numerous forces, valiant, and having troops of every description; but he was afflicted with leprosy, which the physicians and sages had failed to remove; neither their potions, nor powders, nor ointments were of any benefit to him; and none of the physicians was able to cure him. At length there arrived at the city of this king a great sage, stricken in years, who was called the sage Duban: he was acquainted with ancient Greek, Persian, modern Greek, Arabic, and Syriac books, and with medicine and astrology, both with respect to their scientific principles and the rules of their practical applications for good and evil; as well as the properties of plants, dried and fresh; the injurious and the useful: he was versed in the wisdom of the philosophers, and embraced a knowledge of all the medical and other sciences.

After this sage had arrived in the city, and remained in

it a few days, he heard of the case of the King, of the leprosy with which God had afflicted him, and that the physicians and men of science had failed to cure him. In consequence of this information, he passed the next night in deep study; and when the morning came, and diffused its light, and the sun saluted the Ornament of the Good,[4] he attired himself in the richest of his apparel, and presented himself before the King. Having kissed the ground before him, and offered up a prayer for the continuance of his power and happiness, and greeted him in the best manner he was able, he informed him who he was, and said, O King, I have heard of the disease which hath attacked thy person, and that many of the physicians are unacquainted with the means of removing it; and I will cure thee without giving thee to drink any potion, or anointing thee with ointment. When King Yuman heard his words, he wondered, and said to him, How wilt thou do this? By Allah, if thou cure me, I will enrich thee and thy children's children, and I will heap favours upon thee, and whatever thou shalt desire shall be thine, and thou shalt be my companion and my friend. —He then bestowed upon him a robe of honour, and other presents, and said to him, Wilt thou cure me of this disease without potion or ointment? He answered, Yes; I will cure thee without any discomfort to thy person. And the King was extremely astonished, and said, O Sage, at what time, and on what day, shall that which thou hast proposed to me be done? Hasten it, O my Son.—He answered, I hear and obey.

He then went out from the presence of the King, and hired a house, in which he deposited his books, and medicines, and drugs. Having done this, he selected certain of his medicines and drugs, and made a goff-stick, with a hollow handle, into which he introduced them; after which he made a ball for it, skilfully adapted; and on the following day, after he had finished these, he went again to the King, and kissed the ground before him, and directed him to repair to the horse-course, and to play with the ball and goff-stick. The King, attended by his Emirs and Chamber-

[4] The Prophet Mohammad, who said "the sun never riseth until it hath saluted me."

lains and Wezirs, went thither, and, as soon as he arrived
there, the sage Duban presented himself before him, and
handed to him the goff-stick, saying, Take this goff-stick,
and grasp it thus, and ride along the horse-course, and strike
the ball with it with all thy force, until the palm of thy hand
and thy whole body become moist with perspiration, when
the medicine will penetrate into thy hand, and pervade thy
whole body; and when thou hast done this, and the medicine remains in thee, return to thy palace, and enter the
bath, and wash thyself, and sleep; then shalt thou find thyself cured: and peace be on thee. So King Yunan took
the goff-stick from the sage, and grasped it in his hand, and
mounted his horse; and the ball was thrown before him,
and he urged his horse after it until he overtook it, when he
struck it with all his force; and when he had continued this
exercise as long as was necessary, and bathed and slept, he
looked upon his skin, and not a vestige of the leprosy
remained: it was clear as white silver. Upon this he
rejoiced exceedingly; his heart was dilated, and he was full
of happiness.

On the following morning he entered the council-chamber,
and sat upon his throne; and the Chamberlains and great
officers of his court came before him. The sage Duban also
presented himself; and when the King saw him, he rose to
him in haste, and seated him by his side. Services of food
were then spread before them, and the sage ate with the
King, and remained as his guest all the day; and when the
night approached, the King gave him two thousand pieces
of gold, besides dresses of honour and other presents, and
mounted him on his own horse, and so the sage returned to
his house. And the King was astonished at his skill; saying, This man hath cured me by an external process, without
anointing me with ointment: by Allah, this is consummate
science; and it is incumbent on me to bestow favours and
honours upon him, and to make him my companion and
familiar friend as long as I live. He passed the night happy
and joyful on account of his recovery, and when he arose,
he went forth again, and sat upon his throne; the officers of
his court standing before him, and the Emirs and Wezirs
sitting on his right hand and on his left; and he called for

the sage Duban, who came, and kissed the ground before him; and the king rose, and seated him by his side, and ate with him, and greeted him with compliments: he bestowed upon him again a robe of honour and other presents, and after conversing with him till the approach of night, gave orders that five other robes of honour should be given to him, and a thousand pieces of gold; and the sage departed, and returned to his house.

Again, when the next morning came, the King went as usual to his council-chamber, and the Emirs and Wezirs and Chamberlains surrounded him. Now there was, among his Wezirs, one of ill aspect, and of evil star; sordid, avaricious, and of an envious and malicious disposition; and when he saw that the King had made the sage Duban his friend, and bestowed upon him these favours, he envied him his distinction, and meditated evil against him; agreeably with the adage which saith, There is no one void of envy;—and another, which saith, Tyranny lurketh in the soul: power manifesteth it, and weakness concealeth it. So he approached the King, and kissed the ground before him, and said, O King of the age, thou art he whose goodness extendeth to all men, and I have an important piece of advice to give thee: if I were to conceal it from thee, I should be a baseborn wretch: therefore, if thou order me to impart it, I will do so. The King, disturbed by these words of the Wezir, said, What is thy advice? He answered, O glorious King, it hath been said, by the ancients, He who looketh not to results, fortune will not attend him:—now I have seen the King in a way that is not right; since he hath bestowed favours upon his enemy, and upon him who desireth the downfall of his dominion: he hath treated him with kindness, and honoured him with the highest honours, and admitted him to the closest intimacy: I therefore fear, for the King, the consequence of this conduct.—At this the King was troubled and his countenance changed; and he said, Who is he whom thou regardest as mine enemy, and to whom I shew kindness? He replied, O King, if thou hast been asleep, awake! I allude to the sage Duban.—The King said, He is my intimate companion, and the dearest of men in my estimation; for he restored me by a thing that I merely held in my hand, and cured me of my disease which the physicians were unable to remove, and there is not now to be found one like to him in the whole world, from west to east. Wherefore, then, dost thou utter these words against him? I will, from this day, appoint him a regular salary and maintenance, and give him every month a thousand pieces of gold; and if I give him a share of my kingdom it were but a small thing to do unto him. I do not think that thou hast said this from any other motive than that of envy. If I didst what thou desirest, I should repent after it, as the man repented who killed his parrot.

The Story of the Husband and the Parrot

THERE was a certain merchant, of an exceedingly jealous disposition, having a wife endowed with perfect beauty, who had prevented him from leaving his home; but an event happened which obliged him to make a journey; and when he found his doing so to be indispensable, he went to the market in which birds were sold, and bought a parrot, which he placed in his house to act as a spy, that, on his return, she might inform him of what passed during his absence; for this parrot was cunning and intelligent, and remembered whatever she heard. So, when he had made his journey, and accomplished his business, he returned, and caused the parrot to be brought to him, and asked her respecting the conduct of his wife. She answered, Thy wife has a lover, who visited her every night during thy absence,—and when the man heard this, he fell into a violent rage, and went to his wife, and gave her a severe beating.

The woman imagined that one of the female slaves had informed him of what had passed between her and her paramour during his absence: she therefore called them together, and made them swear; and they all swore that they had not told their master anything of the matter; but confessed that they had heard the parrot relate to him what had passed. Having thus established, on the testimony of the slaves, the fact of the parrot's having informed her husband of her intrigue, she ordered one of these slaves to grind with a hand-mill under the cage, another to sprinkle water from above, and a third to move a mirror from side to side, during the next night on which her husband was absent; and on the following morning, when the man returned from an entertainment at which he had been present, and inquired again of the parrot what had passed that night during his absence, the bird answered, O my master, I could neither see nor hear anything, on account of the excessive darkness, and thunder, and lightning, and rain. Now this happened during summer: so he said to her, What strange words are these? It is now summer, when nothing of what thou hast described ever happens.—The parrot, however, swore by Allah the Great that what she had said was true; and that it had so happened: upon which the man, not understanding the case, nor knowing the plot, became violently enraged, and took out the bird from the cage, and threw her down upon the ground with such violence that he killed her.

But after some days, one of his female slaves informed him of the truth; yet he would not believe it, until he saw his wife's paramour going out from his house; when he drew his sword, and slew the traitor by a blow on the back of his neck: so also did he to his treacherous wife; and thus both of them went, laden with the sin which they had committed, to the fire; and the merchant discovered that the parrot had informed him truly of what she had seen; and he mourned grievously for her loss.

When the Wezir heard these words of King Yunan, he said, O King of great dignity, what hath this crafty sage— this man from whom nought but mischief proceedeth—done unto me, that I should be his enemy, and speak evil of him, and plot with thee to destroy him? I have informed thee respecting him in compassion for thee, and in fear of his despoiling thee of thy happiness; and if my words be not true, destroy me, as the Wezir of Es-Sindibad was destroyed. —The King asked, How was that? And the Wezir thus answered:—

The Story of the Envious Wezir and the Prince and the Ghuleh

The King above mentioned had a son who was ardently fond of the chase; and he had a Wezir whom he charged to be always with his son wherever he went. One day the son went forth to hunt, and his father's Wezir was with him; and as they rode together, they saw a great wild beast; upon which the Wezir exclaimed to the Prince, Away after this wild beast! The King's son pursued it until he was out of the sight of his attendants, and the beast also escaped from before his eyes in the desert; and while the Prince wandered in perplexity, not knowing whither to direct his course, he met in his way a damsel, who was weeping. He said to her, Who art thou?—and she answered, I am a daughter of one of the kings of India; I was in the desert, and slumber overtook me, and I fell from my horse in a state of insensibility, and being thus separated from my attendants, I lost my way. The Prince, on hearing this, pitied her forlorn state, and placed her behind him on his horse; and as they proceeded, they passed by a ruin, and the damsel said to him, O my master, I would alight here for a little while. The Prince therefore lifted her from his horse at this ruin; but she delayed so long to return, that he wondered wherefore she had loitered so, and entering after her, without her knowledge, perceived that she was a Ghuleh,[5] and heard her say, My children, I have brought you to-day a fat young man:—on which they exclaimed, Bring him in to us, O mother! that we may fill our stomachs with his flesh. When the Prince heard their words, he felt assured of destruction; the muscles of his sides quivered, and fear overcame him, and he retreated. The Ghuleh then came forth, and, seeing that he appeared alarmed and fearful, and that he was trembling, said to him, Wherefore dost thou fear? He answered, I have an enemy of whom I am in fear. The Ghuleh said, Thou assertest thyself to be the son of the King. He replied, Yes.—Then, said she, wherefore dost thou not give some money to thine enemy,

[5] A female Ghul, that eats men.

and so conciliate him? He answered, He will not be appeased with money, nor with anything but life; and therefore do I fear him: I am an injured man. She then said to him, if thou be an injured man, as thou affirmest, beg aid of God against thine oppressor, and He will avert from thee his mischievous design, and that of every other person whom thou fearest. Upon this, therefore, the Prince raised his head towards heaven, and said, O Thou who answerest the distressed when he prayeth to Thee, and dispellest evil, assist me, and cause mine enemy to depart from me; for Thou art able to do whatsoever Thou wilt!—and the Ghuleh no sooner heard his prayer, than she departed from him. The Prince then returned to his father, and informed him of the conduct of the Wezir; upon which the King gave orders that the minister should be put to death.——

And thou, O King, continued the Wezir of King Yunan, if thou trust in this sage, he will kill thee in the foulest manner. If thou continue to bestow favours upon him, and to make him thine intimate companion, he will plot thy destruction. Dost thou not see that he hath cured thee of the disease by external means, by a thing that thou heldest in thy hand? Therefore thou art not secure against his killing thee by a thing that thou shalt hold in the same manner.—King Yunan answered, Thou hast spoken truth: the case is as thou hast said, O faithful Wezir: it is probable that this sage came as a spy to accomplish my death; and if he cured me by a thing I held in my hand, he may destroy me by a thing that I may smell: what then, O Wezir, shall be done respecting him? The Wezir answered, Send to him immediately, and desire him to come hither; and when he is come, strike off his head, and so shalt thou avert from thee his evil design, and be secure from him. Betray him before he betray thee.—The King said, Thou hast spoken right.

Immediately, therefore, he sent for the sage, who came, full of joy, not knowing what the Compassionate had decreed against him, and addressed the King with these words of the poet—

If I fail any day to render thee due thanks, tell me for whom I
  have composed my verse and prose.

Thou hast loaded me with favours unsolicited, bestowed without
    delay on thy part, or excuse.
How then should I abstain from praising thee as thou deservest,
    and lauding thee both with my heart and voice?
Nay, I will thank thee for thy benefits conferred upon me: they are
    light upon my tongue, though weighty to my back.

Knowest thou, said the King, wherefore I have summoned
thee? The sage answered, None knoweth what is secret
but God, whose name be exalted! Then said the King, I
have summoned thee that I may take away thy life. The
sage, in the utmost astonishment at this announcement, said,
O King, wherefore wouldst thou kill me, and what offence
hath been committed by me? The King answered, It hath
been told me that thou art a spy, and that thou hast come
hither to kill me: but I will prevent thee by killing thee
first:—and so saying, he called out to the executioner, Strike
off the head of this traitor, and relieve me from his wickedness.—Spare me, said the sage, and so may God spare thee;
and destroy me not, lest God destroy thee.—And he repeated
these words several times, like as I did, O 'Efrit; but thou
wouldst not let me go, desiring to destroy me.

King Yunan then said to the sage Duban, I shall not be
secure unless I kill thee; for thou curedst me by a thing
that I held in my hand, and I have no security against thy
killing me by a thing that I may smell, or by some other
means.—O King, said the sage, is this my recompense from
thee? Dost thou return evil for good?—The King answered,
Thou must be slain without delay. When the sage, therefore, was convinced that the King intended to put him to
death, and that his fate was inevitable, he lamented the
benefit that he had done to the undeserving. The executioner then advanced, and bandaged his eyes, and, having
drawn his sword, said, Give permission. Upon this the sage
wept, and said again, Spare me, and so may God spare
thee; and destroy me not, lest God destroy thee! Wouldst
thou return me the recompense of the crocodile?—What,
said the King, is the story of the crocodile? The sage
answered, I cannot relate it while in this condition; but
I conjure thee by Allah to spare me, and so may He spare
thee. And he wept bitterly. Then one of the chief officers

of the King arose, and said, O King, give up to me the blood of this sage; for we have not seen him commit any offence against thee; nor have we seen him do aught but cure thee of thy disease, which wearied the other physicians and sages. The King answered, Ye know not the reason wherefore I would kill the sage: it is this, that if I suffered him to live, I should myself inevitably perish; for he who cured me of the disease under which I suffered by a thing that I held in my hand, may kill me by a thing that I may smell; and I fear that he would do so, and would receive an appointment on account of it; seeing that it is probable he is a spy who hath come hither to kill me; I must therefore kill him, and then shall I feel myself safe.—The sage then said again, Spare me, and so may God spare thee; and destroy me not, lest God destroy thee.

But he now felt certain, O 'Efrit, that the King would put him to death, and that there was no escape for him; so he said, O King, if my death is indispensable, grant me some respite, that I may return to my house, and acquit myself of my duties, and give directions to my family and neighbours to bury me, and dispose of my medical books; and among my books is one of the most especial value, which I offer as a present to thee, that thou mayest treasure it in thy library.— And what, said the King, is this book? He answered, It contains things not to be enumerated; and the smallest of the secret virtues that it possesses is this; that, when thou hast cut off my head, if thou open this book, and count three leaves, and then read three lines on the page to the left, the head will speak to thee, and answer whatever thou shalt ask. At this the King was excessively astonished, and shook with delight, and said to him, O Sage, when I have cut off thy head will it speak? He answered, Yes, O King; and this is a wonderful thing.

The King then sent him in the custody of guards; and the sage descended to his house, and settled all his affairs on that day; and on the following day he went up to the court: and the Emirs and Wezirs, and Chamberlains and Deputies, and all the great officers of the state, went thither also: and the court resembled a flower-garden. And when the sage had entered, he presented himself before the King, bearing an old book, and a small pot containing a powder: and he sat down, and said, Bring me a tray. So they brought him one; and he poured out the powder into it, and spread it. He then said, O King, take this book, and do nothing with it until thou hast cut off my head; and when thou hast done so, place it upon this tray, and order some one to press it down upon the powder; and when this is done, the blood will be stanched: then open the book. As soon as the sage had said this, the King gave orders to strike off his head; and it was done. The King then opened the book, and found that its leaves were stuck together; so he put his finger to his mouth, and moistened it with his spittle, and opened the first leaf, and the second, and the third; but the leaves were not opened without difficulty. He opened six leaves, and looked at them; but found upon them no writing. So he said, O Sage, there is nothing written in it. The head of the sage answered, Turn over more leaves. The King did so; and in a little while, the poison penetrated into his system; for the book was poisoned; and the King fell back, and cried out, The poison hath penetrated into me!—and upon this, the head of the sage Duban repeated these verses:—

They made use of their power, and used it tyrannically; and soon it
    became as though it never had existed.
Had they acted equitably, they had experienced equity; but they
    oppressed; wherefore fortune oppressed them with calamities
    and trials.
Then did the case itself announce to them, This is the reward of
    your conduct, and fortune is blameless.

And when the head of the sage Duban had uttered these words, the King immediately fell down dead.——

Now, O 'Efrit, continued the fisherman, know that if King Yunan had spared the sage, Duban, God had spared him; but he refused, and desired his destruction; therefore God destroyed him; and thou, O 'Efrit, if thou hadst spared me, God had spared thee, and I had spared thee; but thou desiredst my death; therefore will I put thee to death imprisoned in this bottle, and will throw thee here into the sea. The Marid, upon this, cried out, and said, I conjure thee by Allah, O fisherman, that thou do it not: spare me in generosity, and be not angry with me for what I did; but if I have done evil, do thou good, according to the proverb,— O thou benefactor of him who hath done evil, the action that he hath done is sufficient for him:—do not therefore as Umameh did to 'Atikeh.—And what, said the fisherman, was their case? The 'Efrit answered, This is not a time for telling stories, when I am in this prison; but when thou liberatest me, I will relate to thee their case. The fisherman said, Thou must be thrown into the sea, and there shall be no way of escape for thee from it; for I endeavoured to propitiate thee, and humbled myself before thee, yet thou wouldest nothing but my destruction, though I had committed no offence to deserve it, and had done no evil to thee whatever, but only good, delivering thee from thy confinement; and when thou didst thus unto me, I perceived that thou wast radically corrupt: and I would have thee know, that my motive for throwing thee into this sea, is that I may acquaint with thy story every one that shall take thee out, and caution him against thee, that he may cast thee in again: thus shalt thou remain in this sea to the end of time, and experience varieties of torment.—The 'Efrit then said, Liberate me, for this is an opportunity for thee to display humanity; and I vow to thee that I will never do thee harm; but, on the contrary, will do thee a service that shall enrich thee for ever.

Upon this the fisherman accepted his covenant that he would not hurt him, but that he would do him good; and when he had bound him by oaths and vows, and made him swear by the Most Great Name of God, he opened to him; and the smoke ascended until it had all come forth, and then collected together, and became, as before, an 'Efrit of hideous form. The 'Efrit then kicked the bottle into the sea. When the fisherman saw him do this, he made sure of destruction, and said, This is no sign of good:—but afterwards he fortified his heart, and said, O 'Efrit, God, whose name be exalted, hath said, Perform the covenant, for the covenant shall be inquired into:[6]—and thou hast covenanted with me, and sworn that thou wilt not act

[6] Kur'an, xvii. 36.

treacherously towards me; therefore, if thou so act, God
will recompense thee; for He is jealous; He respiteth, but
suffereth not to escape; and remember that I said to thee
as said the sage Duban to King Yunan, Spare me, and so
may God spare thee.

The 'Efrit laughed, and walking on before him, said, O
fisherman, follow me. The fisherman did so, not believing
in his escape, until they had quitted the neighbourhood of
the city, and ascended a mountain, and descended into a
wide desert tract, in the midst of which was a lake of water.
Here the 'Efrit stopped, and ordered the fisherman to cast
his net and take some fish; and the fisherman, looking into
the lake, saw in it fish of different colours, white and red
and blue and yellow; at which he was astonished; and he
cast his net, and drew it in, and found in it four fish, each
fish of a different colour from the others, at the sight of
which he rejoiced. The 'Efrit then said to him, Take them
to the Sultan, and present them to him, and he will give
thee what will enrich thee; and for the sake of God accept
my excuse, for, at present, I know no other way of rewarding thee, having been in the sea a thousand and eight
hundred years, and not seen the surface of the earth until
now; but take not fish from the lake more than once each
day: and now I commend thee to the care of God.—Having
thus said, he struck the earth with his feet, and it clove
asunder, and swallowed him.

The fisherman then went back to the city, wondering at
all that had befallen him with the 'Efrit, and carried the fish
to his house; and he took an earthen bowl, and, having
filled it with water, put the fish into it; and they struggled
in the water: and when he had done this, he placed the
bowl upon his head, and repaired to the King's palace, as
the 'Efrit had commanded him, and, going up unto the
King, presented to him the fish; and the King was excessively astonished at them, for he had never seen any like
them in the course of his life; and he said, Give these fish
to the slave cook-maid. This maid had been sent as a
present to him by the King of the Greeks, three days
before; and he had not yet tried her skill. The Wezir,
therefore, ordered her to fry the fish, and said to her, O

maid, the King saith unto thee, I have not reserved my tear
but for the time of my difficulty:—to-day, then, gratify us by
a specimen of thy excellent cookery, for a person hath
brought these fish as a present to the Sultan. After having
thus charged her, the Wezir returned, and the King ordered
him to give the fisherman four hundred pieces of gold: so
the Wezir gave them to him; and he took them in his lap,
and returned to his home and his wife, joyful and happy, and
bought what was needful for his family.

Such were the events that befell the fisherman: now we
must relate what happened to the maid.—She took the fish,
and cleaned them, and arranged them in the frying-pan, and
left them until one side was cooked, when she turned them
upon the other side; and lo, the wall of the kitchen clove
asunder, and there came forth from it a damsel of tall
stature, smooth-cheeked, of perfect form, with eyes adorned
with kohl, beautiful in countenance, and with heavy, swelling
hips; wearing a kufiyeh interwoven with blue silk; with
rings in her ears, and bracelets on her wrists, and rings set
with precious jewels on her fingers; and in her hand was a
rod of Indian cane: and she dipped the end of the rod in
the frying-pan, and said, O fish, are ye remaining faithful to
your covenant? At the sight of this, the cook-maid fainted.
The damsel then repeated the same words a second and a
third time; after which the fish raised their heads from the
frying-pan, and answered, Yes, yes. They then repeated
the following verse:—

If thou return, we return; and if thou come, we come; and if thou
    forsake, we verily do the same.

And upon this the damsel overturned the frying-pan, and
departed by the way she had entered, and the wall of the
kitchen closed up again. The cook-maid then arose, and
beheld the four fish burnt like charcoal; and she exclaimed,
In his first encounter his staff broke!—and as she sat re-
proaching herself, she beheld the Wezir standing at her
head; and he said to her, Bring the fish to the Sultan:—
and she wept, and informed him of what had happened.

The Wezir was astonished at her words, and exclaimed,
This is indeed a wonderful event;—and he sent for the

fisherman, and when he was brought, he said to him, O fisherman, thou must bring to us four fish like those which thou broughtest before. The fisherman accordingly went forth to the lake, and threw his net, and when he had drawn it in he found in it four fish as before; and he took them to the Wezir, who went with them to the maid, and said to her, Rise, and fry them in my presence, that I may witness this occurrence. The maid, therefore, prepared the fish, and put them in the frying-pan, and they had remained but a little while, when the wall clove asunder, and the damsel appeared, clad as before, and holding the rod; and she dipped the end of the rod in the frying-pan, and said, O fish, O fish, are ye remaining faithful to your old covenant? Upon which they raised their heads, and answered as before; and the damsel overturned the frying-pan with the rod, and returned by the way she had entered, and the wall closed up again.

The Wezir then said, This is an event which cannot be concealed from the King:—so he went to him, and informed him of what had happened in his presence; and the King said, I must see this with my own eyes. He sent, therefore, to the fisherman, and commanded him to bring four fish like the former, granting him a delay of three days. And the fisherman repaired to the lake, and brought the fish thence to the King, who ordered again that four hundred pieces of gold should be given to him; and then, turning to the Wezir, said to him, Cook the fish thyself here before me. The Wezir answered, I hear and obey. He brought the frying-pan, and after he had cleaned the fish, threw them into it; and as soon as he had turned them, the wall clove asunder, and there came forth from it a negro, in size like a bull, or like one of the tribe of 'Ad,[7] having in his hand a branch of a green tree; and he said, with a clear but terrifying voice, O fish, O fish, are ye remaining faithful to your old covenant? Upon which they raised their heads, and answered as before, Yes, yes:

If thou return, we return ; and if thou come, we come ; and if thou forsake, we verily do the same.

[7] The smallest of the ancient Arab tribe of 'Ad is said to have been sixty cubits high.

The black then approached the frying-pan, and overturned it with the branch, and the fish became like charcoal, and he went away as he had come.

When he had thus disappeared from before their eyes, the King said, This is an event respecting which it is impossible to keep silence, and there must, undoubtedly, be some strange circumstance connected with these fish. He then ordered that the fisherman should be brought before him, and when he had come, he said to him, Whence came these fish? The fisherman answered, From a lake between four mountains behind this mountain which is without thy city. The King said to him, How many days' journey distant? He answered, O our lord the Sultan, a journey of half-an-hour. And the Sultan was astonished, and ordered his troops to go out immediately with him and the fisherman, who began to curse the 'Efrit. They proceeded until they had ascended the mountain, and descended into a wide desert tract which they had never before seen in their whole lives; and the Sultan and all the troops wondered at the sight of this desert, which was between four mountains, and at the fish, which were of four colors, red and white and yellow and blue. The King paused in astonishment, and said to the troops, and to the other attendants who were with him, Hath any one of you before seen this lake in this place? They all answered, No. Then said the King, By Allah, I will not enter my city, nor will I sit upon my throne, until I know the true history of this lake, and of its fish. And upon this he ordered his people to encamp around these mountains; and they did so. He then called for the Wezir, who was a well-informed, sensible, prudent, and learned man; and when he had presented himself before him, he said to him, I desire to do a thing with which I will acquaint thee; and it is this:—I have resolved to depart alone this night, to seek for information respecting this lake and its fish: therefore, sit thou at the door of my pavilion, and say to the Emirs and Wezirs and Chamberlains, The Sultan is sick, and hath commanded me not to allow any person to go in unto him:—and acquaint no one with my intention.

The Wezir was unable to oppose his design; so the King

disguised himself, and slung on his sword, and withdrew himself from the midst of his troops. He journeyed the whole of the night, until the morning, and proceeded until the heat became oppressive to him: he then paused to rest; after which he again proceeded the remainder of the day and the second night until the morning, when there appeared before him, in the distance, something black, at the sight of which he rejoiced, and said, Perhaps I shall there find some person who will inform me of the history of the lake and its fish. And when he approached this black object, he found it to be a palace built of black stones, and overlaid with iron; and one of the leaves of its door was open, and the other shut. The King was glad, and he stood at the door, and knocked gently, but heard no answer; he knocked a second and a third time, but again heard no answer: then he knocked a fourth time, and with violence; but no one answered. So he said, It is doubtless empty:—and he took courage, and entered from the door into the passage, and cried out, saying, O inhabitants of the palace, I am a stranger and a traveller! have ye any provision? And he repeated these words a second and a third time; but heard no answer. And upon this he fortified his heart, and emboldened himself, and proceeded from the passage into the midst of the palace; but he found no one there, and only saw that it was furnished, and that there was, in the centre of it, a fountain with four lions of red gold, which poured forth the water from their mouths, like pearls and jewels: around this were birds; and over the top of the palace was extended a net which prevented their flying out. At the sight of these objects he was astonished, and he was grieved that he saw no person there whom he could ask for information respecting the lake, and the fish, and the mountains, and the palace. He then sat down between the doors, reflecting upon these things; and as he thus sat, he heard a voice of lamentation from a sorrowful heart, chanting these verses:—

O fortune, thou pitiest me not, nor releasest me! See my heart is
 straitened between affliction and peril!
Will not you [O my wife] have compassion on the mighty whom
 love hath abased, and the wealthy who is reduced to
 indigence?

We were jealous even of the zephyr which passed over you: but
    when the divine decree is issued, the eye becometh blind!
What resource hath the archer when, in the hour of conflict, he
    desireth to discharge the arrow, but findeth his bow-string
    broken?
And when troubles are multiplied upon the noble-minded, where
    shall he find refuge from fate and from destiny?

When the Sultan heard this lamentation, he sprang upon
his feet, and, seeking the direction whence it proceeded,
found a curtain suspended before the door of a chamber;
and he raised it, and beheld behind it a young man sitting
on a couch raised to the height of a cubit from the floor.
He was a handsome youth, well-shaped, and of eloquent
speech, with shining forehead, and rosy cheek, marked with
a mole resembling ambergris. The King was rejoiced at
seeing him, and saluted him; and the young man (who
remained sitting, and was clad with a vest of silk, embroidered with gold, but who exhibited traces of grief) returned
his salutation, and said to him, O my master, excuse my not
rising.—O youth! said the King, inform me respecting the
lake, and its fish of various colours, and respecting this
palace, and the reason of thy being alone in it, and of thy
lamentation. When the young man heard these words,
tears trickled down his cheeks, and he wept bitterly. And
the King was astonished, and said to him, What causeth
thee to weep, O youth? He answered, How can I refrain
from weeping, when this is my state?—and so saying, he
stretched forth his hand, and lifted up the skirts of his
clothing; and lo, half of him, from his waist to the soles of
his feet, was stone; and from his waist to the hair of his
head, he was like other men. He then said, Know, O King,
that the story of the fish is extraordinary; if it were engraved
upon the intellect, it would be a lesson to him who would be
admonished:—and he related as follows:—

The Story of the Young King of the Black Islands

My father was king of the city which was here situate:
his name was Mahmud, and he was lord of the Black Islands,
and of the four mountains. After a reign of seventy years,

he died, and I succeeded to his throne; whereupon I took
as my wife the daughter of my uncle; and she loved me
excessively, so that when I absented myself from her, she
would neither eat nor drink till she saw me again. She
remained under my protection five years. After this, she
went one day to the bath; and I had commanded the cook
to prepare the supper, and entered this palace, and slept in
my usual place. I had ordered two maids to fan me; and
one of them sat at my head, and the other at my feet; but I
was restless, because my wife was not with me; and I could
not sleep. My eyes were closed, but my spirit was awake;
and I heard the maid at my head say to her at my feet, O
Mes'udeh, verily our lord is unfortunate in his youth, and
what a pity is it that it should be passed with our depraved,
wicked mistress!—Perdition to unfaithful wives! replied the
other: but (added she) such a person as our lord, so endowed by nature, is not suited to this profligate woman, who
passes every night absent from his bed.—Verily, rejoined she
at my head, our lord is careless in not making any inquiry
respecting her.—Wo to thee! said the other: hath our lord
any knowledge of her conduct, or doth she leave him to his
choice? Nay, on the contrary, she contriveth to defraud
him by means of the cup of wine which he drinketh every
night before he sleepeth, putting benj[8] into it; in consequence of which he sleepeth so soundly that he knoweth not
what happeneth, nor whither she goeth, nor what she doeth;
for, after she hath given him the wine to drink, she dresseth
herself, and goeth out from him, and is absent until daybreak, when she returneth to him, and burneth a perfume
under his nose, upon which he awaketh from his sleep.

When I heard this conversation of the maids, the light
became darkness before my face, and I was hardly conscious
of the approach of night, when my cousin returned from
the bath. The table was prepared, and we ate, and sat a
while drinking our wine as usual. I then called for the
wine which I was accustomed to drink before I lay down to
sleep, and she handed to me the cup; but I turned away,
and, pretending to drink it as I was wont to do, poured it
into my bosom, and immediately lay down: upon which

[8] Bhang, hemp.

she said, Sleep on; I wish that thou wouldst never wake
again! By Allah, I abhor thee, and abhor thy person, and
my soul is weary of thy company!—She then arose, and
attired herself in the most magnificent of her apparel, and,
having perfumed herself, and slung on a sword, opened the
door of the palace, and went out. I got up immediately,
and followed her until she had quitted the palace, and
passed through the streets of the city, and arrived at the
city-gates, when she pronounced some words that I understood not; whereupon the locks fell off, and the gates
opened, and she went out, I still following her, without her
knowledge. Thence she proceeded to a space among the
mounds, and arrived at a strong edifice, in which was a
kubbeh[9] constructed of mud, with a door, which she entered.
I then climbed upon the roof of the kubbeh, and, looking
down upon her through an aperture, saw that she was
visiting a black slave, whose large lips, one of which over-
lapped the other, gathered up the sand from the pebbly
floor, while he lay, in a filthy and wet condition, upon a
few stalks of sugar-cane.

She kissed the ground before this slave; and he raised
his head towards her, and said, Wo to thee! Wherefore
hast thou remained away until this hour? The other blacks
have been here drinking wine, and each of them has gone
away with his mistress; and I refused to drink on thy
account.—She answered, O my master, and beloved of my
heart, knowest thou not that I am married to my cousin,
and that I abhor every man who resembles him, and hate
myself while I am in his company? If I did not fear to
displease thee, I would reduce the city to ruins, so that the
owl and the raven should cry in it, and would transport its
stones beyond Mount Kaf.[10]—Thou liest, thou infamous
woman, replied the slave; and I swear by the generosity
of the blacks (and if I speak not truth, may our valour be as
the valour of the whites), that if thou loiter as thou hast
now done till this hour, I will no longer give thee my
company, nor approach thy person, thou faithless one!
Dost thou inconvenience me for the sake of thine own

[9] A building with a dome.
[10] The chain of mountains believed by Muslims to encircle the earth.

pleasure, thou filthy wretch, and vilest of the whites?—
When I heard (continued the King) their words, and witnessed what passed between them, the world became dark
before my face, and I knew not where I was.—My cousin still
stood weeping, and abasing herself before him, and said,
O my beloved, and treasure of my heart, there remaineth
to me none but thee for whom I care, and if thou cast me
off, alas for me! O my beloved! O light of mine eye!—
Thus she continued to weep, and to humble herself before
him, until he became pacified towards her; upon which
she rejoiced, and arose, and, having disrobed herself, said
to him, O my master, hast thou here anything that thy maid
may eat? He answered, Uncover the dough-pan; it contains some cooked rats' bones: eat of them, and pick them;
and take this earthen pot: thou wilt find in it some buzah[11]
to drink. So she arose, and ate and drank, and washed her
hands; after which she lay down by the side of the slave,
upon the stalks of sugar-cane, and covered herself with his
tattered clothes and rags.

When I saw her do this, I became unconscious of my
existence, and, descending from the roof of the kubbeh,
entered, and took the sword from the side of my cousin,
with the intention of killing them both. I struck the slave
upon his neck, and thought that he was killed; but the
blow, which I gave with the view of severing his head, only
cut the gullet and skin and flesh; and when I thought that
I had killed him, he uttered a loud snore, upon which my
cousin started up, and, as soon as I had gone, took the
sword, and returned it to its scabbard, and came back to
the city and to the palace, and lay down again in my bed,
in which she remained until the morning.

On the following day, I observed that my cousin had
cut off her hair, and put on the apparel of mourning; and
she said to me, O my cousin, blame me not for what I do;
for I have received news that my mother is dead, and that
my father hath been slain in a holy war, and that one of my
two brothers hath died of a poisonous sting, and the other
by the fall of a house: it is natural, therefore, that I should
weep and mourn. On hearing these words, I abstained

[11] Barley-beer.

from upbraiding her, and said, Do what seemeth fit to thee; for I will not oppose thee. Accordingly, she continued mourning and weeping and wailing a whole year; after which she said to me, I have a desire to build for myself, in thy palace, a tomb, with a kubbeh, that I may repair thither alone to mourn, and I will call it the House of Lamentations. I replied, Do what thou seest fit. So she built for herself a house for mourning, with a kubbeh in the middle of it, like the tomb of a saint; after which she removed thither the slave, and there she lodged him. He was in a state of excessive weakness, and unable to render her any service, though he drank wine; and from the day on which I had wounded him, he had never spoken; yet he remained alive, because the appointed term of his life had not expired. My cousin every day visited him in this tomb early and late, to weep and mourn over him, and took to him wine to drink, and boiled meats; and thus she continued to do, morning and evening, until the expiration of the second year, while I patiently suffered her, till, one day, I entered her apartments unawares, and found her weeping, and slapping her face, and repeating these verses:—

I have lost my existence among mankind since your absence; for
    my heart loveth none but you.
Take my body, then, in mercy, to the place where you are laid;
    and there bury me by your side:
And if, at my grave, you utter my name, the moaning of my bones
    shall answer to your call.

As soon as he had finished the recitation of these verses, I said to her, holding my drawn sword in my hand, This is the language of those faithless women who renounce the ties of affinity, and regard not lawful fellowship!—and I was about to strike her with the sword, and had lifted up my arm to do so, when she rose—for she knew that it was I who had wounded the slave—and, standing before me, pronounced some words which I understood not, and said, May God, by means of my enchantment, make thee to be half of stone, and half of the substance of man!—whereupon I became as thou seest, unable to move, neither dead nor alive; and when I had been reduced to this state, she

enchanted the city and its markets and fields. The inhabitants of our city were of four classes; Muslims and
Christians, and Jews and Magians; and she transformed
them into fish: the white are the Muslims; the red, the
Magians; the blue, the Christians; and the yellow, the Jews.
She transformed, also, the four islands into four mountains,
and placed them around the lake; and from that time she
has continued every day to torture me, inflicting upon me a
hundred lashes with a leathern whip, until the blood flows
from my wounds; after which she puts on my upper half a
vest of hair-cloth, beneath these garments.—Having said thus,
the young man wept, and ejaculated the following verses:—

Give me patience, O Allah, to bear what Thou decreest! I will
be patient, if so I may obtain thine approval.
I am straitened, indeed, by the calamity that hath befallen me: but
the Family of the favoured Prophet shall intercede for me!

Upon this, the King, looking towards the young man,
said to him, O youth, thou hast increased my anxiety. And
where (he added) is this woman?—The young man answered,
She is in the tomb where the slave is lying, in the kubbeh;
and every day, before she visits him, she strips me of my
clothing, and inflicts upon me a hundred lashes with the
whip, while I weep and cry out, unable to move so as to
repulse her. After thus torturing me, she repairs early to
the slave, with the wine and boiled meat.—By Allah, O
youth, said the King, I will do thee an act of kindness for
which I shall be remembered, and a favour which historians
shall record in a biography after me.

He then sat and conversed with him until the approach
of night, upon which he arose, and waited till the first dawn
of day, when he took off his clothes, and slung on his sword,
and went to the place where the slave lay. After remarking
the candles and lamps, and perfumes and ointments, he approached the slave, and with a blow of his sword slew him;
he then carried him on his back, and threw him into a well
which he found in the palace, and returning to the kubbeh,
clad himself with the slave's clothes, and lay down with the
drawn sword by his side. Soon after, the vile enchantress
went to her cousin, and, having pulled off his clothes, took

the whip and beat him, while he cried, Ah! it is enough for me to be in this state! Have pity on me then!—Didst thou shew pity to me, she exclaimed, and didst thou spare my lover?—She then put on him the hair-cloth vest and his outer garments, and repaired to the slave with a cup of wine, and a bowl of boiled meat. Entering the tomb, she wept and wailed, exclaiming, O my master, answer me! O my master, speak to me!—and poured forth her lamentation in the words of this verse:—

How long shall this aversion and harshness continue? Sufficient is the evil which my passion hath brought upon me!

Then, weeping, as before, she exclaimed again, O my master, answer me and speak to me! Upon this the King, speaking in a low voice, and adapting his tongue to the pronunciation of the blacks ejaculated, Ah! Ah! there is no strength nor power but in God! On hearing these words, she screamed with joy, and fell down in a swoon; and when she recovered, she exclaimed, Possibly my master is restored to health! The King, again lowering his voice, as if from weakness, replied, Thou profligate wretch, thou deservest not that I should address thee.—Wherefore? said she. He answered, Because all the day long thou tormentest thy husband, while he calleth out, and imploreth the aid of God, so that thou hast prevented my sleeping from the commencement of darkness until morning: thy husband hath not ceased to humble himself, and to imprecate vengeance upon thee, till he hath distracted me; and had it not been for this, I had recovered my strength: this it is which hath prevented my answering thee.—Then, with thy permission, she replied, I will liberate him from his present sufferings.—Liberate him, said the King, and give us ease.

She replied, I hear and obey;—and immediately arose, and went out from the kubbeh to the palace, and, taking a cup, filled it with water, and pronounced certain words over it, upon which it began to boil like a cauldron. She then sprinkled some of it upon her cousin, saying, By virtue of what I have uttered, be changed from thy present state to that in which thou wast at first!—and instantly he shook, and stood upon his feet, rejoicing in his liberation, and exclaimed, I testify that there is no deity but God, and that Mohammad is God's Apostle; God bless and save him! She then said to him, Depart, and return not hither, or I will kill thee:—and she cried out in his face: so he departed from before her, and she returned to the kubbeh, and said, O my master, come forth to me that I may behold thee. He replied, with a weak voice, What hast thou done? Thou hast relieved me from the branch, but hast not relieved me from the root.—O my beloved, she said, and what is the root? He answered, The people of this city, and of the four islands: every night, at the middle hour, the fish raise their heads, and imprecate vengeance upon me and upon thee; and this is the cause that preventeth the return of vigour to my body; therefore, liberate them, and come, and take my hand, and raise me; for vigour hath already in part returned to me.

On hearing these words of the King, whom she imagined to be the slave, she said to him with joy, O my master, on my head and my eye! In the name of Allah!—and she sprang up, full of happiness, and hastened to the lake, where, taking a little of its water, she pronounced over it some unintelligible words, whereupon the fish became agitated, and raised their heads, and immediately became converted into men as before. Thus was the enchantment removed from the inhabitants of the city, and the city became repeopled, and the market-streets re-erected, and every one returned to his occupation: the mountains also became changed into islands as they were at the first. The enchantress then returned immediately to the King, whom she still imagined to be the slave, and said to him, O my beloved, stretch forth thy honoured hand, that I may kiss it.—Approach me, said the King in a low voice. So she drew near to him; and he, having his keen-edged sword ready in his hand, thrust it into her bosom, and the point protruded from her back: he then struck her again, and clove her in twain, and went forth.

He found the young man who had been enchanted waiting his return, and congratulated him on his safety; and the young prince kissed his hand, and thanked him. The King then said to him, Wilt thou remain in thy city, or come with me to my capital?—O King of the age, said the young man,

dost thou know the distance that is between thee and thy
city? The King answered, Two days and a half.—O King,
replied the young man, if thou hast been asleep, awake: between thee and thy city is a distance of a year's journey to
him who travelleth with diligence; and thou camest in two
days and a half only because the city was enchanted: but,
O King, I will never quit thee for the twinkling of an eye.
The King rejoiced at his words, and said, Praise be to God,
who hath in his beneficence given thee to me: thou art my
son; for during my whole life, I have never been blest with
a son:—and they embraced each other, and rejoiced exceedingly. They then went together into the palace, where the
King who had been enchanted informed the officers of his
court that he was about to perform the holy pilgrimage: so
they prepared for him everything that he required; and he
departed with the Sultan; his heart burning with reflections
upon his city, because he had been deprived of the sight of
it for the space of a year.

He set forth, accompanied by fifty memluks, and provided with presents, and they continued their journey night
and day for a whole year, after which they drew near to the
city of the Sultan, and the Wezir and the troops, who had
lost all hope of his return, came forth to meet him. The
troops, approaching him, kissed the ground before him, and
congratulated him on his safe return; and he entered the
city, and sat upon the throne. He then acquainted the Wezir
with all that had happened to the young King; on hearing
which, the Wezir congratulated the latter, also, on his safety;
and when all things were restored to order, the Sultan bestowed presents upon a number of his subjects, and said to
the Wezir, Bring to me the fisherman who presented to me
the fish. So he sent to this fisherman, who had been the
cause of the restoration of the inhabitants of the enchanted
city, and brought him; and the King invested him with a
dress of honour, and inquired of him respecting his circumstances, and whether he had any children. The fisherman
informed him that he had a son and two daughters; and the
King, on hearing this, took as his wife one of the daughters,
and the young prince married the other. The King also conferred upon the son the office of treasurer. He then sent

the Wezir to the city of the young prince, the capital of the
Black Islands, and invested him with its sovereignty, des-
patching with him the fifty memluks who had accompanied
him thence, with numerous robes of honour to all the Emirs;
and the Wezir kissed his hands, and set forth on his journey;
while the Sultan and the young prince remained. And as to
the fisherman, he became the wealthiest of the people of his
age; and his daughters continued to be the wives of the Kings
until they died.

But this (added Shahrazad) is not more wonderful than
what happened to the porter.

THE STORY OF THE PORTER AND THE LADIES OF BAGHDAD, AND OF THE THREE ROYAL MENDICANTS, ETC.

THERE was a man of the city of Baghdad, who was un-married, and he was a porter; and one day, as he sat in the market, reclining against his crate, there accosted him a female wrapped in an izar of the manufacture of El-Mosil,[1] composed of gold-embroidered silk, with a border of gold lace at each end, who raised her face-veil, and displayed beneath it a pair of black eyes, with lids bordered by long lashes, exhibiting a tender expression, and features of perfect beauty; and she said, with a sweet voice, Bring thy crate, and follow me.

The porter had scarcely heard her words when he took up his crate, and he followed her until she stopped at the door of a house, and knocked; whereupon there came down to her a Christian, and she gave him a piece of gold, and received for it a quantity of olives, and two large vessels of wine, which she placed in the crate, saying to the porter, Take it up, and follow me. The porter exclaimed, This is, indeed, a fortunate day!—and he took up the crate, and followed her. She next stopped at the shop of a fruiterer, and bought of him Syrian apples, and 'Othmani quinces, and peaches of 'Oman, and jasmine of Aleppo, and water-lilies of Damascus, and cucumbers of the Nile, and Egyptian limes, and Sultani citrons, and sweet-scented myrtle, and sprigs of the henna-tree, and chamomile, and anemones, and violets, and pomegranate-flowers, and eglantine: all these she put into the porter's crate, and said to him, Take it up. So he took it up, and followed her until she stopped at the shop of a butcher, to whom she said, Cut off ten pounds of

---

[1] " Mosul," a city long famous for its fine stuffs.

meat;—and he cut it off for her, and she wrapped it in a
leaf of a banana-tree, and put it in the crate, and said again,
Take it up, O porter:—and he did so, and followed her.
She next stopped at the shop of a seller of dry fruits, and
took some of every kind of these, and desired the porter to
take up his burden. Having obeyed, he followed her until
she stopped at the shop of a confectioner, where she bought
a dish, and filled it with sweets of every kind that he had,
which she put into the crate; whereupon the porter ventured
to say, If thou hadst informed me beforehand, I had brought
with me a mule to carry all these things. The lady smiled
at his remark, and next stopped at the shop of a perfumer,
of whom she bought ten kinds of scented waters; rose-
water, and orange-flower-water, and willow-flower-water, &c.;
together with some sugar, and a sprinkling-bottle of rose-
water infused with musk, and some frankincense, and aloes-
wood, and ambergris, and musk, and wax candles; and,
placing all these in the crate, she said, Take up thy crate,
and follow me. He, therefore, took it up, and followed her
until she came to a handsome house, before which was a
spacious court. It was a lofty structure, with a door of two
leaves, composed of ebony, overlaid with plates of red gold.
    The young lady stopped at this door, and knocked
gently; whereupon both its leaves were opened, and the
porter, looking to see who opened it, found it to be a damsel
of tall stature, high-bosomed, fair and beautiful, and of
elegant form, with a forehead like the bright new moon,
eyes like those of gazelles, eyebrows like the new moon of
Ramadan, cheeks resembling anemones, and a mouth like
the seal of Suleyman: her countenance was like the full
moon in its splendour, and the forms of her bosom resembled
two pomegranates of equal size. When the porter beheld
her, she captived his reason, the crate nearly fell from his
head, and he exclaimed, Never in my life have I seen a
more fortunate day than this! The lady-portress, standing
within the door, said to the cateress and the porter, Ye are
welcome:—and they entered, and proceeded to a spacious
saloon, decorated with various colours, and beautifully constructed, with carved wood-work, and fountains, and benches
of different kinds, and closets with curtains hanging before

them; there was also in it, at the upper end, a couch of
alabaster inlaid with large pearls and jewels, with mos-
quito-curtain of red satin suspended over it, and within this
was a young lady with eyes possessing the enchantment of
Babil,[2] and a figure like the letter Alif, with a face that put
to shame the shining sun: she was like one of the brilliant
planets, or rather, one of the most high-born of the maidens
of Arabia. This third lady, rising from the couch, advanced
with a slow and elegant gait to the middle of the saloon,
where her sisters were standing, and said to them, Why
stand ye still? Lift down the burden from the head of
this poor porter:—whereupon the cateress placed herself
before him, and the portress behind him, and, the third
lady assisting them, they lifted it down from his head.
They then took out the contents of the crate, and, having
put everything in its place, gave to the porter two pieces of
gold, saying to him Depart, O porter.

The porter, however, stood looking at the ladies, and
admiring their beauty and their agreeable dispositions; for
he had never seen any more handsome; and when he
observed that they had not a man among them, and gazed
upon the wine, and fruits, and sweet-scented flowers, which
were there, he was full of astonishment, and hesitated to go
out; upon which one of the ladies said to him, Why dost
thou not go? dost thou deem thy hire too little? Then
turning to one of her sisters, she said to her, Give him
another piece of gold.—By Allah, O my mistress, exclaimed
the porter, my hire is but two half-dirhems, and I thought
not what ye have given me too little; but my heart and
mind were occupied with reflections upon you and your
state, ye being alone, with no man among you, not one to
amuse you with his company; for ye know that the men-
areh[3] standeth not firmly but on four walls: now ye have
not a fourth, and the pleasure of women is not complete without men: ye are three only, and have need of a
fourth, who should be a man, a person of sense, discreet,

[2] Babil, or Babel, is regarded by the Muslims as the fountain-head of the
science of magic, which was, and, as most think, still is, taught there to
mankind by two fallen angels, named Harut and Marut (Kur'an, ii. 96),
who are there suspended by the feet in a great pit closed by a mass of rock.
[3] Minaret.

acute, and a concealer of secrets.—We are maidens, they replied; and fear to impart our secret to him who will not keep it; for we have read, in a certain history, this verse:—

Guard thy secret from another: intrust it not: for he who intrusteth
    a secret hath lost it.

—By your existence, said the porter, I am a man of sense, and trustworthy: I have read various books, and perused histories: I make known what is fair, and conceal what is foul, and act in accordance with the saying of the poet:—

None keepeth a secret but a faithful person: with the best of man-
    kind it remaineth concealed.
A secret is with me as in a house with a lock, whose key is lost,
    and whose door is sealed.

When the ladies heard the verses which he quoted, and the words with which he addressed them, they said to him, Thou knowest that we have expended here a considerable sum of money: hast thou then wherewith to requite us? We will not suffer thee to remain with us unless thou contribute a sum of money; for thou desirest to sit with us, and to be our cup-companion, and to gaze upon our beautiful faces.— If friendship is without money, said the mistress of the house, it is not equivalent to the weight of a grain:—and the por- tress added, If thou hast nothing, depart with nothing:— but the cateress said, O sister, let us suffer him; for, verily, he hath not been deficient in his services for us this day: another had not been so patient with us: whatever, therefore, falls to his share of the expense, I will defray for him.—At this the porter rejoiced, and exclaimed, By Allah, I obtained my first and only pay this day from none but thee:—and the other ladies said to him, Sit down: thou art welcome.

The cateress then arose, and, having tightened her girdle, arranged the bottles, and strained the wine, and prepared the table by the pool of the fountain. She made ready all that they required, brought the wine, and sat down with her sisters; the porter also sitting with them, thinking he was in a dream. And when they had seated themselves, the cater- ess took a jar of wine, and filled the first cup, and drank it: she then filled another, and handed it to one of her sisters;

and in like manner she did to her other sister; after which she filled again, and handed the cup to the porter, who, having taken it from her hand, repeated this verse:—

I will drink the wine, and enjoy health; for, verily, this beverage
    is a remedy for disease.

The wine continued to circulate among them, and the porter, taking his part in the revels, dancing and singing with them, and enjoying the fragrant odours, began to hug and kiss them, while one slapped him, and another pulled him, and the third beat him with sweet-scented flowers, till, at length, the wine made sport with their reason; and they threw off all restraint, indulging their merriment with as much freedom as if no man had been present.

Thus they continued until the approach of night, when they said to the porter, Depart, and shew us the breadth of thy shoulders;—but he replied, Verily the departure of my soul from my body were more easy to me than my departure from your company; therefore suffer us to join the night to the day, and then each of us shall return to his own, or her own, affairs. The cateress, also, again interceded for him, saying, By my life I conjure you that ye suffer him to pass the night with us, that we may laugh at his drolleries, for he is a witty rogue. So they said to him, Thou shalt pass the night with us on this condition, that thou submit to our authority, and ask not an explanation of anything that thou shalt see. He replied, Good.—Rise then, said they, and read what is inscribed upon the door. Accordingly, he went to the door, and found the following inscription upon it in letters of gold, Speak not of that which doth not concern thee, lest thou hear that which will not please thee:—and he said, Bear witness to my promise that I will not speak of that which doth not concern me.

The cateress then arose, and prepared for them a repast; and, after they had eaten a little, they lighted the candles and burned some aloes-wood. This done, they sat down again to the table; and, while they were eating and drinking, they heard a knocking at the door; whereupon, without causing any interruption to their meal, one of them went to the door, and, on her return, said, Our pleasure this night is now complete, for I have found, at the door, three foreigners[4] with shaven chins, and each of them is blind of the left eye: it is an extraordinary coincidence. They are strangers newly arrived, and each of them has a ridiculous appearance: if they come in, therefore, we shall be amused with laughing at them.—The lady ceased not with these words, but continued to persuade her sisters until they consented, and said, Let them enter; but make it a condition with them that they speak not of that which doth not concern them, lest they hear that which will not please them. Upon this she rejoiced, and having gone again to the door, brought in the three men blind of one eye and with shaven chins, and they had thin and twisted mustaches. Being mendicants, they saluted and drew back; but the ladies rose to them, and seated them; and when these three men looked at the porter, they saw that he was intoxicated; and, observing him narrowly, they thought that he was one of their own class, and said, He is a mendicant like ourselves, and will amuse us by his conversation:—but the porter, hearing what they said, arose, and rolled his eyes, and exclaimed to them, Sit quiet, and abstain from impertinent remarks. Have ye not read the inscription upon the door?—The ladies, laughing, said to each other, Between the mendicants and the porter we shall find matter for amusement. They then placed before the former some food, and they ate, and then sat to drink. The portress handed to them the wine, and, as the cup was circulating among them, the porter said to them, Brothers, have ye any tale or strange anecdote wherewith to amuse us? The mendicants, heated by the wine, asked for musical instruments; and the portress brought them a tambourine of the manufacture of El-Mosil, with a lute of El-Irak, and a Persian harp; whereupon they all arose; and one took the tambourine; another, the lute; and the third, the harp: and they played upon these instruments, the ladies accompanying them with loud songs; and while they were thus diverting themselves, a person knocked at the door. The portress, therefore, went to see who was there; and the cause of the knocking was this.

The Khalifeh Harun Er-Rashid had gone forth this

[4 Or perhaps Kalenderi darwishes.]

night to see and hear what news he could collect, accompanied by Ja'far his Wezir, and Mesrur his executioner. It was his custom to disguise himself in the attire of a merchant; and this night, as he went through the city, he happened to pass, with his attendants, by the house of these ladies, and hearing the sounds of the musical instruments, he said to Ja'far, I have a desire to enter this house, and to see who is giving this concert.—They are a party who have become intoxicated, replied Ja'far, and I fear that we may experience some ill usage from them;—but the Khalifeh said, We must enter, and I would that you devise some stratagem by which we may obtain admission to the inmates. Ja'far therefore answered, I hear and obey:—and he advanced, and knocked at the door; and when the portress came and opened the door, he said to her, My mistress, we are merchants from Tabariyeh,[5] and have been in Baghdad ten days; we have brought with us merchandise, and taken lodgings in a Khan; and a merchant invited us to an entertainment this night: accordingly, we went to his house, and he placed food before us, and we ate, and sat a while drinking together, after which he gave us leave to depart; and going out in the dark, and being strangers, we missed our way to the Khan: we trust, therefore in your generosity that you will admit us to pass the night in your house; by doing which you will obtain a reward in heaven.—The portress, looking at them, and observing that they were in the garb of merchants, and that they bore an appearance of respectability, returned, and consulted her two companions; and they said to her, Admit them:—so she returned, and opened to them the door. They said to her, Shall we enter with thy permission? She answered, Come in. The Khalifeh, therefore, entered, with Ja'far and Mesrur; and when the ladies saw them, they rose to them, and served them, saying, Welcome are our guests; but we have a condition to impose upon you, that ye speak not of that which doth not concern you, lest ye hear that which will not please you. They answered, Good:—and when they had sat down to drink, the Khalifeh looked at the three mendicants, and was surprised at observing that each of them was blind of

the left eye; and he gazed upon the ladies, and was perplexed and amazed at their fairness and beauty. And when
the others proceeded to drink and converse, the ladies
brought wine to the Khalifeh; but he said, I am a pilgrim;
—and drew back from them. Whereupon the portress
spread before him an embroidered cloth, and placed upon
it a China bottle, into which she poured some willow-flower-
water, adding to it a lump of ice, and sweetening it with
sugar, while the Khalifeh thanked her, and said within
himself, To-morrow I must reward her for this kind action.

The party continued their carousal, and, when the wine
took effect upon them, the mistress of the house arose, and
waited upon them; and afterwards, taking the hand of the
cateress, said, Arise, O my sister, that we may fulfil our
debt. She replied, Good. The portress then rose, and,
after she had cleared the middle of the saloon, placed the
mendicants at the further end, beyond the doors; after
which, the ladies called to the porter, saying, How slight
is thy friendship! thou art not a stranger, but one of the
family. So the porter arose, and girded himself, and said,
What would ye?—to which one of the ladies answered,
Stand where thou art:—and presently the cateress said to
him, Assist me:—and he saw two black bitches, with chains
attached to their necks, and drew them to the middle of
the saloon; whereupon the mistress of the house arose from
her place, and tucked up her sleeve above her wrist, and,
taking a whip, said to the porter, Bring to me one of them.
Accordingly, he dragged one forward by the chain. The
bitch whined, and shook her head at the lady; but the
latter fell to beating her upon the head, notwithstanding
her howling, until her arms were tired, when she threw the
whip from her hand, and pressed the bitch to her bosom,
and wiped away her tears, and kissed her head; after which
she said to the porter, Take her back and bring the other;
—and he brought her, and she did to her as she had done to
the first. At the sight of this, the mind of the Khalifeh
was troubled, and his heart was contracted, and he winked
to Ja'far that he should ask her the reason; but he replied
by a sign, Speak not.

The mistress of the house then looked towards the

portress and said to her, Arise to perform what thou hast
to do. She replied, Good:—and the mistress of the house
seated herself upon a couch of alabaster, overlaid with gold
and silver, and said to the portress and the cateress, Now
perform your parts. The portress then seated herself
upon a couch by her; and the cateress, having entered a
closet, brought out from it a bag of satin with green fringes,
and, placing herself before the lady of the house, shook it,
and took out from it a lute; and she tuned its strings, and
sang to it these verses:—

Restore to my eyelids the sleep which hath been ravished; and
    inform me of my reason, whither it hath fled.
I discovered, when I took up my abode with love, that slumber
    had become an enemy to my eyes.
They said, We saw thee to be one of the upright; what, then, hath
    seduced thee? I answered, Seek the cause from his glance.
Verily I excuse him for the shedding of my blood, admitting that
    I urged him to the deed by vexation.
He cast his sun-like image upon the mirror of my mind, and its
    reflection kindled a flame in my vitals.

When the portress had heard this song, she exclaimed,
Allah approve thee!—and she rent her clothes, and fell
upon the floor in a swoon; and when her bosom was thus
uncovered, the Khalifeh saw upon her the marks of beating,
as if from mikra'ahs[5] and whips; at which he was greatly
surprised. The cateress immediately arose, sprinkled water
upon her face, and brought her another dress, which she put
on. The Khalifeh then said to Ja'far, Seest thou not this
woman, and the marks of beating upon her? I cannot keep
silence respecting this affair, nor be at rest, until I know the
truth of the history of this damsel, and that of these two
bitches. But Ja'far replied, O our lord, they have made a
covenant with us that we shall not speak excepting of that
which concerneth us, lest we hear that which will not please
us.—The cateress then took the lute again, and, placing it
against her bosom, touched the chords with the ends of her
fingers, and thus sang to it:—

If of love we complain, what shall we say? Or consuming through
    desire, how can we escape?

[5] Palm sticks.

Or if we send a messenger to interpret for us, he cannot convey
the lover's complaint.

Or if we would be patient, short were our existence after the loss
of those we love.

Nought remaineth to us but grief and mourning, and tears stream-
ing down our cheeks.

O you who are absent from my sight, but constantly dwelling
within my heart!

Have you kept your faith to an impassioned lover, who, while
time endureth will never change?

Or, in absence have you forgotten that lover who, on your account,
is wasting away?

When the day of judgment shall bring us together, I will beg of
our Lord a protractive trial.

On hearing these verses of the cateress, the portress again
rent her clothes, and cried out, and fell upon the floor in a
swoon; and the cateress, as before, put on her another
dress, after she had sprinkled some water upon her face.

The mendicants, when they witnessed this scene, said,
Would that we had never entered this house, but rather had
passed the night upon the [rubbish-]mounds; for our night
hath been rendered foul by an event that breaketh the back!
The Khalifeh, looking towards them, then said, Wherefore
is it so with you? They answered, Our hearts are troubled
by this occurrence.—Are ye not, he asked, of this house?—
No, they answered; nor did we imagine that this house
belonged to any but the man who is sitting with you:—upon
which the porter said, Verily, I have never seen this place
before this night; and I would that I had passed the night
upon the mounds rather than here. They then observed,
one to another, We are seven men, and they are but three
women; we will, therefore, ask them of their history; and
if they answer us not willingly they shall do it in spite of
themselves:—and they all agreed to this, excepting Ja'far,
who said, This is not a right determination; leave them to
themselves, for we are their guests, and they made a covenant
with us which we should fulfil: there remaineth but little of
the night, and each of us shall soon go his way. Then,
winking to the Khalifeh, he said, There remaineth but an
hour; and to-morrow we will bring them before thee, and
thou shalt ask them their story. But the Khalifeh refused
to do so, and said, I have not patience to wait so long for

their history.—Words followed words, and at last they said, Who shall put the question to them?—and one answered, The porter.

The ladies then said to them, O people, of what are ye talking?—whereupon the porter approached the mistress of the house, and said to her, O my mistress, I ask thee, and conjure thee by Allah, to tell us the story of the two bitches, and for what reason thou didst beat them, and then didst weep, and kiss them, and that thou acquaint us with the cause of thy sister's having been beaten with mikra'ahs: that is our question, and peace be on you.—Is this true that he saith of you? inquired the lady, of the other men; and they all answered, Yes,—excepting Ja'far, who was silent. When the lady heard their answer, she said, Verily, O our guests, ye have wronged us excessively; for we made a covenant with you beforehand, that he who should speak of that which concerned him not should hear that which would not please him. Is it not enough that we have admitted you into our house, and fed you with our provisions? But it is not so much your fault as the fault of her who introduced you to us.—She then tucked up her sleeve above her wrist, and struck the floor three times, saying, Come ye quickly!— and immediately the door of a closet opened, and there came forth from it seven black slaves, each having in his hand a drawn sword. The lady said to them, Tie behind them the hands of these men of many words, and bind each of them to another:—and they did so, and said, O virtuous lady, dost thou permit us to strike off their heads? She answered, Give them a short respite, until I shall have inquired of them their histories, before ye behead them.—By Allah, O my mistress, exclaimed the porter, kill me not for the offence of others: for they have all transgressed and committed an offence, excepting me. Verily our night had been pleasant if we had been preserved from these mendicants, whose presence is enough to convert a well-peopled city into a heap of ruins!—He then repeated this couplet:—

How good is it to pardon one able to resist! and how much more
    so, one who is helpless!
For the sake of the friendship that subsisted between us, destroy
    not one for the crime of another!

On hearing these words of the porter, the lady laughed after her anger. Then approaching the men, she said, Acquaint me with your histories, for there remaineth of your lives no more than an hour. Were ye not persons of honourable and high condition, or governors, I would hasten your recompense.—The Khalifeh said to Ja'far, Woe to thee, O Ja'far! make known to her who we are; otherwise she will kill us. —It were what we deserve, replied he.—Jesting, said the Khalifeh, is not befitting in a time for seriousness: each has its proper occasion.—The lady then approached the mendicants, and said to them, Are ye brothers? They answered, No, indeed; we are only poor foreigners. She said then to one of them, Wast thou born blind of one eye?—No, verily, he answered; but a wonderful event happened to me when my eye was destroyed, and the story of it, if engraved on the understanding, would serve as a lesson to him who would be admonished. She asked the second and the third also; and they answered her as the first; adding, Each of us is from a different country, and our history is wonderful and extraordinary. The lady then looked towards them and said, Each of you shall relate his story, and the cause of his coming to our abode, and then stroke his head, and go his way.

The first who advanced was the porter, who said, O my mistress, I am a porter; and this cateress loaded me, and brought me hither, and what hath happened to me here in your company ye know. This is my story; and peace be on you.—Stroke thy head, then, said she, and go:—but he replied, By Allah, I will not go until I shall have heard the story of my companions.—The first mendicant then advanced, and related as follows:—

THE STORY OF THE FIRST ROYAL MENDICANT

KNOW, O my mistress, that the cause of my having shaved my beard, and of the loss of my eye, was this:—My father was a King, and he had a brother who was also a King, and who resided in another capital. It happened that my mother gave birth to me on the same day on which the son of my uncle was born; and years and days passed away until we attained to manhood. Now, it was my custom, some years, to visit my uncle, and to remain with him several months; and on one of these occasions my cousin paid me great honour; he slaughtered sheep for me, and strained the wine for me, and we sat down to drink; and when the wine had affected us, he said to me, O son of my uncle, I have need of thine assistance in an affair of interest to me, and I beg that thou wilt not oppose me in that which I desire to do. I replied, I am altogether at thy service:—and he made me swear to him by great oaths, and, rising immediately, absented himself for a little while, and then returned, followed by a woman decked with ornaments, and perfumed, and wearing a dress of extraordinary value. He looked towards me, while the woman stood behind him, and said, Take this woman, and go before me to the burial-ground which is in such a place:—and he described it to me, and I knew it. He then added, Enter the burial-ground, and there wait for me.

I could not oppose him, nor refuse to comply with his request, on account of the oaths which I had sworn to him; so I took the woman, and went with her to the burial-ground; and when we had sat there a short time, my cousin came, bearing a basin of water, and a bag containing some plaster, and a small adze. Going to a tomb in the midst of the burial-ground, he took the adze, and disunited the stones, which he placed on one side; he then dug up the earth with the adze, and uncovered a flat stone, of the size of a small door, under which there appeared a vaulted staircase. Having done this, he made a sign to the woman, and said to her, Do according to thy choice:—whereupon she descended the stairs. He then looked towards me, and said, O son of my uncle, complete thy kindness when I have descended into this place, by replacing the trap-door and the earth above it as they were before: then, this plaster which is in the bag, and this water which is in the basin, do thou knead together, and plaster the stones of the tomb as they were, so that no man may know it, and say, This hath been lately opened, but its interior is old:—for, during the space of a whole year I have been preparing this, and no one knew it but God: this is what I would have thee do. He then said to me, May God never deprive thy friends of thy presence, O son of my uncle!—and, having uttered these words, he descended the stairs.

When he had disappeared from before my eyes, I replaced the trap-door, and busied myself with doing as he had ordered me, until the tomb was restored to the state in which it was at first; after which I returned to the palace of my uncle, who was then absent on a hunting excursion. I slept that night, and when the morning came, I reflected upon what had occurred between me and my cousin, and repented of what I had done for him, when repentance was of no avail. I then went out to the burial-ground, and searched for the tomb; but could not discover it. I ceased not in my search until the approach of night; and, not finding the way to it, returned again to the palace; and I neither ate nor drank; my heart was troubled respecting my cousin, since I knew not what had become of him; and I fell into excessive grief. I passed the night sorrowful until the morning, and went again to the burial-ground, reflecting upon the action of my cousin, and repenting of my compliance with his request; and I searched among all the tombs; but discovered not that for which I looked. Thus I persevered in my search seven days without success.

My trouble continued and increased until I was almost mad; and I found no relief but in departing, and returning to my father; but on my arrival at his capital, a party at the city-gate sprang upon me and bound me. I was struck with the utmost astonishment, considering that I was the son of the Sultan of the city, and that these were the servants of my father and of myself: excessive fear of them overcame me, and I said within myself, What hath happened to my father? I asked, of those who had bound me, the cause of this conduct; but they returned me no answer, till after a while, when one of them, who had been my servant, said to me, Fortune hath betrayed thy father, the troops have been false to him, and the Wezir hath killed him; and we were lying in wait to take thee.—They took me, and I was as one dead, by reason of this news which I had heard respecting my father; and I stood before the Wezir who had killed my father.

Now, there was an old enmity subsisting between me and

him; and the cause of it was this:—I was fond of shooting
with the crossbow; and it happened, one day, that as I was
standing on the roof of my palace, a bird alighted on the
roof of the palace of the Wezir, who was standing there at
the time, and I aimed at the bird; but the bullet missed it, and
struck the eye of the Wezir, and knocked it out, in accordance
with the appointment of fate and destiny, as the poet hath
said:—

We trod the steps appointed for us: and the man whose steps are
    appointed must tread them.
He whose death is decreed to take place in one land will not die
    in any land but that.

When I had thus put out the eye of the Wezir, he could say
nothing, because my father was King of the city. This was
the cause of the enmity between him and me: and when I
stood before him, with my hands bound behind me, he gave
the order to strike off my head. I said to him, Wouldst thou
kill me for no offence?—What offence, he exclaimed, could be
greater than this?—and he pointed to the place of the eye
which was put out. I did that, said I, unintentionally. He
replied, If thou didst it unintentionally, I will do the same
to thee purposely:—and immediately he said, Bring him forward to me:—and, when they had done so, he thrust his
finger into my left eye, and pulled it out. Thus I became
deprived of one eye, as ye see me. He then bound me firmly,
and placed me in a chest, and said to the executioner, Take
this fellow, and draw thy sword, and convey him without
the city; then put him to death, and let the wild beasts devour
him.

Accordingly, he went forth with me from the city, and,
having taken me out from the chest, bound hand and foot,
was about to bandage my eye, and kill me; whereupon I wept,
and exclaimed,—

How many brothers have I taken as armour! and such they were;
    but to guard my enemies.
I thought they would be as piercing arrows: and such they were;
    but to enter my heart!

The executioner, who had served my father in the same
capacity, and to whom I had shewn kindnesses, said, on
hearing these verses, O my master, what can I do, being a

slave under command?—but presently he added, Depart with
thy life, and return not to this country, lest thou perish, and
cause me to perish with thee.   The poet saith,—

Flee with thy life if thou fearest oppression, and leave the house to
    tell its builder's fate.
Thou wilt find, for the land that thou quittest, another: but no
    soul wilt thou find to replace thine own.

As soon as he had thus said, I kissed his hands, and believed not in my safety until I had fled from his presence.
The loss of my eye appeared light to me when I considered
my escape from death; and I journeyed to my uncle's capital,
and, presenting myself before him, informed him of what had
befallen my father, and of the manner in which I had lost
my eye: upon which he wept bitterly, and said, Thou hast
added to my trouble and my grief; for thy cousin hath been
lost for some days, and I know not what hath happened to
him, nor can any one give me information respecting him.
Then he wept again, until he became insensible; and when
he recovered, he said, O my son, the loss of thine eye is better
than the loss of thy life.
Upon this I could no longer keep silence respecting his
son, my cousin; so I informed him of all that happened to
him; and on hearing this news he rejoiced exceedingly, and
said, Shew me the tomb.—By Allah, O my uncle, I replied,
I know not where it is; for I went afterwards several times
to search for it, and could not recognize its place. We, however, went together to the burial-ground, and, looking to the
right and left, I discovered it; and both I and my uncle rejoiced. I then entered the tomb with him, and when we had
removed the earth, and lifted up the trap-door, we descended
fifty steps, and, arriving at the bottom of the stairs, there
issued forth upon us a smoke which blinded our eyes; whereupon my uncle pronounced those words which relieve from
fear him who uttereth them,—There is no strength nor power
but in God, the High, the Great!—After this, we proceeded,
and found ourselves in a saloon, filled with flour and grain,
and various eatables; and we saw there a curtain suspended
over a couch, upon which my uncle looked, and found there
his son and the woman who had descended with him, lying

side by side, and converted into black charcoal, as if they had been thrown into a pit of fire. And when he beheld this spectacle, he spat in his son's face, and exclaimed, This is what thou deservest, O thou wretch! This is the punishment of the present world, and there remaineth the punishment of the other world, which will be more severe and lasting!—and he struck him with his shoes. Astonished at this action, and grieved for my cousin, seeing him and the damsel thus converted into charcoal, I said, By Allah, O my uncle, moderate the trouble of thy heart, for my mind is perplexed by that which hath happened to thy son, and by thinking how it hath come to pass that he and the damsel are converted into black charcoal. Dost thou not deem it enough for him to be in this state, that thou beatest him with thy shoes?

O son of my brother, he replied, this my son was, from his early years, inflamed with love for his [foster-]sister, and I used to forbid him from entertaining this passion for her, and to say within myself, They are now children, but when they grow older a base act will be committed by them:—and, indeed, I heard that such had been the case, but I believed it not. I, however, reprimanded him severely, and said to him, Beware of so foul an action, which none before thee hath committed, nor will any commit after thee: otherwise we shall suffer disgrace and disparagement among the Kings until we die, and our history will spread abroad with the caravans: have a care for thyself that such an action proceed not from thee; for I should be incensed against thee, and kill thee. I then separated him from her, and her from him: but the vile woman loved him excessively; the Devil got possession of them both; and when my son saw that I had separated him, he secretly made this place beneath the earth, and, having conveyed hither the provisions which thou seest, took advantage of my inadvertence when I had gone out to hunt, and came hither: but the Truth (whose perfection be extolled, and whose name be exalted!) was jealously vigilant over them, and consumed them by fire; and the punishment of the world to come will be more severe and lasting.—He then wept, and I wept with him; and he said to me, Thou art my son in his stead.—I remained a while reflecting upon the world and its vicissitudes, upon the murder of my father by the Wezir, and his usurping his throne, and the loss of my eye, and the strange events which had happened to my cousin, and I wept again.

We then ascended, and, having replaced the trap-door and the earth above it, and restored the tomb to its former state, returned to our abode; but scarcely had we seated ourselves when we heard the sounds of drums and trumpets, warriors galloped about, and the air was filled with dust raised by the horses' hoofs. Our minds were perplexed, not knowing what had happened, and the King, asking the news, was answered, The Wezir of thy brother hath slain him and his soldiers and guards, and come with his army to assault the city unawares; and the inhabitants, being unable to withstand, have submitted to him:—whereupon I said within myself, If I fall into his hand, he will slay me.—Griefs overwhelmed me, and I thought of the calamities which had befallen my father and my mother, and knew not what to do; for if I appeared, the people of the city would know me, and the troops of my father would hasten to kill and destroy me. I knew no way of escape but to shave off my beard; so I shaved it, and, having changed my clothes, departed from the city, and came hither, to this abode of peace, in the hope that some person would introduce me to the Prince of the Faithful, the Khalifeh of the Lord of all creatures, that I might relate to him my story, and all that had befallen me. I arrived in this city this night; and as I stood perplexed, not knowing whither to direct my steps, I saw this mendicant, and saluted him, and said, I am a stranger. He replied, And I, too, am a stranger:—and while we were thus addressing each other, our companion, this third person, came up to us, and, saluting us, said, I am a stranger. We replied, And we, also, are strangers. So we walked on together, and darkness overtook us, and destiny directed us unto your abode:—This was the cause of the shaving of my beard, and of the loss of my eye.

The lady then said to him, Stroke thy head, and depart;—but he replied, I will not depart until I have heard the stories of the others. And they wondered at his tale; and the Khalifeh said to Ja'far, Verily I have never known the like of that which hath happened to this mendicant.

The second mendicant then advanced, and, having kissed the ground, said,—

The Story of the Second Royal Mendicant

O MY mistress, I was not born with only one eye; but my story is wonderful, and, if written, would serve as a lesson to him who would be admonished. I am a King, and son of a King: I read the Kur'an according to the seven readings, and perused various works under the tuition of different learned professors of their subjects: I studied the science of the stars, and the writings of the poets, and made myself a proficient in all the sciences; so that I surpassed the people of my age. My hand-writing was extolled among all the scribes, my fame spread among all countries, and my history among all Kings; and the King of India, hearing of me, requested my father to allow me to visit him, sending him various gifts and curious presents, such as were suitable to Kings. My father, therefore, prepared for me six ships, and we proceeded by sea for the space of a whole month, after which we came to land; and, having disembarked some horses which we had with us in the ship, we loaded ten camels with presents, and commenced our journey; but soon there appeared a cloud of dust, which rose and spread until it filled the air before us, and, after a while, cleared a little, and discovered to us, in the midst of it, sixty horsemen like fierce lions, whom we perceived to be Arab highwaymen; and when they saw us, that we were a small company with ten loads of presents for the King of India, they galloped towards us, pointing their spears at us. We made signs to them with our fingers, and said, We are ambassadors to the honoured King of India; therefore do us no injury:—but they replied, We are not in his territories, nor under his government. They slew certain of the young men, and the rest fled. I also fled, after I had received a severe wound; the Arabs being employed, without further regard to us, in taking possession of the treasure and presents which we had with us.

I proceeded without knowing whither to direct my course, reduced from a mighty to an abject state, and journeyed till I arrived at the summit of a mountain, where I took shelter in a cavern until the next morning. I then resumed my journey, and arrived at a flourishing city: the winter, with its cold, had passed away, and the spring had come, with its flowers; and I rejoiced at my arrival there, being wearied with my journey, anxious and pallid. My condition being thus changed, I knew not whither to bend my steps; and, turning to a tailor sitting in his shop, I saluted him, and he returned my salutation, and welcomed me, and wished me joy, asking me the reason of my having come thither. I acquainted him, therefore, with what had befallen me from first to last, and he was grieved for me, and said, O young man, reveal not thy case, for I fear what the King of this city might do to thee, since he is the greatest of thy father's enemies, and hath a debt of blood against him. He then placed some food and drink before me, and we ate together, and I conversed with him till night, when he lodged me in a place by his shop, and brought me a bed and coverlet; and, after I had remained with him three days, he said to me, Dost thou not know any trade by which to make gain? I answered, I am acquainted with the law, a student of sciences, a writer, and an arithmetician.—Thy occupation, he said, is profitless in our country: there is no one in our city acquainted with science or writing, but only with getting money. Verily, I replied, I know nothing but what I have told thee.—Gird thyself, then, said he, and take an axe and a rope, and cut firewood in the desert, and so obtain thy subsistence until God dispel thy affliction; but acquaint no one with thy history, else they will kill thee. He then bought for me an axe and a rope, and sent me with a party of woodcutters, giving them a charge respecting me. Accordingly, I went forth with them, and cut some wood, and brought back a load upon my head, and sold it for half a piece of gold, part of which I expended in food, laying by the remainder.

Thus I continued for the space of a year, after which I went one day into the desert, according to my custom, to cut firewood; and, finding there a tract with abundance of wood, I entered it, and came to a tree, around which I dug; and as I was removing the earth from its roots, the axe struck against a ring of brass; and I cleared away the earth from it, and found that it was affixed to a trapdoor of wood, which I immediately removed. Beneath it appeared a staircase, which I descended; and at the bottom of this I entered a door, and beheld a palace, strongly constructed, where I found a lady, like a pearl of high price, whose aspect banished from the heart all anxiety and grief and affliction. At the sight of her I prostrated myself in adoration of her Creator for the fairness and beauty which He had displayed in her person; and she, looking towards me, said, Art thou a man or a Jinni? I answered her, I am a man.—And who, she asked, hath brought thee to this place, in which I have lived five and twenty years without ever seeing a human being?—Her words sounded sweetly to me, and I answered her, O my mistress, God hath brought me to thy abode, and I hope will put an end to my anxiety and grief:—and I related to her my story from beginning to end. She was grieved at my case, and wept, and said, I also will acquaint thee with my story. Know that I am the daughter of the King of the further parts of India, the lord of the Ebony Island. My father had married me to the son of my uncle; but on the night of my bridal festivities, an 'Efrit named Jarjaris, the son of Rejmus, the son of Iblis, carried me off, and, soaring with me through the air, alighted in this place, to which he conveyed all things necessary for me, such as ornaments, and garments, and linen, and furniture, and food, and drink; and once in every ten days he cometh to me, and spendeth a night here; and he hath appointed with me, that, in case of my wanting any thing by night or day, I should touch with my hand these two lines which are inscribed upon the kubbeh, and as soon as I remove my hand I see him before me. Four days have now passed since he was last with me, and there remain, therefore, six days before he will come again; wilt thou then remain with me five days, and depart one day before his visit?—I answered, Yes;—rejoicing at the proposal; and she arose, and, taking me by the hand, conducted me through an arched door to a small and elegant bath, where I took off my clothes, while she seated herself upon a mattress. After this, she seated me by her side, and brought me some sherbet of sugar infused with musk, and handed it to me to drink: she then placed some food before me, and after we had eaten and conversed together, she said to me, Sleep, and rest thyself; for thou are fatigued.

I slept, O my mistress, and forgot all that had befallen me; and when I awoke, I found her rubbing my feet; upon which I called to her, and we sat down again and conversed awhile; and she said to me, By Allah, I was straitened in my heart, living here alone, without any person to talk with me, five and twenty years. Praise be to God who hath sent thee to me.—I thanked her for her kind expressions; and love of her took possession of my heart, and my anxiety and grief fled away. We then sat down to drink together; and I remained by her side all the night, delighted with her company, for I had never seen her like in my whole life; and in the morning, when we were both full of joy, I said to her, Shall I take thee up from this subterranean place, and release thee from the Jinni? But she laughed, and replied, Be content, and hold thy peace; for, of every ten days, one day shall be for the 'Efrit, and nine for thee. I persisted, however, being overcome with passion; and said, I will this instant demolish this kubbeh upon which the inscription is engraved, and let the 'Efrit come, that I may slay him: for I am predestined to kill 'Efrits. She entreated me to refrain; but, paying no attention to her words, I kicked the kubbeh with violence; upon which she exclaimed, The 'Efrit hath arrived! Did I not caution thee against this? Verily thou hast brought a calamity upon me; but save thyself, and ascend by the way that thou camest.

In the excess of my fear I forgot my sandals and my axe, and when I had ascended two steps, turning round to look for them, I saw that the ground had opened, and there rose from it an 'Efrit of hideous aspect, who said, Wherefore is this disturbance with which thou hast alarmed me, and what misfortune hath befallen thee? She answered, No misfortune hath happened to me, excepting that my heart was contracted, and I desired to drink some wine to dilate it, and, rising to perform my purpose, I fell against the kubbeh.—Thou liest, vile woman, he exclaimed;—and, looking about the palace to the right and left, he saw the sandals and axe; and said to her, These are the property of none but a man. Who hath visited thee?—I have not seen them, she answered, until this instant: probably they caught to thee.—This language, said he, is absurd, and will have no effect upon me, thou shameless woman!—and, so saying, he stripped her of her clothing, and tied her down, with her arms and legs extended, to four stakes, and began to beat her, urging her to confess what had happened.

For myself, being unable to endure her cries, I ascended the stairs, overpowered by fear, and, arriving at the top, replaced the trap-door as it was at first, and covered it over with earth. I repented bitterly of what I had done, and reflecting upon the lady and her beauty, and how this wretch was torturing her after she had lived with him five and twenty years, and that he tortured her only on my account, and reflecting also upon my father and his kingdom, and how I had been reduced to the condition of a wood-cutter, I repeated this verse:—

When fortune bringeth thee affliction, console thyself by remembering that one day thou must see prosperity, and another day, difficulty.

Returning to my companion, the tailor, I found him awaiting my return as if he were placed in a pan upon burning coals. I passed last night, said he, with anxious heart on thy account, fearing for thee from some wild beast or other calamity. Praise be to God for thy safe return.—I thanked him for his tender concern for me, and entered my apartment; and as I sat meditating upon that which had befallen me, and blaming myself for having kicked the kubbeh, my friend the tailor came in to me, and said, In the shop is a foreigner, who asks for thee, and he has thy axe and sandals; he came with them to the wood-cutters, and said to them, I went out at the time of the call of the Mu'eddin to morning-prayer, and stumbled upon these, and know not to whom they belong: can ye guide me to their owner?—The wood-cutters, therefore, directed him to thee: he is sitting in my shop; so go out to him and thank him, and take thy axe and thy sandals.—On hearing these words, my countenance turned pale, and my whole state became changed; and while I was in this condition, the floor of my chamber clove asunder, and there rose from it the stranger, and lo, he was the 'Efrit; he had tortured the lady with the utmost cruelty;

but she would confess nothing: so he took the axe and the sandals, and said to her, If I am Jarjaris, of the descendants of Iblís, I will bring the owner of this axe and these sandals. Accordingly, he came, with the pretence before mentioned, to the wood-cutters, and, having entered my chamber without granting me any delay, seized me, and soared with me through the air: he then descended, and dived into the earth, and brought me up into the place where I was before.

Here I beheld the lady stripped of her clothing, and with blood flowing from her sides; and tears trickled from my eyes. The 'Efrít then took hold of her, and said, Vile woman, this is thy lover:—whereupon she looked at me, and replied, I know him not, nor have I ever seen him until this instant. The 'Efrít said to her, With all this torture wilt thou not confess? She answered, Never in my life have I seen him before, and it is not lawful in the sight of God that I should speak falsely against him.—Then, said he, if thou know him not, take this sword and strike off his head. She took the sword, and came to me, and stood over my head: but I made a sign to her with my eyebrow, while tears ran down my cheeks. She replied in a similar manner, Thou art he who hath done all this to me:—I made a sign to her, however, that this was a time for pardon, conveying my meaning in the manner thus described by the poet:—

Our signal in love is the glance of our eyes; and every intelligent
        person understandeth the sign.
Our eyebrows carry on an intercourse between us: we are silent;
        but love speaketh.

And when she understood me, she threw the sword from her hand, O my mistress, and the 'Efrít handed it to me, saying, Strike off her head, and I will liberate thee, and do thee no harm. I replied, Good:—and, quickly approaching her, raised my hand; but she made a sign as though she would say, I did no injury to thee:—whereupon my eyes poured with tears, and, throwing down the sword, I said, O mighty 'Efrít, and valiant hero, if a woman, deficient in sense and religion, seeth it not lawful to strike off my head, how is it lawful for me to do so to her, and especially when I have never seen her before in my life? I will never do it,

though I should drink the cup of death and destruction.—
There is affection between you, said the 'Efrit, and, taking
the sword, he struck off one of the hands of the lady; then,
the other; after this, her right foot; and then, her left foot:
thus with four blows he cut off her four extremities, while I
looked on, expecting my own death. She then made a sign
to me with her eye; and the 'Efrit, observing her, exclaimed,
Now thou hast been guilty of incontinence with thine eye!
—and, with a blow of his sword, struck off her head; after
which, he turned towards me, and said, O man, it is allowed
us by our law, if a wife be guilty of incontinence, to put her
to death. This woman I carried off on her wedding-night,
when she was twelve years of age, and she was acquainted
with no man but me; and I used to pass one night with her
in the course of every ten days in the garb of a foreigner;
and when I discovered of a certainty that she had been unfaithful to me, I killed her: but as for thee, I am not convinced that thou hast wronged me with respect to her; yet
I must not leave thee unpunished: choose, therefore, what
injury I shall do to thee.

Upon this, O my mistress, I rejoiced exceedingly, and,
eager to obtain his pardon, I said to him, What shall I
choose from thy hands?—Choose he answered, into what
form I shall change thee; either the form of a dog, or that
of an ass, or that of an ape. I replied, in my desire of
forgiveness, Verily, if thou wilt pardon me, God will pardon
thee in recompense for thy shewing mercy to a Muslim who
hath done thee no injury:—and I humbled myself in the
most abject manner, and said to him, Pardon me as the
envied man did the envier.—And how was that? said he.
I answered as follows:—

THE STORY OF THE ENVIER AND THE ENVIED

KNOW, O my master, that there was a certain man who
had a neighbour that envied him; and the more this person
envied him, so much the more did God increase the prosperity of the former. Thus it continued a long time; but
when the envied man found that his neighbour persisted
in troubling him, he removed to a place where there was a

deserted well; and there he built for himself an oratory, and occupied himself in the worship of God. Numerous Fakirs⁶ assembled around him, and he acquired great esteem, people repairing to him from every quarter, placing firm reliance upon his sanctity; and his fame reached the ears of his envious neighbour, who mounted his horse, and went to visit him; and when the envied man saw him, he saluted him, and payed him the utmost civility. The envier then said to him, I have come hither to inform thee of a matter in which thou wilt find advantage, and for which I shall obtain a recompense in heaven. The envied man replied, May God requite thee for me with every blessing. Then, said the envier, order the Fakirs to retire to their cells, for the information that I am about to give thee I would have no one overhear. So he ordered them to enter their cells; and the envier said to him, Arise, and let us walk together, and converse; and they walked on until they came to the deserted well before mentioned, when the envier pushed the envied man into this well, without the knowledge of any one, and went his way, imagining that he had killed him.

But this well was inhabited by Jinn, who received him unhurt, and seated him upon a large stone; and when they had done this, one of them said to the others, Do ye know this man? They answered, We know him not.—This, said he, is the envied man who fled from him who envied him, and took up his abode in this quarter, in the neighbouring oratory, and who entertaineth us by his zikr⁷ and his readings; and when his envier heard of him, he came hither to him, and, devising a stratagem against him, threw him down here. His fame hath this night reached the Sultan of this city, who hath purposed to visit him to-morrow, on account of the affliction which hath befallen his daughter.—And what, said they, hath happened to his daughter? He answered, Madness; for Meymun, the son of Demdem, hath become inflamed with love for her; and her cure is the easiest of things. They asked him, What is it?—and

---

⁶ Poor persons who especially occupy themselves in religious exercises.
⁷ Zikrs consist in repeating the name of God, or the profession of his unity, etc., in chorus, accompanying the words by certain motions of the head, hands, or whole body.

he answered, The black cat that is with him in the oratory hath at the end of her tail a white spot, of the size of a piece of silver; and from this white spot should be taken seven hairs, and with these the damsel should be fumigated, and the Marid would depart from over her head, and not return to her; so she would be instantly cured. And now it is our duty to take him out.

When the morning came, the Fakirs saw the sheykh rising out of the well; and he became magnified in their eyes. And when he entered the oratory, he took from the white spot at the end of the cat's tail seven hairs, and placed them in a portfolio by him; and at sunrise the King came to him, and when the sheykh saw him, he said to him, O King, thou hast come to visit me in order that I may cure thy daughter. The King replied, Yes, O virtuous Sheykh.—Then, said the sheykh, send some person to bring her hither; and I trust in God, whose name be exalted, that she may be instantly cured. And when the King had brought his daughter, the sheykh beheld her bound, and, seating her, suspended a curtain over her, and took out the hairs, and fumigated her with them; whereupon the Marid cried out from over her head, and left her; and the damsel immediately recovered her reason, and, veiling her face, said to her father, What is this, and wherefore didst thou bring me to this place? He answered her, Thou hast nothing to fear;—and rejoiced greatly. He kissed the hand of the envied sheykh, and said to the great men of his court who were with him, What shall be the recompense of this sheykh for that which he hath done? They answered, His recompense should be that thou marry him to her.—Ye have spoken truly, said the King:—and he gave her in marriage to him, and thus the sheykh became a connection of the King; and after some days the King died, and he was made King in his place.

And it happened one day that this envied King was riding with his troops, and he saw his envier approaching; and when this man came before him he seated him upon a horse with high distinction and honour, and, taking him to his palace, gave him a thousand pieces of gold, and a costly dress; after which he sent him back from the city, with attendants to escort him to his house, and reproached him for nothing.—Consider, then, O 'Efrit, the pardon of the envied to the envier, and his kindness to him, notwithstanding the injuries he had done him.—

The 'Efrit, when he had heard this story, replied, Lengthen not thy words to me: as to my killing thee, fear it not; and as to my pardoning thee, covet it not; but as to my enchanting thee, there is no escape from it;—and, so saying, he clove the earth asunder, and soared with me through the sky to such a height that I beheld the world beneath me as though it were a bowl of water; then, alighting upon a mountain, he took up a little dust, and, having muttered and pronounced certain words over it, sprinkled me with it, saying, Quit this form, and take the form of an ape!—whereupon I became like an ape of a hundred years of age.

When I saw myself changed into this ugly form, I wept for myself, but determined to be patient under the tyranny of fortune, knowing it to be constant to no one. I descended from the summit of the mountain, and, after having journeyed for the space of a month, arrived at the seashore; and, when I had stood there a short time, I saw a vessel in the midst of the sea, with a favourable wind approaching the land; I therefore hid myself behind a rock on the beach, and when the ship came close up, I sprang into the midst of it. But as soon as the persons on board saw me, one of them cried, Turn out this unlucky brute from the ship:—another said, Let us kill him:—and a third exclaimed, I will kill him with this sword. I, however, caught hold of the end of the sword, and tears flowed from my eyes; at the sight of which the captain took compassion on me, and said to the passengers, O merchants, this ape hath sought my aid, and I give it him; he is under my protection; let no one, therefore, oppose or trouble him. He then treated me with kindness, and whatever he said to me I understood, and all that he required to be done I performed as his servant.

We continued our voyage for fifty days with a fair wind, and cast anchor under a large city containing a population

which no one but God, whose name be exalted, could
reckon; and when we had moored our vessel, there came
to us some memluks from the King of the city, who came
on board the ship, and complimented the merchants on
their safe arrival, saying, Our King greeteth you, rejoicing
in your safety, and hath sent to you this roll of paper, desiring that each of you shall write a line upon it; for the
King had a Wezir who was an eminent calligraphist, and he
is dead, and the King hath sworn that he will not appoint
any person to his office who cannot write equally well.
Though in the form of an ape, I arose and snatched the
paper from their hands; upon which, fearing that I would
tear it and throw it into the sea, they cried out against me,
and would have killed me; but I made signs to them that
I would write, and the captain said to them, Suffer him to
write, and if he scribble we will turn him away; but if he
write well I will adopt him as my son; for I have never
seen a more intelligent ape. So I took the pen, and demanded the ink, and wrote in an epistolary hand this
couplet:—

Fame hath recorded the virtues of the noble; but no one hath
    been able to reckon thine.
May God not deprive mankind of such a father; for thou art the
    parent of every excellence.

Then, in a more formal, large hand, I wrote the following
verses:—

There is no writer that shall not perish; but what his hand hath
    written endureth ever.
Write, therefore, nothing but what will please thee when thou
    shalt see it on the day of resurrection.

Two other specimens I wrote, in two different and smaller
hands, and returned the paper to the memluks, who took it
back to the King; and when he saw what was written upon
it, the hand of no one pleased him excepting mine; and he
said to his attendants, Go to the author of this hand-writing,
put upon him this dress, and mount him upon a mule, and
conduct him, with the band of music before him, to my
presence. On hearing this order, they smiled; and the
King was angry with them, and said, How is it that I give

you an order, and ye laugh at me? They answered, O King,
we laugh not at thy words, but because he who wrote this
is an ape, and not a son of Adam: he is with the captain
of the ship newly arrived.

The King was astonished at their words; he shook with
delight, and said, I would purchase this ape. He then sent
some messengers to the ship, with the mule and the dress
of honour, saying to them, Ye must clothe him with this
dress, and mount him upon the mule, and bring him hither.
So they came to the ship, and, taking me from the captain,
clad me with the dress; and the people were astonished,
and flocked to amuse themselves with the sight of me. And
when they brought me to the King, and I beheld him, I
kissed the ground before him three times, and he ordered
me to sit down: so I sat down upon my knees; and the
persons present were surprised at my polite manners, and
especially the King, who presently ordered his people to
retire. They, therefore, did so; none remaining but the
King, and a eunuch, and a young memluk, and myself.
The King then commanded that a repast should be brought;
and they placed before him a service of viands, such as
gratified the appetite and delighted the eye; and the King
made a sign to me that I should eat; whereupon I arose,
and, having kissed the ground before him seven times, sat
down to eat with him; and when the table was removed, I
washed my hands, and, taking the ink-case, and pen and
paper, I wrote these two verses:—

Great is my appetite for thee, O Kunafeh![8] I cannot be happy
    nor endure without thee.
Be thou every day and night my food; and may drops of honey
    not be wanting to moisten thee.

Having done this, I arose, and seated myself at a distance;
and the King, looking at what I had written, read it with
astonishment, and exclaimed, Can an ape possess such
fluency and such skill in calligraphy? This is, indeed, a
wonder of wonders!—Afterwards, a chess-table was brought
to the King, and he said to me, Wilt thou play? By a
motion of my head I answered, Yes:—and I advanced, and

[8] A kind of pastry resembling vermicelli, made of wheat-flour. It is
moistened with clarified butter—then baked, and sweetened with honey or
sugar.

arranged the pieces. I played with him twice, and beat him; and the King was perplexed, and said, Were this a man, he would surpass all the people of his age.

He then said to his eunuch, Go to thy mistress, and say to her, Answer the summons of the King:—that she may come and gratify her curiosity by the sight of this wonderful ape. The eunuch, therefore, went, and returned with his mistress, the King's daughter, who, as soon as she saw me, veiled her face, and said, O my father, how is it that thou art pleased to send for me and suffer strange men to see me?—O my daughter, answered the King, there is no one here but the young memluk, and the eunuch who brought thee up, and this ape, with myself, thy father: from whom, then, dost thou veil thy face?—This ape, said she, is the son of a King, and the name of his father is Eymar: he is enchanted, and it was the 'Efrit Jarjaris, a descendant of Iblis, who transformed him, after having slain his own wife, the daughter of King Aknamus. This, whom thou sup-posedst to be an ape, is a learned and wise man.—The King was amazed at his daughter's words, and, looking towards me, said, Is it true that she saith of thee? I answered, by a motion of my head, Yes:—and wept. The King then said to his daughter, By what means didst thou discover that he was enchanted?—O my father, she answered, I had with me, in my younger years, an old woman who was a cunning enchantress, and she taught me the art of en-chantment: I have committed its rules to memory, and know it thoroughly, being acquainted with a hundred and seventy modes of performing it, by the least of which I could transport the stones of thy city beyond Mount Kaf, and make its site to be an abyss of the sea, and convert its inhabitants into fish in the midst of it.—I conjure thee, then, by the name of Allah, said her father, to restore this young man, that I may make him my Wezir. Is it possible that thou possessedst this excellence, and I knew it not? Restore him, that I may make him my Wezir, for he is a polite and intelligent youth.

She replied, With pleasure:—and, taking a knife upon which were engraved some Hebrew names, marked with it a circle in the midst of the palace. Within this she wrote certain names and talismans, and then she pronounced invocations, and uttered unintelligible words; and soon the palace around us became immersed in gloom to such a degree, that we thought the whole world was overspread; and lo, the 'Efrit appeared before us in a most hideous shape, with hands like winnowing-forks, and legs like masts, and eyes like burning torches; so that we were terrified at him. The King's daughter exclaimed, No welcome to thee! —to which the 'Efrit, assuming the form of a lion, replied, Thou traitress, how is it that thou hast broken thine oath? Did we not swear that we would not oppose one another?— Thou wretch, said she, when didst thou receive an oath?— The 'Efrit, still in the form of a lion, then exclaimed, Take what awaiteth thee!—and, opening his mouth, rushed upon the lady; but she instantly plucked a hair from her head and muttered with her lips, whereupon the hair became converted into a piercing sword, with which she struck the lion, and he was cleft in twain by the blow; but his head became changed into a scorpion. The lady immediately transformed herself into an enormous serpent, and crept after the execrable wretch in the shape of a scorpion, and a sharp contest ensued between them; after which, the scorpion became an eagle, and the serpent, changing to a vulture, pursued the eagle for a length of time. The latter then transformed himself into a black cat, and the King's daughter became a wolf, and they fought together long and fiercely, till the cat, seeing himself overcome, changed himself into a large red pomegranate, which fell into a pool; but, the wolf pursuing it, it ascended into the air, and then fell upon the pavement of the palace, and broke in pieces, its grains becoming scattered, each apart from the others, and all spread about the whole space of ground enclosed by the palace. The wolf, upon this, transformed itself into a cock, in order to pick up the grains, and not leave one of them; but, according to the decree of fate, one grain remained hidden by the side of the pool of the fountain. The cock began to cry, and flapped its wings, and made a sign to us with its beak; but we understood not what it would say. It then uttered at us such a cry, that we thought the palace had fallen down upon us; and it ran about the whole of the ground, until it saw the grain that had lain hid by the side of the pool, when it pounced upon it, to pick it up; but it fell into the midst of the water, and became transformed into a fish, and sank into the water; upon which the cock became a fish of a larger size, and plunged in after the other. For a while it was absent from our sight; but, at length, we heard a loud cry, and trembled at the sound; after which, the 'Efrit rose as a flame of fire, casting fire from his mouth, and fire and smoke from his eyes and nostrils: the King's daughter also became as a vast body of fire; and we would have plunged into the water from fear of our being burnt and destroyed; but suddenly the 'Efrit cried out from within the fire, and came towards us upon the liwan,[9] blowing fire at our faces. The lady, however, overtook him, and blew fire in like manner in his face; and some sparks struck us both from her and from him: her sparks did us no harm; but one from him struck me in my eye, and destroyed it, I being still in the form of an ape; and a spark from him reached the face of the King, and burned the lower half, with his beard and mouth, and struck out his lower teeth: another spark also fell upon the breast of the eunuch; who was burnt, and died immediately. We expected destruction, and gave up all hope of preserving our lives; but while we were in this state, a voice exclaimed, God is most great! God is most great! He hath conquered and aided, and abandoned the denier of the faith of Mohammad, the chief of mankind.[10] —The person from whom this voice proceeded was the King's daughter: she had burnt the 'Efrit; and when we looked towards him, we perceived that he had become a heap of ashes.

The lady then came to us, and said, Bring me a cup of water:—and when it was brought to her, she pronounced over it some words which we understood not, and, sprinkling me with it, said, Be restored, by virtue of the name of the Truth, and by virtue of the most great name of God, to thy original form!—whereupon I became a man as I was at first, excepting that my eye was destroyed. After this, she

[9] Dais.
[10] This was, and I believe still is, a common battle-cry of the Arabs, and more commonly used on the occasion of a victory.

cried out, The fire! the fire! O my father, I shall no longer live, for I am predestined to be killed. Had he been a human being, I had killed him at the first of the encounter. I experienced no difficulty till the scattering of the grains of the pomegranate, when I picked them up excepting the one in which was the life of the Jinni: had I picked up that, he had instantly died; but I saw it not, as fate and destiny had appointed; and suddenly he came upon me, and a fierce contest ensued between us under the earth, and in the air, and in the water; and every time that he tried against me a new mode, I employed against him one more potent, until he tried against me the mode of fire; and rarely does one escape against whom the mode of fire is employed. Destiny, however, aided me, so that I burned him first; but I exhorted him previously to embrace the faith of El-Islam. Now I die; and may God supply my place to you.—Having thus said, she ceased not to pray for relief from the fire; and lo, a spark ascended to her breast, and thence to her face; and when it reached her face, she wept, and exclaimed, I testify that there is no deity but God, and I testify that Mohammad is God's Apostle!—We then looked towards her, and saw that she had become a heap of ashes by the side of the ashes of the 'Efrit.

We were plunged into grief on her account, and I wished that I had been in her place rather than have seen that sweet-faced creature who had done me this kindness reduced to a heap of ashes: but the decree of God cannot be averted. The King, on beholding his daughter in this state, plucked out what remained of his beard, and slapped his face, and rent his clothes; and I also did the same, while we both wept for her. Then came the chamberlains and other great officers of the court, who, finding the King in a state of insensibility, with two heaps of ashes before him, were astonished, and remained encompassing him until he recovered from his fit, when he informed them of what had befallen his daughter with the 'Efrit; and great was their affliction. The women shrieked, with the female slaves, and continued their mourning seven days. After this, the King gave orders to build, over the ashes of his daughter, a great tomb with a dome, and illuminated it with candles and lamps: but the

ashes of the 'Efrit they scattered in the wind, exposing them
to the curse of God. The King then fell sick, and was near
unto death: his illness lasted a month; but after this he recovered his health, and, summoning me to his presence, said
to me, O young man, we passed our days in the enjoyment
of the utmost happiness, secure from the vicissitudes of
fortune, until thou camest to us, when troubles overcame us.
Would that we had never seen thee, nor thy ugly form, on
account of which we have been reduced to this state of pri-
vation; for, in the first place, I have lost my daughter, who
was worth a hundred men; and, secondly, I have suffered this
burning, and lost my teeth: my eunuch also is dead: but it
was not in thy power to prevent these afflictions: the decree
of God hath been fulfilled on us and on thee; and praise
be to God that my daughter restored thee, though she destroyed herself. Now, however, depart, O my son, from
my city. It is enough that hath happened on thy account;
but as it was decreed against us and thee, depart in peace.

So I departed, O my mistress, from his presence; but
before I quitted the city, I entered a public bath, and shaved
my beard. I traversed various regions, and passed through
great cities, and bent my course to the Abode of Peace,
Baghdad, in the hope of obtaining an interview with the
Prince of the Faithful, that I might relate to him all that
had befallen me.

The third mendicant then advanced, and thus related his
story:—

The Story of the Third Royal Mendicant

O ILLUSTRIOUS lady, my story is not like those of my two
companions, but more wonderful: the course of fate and
destiny brought upon them events against which they could
not guard; but as to myself, the shaving of my beard and
the loss of my eye were occasioned by my provoking fate
and misfortune; and the cause was this:—

I was a King, and the son of a King; and when my
father died, I succeeded to his throne, and governed my
subjects with justice and beneficence. I took pleasure in
sea-voyages; and my capital was on the shore of an ex-

tensive sea, interspersed with fortified and garrisoned islands, which I desired, for my amusement, to visit; I therefore embarked with a fleet of ten ships, and took with me provisions sufficient for a whole month. I proceeded twenty days, after which there arose against us a contrary wind; but at daybreak it ceased, and the sea became calm, and we arrived at an island, where we landed, and cooked some provisions and ate; after which we remained there two days. We then continued our voyage; and when twenty days more had passed, we found ourselves in strange waters, unknown to the captain, and desired the watch to look out from the mast-head: so he went aloft, and when he had come down he said to the captain, I saw, on my right hand, fish floating upon the surface of the water; and looking towards the midst of the sea, I perceived something looming in the distance, sometimes black and sometimes white.

When the captain heard this report of the watch, he threw his turban on the deck, and plucked his beard, and said to those who were with him, Receive warning of our destruction, which will befall all of us: not one will escape! So saying, he began to weep; and all of us in like manner bewailed our lot. I desired him to inform us of that which the watch had seen. O my lord, he replied, know that we have wandered from our course since the commencement of the contrary wind that was followed in the morning by a calm, in consequence of which we remained stationary two days; from that period we have deviated from our course for twenty-one days, and we have no wind to carry us back from the fate which awaits us after this day: to-morrow we shall arrive at a mountain of black stone, called loadstone: the current is now bearing us violently towards it, and the ships will fall in pieces, and every nail in them will fly to the mountain, and adhere to it; for God hath given to the loadstone a secret property by virtue of which everything of iron is attracted toward it. On that mountain is such a quantity of iron as no one knoweth but God, whose name be exalted; for from times of old great numbers of ships have been destroyed by the influence of that mountain. There is, upon the summit of the mountain, a cupola of brass supported by ten columns, and upon the top of this cupola is a horseman upon a horse of brass, having in his hand a brazen spear, and upon his breast suspended a tablet of lead, upon which are engraved mysterious names and talismans; and as long, O King, as this horseman remains upon the horse, so long will every ship that approaches be destroyed, with every person on board, and all the iron contained in it will cleave to the mountain: no one will be safe until the horseman shall have fallen from the horse.—The captain then wept bitterly; and we felt assured that our destruction was inevitable, and every one of us bade adieu to his friend.

On the following morning we drew near to the mountain; the current carried us toward it with violence, and when the ships were almost close to it, they fell asunder, and all the nails, and everything else that was of iron, flew from them towards the loadstone. It was near the close of day when the ships fell in pieces. Some of us were drowned, and some escaped; but the greater number were drowned, and of those who saved their lives none knew what became of the others, so stupefied were they by the waves and the boisterous wind. As for myself, O my mistress, God, whose name be exalted, spared me on account of the trouble and torment and affliction that He had predestined to befall me. I placed myself upon a plank, and the wind and waves cast it upon the mountain; and when I had landed, I found a practicable way to the summit, resembling steps cut in the rock: so I exclaimed, In the name of God!—and offered up a prayer, and attempted the ascent, holding fast by the notches; and presently God stilled the wind and assisted me in my endeavours, so that I arrived in safety at the summit. Rejoicing greatly in my escape, I immediately entered the cupola, and performed the prayers of two rek'ahs[11] in gratitude to God for my preservation; after which I slept beneath the cupola, and heard a voice saying to me, O son of Khasib, when thou awakest from thy sleep, dig beneath thy feet, and thou wilt find a bow of brass, and three arrows of lead, whereon are engraved talismans: then take the

[11] [Bowings]: the repetition of a set form of words, chiefly from the Kur'an, and ejaculations of "God is most great!" etc., accompanied by particular postures; part of the words being repeated in an erect posture; part, sitting; and part, in other postures: an inclination of the head and body, followed by two prostrations, distinguishing each rek'ah.

bow and arrows and shoot at the horseman that is upon the top of the cupola, and relieve mankind from this great affliction; for when thou hast shot at the horseman he will fall into the sea; the bow will also fall, and do thou bury it in its place; and as soon as thou hast done this, the sea will swell and rise until it attains the summit of the mountain; and there will appear upon it a boat bearing a man, different from him whom thou shalt have cast down, and he will come to thee, having an oar in his hand: then do thou embark with him; but utter not the name of God; and he will convey thee in ten days to a safe sea, where, on thy arrival, thou wilt find one who will take thee to thy city. All this shall be done if thou utter not the name of God.

Awaking from my sleep, I sprang up, and did as the voice had directed. I shot at the horseman, and he fell into the sea; and the bow having fallen from my hand, I buried it: the sea then became troubled, and rose to the summit of the mountain, and when I had stood waiting there a little while, I beheld a boat in the midst of the sea, approaching me. I praised God, whose name be exalted, and when the boat came to me I found in it a man of brass, with a tablet of lead upon his breast, engraven with names and talismans. Without uttering a word, I embarked in the boat, and the man rowed me ten successive days, after which I beheld the islands of security, whereupon, in the excess of my joy, I exclaimed, In the name of God! There is no deity but God! God is most great!—and as soon as I had done this, he cast me out of the boat, and sank in the sea.

Being able to swim, I swam until night, when my arms and shoulders were tired, and, in this perilous situation, I repeated the profession of the faith, and gave myself up as lost; but the sea rose with the violence of the wind, and a wave like a vast castle threw me upon the land, in order to the accomplishment of the purpose of God. I ascended the shore, and after I had wrung out my clothes, and spread them upon the ground to dry, I slept; and in the morning I put on my clothes again, and, looking about to see which way I should go, I found a tract covered with trees, to which I advanced; and when I had walked round it, I found that I was upon a small island in the midst of the sea; upon which I said within myself, Every time that I escape from one calamity I fall into another that is worse:—but while I was reflecting upon my unfortunate case, and wishing for death, I beheld a vessel bearing a number of men. I arose immediately, and climbed into a tree; and lo, the vessel came to the shore, and there landed from it ten black slaves bearing axes. They proceeded to the middle of the island, and, digging up the earth, uncovered and lifted up a trap-door, after which they returned to the vessel, and brought from it bread and flour and clarified butter and honey and sheep and everything that the wants of an inhabitant would require, continuing to pass backwards and forwards between the vessel and the trap-door, bringing loads from the former, and entering the latter, until they had removed all the stores from the ship. They then came out of the vessel with various clothes of the most beautiful description, and in the midst of them was an old sheykh enfeebled and wasted by extreme age, leading by the hand a young man cast in the mould of graceful symmetry, and invested with such perfect beauty as deserved to be a subject for proverbs. He was like a fresh and slender twig, enchanting and captivating every heart by his elegant form. The party proceeded to the trap-door, and, entering it, became concealed from my eyes.

They remained beneath about two hours, or more; after which, the sheykh and the slaves came out; but the youth came not with them; and they replaced the earth, and embarked and set sail. Soon after, I descended from the tree, and went to the excavation. I removed the earth, and, entering the aperture, saw a flight of wooden steps, which I descended; and, at the bottom, I beheld a handsome dwelling-place, furnished with a variety of silken carpets; and there was the youth, sitting upon a high mattress, with sweet-smelling flowers and fruits placed before him. On seeing me, his countenance became pale; but I saluted him, and said, Let thy mind be composed, O my Master: thou hast nothing to fear, O delight of my eye; for I am a man, and the son of a King, like thyself: fate hath impelled me to thee, that I may cheer thee in thy solitude. The youth, when he heard me thus address him, and was convinced that

I was one of his own species, rejoiced exceedingly at my arrival, his colour returned, and, desiring me to approach him, he said, O my brother, my story is wonderful: my father is a jeweller: he had slaves who made voyages by his orders, for the purposes of commerce, and he had dealings with Kings; but he had never been blest with a son; and he dreamt that he was soon to have a son, but one whose life would be short; and he awoke sorrowful. Shortly after, in accordance with the decrees of God, my mother conceived me, and when her time was complete, she gave birth to me; and my father was greatly rejoiced: the astrologers, however, came to him, and said, Thy son will live fifteen years: his fate is intimated by the fact that there is, in the sea, a mountain called the Mountain of Loadstone, whereon is a horseman on a horse of brass, on the former of which is a tablet of lead suspended to his neck; and when the horseman shall be thrown down from his horse, thy son will be slain: the person who is to slay him is he who will throw down the horseman, and his name is King 'Ajib, the son of King Khasib. My father was greatly afflicted at this announcement; and when he had reared me until I had nearly attained the age of fifteen years, the astrologers came again, and informed him that the horseman had fallen into the sea, and that it had been thrown down by King 'Ajib, the son of King Khasib; on hearing which, he prepared for me this dwelling, and here left me to remain until the completion of the term, of which there now remain ten days. All this he did from fear lest King 'Ajib should kill me.

When I heard this, I was filled with wonder, and said within myself, I am King 'Ajib, the son of King Khasib, and it was I who threw down the horseman; but, by Allah, I will neither kill him nor do him any injury. Then said I to the youth, Far from thee be both destruction and harm, if it be the will of God, whose name be exalted: thou hast nothing to fear: I will remain with thee to serve thee, and will go forth with thee to thy father, and beg of him to send me back to my country, for the which he will obtain a reward. The youth rejoiced at my words, and I sat and conversed with him until night, when I spread his bed for him, and covered him, and slept near to his side. And in the morning

I brought him water, and he washed his face, and said to me, May God requite thee for me with every blessing. If I escape from King 'Ajib, I will make my father reward thee with abundant favours. Never, I replied, may the day arrive that would bring thee misfortune. I then placed before him some refreshments, and after we had eaten together, we passed the day conversing with the utmost cheerfulness.

I continued to serve him for nine days; and on the tenth day the youth rejoiced at finding himself in safety, and said to me, O my brother, I wish that thou wouldst in thy kindness warm for me some water, that I may wash myself and change my clothes; for I have smelt the odour of escape from death, in consequence of thy assistance.—With pleasure, I replied;—and I arose, and warmed the water; after which, he entered a place concealed from my view, and, having washed himself and changed his clothes, laid himself upon the mattress to rest after his bath. He then said to me, Cut up for me, O my brother, a water-melon, and mix its juice with some sugar:—so I arose, and taking a melon, brought it upon a plate, and said to him, Knowest thou, O my master, where is the knife?—See, here it is, he answered, upon the shelf over my head. I sprang up hastily, and took it from its sheath, and as I was drawing back, my foot slipped, as God had decreed, and I fell upon the youth, grasping in my hand the knife, which entered his body, and he died instantly. When I perceived that he was dead, and that I had killed him, I uttered a loud shriek, and beat my face and rent my clothes, saying, This is, indeed, a calamity! O what a calamity! O my Lord, I implore thy pardon, and declare to Thee my innocence of his death! Would that I had died before him! How long shall I devour trouble after trouble!

With these reflections I ascended the steps, and, having replaced the trap-door, returned to my first station, and looked over the sea, where I saw the vessel that had come before, approaching, and cleaving the waves in its rapid course. Upon this I said within myself, Now will the men come forth from the vessel, and find the youth slain, and they will slay me also:—so I climbed into a tree, and concealed myself among its leaves, and sat there till the vessel arrived and cast anchor, when the slaves landed with the old sheykh, the father of the youth, and went to the place, and removed the earth. They were surprised at finding it moist, and when they had descended the steps, they discovered the youth lying on his back, exhibiting a face beaming with beauty, though dead, and clad in white and clean clothing, with the knife remaining in his body. They all wept at the sight, and the father fell down in a swoon, which lasted so long that the slaves thought he was dead. At length, however, he recovered, and came out with the slaves, who had wrapped the body of the youth in his clothes. They then took back all that was in the subterranean dwelling to the vessel, and departed.

I remained, O my mistress, by day hiding myself in a tree, and at night walking about the open part of the island. Thus I continued for the space of two months; and I perceived that, on the western side of the island, the water of the sea every day retired, until, after three months, the land that had been beneath it became dry. Rejoicing at this, and feeling confident now in my escape, I traversed this dry tract, and arrived at an expanse of sand; whereupon I emboldened myself, and crossed it. I then saw in the distance an appearance of fire, and, advancing towards it, found it to be a palace, overlaid with plates of copper, which, reflecting the rays of the sun, seemed from a distance to be fire: and when I drew near to it, reflecting upon this sight, there approached me an old sheykh, accompanied by ten young men who were all blind of one eye, at which I was extremely surprised. As soon as they saw me, they saluted me, and asked me my story, which I related to them from first to last; and they were filled with wonder. They then conducted me into the palace, where I saw ten benches, upon each of which was a mattress covered with a blue stuff;[12] and each of the young men seated himself upon one of these benches, while the sheykh took his place upon a smaller one; after which they said to me, Sit down, O young man, and ask no question respecting our condition, nor respecting our being blind of one eye. Then the sheykh arose, and brought to each of them some food, and the same

[12] The colour of mourning.

to me also; and next he brought to each of us some wine: and after we had eaten, we sat drinking together until the time for sleep, when the young men said to the sheykh, Bring to us our accustomed supply :—upon which the sheykh arose, and entered a closet, from which he brought upon his head, ten covered trays. Placing these upon the floor, he lighted ten candles, and stuck one of them upon each tray; and, having done this he removed the covers, and there appeared beneath them ashes mixed with pounded charcoal. The young men then tucked up their sleeves above the elbow, and blackened their faces, and slapped their cheeks, exclaiming, We were reposing at our ease, and our impertinent curiosity suffered us not to remain so! Thus they did until the morning, when the sheykh brought them some hot water, and they washed their faces, and put on other clothes.

On witnessing this conduct, my reason was confounded, my heart was so troubled that I forgot my own misfortunes, and I asked them the cause of their strange behaviour; upon which they looked towards me, and said, O young man, ask not respecting that which doth not concern thee; but be silent; for in silence is security from error.—I remained with them a whole month, during which every night they did the same; and at length I said to them, I conjure you by Allah to remove this disquiet from my mind, and to inform me of the cause of your acting in this manner, and of your exclaiming, We were reposing at our ease, and our impertinent curiosity suffered us not to remain so!—if ye inform me not, I will leave you, and go my way; for the proverb saith, When the eye seeth not, the heart doth not grieve.—On hearing these words, they replied, We have not concealed this affair from thee but in our concern for thy welfare, lest thou shouldst become like us, and the same affliction that hath befallen us happen also to thee. I said, however, Ye must positively inform me of this matter.—We give thee good advice, said they, and do thou receive it, and ask us not respecting our case; otherwise thou wilt become blind of one eye, like us:—but I still persisted in my request; whereupon they said, O young man, if this befall thee, know that thou wilt be banished from our company.

They then all arose, and, taking a ram, slaughtered and skinned it, and said to me, Take this knife with thee, and introduce thyself into the skin of the ram, and we will sew thee up in it, and go away; whereupon a bird called the rukh will come to thee, and, taking thee up by its talons, will fly away with thee, and set thee down upon a mountain: then cut open the skin with this knife, and get out, and the bird will fly away. Thou must arise, as soon as it hath gone, and journey for half a day, and thou wilt see before thee a lofty palace, encased with red gold, set with various precious stones, such as emeralds and rubies, &c.; and if thou enter it thy case will be as ours; for our entrance into that palace was the cause of our being blind of one eye; and if one of us would relate to thee all that hath befallen him, his story would be too long for thee to hear.

They then sewed me up in the skin, and entered their palace; and soon after, there came an enormous white bird, which seized me, and flew away with me, and set me down upon the mountain; whereupon I cut open the skin, and got out; and the bird, as soon as it saw me, flew away. I rose up quickly, and proceeded towards the palace, which I found to be as they had described it to me; and when I had entered it, I beheld, at the upper end of a saloon, forty young damsels, beautiful as so many moons, and magnificently attired, who, as soon as they saw me, exclaimed, Welcome! Welcome! O our master and our lord! We have been for a month expecting thee. Praise be to God who hath blessed us with one who is worthy of us, and one of whom we are worthy!—After having thus greeted me, they seated me upon a mattress, and said, Thou art from this day our master and prince, and we are thy handmaids, and entirely under thy authority. They then brought to me some refreshments, and when I had eaten and drunk, they sat and conversed with me, full of joy and happiness. So lovely were these ladies, that even a devotee, if he saw them, would gladly consent to be their servant, and to comply with all that they would desire. At the approach of night they all assembled around me, and placed before me a table of fresh and dried fruits, with other delicacies that the tongue cannot describe, and wine; and one began to sing, while another played upon the lute. The wine-cups circulated among us, and joy overcame me to such a degree as to obliterate from my mind every earthly care, and make me exclaim, This is indeed a delightful life! I passed a night of such enjoyment as I had never before experienced; and on the morrow I entered the bath; and, after I had washed myself, they brought me a suit of the richest clothing, and we again sat down to a repast.

In this manner I lived with them a whole year; but on the first day of the new year, they seated themselves around me, and began to weep, and bade me farewell, clinging to my skirts.—What calamity hath befallen you? said I. Ye have broken my heart.—They answered, Would that we had never known thee; for we have associated with many men, but have seen none like thee. May God, therefore, not deprive us of thy company.—And they wept afresh. I said to them, I wish that you would acquaint me with the cause of this weeping.—Thou, they replied, art the cause; yet now, if thou wilt attend to what we tell thee, we shall never be parted; but if thou act contrary to it, we are separated from this time; and our hearts whisper to us that thou wilt not regard our warning.—Inform me, said I, and I will attend to your directions:—and they replied, If then thou wouldst inquire respecting our history, know that we are the daughters of Kings: for many years it hath been our custom to assemble here, and every year we absent ourselves during a period of forty days; then returning, we indulge ourselves for a year in feasting and drinking. This is our usual practice; and now we fear that thou wilt disregard our directions when we are absent from thee. We deliver to thee the keys of the palace, which are a hundred in number, belonging to a hundred closets. Open each of these, and amuse thyself, and eat and drink, and refresh thyself, excepting the closet that hath a door of red gold; for if thou open this, the consequence will be a separation between us and thee. We conjure thee, therefore, to observe our direction, and to be patient during this period.—Upon hearing this, I swore to them that I would never open the closet to which they alluded; and they departed, urging me to be faithful to my promise.

I remained alone in the palace, and at the approach of evening I opened the first closet, and, entering it, found a mansion like paradise, with a garden containing green trees loaded with ripe fruits, abounding with singing birds, and watered by copious streams. My heart was soothed by the sight, and I wandered among the trees, scenting the fragrance of the flowers, and listening to the warbling of the birds as they sang the praises of the One, the Almighty. After admiring the mingled colours of the apple resembling the hue upon the cheek of a beloved mistress and the sallow countenance of the perplexed and timid lover, the sweet-smelling quince diffusing an odour like musk and ambergris, and the plum shining as the ruby, I retired from this place, and, having locked the door, opened that of the next closet, within which I beheld a spacious tract planted with numerous palm-trees, and watered by a river flowing among rose-trees, and jasmine, and marjoram, and eglantine, and narcissus, and gilliflower, the odours of which diffused in every direction by the wind, inspired me with the utmost delight. I locked again the door of the second closet, and opened that of the third. Within this I found a large saloon, paved with marbles of various colours, and with costly minerals and precious gems, and containing cages constructed of sandal and aloes-wood with singing birds within them, and others upon the branches of trees which were planted there. My heart was charmed, my trouble was dissipated, and I slept there until the morning. I then opened the door of the fourth closet, and within this door I found a great building in which were forty closets with open doors; and, entering these, I beheld pearls, and rubies, and chrysolites, and emeralds, and other precious jewels such as the tongue cannot describe. I was astonished at the sight and said, Such things as these, I imagine, are not found in the treasury of any King. I am now the King of my age, and all these treasures, through the goodness of God, are mine, together with forty damsels under my authority who have no man to share them with me.

Thus I continued to amuse myself, passing from one place to another, until thirty-nine days had elapsed, and I had opened the doors of all the closets excepting that which they had forbidden me to open. My heart was then disturbed by curiosity respecting this hundredth closet, and the Devil, in order to plunge me into misery, induced me to open it. I had not patience to abstain, though there remained of the appointed period only one day: So I approached the closet, and opened the door; and when I had entered, I perceived a fragrant odour, such as I had never before smelt, which intoxicated me so that I fell down insensible, and remained some time in this state: but at length recovering, I fortified my heart, and proceeded. I found the floor overspr :d with saffron, and the place illuminated by golden lamps and by candles, which diffused the odours of musk and ambergris; and two large perfuming-vessels filled with aloes-wood and ambergris, and a perfume compounded with honey, spread fragrance through the whole place. I saw also a black horse, of the hue of the darkest night, before which was a manger of white crystal filled with cleansed sesame, and another, similar to it, containing rose-water infused with musk: he was saddled and bridled, and his saddle was of red gold. Wondering at the sight of him, I said within myself, This must be an animal of extraordinary qualities;—and, seduced by the Devil, I led him out, and mounted him; but he moved not from his place: I kicked him with my heel; but still he moved not: so I took a mikra'ah and struck him with it; and as soon as he felt the blow he uttered a sound like thunder, and, expanding a pair of wings, soared with me to an immense height through the air, and then alighted upon the roof of another palace, where he threw me from his back, and, by a violent blow with his tail upon my face, as I sat on the roof, struck out my eye, and left me.

In this state I descended from the roof, and below I found the one-eyed young men before mentioned, who, as soon as they beheld me, exclaimed, No welcome to thee!— Receive me, said I, into your company:—but they replied, By Allah, thou shalt not remain with us:—so I departed from them, with mournful heart and weeping eye, and, God having decreed me a safe journey hither, I arrived at Baghdad, after I had shaved my beard, and become a mendicant.

The mistress of the house then looked towards the
Khalifeh and Ja'far and Mesrur, and said to them, Acquaint
me with your histories:—upon which Ja'far advanced towards her, and related to her the same story that he had
told to the portress before they entered; and when she had
heard it, she liberated them all.   They accordingly departed, and when they had gone out into the street, the
Khalifeh inquired of the mendicants whither they were
going.   They answered that they knew not whither to go:
whereupon he desired them to accompany his party; and
then said to Ja'far, Take them home with thee, and bring
them before me to-morrow, and we will see the result.
Ja'far, therefore, did as he was commanded, and the Khalifeh
returned to his palace; but he was unable to sleep during
the remainder of the night.

On the following morning he sat upon his throne, and
when his courtiers had presented themselves before him,
and departed, excepting Ja'far, he said to him, Bring before
me the three ladies and the two bitches and the mendicants.
So Ja'far arose, and brought them, and, placing the ladies
behind the curtains, said to them, We have forgiven you
on account of your previous kindness to us, and because
ye knew us not; and now I acquaint you that ye are in
the presence of the fifth of the sons of El-'Abbas, Harun
Er-Rashid; therefore relate to him nothing but the truth.
And when the ladies heard the words which Ja'far addressed to them on the part of the Khalifeh, the eldest of
them advanced, and thus related her story:—

THE STORY OF THE FIRST OF THE THREE LADIES OF BAGHDAD

O PRINCE OF THE FAITHFUL, my story is wonderful; for
these two bitches are my sisters, born to my father, but
of another mother; and I am the youngest of the three.
After the death of our father, who left us five thousand
pieces of gold, these my two sisters married, and when
they had resided some time with their husbands, each of
the latter prepared a stock of merchandise, and received
from his wife a thousand pieces of gold, and they all set

forth on a journey together, leaving me here; but after they had been absent four years, my sisters' husbands lost all their property, and abandoned them in a strange land, and they returned to me in the garb of beggars. When I first saw them in this state, I knew them not; and, as soon as I recognised them, I exclaimed, How is it that ye are in this condition?—O our sister, they answered, thy inquiry now is of no use: the Pen hath written what God hath decreed.—I sent them, therefore, to the bath, and, having clad them in new apparel, said to them, O my sisters, ye are my elders, and I am young; so ye shall be to me in the places of my father and mother. The inheritance which I shared with you God hath blessed; partake then of its increase, for my affairs are prosperous; and I and ye shall fare alike.—I treated them with the utmost kindness, and during a whole year they remained with me, and enriched themselves by the money that I had given them; but after this period they said to me, It will be more agreeable to us to marry again, for we can no longer abstain from doing so.—O my sisters, I replied, ye have seen no happiness in marriage: a good husband in this age is rarely found, and ye have already had experience of the marriage-state. They, however, heeded not my words; but married against my consent: yet I gave them dowries from my own property, and continued to them my protection. They went to their husbands, and the latter, after they had resided with them a short time, defrauded them of all that they possessed, and, setting forth on a journey, left them destitute: so again they returned to me, and, in a state of nudity, implored my forgiveness, saying, Be not angry with us; for though thou art younger than we, thou hast more mature sense; and we promise thee that we will never again mention the subject of marriage. I replied, Ye are welcome, O my sisters; for I have no one dearer to me than yourselves:—and I received them, and treated them with every kindness, and we remained happily together for the space of a year.

After this I resolved to fit out a vessel for a mercantile voyage: accordingly, I stocked a large ship with various goods and necessary provisions, and said to my sisters, Will ye rather stay at home during my voyage, or will ye

go with me?—to which they answered, We will accompany
thee during the voyage, for we cannot endure to be separated
from thee. I therefore took them with me, and we set sail;
but first I divided my property into two equal portions; one
of which I took with me, and the other I concealed, saying
within myself, Perhaps some evil accident may happen to
the ship, and our lives may be prolonged; in which case,
when we return we shall find that which will be of service
to us.—We continued our voyage by day and night, till at
length the vessel pursued a wrong course, and the captain
knew not whither to steer. The ship had entered a different
sea from that which we wished to cross, and for some time
we knew it not; but for ten days we had a pleasant wind,
and after this, a city loomed before us in the distance. We
asked the captain what was the name of this city; and he
answered, I know it not; I have never seen it till this day,
nor have I ever before in the course of my life navigated
this sea: but as we have come hither in safety, ye have
nothing to do but to enter this city and land your goods,
and, if ye find opportunity, sell or exchange there: if not,
we will rest there two days, and take in fresh provisions,
So we entered the port of the city, and the captain landed,
and after a while returned to us, saying, Arise, and go up
into the city, and wonder at that which God hath done
unto his creatures, and pray to be preserved from his anger.
And when we had entered the city, we found all its inhabitants converted into black stones. We were amazed
at the sight, and as we walked through the market-streets,
finding the merchandise and the gold and silver remaining
in their original state, we rejoiced, and said, This must have
been occasioned by some wonderful circumstance. We then
separated in the streets, each of us attracted from his companions by the wealth and stuffs in the shops.

As for myself, I ascended to the citadel, which I found
to be a building of admirable construction; and, entering
the King's palace, I found all the vessels of gold and silver
remaining in their places, and the King himself seated in
the midst of his Chamberlains and Viceroys and Wezirs,
and clad in apparel of astonishing richness. Drawing nearer
to him, I perceived that he was sitting upon a throne adorned

with pearls and jewels, every one of the pearls shining like
a star: his dress was embroidered with gold, and around
him stood fifty memluks, attired in silks of various descriptions, and having in their hands drawn swords. Stupefied
at this spectacle, I proceeded, and entered the saloon of
the Harim, upon the walls of which were hung silken
curtains; and here I beheld the Queen, attired in a dress
embroidered with fresh pearls, and having upon her head
a diadem adorned with various jewels, and necklaces of
different kinds on her neck. All her clothing and ornaments
remained as they were at first, though she herself was converted into black stone. Here also I found an open door,
and, entering it, I saw a flight of seven steps, by which I
ascended to an apartment paved with marble, furnished
with gold-embroidered carpets, and containing a couch of
alabaster, ornamented with pearls and jewels; but my eyes
were first attracted by a gleam of light, and when I approached the spot whence it proceeded, I found a brilliant
jewel, of the size of an ostrich's egg, placed upon a small
stool, diffusing a light like that of a candle. The coverings
of the couch above mentioned were of various kinds of silk,
the richness of which would surprise every beholder; and
I looked at them with wonder. In this apartment I likewise observed some lighted candles, and reflected that there
must then have been some person there to light them. I
passed thence to another part of the palace, and continued
to explore the different apartments, forgetting myself in the
amazement of my mind at all these strange circumstances,
and immersed in thoughts respecting what I beheld, until the
commencement of night, when I would have departed; but
could not find the door; so I returned to the place in which
were the lighted candles, and there I laid myself upon the
couch, and, covering myself with a quilt, repeated some
words of the Kur'an and endeavoured to compose myself
to sleep; but I could not. I continued restless: and at
midnight I heard a recitation of the Kur'an, performed by
a melodious and soft voice; upon which I arose, and, looking about, saw a closet with an open door, and I entered
it, and found that it was an oratory: lighted lamps were
suspended in it, and upon a prayer carpet spread on the

floor sat a young man of handsome aspect. Wondering that
he had escaped the fate of the other inhabitants of the city,
I saluted him; and he raised his eyes, and returned my
salutation: and I then said to him, I conjure thee by the
truth of that which thou art reading in the Book of God,
that thou answer the question which I am about to ask
thee:—whereupon he smiled, and replied, Do thou first
acquaint me with the cause of thine entrance into this
place, and then I will answer thy question: so I told him
my story, and inquired of him the history of this city. Wait
a little, said he;—and he closed the Kur'an, and, having
put it in a bag of satin, seated me by his side. As I now
beheld him, his countenance appeared like the full moon, and
his whole person exhibited such perfect elegance and loveliness, that a single glance at him drew from me a thousand
sighs, and kindled a fire in my heart. I repeated my request
that he would give me an account of the city; and, replying,
I hear and obey, he thus addressed me:—

Know that this city belonged to my father and his
family and subjects; and he is the King whom thou hast
seen converted into stone; and the Queen whom thou hast
seen is my mother. They were all Magians, worshipping
fire in the place of the Almighty King; and they swore by
the fire and the light, and the shade and the heat, and the
revolving orb. My father had no son, till, in his declining
years, he was blest with me, whom he reared until I attained
to manhood. But, happily for me, there was, in our family,
an old woman, far advanced in age, who was a Muslimeh,
believing in God and his Apostle in her heart, though she
conformed with my family in outward observances; and my
father confided in her, on account of the faithfulness and
modesty that he had observed in her character, and shewed
her great favour, firmly believing that she held the same
faith as himself; therefore, when I had passed my infancy,
he committed me to her care, saying, Take him, and rear
him, and instruct him in the ordinances of our faith, and
educate him and serve him in the best manner. The old
woman accordingly received me, but took care to instruct
me in the faith of El-Islam, teaching me the laws of purifi-
cation, and the divine ordinances of ablution, together with

the forms of prayer; after which she made me commit to
memory the whole of the Kur'an. She then charged me to
keep my faith a secret from my father, lest he should kill
me; and I did so; and a few days after, the old woman
died. The inhabitants of the city had now increased in
their impiety and arrogance, and in their dereliction of the
truth; and while they were in this state, they heard a crier
proclaim with a voice like thunder, so as to be audible to
both the near and the distant, O inhabitants of this city,
abstain from the worship of fire, and worship the Almighty
King!—The people were struck with consternation, and,
flocking to my father, the King of the city, said to him,
What is this alarming voice which hath astounded us by its
terrible sound?—but he answered them, Let not the voice
terrify you, nor let it turn you from your faith:—and their
hearts inclined to his words; so they persevered in the
worship of fire, and remained obstinate in their impiety
during another year, until the return of the period at which
they had heard the voice the first time. It was then heard
a second time; and again, in the next year, they heard it a
third time; but still they persisted in their evil ways, until,
drawing down upon themselves the abhorrence and indignation of Heaven, one morning, shortly after daybreak, they
were converted into black stones, together with their beasts
and all their cattle. Not one of the inhabitants of the city
escaped, excepting me; and from the day on which this
catastrophe happened, I have continued occupied as thou
seest, in prayer, and fasting, and reading the Kur'an: but I
have become weary of this solitary state, having no one to
cheer me with his company.

On hearing these words, I said to him, Wilt thou go with
me to the city of Baghdad, and visit its learned men and
lawyers, and increase thy knowledge? If so, I will be thy
handmaid, though I am the mistress of my family, and have
authority over a household of men. I have here a ship
laden with merchandise, and destiny hath driven us to this
city, in order that we might become acquainted with these
events: our meeting was predestined.—In this manner I
continued to persuade him until he gave his consent. I
slept that night at his feet, unconscious of my state through

excessive joy; and in the morning we rose, and, entering the treasuries, took away a quantity of the lighter and most valuable of the articles that they contained, and descended from the citadel into the city, where we met the slaves and the captain, who were searching for me. They were rejoiced at seeing me, and, to their questions respecting my absence, I replied by informing them of all that I had seen, and related to them the history of the young man, and the cause of the transmutation of the people of the city, and of all that had befallen them, which filled them with wonder. But when my two sisters saw me with the young man, they envied me on his account, and malevolently plotted against me.

We embarked again, and I experienced the utmost happiness, chiefly owing to the company of the young man; and after we had waited a while till the wind was favourable, we spread our sails, and departed. My sisters sat with me and the young man; and, in their conversation with me, said, O our sister, what dost thou purpose to do with this handsome youth? I answered, I desire to take him as my husband:—and, turning to him, and approaching him, I said, O, my master, I wish to make a proposal to thee, and do not thou oppose it. He replied, I hear and obey:—and I then looked towards my sisters, and said to them, This young man is all that I desire, and all the wealth that is here is yours.—Excellent, they replied, is thy determination:—yet still they designed evil against me.—We continued our voyage with a favourable wind, and, quitting the sea of peril, entered the sea of security, across which we proceeded for some days, until we drew near to the city of El-Basrah, the buildings of which loomed before us at the approach of evening; but as soon as we had fallen asleep, my sisters took us up in our bed, both myself and the young man, and threw us into the sea. The youth, being unable to swim, was drowned; God recorded him among the company of the martyrs; while I was registered among those whose life was yet to be preserved: and, accordingly, as soon as I awoke and found myself in the sea, the providence of God supplied me with a piece of timber, upon which I placed myself, and the waves cast me upon the shore of an island.

During the remainder of the night I walked along this island, and in the morning I saw a neck of land, bearing the marks of a man's feet, and uniting with the main land. The sun having now risen, I dried my clothes in its rays, and proceeded along the path that I had discovered until I drew near to the shore upon which stands the city, when I beheld a snake approaching me, and followed by a serpent which was endeavouring to destroy it: the tongue of the snake was hanging from its mouth in consequence of excessive fatigue, and it excited my compassion; so I took up a stone, and threw it at the head of the serpent, which instantly died: the snake then extended a pair of wings, and soared aloft into the sky, leaving me in wonder at the sight. At the time of this occurrence I had become so fatigued, that I now laid myself down and slept; but I awoke after a little while, and found a damsel seated at my feet, and gently rubbing them with her hands; upon which I immediately sat up, feeling ashamed that she should perform this service for me, and said to her, Who art thou, and what dost thou want?—How soon hast thou forgotten me! she exclaimed: I am she to whom thou hast just done a kindness, by killing my enemy: I am the snake whom thou savedst from the serpent; for I am a Jinniyeh, and the serpent was a Jinni at enmity with me; and none but thou delivered me from him: therefore, as soon as thou didst this, I flew to the ship from which thy sisters cast thee, and transported all that it contained to thy house; I then sunk it; but as to thy sisters, I transformed them by enchantment into two black bitches; for I knew all that they had done to thee: the young man, however, is drowned.—Having thus said, she took me up, and placed me with the two black bitches on the roof of my house: and I found all the treasures that the ship had contained collected in the midst of my house: nothing was lost. She then said to me, I swear by that which was engraved upon the seal of Suleyman, that, if thou do not inflict three hundred lashes upon each of these bitches every day, I will come and transform thee in the like manner:—so I replied, I hear and obey:—and have continued ever since to inflict upon them these stripes, though pitying them while I do so.

The Khalifeh heard this story with astonishment. and
then said to the second lady, And what occasioned the
stripes of which thou bearest the marks?   She answered as
follows:—

The Story of the Second of the Three Ladies of Baghdad

PRINCE OF THE FAITHFUL, my father, at his death, left
considerable property; and soon after that event I married
to one of the wealthiest men of the age, who, when I had
lived with him a year, died, and I inherited from him eighty
thousand pieces of gold, the portion that fell to me according to the law; with part of which I made for myself ten
suits of clothing, each of the value of a thousand pieces of
gold.   And as I was sitting one day, there entered my
apartment an old woman, disgustingly ugly, who saluted
me, and said, I have an orphan daughter whose marriage I
am to celebrate this night, and I would have thee obtain a
reward and recompense in heaven by thy being present at
her nuptial festivity; for she is broken-hearted, having none
to befriend her but God, whose name be exalted.   She then
wept, and kissed my feet; and, being moved with pity and
compassion, I assented, upon which she desired me to prepare myself, telling me that she would come at the hour of
nightfall and take me; and so saying, she kissed my hand,
and departed.

I arose immediately, and attired myself, and when I had
completed my preparations, the old woman returned, saying,
O my mistress, the ladies of the city have arrived, and I
have informed them of thy coming, and they are waiting
with joy to receive thee:—so I put on my outer garments,
and, taking my female slaves with me, proceeded until we
arrived at a street in which a soft wind was delightfully
playing, where we saw a gateway over-arched with a marble
vault, admirably constructed, forming the entrance to a
palace which rose from the earth to the clouds.   On our
arrival there, the old woman knocked at the door, and,
when it was opened, we entered a carpeted passage, illuminated by lamps and candles, and decorated with jewels and

precious metals. Through this passage we passed into a
saloon of unequalled magnificence, furnished with mattresses
covered with silk, lighted by hanging lamps and by candles,
and having, at its upper end, a couch of alabaster decorated
with pearls and jewels, and canopied by curtains of satin,
from which there came forth a lady beautiful as the moon,
who exclaimed to me, Most welcome art thou, O my sister:
thou delightest me by thy company, and refreshest my heart.
She then sat down again, and said to me, O my sister, I
have a brother who hath seen thee at a festivity: he is a
young man, more handsome than myself, and, his heart
being violently inflamed with love of thee, he hath bribed
this old woman to go to thee, and to employ this artifice in
order to obtain for me an interview with thee. He desireth
to marry thee according to the ordinance of God and his
Apostle, and in that which is lawful there is no disgrace.—
When I heard these words, and saw myself thus confined in
the house so that I could not escape, I replied, I hear, and
obey:—and the lady, rejoicing at my consent, clapped her
hands, and opened a door, upon which there came out from
it a young man so surpassingly handsome, that my heart
immediately inclined to him. No sooner had he sat down
than the Kadi and four witnesses entered, and saluted us,
and proceeded to perform the ceremony of the marriage-
contract between me and the young man; which having
done, they departed; and when they had retired, the young
man looked towards me, and said, May our night be blessed.
He then informed me that he desired to impose a covenant
upon me, and, bringing a copy of the Kur'an, said, Swear
that thou wilt not indulge a preference, nor at all incline, to
any man but me:—and when I had sworn to this effect he
rejoiced exceedingly, and embraced me; and the love of
him took entire possession of my heart.

We lived together in the utmost happiness for the space
of a month, after which I begged that he would allow me
to go to the bazar, in order to purchase some stuffs for
dress, and, having obtained his permission, went thither in
company with the old woman, and seated myself at the shop
of a young merchant with whom she was acquainted, and
whose father, as she informed me, had died, and left him

great wealth. She desired him to shew me his most costly stuffs; and while he was occupied in doing so, she began to utter various flattering expressions in praise of him; but I said to her, We have no concern with the praises that thou bestowest upon him; we desire only to make our purchase, and to return home. Meanwhile he produced to us what we wanted, and we handed him the money: he refused, however, to take it, saying, It is an offer of hospitality to you for your visit this day:—whereupon I said to the old woman, If he will not take the money, return to him his stuff. But he would not receive it again, and exclaimed, By Allah, I will take nothing from you: all this is a present from me for a single kiss, which I shall value more than the entire contents of my shop.—What will a kiss profit thee? asked the old woman. Then, turning to me, she said, O my daughter, thou hast heard what the youth hath said: no harm will befall thee if he give thee a kiss, and thou shalt take what thou wantest.—Dost thou not know, said I, that I have taken an oath? She answered, Let him kiss thee then without thy speaking, and so it will be of no consequence to thee, and thou shalt take back thy money. Thus she continued to palliate the matter until I put my head (as it were) into the bag, and consented: so I covered my eyes, and held the edge of my veil in such a manner as to prevent the passengers from seeing me, whereupon he put his mouth to my cheek beneath the veil, but instead of merely kissing me, he lacerated my cheek by a violent bite. I fell into a swoon from the pain, and the old woman laid me on her lap till I recovered, when I found the shop closed, and the old woman uttering expressions of grief, and saying, What God hath averted would have been a greater calamity: let us return home, and do thou feign to be ill, and I will come to thee and apply a remedy that shall cure the wound, and thou wilt quickly be restored.

After remaining there some time longer, I rose, and, in a state of great uneasiness and fear, returned to the house, and professed myself ill; upon which my husband came in to me, and said, What hath befallen thee, O my mistress, during this excursion? I answered, I am not well.—And what is this wound, said he, that is upon thy cheek, and in the soft part? I answered, When I asked thy permission, and went out to-day to purchase some stuff for dress, a camel loaded with firewood drove against me in the crowd, and tore my veil, and wounded my cheek as thou seest, for the streets of this city are narrow.—To-morrow, then, he exclaimed, I will go to the governor, and make a complaint to him, and he shall hang every seller of firewood in the city.—By Allah, said I, burden not thyself by an injury to any one; for the truth is, that I was riding upon an ass, which took fright with me, and I fell upon the ground, and a stick lacerated my cheek.—If it be so, then, he replied, I will go to-morrow to Ja'far El-Barmeki, and relate the matter to him, and he shall kill every ass-driver in this city.—Wilt thou, said I, kill all those men on my account when this which befell me was decreed by God?—Undoubtedly, he answered; and, so saying, he seized me violently, and then sprang up, and uttered a loud cry, upon which the door opened, and there came forth from it seven black slaves, who dragged me from my bed, and threw me down in the middle of the apartment; whereupon he ordered one of them to hold me by my shoulders, and to sit upon my head; and another to sit upon my knees and to hold my feet. A third then came, with a sword in his hand, and said, O my lord, shall I strike her with the sword, and cleave her in twain, that each of these may take a half and throw it into the Tigris for the fish to devour? For such is the punishment of her who is unfaithful to her oath and to the laws of love.—My husband answered, Strike her O Sa'ad:—And the slave, with the drawn sword in his hand, said, Repeat the profession of the faith, and reflect what thou wouldst have to be done, that thou mayest give thy testamentary directions, for this is the end of thy life.—Good slave, I replied, release me for a while that I may do so:—and I raised my head, and weeping as I spoke, addressed my husband with these verses:—

You render me lovelorn, and remain at ease. You make my
  wounded eyelids to be restless, and you sleep.
Your abode is between my heart and my eyes; and my heart will
  not relinquish you, nor my tears conceal my passion.

You made a covenant with me that you would remain faithful; but
  when you had gained possession of my heart you deceived me.
Will you not pity my love for you and my moaning? Have you
  yourself been secure from misfortunes?
I conjure you, by Allah, if I die, that you write upon my tomb-
  stone, This was a slave of love.
That, perchance, some mourner who hath felt the same flame may
  pass by the lover's grave, and pity her.

But on hearing these verses, and witnessing my weeping,
he became more incensed, and replied in the words of this
couplet:—

I reject not the beloved of my heart from weariness: her own guilty
  conduct is the cause of her punishment.
She desired that another should share with me her love; but the
  faith of my heart inclineth not to partnership.

I continued to weep, and to endeavour to excite his
compassion, saying within myself, I will humble me before
him, and address him with soft words, that he may at least
refrain from killing me, though he take all that I possess;—
but he cried out to the slave, Cleave her in twain; for she
is no longer of any value to us.—So the slave approached
me, and I now felt assured of my death, and committed
myself to God; but suddenly the old woman came and
threw herself at my husband's feet, and, kissing them,
exclaimed, O my son, by the care with which I nursed thee,
I conjure thee to pardon this damsel, for she hath committed no offence that deserveth such a punishment: thou
art young, and I fear the effect of the imprecations that she
may utter against thee:—and after she had thus addressed
him, she wept, and continued to importune him, until, at
length, he said, I pardon her, but must cause her to bear
upon her person such marks of her offence as shall last for
the remainder of her life. So saying he commanded the
slaves to strip off my vest, and, taking a stick cut from a
quince-tree, he beat me upon my back and my sides until
I became insensible from the violence of the blows, and
despaired of my life. He then ordered the slaves to take
me away as soon as it was night, accompanied by the old
woman, and throw me into my house in which I formerly
resided. They accordingly executed their lord's commands,

and when they had deposited me in my house, I applied myself to the healing of my wounds; but, after I had cured myself, my sides still bore the appearance of having been beaten with mikra'ahs. I continued to apply remedies for four months before I was restored, and then repaired to view the house in which this event had happened; but I found it reduced to ruin, and the whole street pulled down; the site of the house I found occupied by mounds of rubbish, and I knew not the cause.

Under these circumstances, I went to reside with this my sister, who is of the same father as myself, and I found with her these two bitches. Having saluted her, I informed her of all that had befallen me; to which she replied, Who is secure from the afflictions of fortune? Praise be to God who terminated the affair with safety to thy life!—She then related to me her own story, and that of her two sisters, and I remained with her, and neither of us ever mentioned the subject of marriage. Afterwards we were joined by this our other sister, the cateress, who every day goes out to purchase for us whatever we happen to want.

The Khalifeh was astonished at this story, and ordered it to be recorded in a book, as an authentic history, and deposited the book in his library. And he said to the first lady, Knowest thou where the Jinniyeh who enchanted thy sister is to be found? She answered, O Prince of the Faithful, she gave me a lock of her hair, and said, When thou desirest my presence, burn a few of these hairs, and I will be with thee quickly, though I should be beyond Mount Kaf.—Bring then the hair, said the Khalifeh. The lady, therefore, produced it; and the Khalifeh, taking it, burned a portion of it, and when the odour had diffused itself, the palace shook, and they heard a sound of thunder, and lo, the Jinniyeh appeared before them. She was a Muslimeh, and therefore greeted the Khalifeh by saying, Peace be on thee, O Khalifeh of God!—to which he replied, On you be peace, and the mercy of God, and his blessings![13] She then said, Know that this lady hath conferred on me a benefit for which I am unable to requite her; for she rescued me from death, by killing my enemy; and I, having seen

[13] This salutation and its reply are to be given only to and by Muslims.

what her sisters had done to her, determined to take
vengeance upon them; therefore I transformed them by
enchantment into two bitches; and, indeed, I had wished
rather to kill them, fearing lest they should trouble her;
but now, if thou desire their restoration, O Prince of the
Faithful, I will restore them, as a favour to thee and to her;
for I am one of the true believers.—Do so, said the
Khalifeh; and then we will enter upon the consideration
of the affair of the lady who hath been beaten, and examine
her case, and if her veracity be established, I will take
vengeance for her upon him who hath oppressed her. The
Jinniyeh replied, O Prince of the Faithful, I will guide thee
to the discovery of him who acted thus to this lady, and
oppressed her, and took her property: he is thy nearest
relation. She then took a cup of water, and, having pronounced a spell over it, sprinkled the faces of the two
bitches, saying, Be restored to your original human forms!
—whereupon they became again two young ladies.—Extolled
be the perfection of their Creator! Having done this, the
Jinniyeh said, O Prince of the Faithful, he who beat the
lady is thy son El-Emin, who had heard of her beauty and
loveliness:—and she proceeded to relate what had happened.
The Khalifeh was astonished, and exclaimed, Praise be to
God for the restoration of these two bitches which hath been
effected through my means!—and immediately he summoned
before him his son El-Emin, and inquired of him the history
of the lady; and he related to him the truth. He then
sent for Kadis and witnesses, and the first lady and her two
sisters who had been transformed into bitches he married
to the three mendicants who had related that they were the
sons of Kings; and these he made chamberlains of his
court, appointing them all that they required, and allotting
them apartments in the palace of Baghdad. The lady who
had been beaten he restored to his son El-Emin, giving her
a large property, and ordering that the house should be
rebuilt in a more handsome style. Lastly, the lady cateress
he took as his own wife; he admitted her at once to his
own apartment, and, on the following day, he appointed
her a separate lodging for herself, with female slaves to wait
upon her: he also allotted to her a regular income; and
afterwards built for her a palace.

THE STORY OF THE HUMPBACK

THERE was, in ancient times, in the city of El-Basrah, a tailor who enjoyed an ample income, and was fond of sport and merriment. He was in the habit of going out occasionally with his wife, that they might amuse themselves with strange and diverting scenes; and one day they went forth in the afternoon, and, returning home in the evening, met a humpbacked man, whose aspect was such as to excite laughter in the angry, and to dispel anxiety and grief: so they approached him to enjoy the pleasure of gazing at him, and invited him to return with them to their house, and to join with them in a carousal that night.

He assented to their proposal; and after he had gone with them to the house, the tailor went out to the market; night having then approached. He bought some fried fish, and bread and limes and sweetmeat, and, returning with them, placed the fish before the humpback, and they sat down to eat; and the tailor's wife took a large piece of fish, and crammed the humpback with it, and, closing his mouth with her hand, said, By Allah, thou shalt not swallow it but by gulping it at once, and I will not give thee time to chew it. He therefore swallowed it; but it contained a large and sharp bone, which stuck across in his throat, his destiny having so determined, and he expired. The tailor exclaimed, There is no strength nor power but in God, the High, the Great! Alas, that this poor creature should not have died but in this manner by our hands!—Wherefore this idling? exclaimed the woman.—And what can I do? asked her husband.—Arise, she answered, and take him in thy bosom, and cover him with a silk napkin: I will go out first, and do thou follow me, this very night, and say, This is my son, and this

122

is his mother; and we are going to convey him to the physician, that he may give him some medicine.

No sooner had the tailor heard these words than he arose, and took the humpback in his bosom. His wife, accompanying him, exclaimed, O my child! may Allah preserve thee! Where is the part in which thou feelest pain; and where hath this small-pox attacked thee?—So every one who saw them said, They are conveying a child smitten with the small-pox. Thus they proceeded, inquiring, as they went, for the abode of the physician; and the people directed them to the house of a physician who was a Jew; and they knocked at the door, and there came down to them a black slave-girl, who opened the door, and beheld a man carrying (as she imagined) a child, and attended by its mother; and she said, What is your business?—We have a child here, answered the tailor's wife, and we want the physician to see him: take, then, this quarter of a piece of gold, and give it to thy master, and let him come down and see my son; for he is ill. The girl, therefore, went up, and the tailor's wife, entering the vestibule, said to her husband, Leave the humpback here, and let us take ourselves away. And the tailor, accordingly, set him up against the wall, and went out with his wife.

The slave-girl, meanwhile, went in to the Jew, and said to him, Below, in the house, is a sick person, with a woman and a man: and they have given me a quarter of a piece of gold for thee, that thou mayest prescribe for them what may suit his case. And when the Jew saw the quarter of a piece of gold, he rejoiced, and, rising in haste, went down in the dark: and in doing so, his foot struck against the lifeless humpback. O Ezra! he exclaimed—O Heavens and the Ten Commandments! O Aaron, and Joshua son of Nun! It seemeth that I have stumbled against this sick person, and he hath fallen down the stairs and died! And how shall I go forth with one killed from my house? O Ezra's ass![1]

---

[1] 'Ozeyr, or Ezra, " riding on an ass by the ruins of Jerusalem, after it had been destroyed by the Chaldeans, doubted in his mind by what means God could raise the city and its inhabitants again; whereupon God caused him to die, and he remained in that condition a hundred years; at the end of which God restored him to life, and he found a basket of figs and a cruse of wine he had with him, not in the least spoiled or corrupted, but his ass was dead, the bones only remaining; and these, while the Prophet

—He then raised him, and took him up from the court of the house to his wife, and acquainted her with the accident. —And why sittest thou here idle? said she; for if thou remain thus until daybreak our lives will be lost: let me and thee, then, take him up to the terrace, and throw him into the house of our neighbour the Muslim; for he is the steward of the Sultan's kitchen, and often do the cats come to his house, and eat of the food which they find there; as do the mice too; and if he remain there for a night, the dogs will come down to him from the terraces and eat him up entirely. So the Jew and his wife went up, carrying the humpback, and let him down by his hands and feet to the pavement; placing him against the wall; which having done, they descended.

Not long had the humpback been thus deposited when the steward returned to his house, and opened the door, and, going up with a lighted candle in his hand, found a son of Adam standing in the corner next the kitchen; upon which he exclaimed, What is this? By Allah, the thief that hath stolen our goods is none other than a son of Adam, who taketh what he findeth of flesh or grease, even though I keep it concealed from the cats and the dogs; and if I killed all the cats and dogs of the quarter it would be of no use; for he cometh down from the terraces!—And so saying, he took up a great mallet, and struck him with it, and then, drawing close to him, gave him a second blow with it upon the chest, when the humpback fell down, and he found that he was dead; whereupon he grieved, and said, There is no strength nor power but in God! And he feared for himself, and exclaimed, Curse upon the grease and the flesh, and upon this night, in which the destiny of this man hath been accomplished by my hand! Then, looking upon him, and perceiving that he was a humpback, he said, Is it not enough that thou art humpbacked, but must thou also be a robber, and steal the flesh and the grease? O Protector, cover me with thy gracious shelter!—And he lifted him upon his shoulders, and descended, and went forth from the house, towards the close of the night, and stopped not until he

looked on, were raised and cloathed with flesh, becoming an ass again, which, being inspired with life, began immediately to bray."—Sale's Koran, ch. ii., note [p. 31, ed. 1734].

had conveyed him to the commencement of the market-street, where he placed him upon his feet by the side of a shop at the entrance of a lane, and there left him and retired.

Soon after there came a Christian, the Sultan's broker, who, in a state of intoxication, had come forth to visit the bath; and he advanced staggering, until he drew near to the humpback, when he turned his eyes, and beheld one standing by him. Now, some persons had snatched off his turban early in the night, and when he saw the humpback standing there, he concluded that he intended to do the same; so he clenched his fist, and struck him on the neck. Down fell the humpback upon the ground, and the Christian called out to the watchman of the market, while, still in the excess of his intoxication, he continued beating the hump-back, and attempting to throttle him. As he was thus em-ployed, the watchman came, and, finding the Christian kneeling upon the Muslim and beating him, said, Arise, and quit him! He arose, therefore, and the watchman, approach-ing the humpback, saw that he was dead, and exclaimed, How is that the Christian dareth to kill the Muslim? Then seizing the Christian, he bound his hands behind him, and took him to the house of the Wali;[2] the Christian saying within himself, O Heavens! O Virgin! how have I killed this man? and how quickly did he die from a blow of the hand!—Intoxication had departed, and reflection had come.

The humpback and the Christian passed the remainder of the night in the house of the Wali, and the Wali ordered the executioner to proclaim the Christian's crime, and he set up a gallows, and stationed him beneath it. The execu-tioner then came, and threw the rope round his neck, and was about to hang him, when the Sultan's steward pushed through the crowd, seeing the Christian standing beneath the gallows, and the people made way for him, and he said to the executioner, Do it not, for it was I who killed him.—Wherefore didst thou kill him? said the Wali. He answered, I went into my house last night, and saw that he had de-scended from the terrace and stolen my goods; so I struck him with a mallet upon his chest, and he died, and I carried him out, and conveyed him to the market-street, where I set

[2] Chief police magistrate.

him up in such a place, at the entrance of such a lane. Is it not enough for me to have killed a Muslim, that a Christian should be killed on my account? Hang, then, none but me.—The Wali, therefore, when he heard these words, liberated the Christian broker, and said to the executioner, Hang this man, on the ground of his confession. And he took off the rope from the neck of the Christian, and put it round the neck of the steward, and having stationed him beneath the gallows, was about to hang him, when the Jewish physician pushed through the crowd, and called out to the executioner, saying to him, Do it not; for none killed him but I; and the case was this: he came to my house to be cured of a disease, and as I descended to him I struck against him with my foot, and he died: kill not the steward, therefore; but kill me. So the Wali gave orders to hang the Jewish physician; and the executioner took off the rope from the steward's neck, and put it round the neck of the Jew. But, lo, the tailor came, and, forcing his way among the people, said to the executioner, Do it not; for none killed him but I; and it happened thus: I was out amusing myself during the day, and as I was returning at the commencement of the night, I met this humpback in a state of intoxication, with a tambourine, and singing merrily; and I stopped to divert myself by looking at him, and took him to my house. I then bought some fish, and we sat down to eat, and my wife took a piece of fish and a morsel of bread, and crammed them into his mouth, and he was choked, and instantly died. Then I and my wife took him to the house of the Jew, and the girl came down and opened the door, and while she went up to her master, I set up the humpback by the stairs, and went away with my wife: so, when the Jew came down and stumbled against him, he thought that he had killed him. —And he said to the Jew, Is this true? He answered, Yes. The tailor, then looking towards the Wali, said to him, Liberate the Jew, and hang me. And when the Wali heard this he was astonished at the case of the humpback, and said, Verily this is an event that should be recorded in books! And he said to the executioner, Liberate the Jew, and hang the tailor on account of his own confession. So the executioner had him forward, saying, Dost thou put forward this and take back that; and shall we not hang one? And he put the rope round the neck of the tailor.

Now the humpback was the Sultan's buffoon, and the Sultan could not bear him to be out of his sight; and when the humpback had got drunk, and been absent that night and the next day until noon, the King inquired respecting him of some of his attendants, and they answered him, O our lord, the Wali hath taken him forth dead, and gave orders to hang the person who killed him, and there came a second and a third person, each saying, None killed him but I:— and describing to the Wali the cause of his killing him. When the King, therefore, heard this, he called out to the Chamberlain, and said to him, Go down to the Wali, and bring them all hither before me. So the Chamberlain went down, and found that the executioner had almost put to death the tailor, and he called out to him, saying, Do it not:—and informed the Wali that the case had been reported to the King. And he took him, and the humpback borne with him, and the tailor and the Jew and the Christian and the steward, and went up with them all to the King; and when the Wali came into the presence of the King, he kissed the ground, and related to him all that had happened. And the King was astonished, and was moved with merriment, at hearing this tale; and he commanded that it should be written in letters of gold. He then said to those who were present, Have ye ever heard anything like the story of this humpback? And upon this the Christian advanced, and said, O King of the age, if thou permit me I will relate to thee an event that hath occurred to me more wonderful and strange and exciting than the story of the humpback.—Tell us then thy story, said the King. And the Christian related as follows:—

THE STORY TOLD BY THE CHRISTIAN BROKER

Know, O King of the age, that I came to this country with merchandise, and destiny stayed me among your people. I was born in Cairo, and am one of its Copts, and there I was brought up. My father was a broker; and when I had attained to manhood, he died, and I succeeded to his business; and as I was sitting one day, lo, a young man of most handsome aspect, and clad in a dress of the richest description, came to me, riding upon an ass, and when he saw me, saluted me; whereupon I rose to him, to pay him honour, and he produced a handkerchief containing some sesame, and said, What is the value of an ardebb[3] of this? I answered him, A hundred pieces of silver. And he said to me, Take the carriers and the measurers, and repair to the Khan of El-Jawali in the district of Bab en-Nasr:[4] there wilt thou find me. And he left me and went his way, after having given me the handkerchief with the sample of the sesame. So I went about to the purchasers; and the price of each ardebb amounted to a hundred and twenty pieces of silver; and I took with me four carriers, and went to him. I found him waiting my arrival; and when he saw me he rose and opened a magazine, and we measured its contents, and the whole amounted to fifty ardebbs. The young man then said, Thou shalt have, for every ardebb, ten pieces of silver as brokerage; and do thou receive the price and keep it in thy care: the whole sum will be five thousand; and thy share of it, five hundred: so there will remain for me four thousand and five hundred; and when I shall have finished the sale of the goods contained in my store-room, I will come to thee and receive it. I replied, It shall be as thou desirest. And I kissed his hand, and left him. Thus there accrued to me, on that day, a thousand pieces of silver, [besides my brokerage.]

He was absent from me a month, at the expiration of which he came and said to me, Where is the money? I answered, Here it is, ready. And he said, Keep it until I come to thee to receive it. And I remained expecting him; but he was absent from me another month; after which he came again, and said, Where is the money? Whereupon I arose and saluted him, and said to him, Wilt thou eat something with us? He, however, declined, and said, Keep the money until I shall have gone and returned to receive it

---

[3] In Cairo, nearly five bushels.
[4] "Gate of Victory or of Aid:" the easternmost of the northern gates of Cairo built in 1088. The Khan referred to is mentioned by El-Makrizi as being situated at a short distance within the present gate and by the site of the older gate of the same name, and as existing in his time [1417].

And what, said I, was the cause of it? He answered thus :—

Know that I am from Baghdad: my father was one of the chief people of that city; and when I had attained the age of manhood, I heard the wanderers and travellers and merchants conversing respecting the land of Egypt, and their words remained in my heart until my father died, when I took large sums of money, and prepared merchandise consisting of the stuffs of Baghdad and of El-Mosil, and similar precious goods, and, having packed them up, journeyed from Baghdad; and God decreed me safety until I entered this your city. And so saying, he wept, and repeated these verses :—

The blear-eyed escapeth a pit into which the clear-sighted falleth;
And the ignorant, an expression by which the shrewd sage is ruined.
The believer can scarce earn his food, while the impious infidel is
    favoured.
What art or act can a man devise? It is what the Almighty
    appointeth!

I entered Cairo, continued the young man, and deposited the stuffs in the Khan of Mesrur,[6] and, having unbound my packages and put them in the magazines, gave to the servant some money to buy for us something to eat, after which I slept a little; and when I arose, I went to Beyn el-Kasreyn. I then returned, and passed the night; and in the morning following, I opened a bale of stuff, and said within myself, I will arise and go through some of the market-streets, and see the state of the mart. So I took some stuff, and made some of my servants carry it, and proceeded until I arrived at the Keysariyeh[7] of Jaharkas, where the brokers came to me, having heard of my arrival, and took from me the stuff, and cried it about for sale; but the price bidden amounted not to the prime cost. And upon this the Sheykh of the brokers said to me, O my master, I know a plan by which thou mayest profit; and it is this: that thou do as other merchants, and sell thy merchandise upon credit for a certain period, employing a scrivener and a witness and a money-changer, and receive a portion of the profits every Thursday and Monday; so shalt thou make of every piece of silver two; and besides that,

───────────

  [6] [In the Beyn el-Kasreyn or "Betwixt the Palaces," by the present Suk
en-Nahhasin. See Lane-Poole, *Story of Cairo* (1902), pp. 266-270.]
  [7] A superior kind of suk or market.

thou wilt be able to enjoy the amusements afforded by Egypt and its Nile.—The advice is judicious, I replied: and accordingly I took the brokers with me to the Khan, and they conveyed the stuffs to the Keysariyeh, where I sold it to the merchants, writing a bond in their names, which I committed to the money-changer, and taking from him a corresponding bond. I then returned to the Khan, and remained there some days; and every day I took for my breakfast a cup of wine, and had mutton and sweetmeats prepared for me, until the month in which I became entitled to the receipt of the profits, when I seated myself every Thursday and Monday at the shops of the merchants, and the money-changer went with the scrivener and brought me the money.

Thus did I until one day I went to the bath and returned to the Khan, and, entering my lodging, took for my breakfast a cup of wine, and then slept; and when I awoke I ate a fowl, and perfumed myself with essence, and repaired to the shop of a merchant named Bedr-ed-Din the Gardener, who, when he saw me, welcomed me, and conversed with me a while in his shop; and as we were thus engaged, lo, a female came and seated herself by my side. She wore a headkerchief inclined on one side, and the odours of sweet perfumes were diffused from her, and she captivated my reason by her beauty and loveliness as she raised her izar and I beheld her black eyes. She saluted Bedr-ed-Din, and he returned her salutation, and stood conversing with her; and when I heard her speech, love for her took entire possession of my heart. She then said to Bedr-ed-Din, Hast thou a piece of stuff woven with pure gold thread? And he produced to her a piece; and she said, May I take it and go, and then send thee the price? But he answered, It is impossible, O my mistress; for this is the owner of the stuff, and I owe him a portion of the profit.—Woe to thee! said she: it is my custom to take of thee each piece of stuff for a considerable sum of money, giving thee a gain beyond thy wish, and then to send thee the price.—Yes, he rejoined; but I am in absolute want of the price this day. And upon this she took the piece and threw it back to him upon his breast, saying, Verily your class knows not how to respect any person's rank! And she arose, and turned away. I felt then as if my soul went with her, and, rising upon my feet, I said to her, O my mistress, kindly bestow a look upon me, and retrace thine honoured steps. And she returned, and smiled and said, For thy sake I return. And she sat opposite me upon the seat of the shop; and I said to Bedr-ed-Din, What is the price that thou hast agreed to give for this piece? He answered, Eleven hundred pieces of silver. And I said to him, Thy profit shall be a hundred pieces of silver: give me then a paper, and I will write for thee the price upon it. I then took the piece of stuff from him, and wrote him the paper with my own hand, and gave the piece of stuff to the lady, saying to her, Take it and go; and if thou wilt, bring the price to me in the market; or, if thou wilt, it shall be my present to thee. She replied, God recompense thee, and bless thee with my property, and make thee my husband; and may God accept this prayer!—O my mistress, said I, let this piece of stuff be thine, and another like it, and permit me to see thy face. And upon this she raised her veil; and when I beheld her face, the sight drew from me a thousand sighs, and my heart was entangled by her love, so that I no longer remained master of my reason. She then lowered the veil again, and took the piece of stuff, saying, O my master, leave me not desolate. So she departed, while I continued sitting in the market-street until past the hour of afternoon-prayer, with wandering mind, overpowered by love. In the excess of my passion, before I rose I asked the merchant respecting her; and he answered me, She is a rich lady, the daughter of a deceased Emir, who left her great property.

I then took leave of him, and returned to the Khan, and the supper was placed before me; but, reflecting upon her, I could eat nothing. I laid myself down to rest; but sleep came not to me, and I remained awake until the morning, when I arose and put on a suit of clothing different from that which I had worn the day before; and, having drunk a cup of wine, and eaten a few morsels as my breakfast, repaired again to the shop of the merchant, and saluted him, and sat down with him. The lady soon came, wearing a dress more rich than the former, and attended by a slave-girl; and she seated herself, and saluted me instead of Bedr-ed-Din, and said, with an eloquent tongue which I had never heard surpassed in softness or sweetness, Send with me some one to receive the twelve hundred pieces of silver, the price of the piece of stuff.—Wherefore, said I, this haste? She replied, May we never lose thee! And she handed to me the price; and I sat conversing with her, and made a sign to her, which she understood, intimating my wish to visit her: whereupon she rose in haste, expressing displeasure at my hint. My heart clung to her, and I followed in the direction of her steps through the market-street; and lo, a slave-girl came to me, and said, O my master, answer the summons of my mistress. Wondering at this, I said, No one here knoweth me.—How soon, she rejoined, hast thou forgotten her! My mistress is she who was to-day at the shop of the merchant Bedr-ed-Din.—So I went with her until we arrived at the money-changer's; and when her mistress, who was there, beheld me, she drew me to her side, and said, O my beloved, thou hast wounded my heart, and love of thee hath taken possession of it; and from the time that I first saw thee, neither sleep nor food nor drink hath been pleasant to me. I replied, And more than that do I feel; and the state in which I am needs no complaint to testify it.—Then shall I visit thee, O my beloved, she asked, or wilt thou come to me? [For our marriage must be a secret.]—I am a stranger, I answered, and have no place of reception but the Khan; therefore, if thou wilt kindly permit me to go to thine abode, the pleasure will be perfect.—Well, she replied; but to-night is the eve of Friday, and let nothing be done till to-morrow, when, after thou hast joined in the prayers, do thou mount thine ass, and inquire for the Habbaniyeh; and when thou hast arrived there, ask for the house called the Ka'ah of Barakat the Nakib,[8] known by the surname of Abu-Shameh; for there do I reside; and delay not; for I shall be anxiously expecting thee.

On hearing this I rejoiced exceedingly, and we parted; and I returned to the Khan in which I lodged. I passed the whole night sleepless, and was scarcely sure that the daybreak had appeared when I rose and changed my clothes, and, having perfumed myself with essences and sweet scents, took with me fifty pieces of gold in a handkerchief, and walked from the

[8] Chief.

Khan of Mesrur to Bab Zuweyleh,[9] where I mounted an ass, and said to its owner, Go with me to the Habbaniyeh. And in less than the twinkling of an eye he set off, and soon he stopped at a by-street called Darb El-Munakkiri, when I said to him, Enter the street, and inquire for the Ka'ah of the Nakib. He was absent but a little while, and, returning, said, Alight.—Walk on before me, said I, to the Ka'ah. And he went on until he had led me to the house; whereupon I said to him, To-morrow come to me hither to convey me back.— In the name of Allah, he replied: and I handed to him a quarter of a piece of gold, and he took it and departed. I then knocked at the door, and there came forth to me two young virgins in whom the forms of womanhood had just developed themselves, resembling two moons, and they said, Enter; for our mistress is expecting thee, and she hath not slept last night from her excessive love for thee. I entered an upper saloon with seven doors: around it were latticed windows looking upon a garden in which were fruits of every kind, and running streams and singing birds: it was plastered with imperial gypsum, in which a man might see his face reflected: its roof was ornamented with gilding, and sur- rounded by inscriptions in letters of gold upon a ground of ultramarine: it comprised a variety of beauties, and shone in the eyes of beholders: the pavement was of coloured marbles, having in the midst of it a fountain, with four snakes of red gold casting forth water from their mouths like pearls and jewels at the corners of the pool; and it was furnished with carpets of coloured silk, and mattresses.

Having entered, I seated myself; and scarcely had I done so when the lady approached me. She wore a crown set with pearls and jewels; her hands and feet were stained with henna; and her bosom was ornamented with gold. As soon as she beheld me she smiled in my face, and embraced me, saying, Is it true that thou hast come to me, or is this a dream?—I am thy slave, I answered; and she said, Thou art welcome. Verily, from the time when I first saw thee, neither sleep hath been sweet to me nor hath food been pleasant!—In such case have *I* been, I replied;—and we sat down to converse; but I hung down my head towards the

[9] Or Zawileh, the southern gate of (the original) Cairo.

ground, in bashfulness; and not long had I thus remained when a repast was placed before me, consisting of the most exquisite dishes, as fricandoes and hashes and stuffed fowls. I ate with her until we were satisfied; when they brought the basin and ewer, and I washed my hands; after which we perfumed ourselves with rose-water infused with musk, and sat down again to converse; expressing to each other our mutual passion; and her love took such possession of me that all the wealth I possessed seemed worthless in comparison. In this manner we continued to enjoy ourselves until, night approaching, the female slaves brought supper and wine, a complete service; and we drank until midnight. Never in my life had I passed such a night. And when morning came, I arose, and, having thrown to her the handkerchief containing the pieces of gold, I took leave of her and went out; but as I did so she wept, and said, O my master, when shall I see again this lovely face? I answered her, I will be with thee at the commencement of the night. And when I went forth, I found the owner of the ass, who had brought me the day before, waiting for me at the door; and I mounted, and returned with him to the Khan of Mesrur, where I alighted, and gave to him half a piece of gold, saying to him, Come hither at sunset. He replied, On the head be thy command.

I entered the Khan, and ate my breakfast, and then went forth to collect the price of my stuffs; after which I returned. I had prepared for my wife a roasted lamb, and purchased some sweetmeat; and I now called the porter, described to him the house, and gave him his hire. Having done this, I occupied myself again with my business until sunset, when the owner of the ass came, and I took fifty pieces of gold, and put them into a handkerchief. Entering the house, I found that they had wiped the marble and polished the vessels of copper and brass, and filled the lamps and lighted the candles, and dished the supper and strained the wine; and when my wife saw me, she threw her arms around my neck, and said, Thou hast made me desolate by thine absence! The tables were then placed before us, and we ate until we were satisfied, and the slave-girls took away the first table, and placed before us the wine; and we sat drinking, and eating of the dried fruits, and making merry, until midnight.

We then slept until morning, when I arose and handed her the fifty pieces of gold as before, and left her.

Thus I continued to do for a long time, until I passed the night and awoke possessing not a piece of silver nor one of gold; and I said within myself, This is of the work of the Devil! And I repeated these verses:—

Poverty causeth the lustre of a man to grow dim, like the yellow-
    ness of the setting sun.
When absent, he is not remembered among mankind; and when
    present, he shareth not their pleasures.
In the market-streets he shunneth notice; and in desert places he
    poureth forth his tears.
By Allah! a man, among his own relations, when afflicted with
    poverty, is as a stranger!

With these reflections I walked forth into Beyn el-Kasreyn, and proceeded thence to Bab Zuweyleh, where I found the people crowding together, so that the gate was stopped up by their number; and, as destiny willed, I saw there a trooper, and, unintentionally pressing against him, my hand came in contact with his pocket, and I felt it, and found that it contained a purse; and I caught hold of the purse, and took it from his pocket. But the trooper felt that his pocket was lightened, and, putting his hand into it, found nothing; upon which he looked aside at me, and raised his hand with the mace, and struck me upon my head. I fell to the ground, and the people surrounded us, and seized the bridle of the trooper's horse, saying, On account of the crowd dost thou strike this young man such a blow? But he called out to them and said, This is a robber! On hearing this I feared. The people around me said, This is a comely young man, and hath taken nothing. While some, however, believed this, others disbelieved; and after many words, the people dragged me along, desiring to liberate me: but, as it was predestined, there came at this moment the Wali and other magistrates entering the gate, and, seeing the people surrounding me and the trooper, the Wali said, What is the news? The trooper answered, By Allah, O Emir, this is a robber: I had in my pocket a blue purse containing twenty pieces of gold; and he took it while I was pressed by the crowd.—Was any one with thee? asked the Wali. The trooper answered, No. And the

Wali called out to the chief of his servants, saying, Seize him and search him. So he seized me; and protection was withdrawn from me; and the Wali said to him, Strip him of all that is upon him. And when he did so, they found the purse in my clothes: and the Wali, taking it, counted the money, and found it to be twenty pieces of gold, as the trooper had said; whereupon he was enraged, and called out to his attendants, saying, Bring him forward. They, therefore, brought me before him, and he said to me, O young man, tell the truth. Didst thou steal this purse?—And I hung down my head towards the ground, saying within myself, If I answer that I did not steal it, it will be useless, for he hath produced it from my clothes; and if I say I stole it, I fall into trouble. I then raised my head, and said, Yes, I took it. And when the Wali heard these words, he wondered, and called witnesses, who presented themselves, and gave their testimony to my confession.—All this took place at Bab Zuweyleh.—The Wali then ordered the executioner to cut off my hand; and he cut of my right hand; but the heart of the trooper was moved with compassion for me, and he interceded for me that I should not be killed: so the Wali left me and departed. The people however continued around me, and gave me to drink a cup of wine; and the trooper gave me the purse, saying, Thou art a comely youth, and it is not fit that thou shouldst be a thief. And I took it from him, and addressed him with these verses:—

By Allah! good sir, I was not a robber; nor was I a thief, O best of mankind!
But fortune's vicissitudes overthrew me suddenly, and anxiety and trouble and poverty overpowered me.
I cast it not; but it was the Deity who cast an arrow that threw down the kingly diadem from my head.

The trooper then left me and departed, after having given me the purse, and I went my way; but first I wrapped my hand in a piece of rag, and put it in my bosom. My condition thus altered, and my countenance pallid in consequence of my sufferings, I walked to the Ka'ah, and, in a disordered state of mind, threw myself upon the bed. My wife, seeing my complexion thus changed, said to me, What hath pained thee, and wherefore do I see thee thus altered? I answered her, My head acheth, and I am not well. And on hearing this she was vexed, and became ill on my account, and said, Burn not my heart, O my master! Sit up, and raise thy head, and tell me what hath happened to thee this day; for I read a tale in thy face.—Abstain from speaking to me, I replied. And she wept, and said, it seemeth that thou art tired of us; for I see thee to be conducting thyself in a manner contrary to thy usual habit. Then she wept again, and continued addressing me, though I made her no reply, until the approach of night, when she placed some food before me; but I abstained from it, fearing that she should see me eat with my left hand, and said, I have no desire to eat at present. She then said again, Tell me what hath happened to thee this day, and wherefore I see thee anxious and broken-hearted. I answered, I will presently tell thee at my leisure. And she put the wine towards me, saying, Take it; for it will dispel thine anxiety; and thou must drink, and tell me thy story. I replied, therefore, If it must be so, give me to drink with thy hand. And she filled a cup and drank it; and then filled it again and handed it to me, and I took it from her with my left hand, and, while tears ran from my eyes, I repeated these verses:—

When God willeth an event to befall a man who is endowed with
    reason and hearing and sight,
He deafeneth his ears, and blindeth his heart, and draweth his
    reason from him as a hair.
Till, having fulfilled his purpose against him, He restoreth him his
    reason that he may be admonished.

Having thus said, I wept again; and when she saw me do so, she uttered a loud cry, and said, What is the reason of thy weeping? Thou hast burned my heart! And wherefore didst thou take the cup with thy left hand?—I answered her, I have a boil upon my right hand.—Then put it forth, said she, that I may open it for thee.—It is not yet, I replied, the proper time for opening it; and continue not to ask me; for I will not put it forth at present. I then drank the contents of the cup, and she continued to hand me the wine until intoxication overcame me, and I fell asleep in the place where I was sitting; upon which she discovered that my right

arm was without a hand, and, searching me, saw the purse
containing the gold.

Grief, such as none else experienceth, overcame her at the
sight; and she suffered incessant torment on my account until
the morning, when I awoke, and found that she had prepared for me a dish composed of four boiled fowls, which
she placed before me. She then gave me to drink a cup
of wine; and I ate and drank, and put down the purse, and
was about to depart; but she said, Whither wouldst thou go?
I answered, To such a place, to dispel somewhat of the
anxiety which oppresseth my heart.—Go not, said she; but
rather sit down again. So I sat down, and she said to me,
Hath thy love of me become so excessive that thou hast expended all thy wealth upon me, and lost thy hand? I take thee,
then, as witness against me, and God also is witness, that
I will never desert thee; and thou shalt see the truth of my
words.—Immediately, therefore, she sent for witnesses, who
came; and she said to them, Write my contract of marriage
to this young man, and bear witness that I have received the
dowry. And they did as she desired them; after which she
said, Bear witness that all my property which is in this chest,
and all my memluks and female slaves, belong to this young
man. Accordingly, they declared themselves witnesses of her
declaration, and I accepted the property, and they departed
after they had received their fees. She then took me by my
hand, and, having led me to a closet, opened a large chest,
and said to me, See what is containeth in this chest. I looked,
therefore; and lo, it was full of handkerchiefs; and she said,
This is thy property, which I have received from thee: for
every time that thou gavest me a handkerchief containing
fifty pieces of gold, I wrapped it up, and threw it into this
chest: take, then, thy property; for God hath restored it to
thee, and thou art now of high estate. Fate hath afflicted
thee on my account so that thou hast lost thy right hand, and
I am unable to compensate thee: if I should sacrifice my life,
it would be but a small thing, and thy generosity would still
have surpassed mine.—She then added, Now take possession
of thy property. So I received it; and she transferred the
contents of her chest to mine, adding her property to mine
which I had given her. My heart rejoiced, my anxiety

ceased, and I approached and kissed her, and made myself merry by drinking with her; after which she said again, Thou hast sacrificed all thy wealth and thy hand through love of me, and how can I compensate thee? By Allah, if I gave my life for love of thee, it were but a small thing, and I should not do justice to thy claims upon me.—She then wrote a deed of gift transferring to me all her apparel, and her ornaments of gold and jewels, and her houses and other possessions; and she passed that night in grief on my account, having heard my relation of the accident that had befallen me.

Thus we remained less than a month, during which time she became more and more infirm and disordered; and she endured no more than fifty days before she was numbered among the people of the other world. So I prepared her funeral, and deposited her body in the earth, and having caused recitations of the Kur'an to be performed for her, and given a considerable sum of money in alms for her sake, returned from the tomb. I found that she had possessed abundant wealth, and houses and lands, and among her property were the store-rooms of sesame of which I sold to thee the contents of one; and I was not prevented from settling with thee during this period but by my being busied in selling the remainder, the price of which I have not yet entirely received. Now I desire of thee that thou wilt not oppose me in that which I am about to say to thee; since I have eaten of thy food: I give thee the price of the sesame, which is in thy hands.—This which I have told thee was the cause of my eating with my left hand.

I replied, Thou hast treated me with kindness and generosity:—and he then said, Thou must travel with me to my country; for I have bought merchandise of Cairo and Alexandria. Wilt thou accompany me?—I answered, Yes:—and promised him that I would be ready by the first day of the following month. So I sold all that I possessed, and, having bought merchandise with the produce, travelled with the young man to this thy country, where he sold his merchandise and bought other in its stead, after which he returned to the land of Egypt: but it was my lot to remain here, and to experience that which hath befallen me this night during my absence from my native country.—Now is not this, O King

of the age, more wonderful than the story of the humpback?
The King replied, Ye must be hanged, all of you!—And
upon this, the Sultan's steward advanced towards the King,
and said, If thou permit me, I will relate to thee a story
that I happened to hear just before I found this humpback;
and if it be more wonderful than the events relating to him,
wilt thou grant us our lives?—The King answered, Tell thy
story:—and he began thus:—

THE STORY TOLD BY THE SULTAN'S STEWARD

I WAS last night with a party who celebrated a recitation
of the Kur'an, for which purpose they had assembled the
professors of religion and law; and when these reciters had
accomplished their task, the servants spread a repast, comprising among other dishes a zirbajeh. We approached,
therefore, to eat of the zirbajeh; but one of the company
drew back, and refused to partake of it: we conjured him;
yet he swore that he would not eat of it: and we pressed
him again; but he said, Press me not; for I have suffered
enough from eating of this dish. And when he had finished,
we said to him, By Allah, tell us the reason of thine abstain-
ing from eating of this zirbajeh. He replied, Because I
cannot eat of it unless I wash my hands forty times with
kali, and forty times with cyperus, and forty times with soap;
altogether, a hundred and twenty times. And upon this,
the giver of the entertainment ordered his servants, and they
brought water and the other things which this man required:
so he washed his hands as he had described, and advanced,
though with disgust, and, having seated himself, stretched
forth his hand as one in fear, and put it into the zirbajeh,
and began to eat, while we regarded him with the utmost
wonder. His hand trembled, and when he put it forth, we
saw that his thumb was cut off, and that he ate with his four
fingers: we therefore said to him, We conjure thee, by Allah,
to tell us how was thy thumb maimed; was it thus created
by God, or hath some accident happened to it?—O my
brothers, he answered, not only have I lost this thumb,
but also the thumb of the other hand; and each of my feet
is in like manner deprived of the great toe: but see ye:—

and, so saying, he uncovered the stump of the thumb of his other hand, and we found it like the right; and so also his feet, destitute of the great toes. At the sight of this, our wonder increased, and we said to him, We are impatient to hear thy story, and thine account of the cause of the amputation of thy thumbs and great toes, and the reason of thy washing thy hands a hundred and twenty times. So he said,—

Know that my father was a great merchant, the chief of the merchants of the city of Baghdad in the time of the Khalifeh Harun Er-Rashid; but he was ardently addicted to the drinking of wine, and hearing the lute; and when he died, he left nothing. I buried him, and caused recitations of the Kur'an to be performed for him, and, after I had mourned for him days and nights, I opened his shop, and found that he had left in it but few goods, and that his debts were many: however, I induced his creditors to wait, and calmed their minds, and betook myself to selling and buying from week to week, and so paying the creditors.

Thus I continued to do for a considerable period, until I had discharged all the debts and increased my capital; and as I was sitting one day, I beheld a young lady, than whom my eye had never beheld any more beautiful, decked with magnificent ornaments and apparel, riding on a mule, with a slave before her and a slave behind her; and she stopped the mule at the entrance of the market-street, and entered, followed by a eunuch, who said to her, O my mistress, enter, but inform no one who thou art, lest thou open the fire of indignation upon us. The eunuch then further cautioned her; and when she looked at the shops of the merchants, she found none more handsome than mine; so, when she arrived before me, with the eunuch following her, she sat down upon the seat of my shop, and saluted me; and I never heard speech more charming than hers, or words more sweet. She then drew aside the veil from her face, and I directed at her a glance which drew from me a sigh; my heart was captivated by her love, and I continued repeatedly gazing at her face, and recited these two verses:—

Say to the beauty in the dove-coloured veil, Death would indeed
    be welcome to relieve me from my torment.

Favour me with a visit, that so I may live. See, I stretch forth
     my hand to accept thy liberality.

And when she had heard my recitation of them, she answered
thus:—

May I lose my heart if it cease to love you! For verily my heart
     loveth none but you.
If my eye regard any charms but yours, may the sight of you never
     rejoice it after absence!

She then said to me, O youth, hast thou any handsome stuffs?
—O my mistress, I answered, thy slave is a poor man; but
wait until the other merchants open their shops, and then
I will bring thee what thou desirest. So I conversed with
her, drowned in the sea of her love, and bewildered by my
passion for her, until the merchants had opened their shops,
when I arose, and procured all that she wanted, and the
price of these stuffs was five thousand pieces of silver: and
she handed them all to the eunuch, who took them; after
which, they both went out from the market-street, and the
slaves brought to her the mule, and she mounted, without
telling me whence she was, and I was ashamed to mention
the subject to her: consequently, I became answerable for the
price to the merchants, incurring a debt of five thousand
pieces of silver.

   I went home, intoxicated with her love, and they placed
before me the supper, and I ate a morsel; but reflections upon
her beauty and loveliness prevented my eating more. I
desired to sleep, but sleep came not to me; and in this condition I remained for a week. The merchants demanded of
me their money; but I prevailed upon them to wait another
week; and after this week, the lady came again, riding upon
a mule, and attended by a eunuch and two other slaves; and,
having saluted me, said, O my master, we have been tardy
in bringing to thee the price of the stuffs: bring now the
money-changer, and receive it. So the money-changer came,
and the eunuch gave him the money, and I took it, and sat
conversing with her until the market was replenished, and
the merchants opened their shops, when she said to me,
Procure for me such and such things. Accordingly, I procured for her what she desired of the merchants, and she

took the goods and departed without saying anything to me respecting the price. When she had gone, therefore, I repented of what I had done; for I had procured for her what she demanded for the price of a thousand pieces of gold; and as soon as she had disappeared from my sight, I said within myself, What kind of love is this? She hath brought me five thousand pieces of silver, and taken goods for a thousand pieces of gold!—I feared that the result would be my bankruptcy and the loss of the property of others, and said, The merchants know none but me, and this woman is no other than a cheat, who hath imposed upon me by her beauty and loveliness: seeing me to be young, she hath laughed at me, and I asked her not where was her residence.

I remained in a state of perplexity, and her absence was prolonged more than a month. Meanwhile the merchants demanded of me their money, and so pressed me that I offered my possessions for sale, and was on the brink of ruin; but as I was sitting absorbed in reflection, suddenly she alighted at the gate of the market-street, and came in to me. As soon as I beheld her, my solicitude ceased, and I forgot the trouble which I had suffered. She approached, and addressed me with her agreeable conversation, and said, Produce the scales, and weigh thy money:—and she gave me the price of the goods which she had taken, with a surplus; after which, she amused herself by talking with me, and I almost died with joy and happiness. She then said to me, Hast thou a wife? I answered, No: for I am not acquainted with any woman: and wept. So she asked me, What causeth thee to weep? And I answered, A thought that hath come into my mind:—and, taking some pieces of gold, gave them to the eunuch, requesting him to grant me his mediation in the affair; upon which he laughed, and said, She is in love with thee more than thou art with her, and hath no want of the stuffs, but hath done this only from her love of thee: propose to her, therefore, what thou wilt; for she will not oppose thee in that which thou wilt say. Now she observed me giving the pieces of gold to the eunuch, and returned, and resumed her seat; and I said to her, Shew favour to thy slave, and pardon me for that which I am about to say. I then acquainted her with the feelings of my heart, and my declaration pleased her, and she consented to my proposal, saying, This eunuch will come with my letter; and do thou what he shall tell thee;—and she arose, and departed.

I went to the merchants, and delivered to them their money, and all profited except myself; for when she left me I mourned for the interruption of our intercourse, and I slept not during the whole of the next night: but a few days after, her eunuch came to me, and I received him with honour, and asked him respecting his mistress. He answered, She is sick:—and I said to him, Disclose to me her history. He replied, The lady Zubeydeh, the wife of Harun Er-Rashid, brought up this damsel, and she is one of her slaves: she had desired of her mistress to be allowed the liberty of going out and returning at pleasure, and the latter gave her permission: she continued, therefore, to do so until she became a chief confident; after which, she spoke of thee to her mistress, and begged that she would marry her to thee: but her mistress said, I will not do it until I see this young man, and if he have a desire for thee, I will marry thee to him. We therefore wish to introduce thee immediately into the palace; and if thou enter without any one's having knowledge of thy presence, thou wilt succeed in accomplishing thy marriage with her; but if thy plot be discovered, thy head will be struck off. What, then, sayest thou? —I answered, Good: I will go with thee, and await the event that shall befall me there.—As soon, then, as this next night shall have closed in, said the eunuch, repair to the mosque which the lady Zubeydeh hath built on the banks of the Tigris, and there say thy prayers, and pass the night.—Most willingly, I replied.

Accordingly, when the time of nightfall arrived, I went to the mosque, and said my prayers there, and passed the night; and as soon as the morning began to dawn I saw two eunuchs approaching in a small boat, conveying some empty chests, which they brought into the mosque. One of them then departed, and the other remained; and I looked attentively at him, and lo. it was he who had been our intermediary: and soon after, the damsel, my companion, came up to us. I rose to her when she approached, and embraced her; and she kissed me, and wept; and after we had conversed together for a little while, she took me and placed me in a chest, and locked it upon me. The slaves then brought a quantity of stuffs, and filled with them the other chests, which they locked, and conveyed, together with the chest in which I was enclosed, to the boat, accompanied by the damsel; and having embarked them, they plied the oars, and proceeded to the palace of the honoured lady Zubeydeh. The intoxication of love now ceased in me, and reflection came in its place: I repented of what I had done, and prayed God to deliver me from my dangerous predicament.

Meanwhile, they arrived at the gate of the Khalifeh, where they landed, and took out all the chests, and conveyed them into the palace: but the chief of the door-keepers, who had been asleep when they arrived, was awoke by the sounds of their voices, and cried out to the damsel, saying, The chests must be opened, that I may see what is in them:—and he arose, and placed his hand upon the chest in which I was hidden. My reason abandoned me, my heart almost burst from my body, and my limbs trembled; but the damsel said, These are the chests of the lady Zubeydeh, and if thou open them and turn them over, she will be incensed against thee, and we shall all perish. They contain nothing but clothes dyed of various colours, except this chest upon which thou hast put thy hand, in which there are also some bottles filled with the water of Zemzem,[10] and if any of the water run out upon the clothes it will spoil their colours. Now I have advised thee, and it is for thee to decide: so do what thou wilt.—When he heard, therefore, these words, he said to her, Take the chests, and pass on:—and the eunuchs immediately took them up, and with the damsel, conveyed them into the palace: but in an instant, I heard a person crying out, and saying, The Khalifeh! The Khalifeh!

I was bereft of my reason, and seized with a colic from excessive fear; I almost died, and my limbs were affected with a violent shaking. The Khalifeh cried out to the damsel, saying to her, What are these chests? She answered, O my

[10] The well at Mekkeh, believed to possess miraculous virtues.

lord (may God exalt thy dominion!), these chests contain clothes of my mistress Zubeydeh. — Open them, said the Khalifeh, that I may see the clothes.—When I heard this, I felt sure of my destruction. The damsel could not disobey his command; but she replied, O Prince of the Faithful, there is nothing in these chests but clothes of the lady Zubeydeh, and she hath commanded me not to open them to any one. The Khalifeh, however, said, The chests must be opened, all of them, that I may see their contents: — and immediately he called out to the eunuchs to bring them before him. I therefore felt certain that I was on the point of destruction. They then brought before him chest after chest, and opened each to him, and he examined the contents; and when they brought forward the chest in which I was enclosed, I bid adieu to life, and prepared myself for death; but as the eunuchs were about to open it, the damsel said, O Prince of the Faithful, verily this chest containeth things especially appertaining to women; and it is proper, therefore, that it should be opened before the lady Zubeydeh: — and when the Khalifeh heard her words, he ordered the eunuchs to convey all the chests into the interior of the palace. The damsel then hastened, and ordered two eunuchs to carry away the chest in which I was hidden, and they took it to an inner chamber, and went their way: whereupon she quickly opened it, and made a sign to me to come out: so I did as she desired, and entered a closet that was before me, and she locked the door upon me, and closed the chest: and when the eunuchs had brought in all the chests, and had gone back, she opened the door of the closet, and said, Thou hast nothing to fear! May God refresh thine eye! Come forth now, and go up with me, that thou mayest have the happiness of kissing the ground before the lady Zubeydeh.

I therefore went with her, and beheld twenty other female slaves, high-bosomed virgins, and among them was the lady Zubeydeh, who was scarcely able to walk from the weight of the robes and ornaments with which she was decked. As she approached, the female slaves dispersed from around her, and I advanced to her, and kissed the ground before her. She made a sign to me to sit down: so

I seated myself before her; and she began to ask me questions respecting my condition and lineage; to all of which I gave such answers that she was pleased, and said, By Allah, the care which we have bestowed on the education of this damsel hath not been in vain. She then said to me, Know that this damsel is esteemed by us as though she were really our child, and she is a trust committed to thy care by God. Upon this, therefore, I again kissed the ground before her, well pleased to marry the damsel; after which, she commanded me to remain with them ten days. Accordingly, I continued with them during this period; but I knew nothing meanwhile of the damsel; certain of the maids only bringing me my dinner and supper, as my servants. After this, however, the lady Zubeydeh asked permission of her husband, the Prince of the Faithful, to marry her maid, and he granted her request, and ordered that ten thousand pieces of gold should be given to her.

The lady Zubeydeh, therefore, sent for the Kadi and witnesses, and they wrote my contract of marriage to the damsel; and the maids then prepared sweetmeats and exquisite dishes, and distributed them in all the apartments. Thus they continued to do for a period of ten more days; and after the twenty days had passed, they conducted the damsel into the bath, preparatively to my being introduced to her as her husband. They then brought to me a repast comprising a basin of zirbajeh sweetened with sugar, perfumed with rose-water infused with musk, and containing different kinds of fricandoed fowls and a variety of other ingredients, such as astonished the mind; and, by Allah, when this repast was brought, I instantly commenced upon the zirbajeh, and ate of it as much as satisfied me, and wiped my hand, but forgot to wash it. I remained sitting until it became dark; when the maids lighted the candles, and the singing-girls approached with the tambourines, and they continued to display the bride, and to give presents of gold, until she had perambulated the whole of the palace; after which they brought her to me, and disrobed her; and as soon as I was left alone with her, I threw my arms around her neck, scarcely believing in our union: but as I did so, she perceived the smell of the zirbajeh from my hand, and immediately uttered a loud cry: whereupon the female slaves ran in to her from every quarter.

I was violently agitated, not knowing what was the matter; and the slaves who had come in said to her, What hath happened to thee, O our sister?—Take away from me, she exclaimed to them, this madman, whom I imagined to be a man of sense!—What indication of my insanity hath appeared to thee? I asked. Thou madman, said she, wherefore hast thou eaten of the zirbajeh, and not washed thy hand? By Allah, I will not accept thee for thy want of sense, and thy disgusting conduct!—And so saying, she took from her side a whip, and beat me with it upon my back until I became insensible from the number of the stripes. She then said to the other maids, Take him to the magistrate of the city police, that he may cut off his hand with which he ate the zirbajeh without washing it afterwards. On hearing this, I exclaimed, There is no strength nor power but in God! Wilt thou cut off my hand on account of my eating a zirbajeh and neglecting to wash it?—And the maids who were present entreated her, saying to her, O our sister, be not angry with him for what he hath done this time. But she replied, By Allah, I must cut off something from his extremities! And immediately she departed, and was absent from me ten days: after which, she came again, and said to me, O thou black-faced! Am I not worthy of thee? How didst thou dare to eat the zirbajeh and not wash thy hand?— And she called to the maids, who bound my hands behind me, and she took a sharp razor, and cut off both my thumbs and both my great toes, as ye see, O companions; and I swooned away. She then sprinkled upon my wounds some powder, by means of which the blood was stanched; and I said, I will not eat of a zirbajeh as long as I live unless I wash my hands forty times with kali and forty times with cyperus and forty times with soap:—and she exacted of me an oath that I would not eat of this dish unless I washed my hands as I have described to you. Therefore, when this zirbajeh was brought, my colour changed, and I said within myself, This was the cause of the cutting off of my thumbs and great toes:—so, when ye compelled me, I said, I must fulfil the oath which I have sworn.

I then said to him (continued the Sultan's steward), And what happened to thee after that? He answered, When I had thus sworn to her, she was appeased, and I was admitted into her favour and we lived happily together for a considerable time: after which she said, The people of the Khalifeh's palace know not that thou hast resided here with me, and no strange man beside thee hath entered it; nor didst thou enter but through the assistance of the lady Zubeydeh. She then gave me fifty thousand pieces of gold, and said to me, Take these pieces of gold, and go forth and buy for us a spacious house. So I went forth, and purchased a handsome and spacious house, and removed thither all the riches that she possessed, and all that she had treasured up, and her dresses and rarities.—This was the cause of the amputation of my thumbs and great toes.—So we ate (said the Sultan's steward), and departed; and after this, the accident with the humpback happened to me: this is all my story; and peace be on thee.

The King said, This is not more pleasant than the story of the humpback: nay, the story of the humpback is more pleasant than this; and ye must all of you be crucified.—The Jew, however, then came forward, and, having kissed the ground, said, O King of the age, I will relate to thee a story more wonderful than that of the humpback:—and the King said, Relate thy story. So he commenced thus:—

The Story Told by the Jewish Physician

The most wonderful of the events that happened to me in my younger days was this:—I was residing in Damascus, where I learnt and practised my art; and while I was thus occupied, one day there came to me a memluk from the house of the governor of the city: so I went forth with him, and accompanied him to the abode of the governor. I entered, and beheld, at the upper end of a saloon, a couch of alabaster overlaid with plates of gold, upon which was reclining a sick man: he was young; and a person more comely had not been seen in his age. Seating myself at his head, I ejaculated a prayer for his restoration; and he made a sign to me with his eye. I then said to him, O my master,

stretch forth to me thy hand:—whereupon he put forth to me
his left hand; and I was surprised at this, and said within
myself, What self-conceit! I felt his pulse, however, and
wrote a prescription for him, and continued to visit him for
a period of ten days, until he recovered his strength; when
he entered the bath, and washed himself, and came forth:
and the governor conferred upon me a handsome dress of
honour, and appointed me superintendent of the hospital of
Damascus. But when I went with him into the bath, which
they had cleared of all other visitors for us alone, and the
servants had brought the clothes, and taken away those
which he had pulled off within, I perceived that his right
hand had been cruelly amputated; at the sight of which I
wondered, and grieved for him; and looking at his skin, I
observed upon him marks of beating with mikr'ahs, which
caused me to wonder more. The young man then turned
towards me, and said, O doctor of the age, wonder not at
my case; for I will relate to thee my story when we have
gone out from the bath:—and when we had gone forth, and
arrived at the house, and had eaten some food, and rested,
he said to me, Hast thou a desire to divert thyself in the
supper-room? I answered, Yes:—and immediately he ordered the slaves to take up thither the furniture, and to
roast a lamb and bring us some fruit. So the slaves did as
he commanded them: and when they had brought the fruit,
and we had eaten, I said to him, Relate to me thy story:—
and he replied, O doctor of the age, listen to the relation of
the events which have befallen me.

Know that I am of the children of El-Mosil. My paternal
grandfather died leaving ten male children, one of whom
was my father: he was the eldest of them, and they all
grew up and married; and my father was blest with me;
but none of his nine brothers was blest with children. So
I grew up among my uncles, who delighted in me exceedingly; and when I had attained to manhood, I was one day
with my father in the chief mosque of El-Mosil. The day
was Friday; and we performed the congregational prayers,
and all the people went out, except my father and my
uncles, who sat conversing together respecting the wonders
of various countries, and the strange sights of different cities,

until they mentioned Egypt; when one of my uncles said,
The travellers assert, that there is not on the face of the
earth a more agreeable country than Egypt with its Nile:—
and my father added, He who hath not seen Cairo hath
not seen the world: its soil is gold; its Nile is a wonder;
its women are like the black-eyed virgins of Paradise; its
houses are palaces; and its air is temperate; its odour surpassing that of aloes-wood, and cheering the heart: and how
can Cairo be otherwise when it is the metropolis of the
world? Did ye see its gardens in the evening (he continued), with the shade obliquely extending over them, ye
would behold a wonder, and yield with ecstasy to their
attractions.

When I heard these descriptions of Egypt, my mind became wholly engaged by reflections upon that country; and
after they had departed to their homes, I passed the night
sleepless from my excessive longing towards it, and neither
food nor drink was pleasant to me. A few days after, my
uncles prepared to journey thither, and I wept before my
father that I might go with them, so that he prepared a
stock of merchandise for me, and I departed in their company; but he said to them, Suffer him not to enter Egypt,
but leave him at Damascus, that he may there sell his merchandise.

I took leave of my father, and we set forth from El-Mosil,
and continued our journey until we arrived at Aleppo, where
we remained some days; after which we proceeded thence
until we came to Damascus; and we beheld it to be a city
with trees and rivers and fruits and birds, as though it were
a paradise, containing fruits of every kind. We took lodgings in one of the Khans, and my uncles remained there
until they had sold and bought; and they also sold my merchandise, gaining, for every piece of silver, five, so that
I rejoiced at my profit. My uncles then left me, and repaired
to Egypt, and I remained and took up my abode in a handsome Ka'ah, such as the tongue cannot describe; the monthly
rent of which was two pieces of gold.

Here I indulged myself with eating and drinking, squandering away the money that was in my possession; and as
I was sitting one day at the door of the Ka'ah, a damsel ap-

proached me, attired in clothing of the richest description, such as I had never seen surpassed in costliness, and I invited her to come in; whereupon, without hesitation, she entered; and I was delighted at her compliance, and closed the door upon us both. She then uncovered her face, and took off her izar, and I found her to be so surprisingly beautiful that love for her took possession of my heart: so I went and brought a repast consisting of the most delicious viands and fruit and everything else that was requisite for her entertainment, and we ate and sported together; after which we drank till we were intoxicated, and fell asleep, and so we remained until the morning, when I handed her ten pieces of gold; but she swore that she would not accept them from me, and said, Expect me again, O my beloved, after three days: at the hour of sunset I will be with thee: and do thou prepare for us, with these pieces of gold, a repast similar to this which we have just enjoyed. She then gave me ten pieces of gold, and took leave of me, and departed, taking my reason with her. And after the three days had expired, she came again, decked with embroidered stuffs and ornaments and other attire more magnificent than those which she wore on the former occasion. I had prepared for her what was required previously to her arrival; so we now ate and drank and fell asleep as before; and in the morning she gave me again ten pieces of gold, promising to return to me after three more days. I therefore made ready what was requisite, and after the three days she came attired in a dress still more magnificent than the first and second, and said to me, O my master, am I beautiful?—Yea, verily, I answered.— Wilt thou give me leave, she rejoined, to bring with me a damsel more beautiful than myself, and younger than I, that she may sport with us, and we may make merry with her? For she hath requested that she may accompany me, and pass the night in frolicking with us.—And so saying, she gave me twenty pieces of gold, desiring me to prepare a more plentiful repast, on account of the lady who was to come with her; after which, she bade me farewell, and departed.

Accordingly, on the fourth day, I procured what was requisite, as usual, and soon after sunset she came, accompanied by a female wrapped in an izar, and they entered, and seated themselves. I was rejoiced, and lighted the candles, and welcomed them with joy and exultation. They then took off their outer garments, and when the new damsel uncovered her face, I perceived that she was like the full moon: I never beheld a person more beautiful. I arose immediately, and placed before them the food and drink, and we ate and drank, while I continued caressing the new damsel, and filling the wine-cup for her, and drinking with her: but the first lady was affected with a secret jealousy.— By Allah, she said, verily this girl is beautiful! Is she not more charming than I?—Yea, indeed, I answered.—Soon after this I fell asleep, and when I awoke in the morning, I found my hand defiled with blood, and opening my eyes, perceived that the sun had risen; so I attempted to rouse the damsel, my new companion, whereupon her head rolled from her body. The other damsel was gone, and I concluded, therefore, that she had done this from her jealousy; and after reflecting a while, I arose, and took off my clothes, and dug a hole in the Ka'ah, in which I deposited the murdered damsel, afterwards covering her remains with earth, and replacing the marble pavement as it was before. I then dressed myself again, and, taking the remainder of my money, went forth, and repaired to the owner of the Ka'ah, and paid him a year's rent, saying to him, I am about to journey to my uncles in Egypt.

So I departed to Egypt, where I met with my uncles, and they were rejoiced to see me. I found that they had concluded the sale of their merchandise, and they said to me, What is the cause of thy coming? I answered, I had a longing desire to be with you, and feared that my money would not suffice me.—For a year I remained with them, enjoying the pleasures of Egypt and its Nile; and I dipped my hand into the residue of my money, and expended it prodigally in eating and drinking until near the time of my uncles' departure, when I fled from them: so they said, Probably he hath gone before us and returned to Damascus: —and they departed. I then came forth from my concealment, and remained in Cairo three years, squandering away my money until scarcely any of it remained: but meanwhile I sent every year the rent of the Ka'ah at Damascus to its

owner: and after the three years my heart became contracted, for nothing remained in my possession but the rent
for the year.

I therefore journeyed back to Damascus, and alighted at
the Ka'ah. The owner was rejoiced to see me, and I entered
it, and cleansed it of the blood of the murdered damsel, and,
removing a cushion, I found, beneath this, the necklace that
she had worn that night. I took it up and examined it, and
wept a while. After this I remained in the house two days,
and on the third day I entered the bath, and changed my
clothes. I now had no money left; and I went one day to the
market, where (the Devil suggesting it to me, in order to
accomplish the purpose of destiny) I handed the necklace
of jewels to a broker; and he rose to me, and seated me by
his side: then having waited until the market was replenished, he took it, and announced it for sale secretly, without
my knowledge. The price bidden for it amounted to two
thousand pieces of gold; but he came to me and said, This
necklace is of brass, of the counterfeit manufacture of the
Franks, and its price hath amounted to a thousand pieces
of silver. I answered him, Yes: we had made it for a woman,
merely to laugh at her, and my wife has inherited it, and we
desire to sell it: go, therefore, and receive the thousand
pieces of silver. Now when the broker heard this, he
perceived that the affair was suspicious, and went and gave
the necklace to the chief of the market, who took it to the
Wali, and said to him, This necklace was stolen from me,
and we have found the thief, clad in the dress of the sons
of the merchants. And before I knew what had happened,
the officers had surrounded me, and they took me to the Wali,
who questioned me respecting the necklace. I told him,
therefore, the same story that I had told to the broker; but
he laughed, and said, This is not the truth:—and instantly
his people stripped me of my outer clothing, and beat me
with mikra'ahs all over my body, until, through the torture
that I suffered from the blows, I said, I stole it:—reflecting
that it was better I should say I stole it, than confess that its
owner was murdered in my abode; for then they would kill
me to avenge her: and as soon as I had said so, they cut off
my hand, and scalded the stump with boiling oil, and I

swooned away. They then gave me to drink some wine, by swallowing which I recovered my senses; and I took my amputated hand, and returned to the Ka'ah; but its owner said to me, Since this hath happened to thee, leave the Ka'ah, and look for another abode; for thou art accused of an unlawful act.—O my master, I replied, give me two or three days' delay that I may seek for a lodging:—and he assented to this and departed and left me. So I remained alone, and sat weeping, and saying, How can I return to my family with my hand cut off. He who cut it off knoweth not that I am innocent: perhaps, then, God will bring about some event for my relief.

I sat weeping violently; and when the owner of the Ka'ah had departed from me, excessive grief overcame me, and I was sick for two days; and on the third day, suddenly the owner of the Ka'ah came to me, with some officers of the police, and the chief of the market, and accused me again of stealing the necklace. So I went out to them, and said, What is the news?—whereupon, without granting me a moment's delay, they bound my arms behind me, and put a chain around my neck, saying to me, The necklace which was in thy possession hath proved to be the property of the governor of Damascus, its Wezir and its Ruler; it hath been lost from the governor's house for a period of three years, and with it was his daughter.—When I heard these words from them, my limbs trembled, and I said within myself, They will kill me! My death is inevitable! By Allah, I must relate my story to the governor; and if he please he will kill me, or if he please he will pardon me.—And when we arrived at the governor's abode, and they had placed me before him, and he beheld me, he said, Is this he who stole the necklace and went out to sell it? Verily ye have cut off his hand wrongfully.—He then ordered that the chief of the market should be imprisoned, and said to him, Give to this person the compensatory fine for his hand, or I will hang thee and seize all thy property. And he called out to his attendants, who took him and dragged him away.

I was now left with the governor alone, after they had, by his permission, loosed the chain from my neck, and untied the cords which bound my arms; and the governor looking towards me, said to me, O my son, tell me thy story, and speak truth. How did this necklace come into thy possession?—So I replied, O my lord, I will tell thee the truth:—and I related to him all that had happened to me with the first damsel, and how she had brought to me the second, and murdered her from jealousy; on hearing which, he shook his head, and covered his face with his handkerchief, and wept. Then looking towards me, he said, Know, O my son, that the elder damsel was my daughter: I kept her closely; and when she had attained a fit age for marriage, I sent her to the son of her uncle in Cairo; but he died, and she returned to me, having learnt habits of profligacy from the inhabitants of that city; so she visited thee four times; and on the fourth occasion, she brought to thee her younger sister. They were sisters by the same mother, and much attached to each other; and when the event which thou has related occurred to the elder, she imparted her secret to her sister, who asked my permission to go out with her; after which the elder returned alone; and when I questioned her respecting her sister, I found her weeping for her, and she answered, I know no tidings of her:—but she afterwards informed her mother, secretly, of the murder which she had committed; and her mother privately related the affair to me; and she continued to weep for her incessantly, saying, By Allah, I will not cease to weep for her until I die. Thy account, O my son, is true; for I knew the affair before thou toldest it me. See then, O my son, what hath happened: and now I request of thee that thou wilt not oppose me in that which I am about to say; and it is this:—I desire to marry thee to my youngest daughter; for she is not of the same mother as they were: she is a virgin, and I will receive from thee no dowry, but will assign to you both an allowance; and thou shalt be to me as an own son.—I replied, Let it be as thou desirest, O my master. How could I expect to attain unto such happiness?—The governor then sent immediately a courier to bring the property which my father had left me (for he had died since my departure from him), and now I am living in the utmost affluence.

I wondered, said the Jew, at his history; and after I had remained with him three days, he gave me a large sum of money; and I left him, to set forth on a journey; and, arriving in this your country, my residence here pleased me, and I experienced this which hath happened to me with the humpback.

The King, when he had heard this story, said, This is not more wonderful than the story of the humpback, and ye must all of you be hanged, and especially the tailor, who is the source of all the mischief. But he afterwards added, O tailor, if thou tell me a story more wonderful than that of the humpback, I will forgive you your offences. So the tailor advanced, and said,—

The Story Told by the Tailor

Know, O King of the age, that what hath happened to me is more wonderful than the events which have happened to all the others. Before I met the humpback, I was, early in the morning, at an entertainment given to certain trades-men of my acquaintance, consisting of tailors and linen-drapers and carpenters and others; and when the sun had risen, the repast was brought for us to eat; and lo, the master of the house came in to us, accompanied by a strange and handsome young man, of the inhabitants of Baghdad. He was attired in clothes of the handsomest description, and was a most comely person, except that he was lame; and as soon as he had entered and saluted us, we rose to him; but when he was about to seat himself, he observed among us a man who was a barber, whereupon he refused to sit down, and desired to depart from us. We and the master of the house, however, prevented him, and urged him to seat himself; and the host conjured him, saying, What is the reason of thy entering, and then immediately departing? —By Allah, O my master, replied he, offer me no opposition; for the cause of my departure is this barber, who is sitting with you. And when the host heard this, he was exceedingly surprised, and said, How is it that the heart of this young man, who is from Baghdad, is troubled by the presence of this barber? We then looked towards him, and said, Relate to us the cause of thy displeasure against this barber; and the young man replied, O company, a surprising adventure

happened to me with this barber in Baghdad, my city; and
he was the cause of my lameness, and of the breaking of my
leg; and I have sworn that I will not sit in any place where
he is present, nor dwell in any town where he resides: I
quitted Baghdad and took up my abode in this city, and
I will not pass the next night without departing from it.—
Upon this, we said to him, We conjure thee, by Allah, to
relate to us thy adventure with him.—And the countenance
of the barber turned pale when he heard us make this request.
The young man then said,—

Know, O good people, that my father was one of the
chief merchants of Baghdad; and God (whose name be
exalted!) blessed him with no son but myself; and when
I grew up, and had attained to manhood, my father was
admitted to the mercy of God, leaving me wealth and
servants and other dependants; whereupon I began to attire myself in clothes of the handsomest description, and
to feed upon the most delicious meats. Now God (whose
perfection be extolled!) made me to be a hater of women;
and so I continued, until, one day, I was walking through
the streets of Baghdad, when a party of them stopped my
way: I therefore fled from them, and, entering a by-street
which was not a thoroughfare, I reclined upon a mastabah
at its further extremity. Here I had been seated but a
short time when, lo, a window opposite the place where I
sat was opened, and there looked out from it a damsel
like the full moon, such as I had never in my life beheld.
She had some flowers, which she was watering, beneath the
window; and she looked to the right and left, and then
shut the window, and disappeared from before me. Fire
had been shot into my heart, and my mind was absorbed
by her; my hatred of women was turned into love, and I
continued sitting in the same place until sunset, in a state
of distraction from the violence of my passion, when, lo,
the Kadi of the city came riding along, with slaves before
him and servants behind him, and alighted, and entered
the house from which the damsel had looked out: so I knew
that he must be her father.

I then returned to my house, sorrowful and fell upon
my bed, full of anxious thoughts; and my female slaves

came in to me, and seated themselves around me, not knowing what was the matter with me; and I acquainted them
not with my case, nor returned any answers to their questions; and my disorder increased. The neighbours, therefore, came to cheer me with their visits; and among those
who visited me was an old woman, who, as soon as she
saw me, discovered my state; whereupon she seated herself at my head, and, addressing me in a kind manner,
said, O my son, tell me what hath happened to thee? So
I related to her my story, and she said, O my son, this is
the daughter of the Kadi of Baghdad, and she is kept in
close confinement: the place where thou sawest her is her
apartment, and her father occupies a large saloon below,
leaving her alone; and often do I visit her: thou canst
obtain an interview with her only through me: so brace up
thy nerves. When I heard, therefore, what she said, I took
courage, and fortified my heart; and my family rejoiced
that day. I rose up firm in limb, and hoping for complete
restoration; and the old woman departed; but she returned
with her countenance changed, and said, O my son, ask not
what she did when I told her of thy case; for she said, If
thou abstain not, O ill-omened old woman, from this discourse, I will treat thee as thou deservest:—but I must go
to her a second time.

On hearing this, my disorder increased: after some days,
however, the old woman came again, and said, O my son, I
desire of thee a reward for good tidings. My soul returned
to my body at these words, and I replied, Thou shalt receive
from me everything that thou canst wish. She then said, I
went yesterday to the damsel, and when she beheld me with
broken heart and weeping eye, she said to me, O my aunt,
wherefore do I see thee with contracted heart?—and when
she had thus said, I wept, and answered, O my daughter
and mistress, I came to thee yesterday from visiting a youth
who loveth thee, and he is at the point of death on thy
account:—and, her heart being moved with compassion, she
asked, Who is this youth of whom thou speakest? I answered,
He is my son, and the child that is dear to my soul: he saw
thee at the window some days ago, while thou wast watering
thy flowers; and when he beheld thy face, he became dis-

tracted with love for thee: I informed him of the conversation that I had with thee the first time; upon which his disorder increased, and he took to his pillow: he is now dying, and there is no doubt of his fate.—And upon this, her countenance became pale and she said, Is this all on my account?—Yea, by Allah, I answered; and what dost thou order me to do?—Go to him, said she; convey to him my salutation, and tell him that my love is greater than his; and on Friday next, before the congregation prayers, let him come hither: I will give orders to open the door to him, and to bring him up to me, and I will have a short interview with him, and he shall return before my father comes back from the prayers.

When I heard these words of the old woman, the anguish which I had suffered ceased; my heart was set at rest, and I gave her the suit of clothes which I was then wearing, and she departed, saying to me, Cheer up thy heart. I replied, I have no longer any pain. The people of my house, and my friends, communicated, one to another, the good news of my restoration to health, and I remained thus until the Friday, when the old woman came in to me, and asked me respecting my state; so I informed her that I was happy and well. I then dressed and perfumed myself, and sat waiting for the people to go to prayers, that I might repair to the damsel; but the old woman said to me, Thou hast yet more than ample time, and if thou go to the bath and shave, especially for the sake of obliterating the traces of thy disorder, it will be more becoming.—It is a judicious piece of advice, replied I; but I will shave my head first, and then go into the bath.

So I sent for a barber to shave my head, saying to the boy, Go to the market, and bring me a barber, one who is a man of sense, little inclined to impertinence, that he may not make my head ache by his chattering. And the boy went, and brought this sheykh, who, on entering, saluted me; and when I returned his salutation, he said to me, May God dispel thy grief and thine anxiety, and misfortunes and sorrows! I responded, May God accept thy prayer! He then said, Be cheerful, O my master; for health hath returned to thee. Dost thou desire to be shaved or to be

bled?—for it hath been handed down, on the authority of
Ibn-'Abbas[11] that the Prophet said, Whoso shorteneth his
hair on Friday, God will avert from him seventy diseases;—
and it hath been handed down also, on the same authority,
that the Prophet said, Whoso is cupped on Friday will not
be secure from the loss of sight and from frequent disease.
—Abstain, said I, from this useless discourse, and come
immediately, shave my head for I am weak. And he arose,
and, stretching forth his hand, took out a handkerchief, and
opened it; and lo, there was in it an astrolabe, consisting of
seven plates; and he took it, and went into the middle of
the court, where he raised his head towards the sun, and
looked for a considerable time; after which he said to me,
Know that there have passed, of this our day,—which is
Friday, and which is the tenth of Safar, of the year 263 of
the Flight of the Prophet,—upon whom be the most excellent
of blessings and peace!—and the ascendant star of which,
according to the required rules of the science of computation, is the planet Mars,—seven degrees and six minutes;
and it happeneth that Mercury hath come in conjunction
with that planet; and this indicateth that the shaving of
hair is now a most excellent operation: and it hath indicated
to me, also, that thou desirest to confer a benefit upon a
person: and fortunate is he!—but after that, there is an
announcement that presenteth itself to me respecting a
matter which I will not mention to thee.

By Allah, I exclaimed, thou hast wearied me, and dissipated my mind, and augured against me, when I required
thee only to shave my head: arise, then, and shave it; and
prolong not thy discourse to me. But he replied, By Allah,
if thou knewest the truth of the case, thou wouldst demand
of me a further explication; and I counsel thee to do this
day as I direct thee, according to the calculations deduced
from the stars: it is thy duty to praise God, and not to
oppose me; for I am one who giveth thee good advice, and
who regardeth thee with compassion: I would that I were
in thy service for a whole year, that thou mightest do me
justice; and I desire not any pay from thee for so doing.—

[11] One of the most learned of the companions of his cousin Mohammad,
and one of the most celebrated of the relators of his sayings and actions.

When I heard this, I said to him, Verily thou art killing me this day, and there is no escape for me.—O my master, he replied, I am he whom the people call Es-Samit, ["the Silent,"] on account of the paucity of my speech, by which I am distinguished above my brothers: for my eldest brother is named El-Bakbuk; and the second, El-Heddar; and the third, Bakbak[12]; and the fourth is named El-Kuz el-Aswani; and the fifth, El-Feshshar; and the sixth is named Shakalik; and the seventh brother is named Es-Samit; and he is myself.

Now when this barber thus overwhelmed me with his talk, I felt as if my gall-bladder had burst, and said to the boy, Give him a quarter of a piece of gold and let him depart from me for the sake of Allah: for I have no need to shave my head. But the barber on hearing what I said to the boy, exclaimed, What is this that thou hast said, O my lord? By Allah, I will accept from thee no pay unless I serve thee; and serve thee I must; for to do so is incumbent on me, and to perform what thou requirest; and I care not if I receive from thee no money. If thou knowest not my worth, I know thine; and thy father—may Allah have mercy upon him!—treated us with beneficence; for he was a man of generosity. By Allah, thy father sent for me one day, like this blessed day, and when I went to him, he had a number of his friends with him, and he said to me, Take some blood from me. So I took the astrolabe, and observed the altitude for him, and found the ascendant of the hour to be of evil omen, and that the letting of blood would be attended with trouble: I therefore acquainted him with this, and he conformed to my wish, and waited until the arrival of the approved hour, when I took the blood from him. He did not oppose me; but, on the contrary, thanked me; and in like manner all the many present thanked me; and thy father gave me a hundred pieces of gold for services similar to the letting of blood.—May God, said I, shew no mercy to my father for knowing such a man as thou!—and the barber laughed, and exclaimed, There is no deity but God! Mohammad is God's Apostle! Extolled be the perfection of Him who changeth others, but is not changed! I did not imagine thee to be otherwise than a man of sense; but

[12] All three names signify "Chatterer."

thou hast talked nonsense in consequence of thine illness.
God hath mentioned, in his Excellent Book, those who restrain their anger, and who forgive men:—but thou art
excused in every case. I am unacquainted, however, with
the cause of thy haste; and thou knowest that thy father
used to do nothing without consulting me; and it hath
been said, that the person to whom one applies for advice
should be trusted: now thou wilt find no one better acquainted with the affairs of the world than myself, and I
am standing on my feet to serve thee. I am not displeased
with thee, and how then art thou displeased with me? But
I will have patience with thee on account of the favours
which I have received from thy father.—By Allah, said I,
thou hast wearied me with thy discourse, and overcome me
with thy speech! I desire that thou shave my head and
depart from me.

I gave vent to my rage; and would have risen, even if
he had wetted my head, when he said, I knew that displeasure with me had overcome thee; but I will not be
angry with thee, for thy sense is weak, and thou art a youth:
a short time ago I used to carry thee on my shoulder, and
take thee to the school.—Upon this, I said to him, O my
brother, I conjure thee by Allah, depart from me that I may
perform my business, and go thou thy way. Then I rent
my clothes; and when he saw me do this, he took the
razor, and sharpened it, and continued to do so until my soul
almost parted from my body; then advancing to my head,
he shaved a small portion of it; after which he raised his
hand, and said, O my lord, haste is from the Devil;—and
he repeated this couplet:—

Deliberate, and haste not to accomplish thy desire; and be merciful,
    so shalt thou meet with one merciful:
For there is no hand but God's hand is above it; nor oppressor
    that shall not meet with an oppressor.

O my lord (he then continued), I do not imagine that thou
knowest my condition in society; for my hand lighteth
upon the heads of kings and emirs and wezirs and sages
and learned men; and of such a one as myself hath the
poet said,—

The trades altogether are like a necklace, and this barber is the
    chief pearl of the strings.
He excelleth all that are endowed with skill, and under his hands
    are the heads of Kings.

—Leave, said I, that which doth not concern thee! Thou hast
contracted my heart, and troubled my mind.—I fancy that
thou art in haste, he rejoined. I replied, Yes! Yes! Yes!—
Proceed slowly, said he; for verily haste is from the Devil,
and it giveth occasion to repentance and disappointment;
and he upon whom be blessing and peace hath said, The
best of affairs is that which is commenced with deliber-
ation:—and, by Allah, I am in doubt as to thine affair: I
wish, therefore, that thou wouldst make known to me what
thou art hasting to do; and may it be good; for I fear it
is otherwise.

    There now remained, to the appointed time, three hours;
and he threw the razor from his hand in anger, and, taking
the astrolabe, went again to observe the sun; then after he
had waited a long time, he returned, saying, There remain,
to the hour of prayer, three hours, neither more nor less.—
For the sake of Allah, said I, be silent; for thou hast
crumbled my liver!—and thereupon he took the razor, and
sharpened it as he had done the first time, and shaved
another portion of my head. Then stopping again, he said,
I am in anxiety on account of thy hurry: if thou wouldst
acquaint me with the cause of it, it would be better for thee;
for thou knowest that thy father used to do nothing without
consulting me.

    I perceived now that I could not avoid his importunity,
and said within myself, The time of prayer is almost come,
and I desire to go before the people come out from the
service: if I delay a little longer, I know not how to gain
admission to her. I therefore said to him, Be quick, and
cease from this chattering and impertinence; for I desire
to repair to an entertainment with my friends. But when
he heard the mention of the entertainment, he exclaimed,
The day is a blessed day for me! I yesterday conjured a
party of my intimate friends to come and feast with me,
and forgot to prepare for them anything to eat; and now
I have remembered it. Alas for the disgrace that I shall

experience from them!—So I said to him, Be in no anxiety
on this account, since thou hast been told that I am going
to-day to an entertainment; for all the food and drink that
is in my house shall be thine if thou use expedition in my
affair, and quickly finish shaving my head.—May God
recompense thee with every blessing! he replied: describe
to me what thou hast for my guests, that I may know it.—
I have, said I, five dishes of meat, and ten fowls fricandoed,
and a roasted lamb.—Cause them to be brought before me,
he said, that I may see them. So I had them brought to
him, and he exclaimed, Divinely art thou gifted! How
generous is thy soul; But the incense and perfumes are
wanting.—I brought him, therefore, a box containing nedd[13]
and aloes-wood and ambergris and musk, worth fifty pieces
of gold.—The time had now become contracted, like my
own heart; so I said to him, Receive this, and shave the
whole of my head, by the existence of Mohammad, God
bless and save him! But he replied, By Allah, I will not
take it until I see all that it contains. I therefore ordered
the boy, and he opened the box to him; whereupon the
barber threw down the astrolabe from his hand, and seating himself upon the ground, turned over the perfumes and
incense and aloes-wood in the box until my soul almost
quitted my body.

He then advanced, and took the razor, and shaved
another small portion of my head; after which he said, By
Allah, O my son, I know not whether I should thank thee
or thank thy father; for my entertainment to-day is entirely
derived from thy bounty and kindness, and I have no one
among my visitors deserving of it; for my guests are Zeytun
the bath-keeper, and Sali' the wheat-seller, and 'Awkal the
bean-seller, and 'Akresheh the grocer, and Homeyd the
dustman, and 'Akarish the milk-seller, and each of these
hath a peculiar dance which he performeth, and peculiar
verses which he reciteth; and the best of their qualities is,
that they are like thy servant, the memluk who is before
thee; and I, thy slave, know neither loquacity nor impertinence. As to the bath-keeper, he saith, If I go not to

---

[13] A perfume composed of ambergris, musk, and aloes-wood; or simply
ambergris.

the feast, it cometh to my house!—and as to the dustman, he is witty, and full of frolic: often doth he dance, and say, News, with my wife, is not kept in a chest!—and each of my friends hath jests that another hath not: but the description is not like the actual observation. If thou choose, therefore, to come to us, it will be more pleasant both to thee and to us: relinquish, then, thy visit to thy friends of whom thou hast told us that thou desirest to go to them: for the traces of disease are yet upon thee, and probably thou art going to a people of many words, who will talk of that which concerneth them not; or probably there will be among them one impertinent person; and thy soul is already disquieted by disease.—I replied, If it be the will of God, that shall be on some other day:—but he said, It will be more proper that thou first join my party of friends, that thou mayest enjoy their conviviality, and delight thyself with their salt. Act in accordance with the saying of the poet:—

Defer not a pleasure when it can be had; for fortune often destroyeth our plans.

Upon this I laughed from a heart laden with anger, and said to him, Do what I require, that I may go in the care of God, whose name be exalted! and do thou go to thy friends, for they are awaiting thine arrival. He replied, I desire nothing but to introduce thee into the society of these people; for verily they are of the sons of that class among which is no impertinent person; and if thou didst but behold them once, thou wouldst leave all thine own companions.—May God, said I, give thee abundant joy with them, and I must bring them together here some day.—If that be thy wish, he rejoined, and thou wilt first attend the entertainment of thy friends this day, wait until I take this present with which thou hast honoured me, and place it before my friends, that they may eat and drink without waiting for me, and then I will return to thee, and go with thee to thy companions: for there is no false delicacy between me and my companions that should prevent my leaving them; so I will return to thee quickly, and repair with thee whithersoever thou goest.—Upon this I exclaimed, There is no strength nor power but in God, the High, the Great! Go thou to thy companions, and delight thy heart with them, and leave me to repair to mine, and to remain with them this day, for they are waiting my arrival.— But he said, I will not leave thee to go alone.—The place to which I am going, said I, none can enter except myself.—I suppose then, he rejoined, that thou hast an appointment to-day with some female: otherwise, thou wouldst take me with thee; for I am more deserving than all other men, and will assist thee to attain what thou desirest. I fear that thou art going to visit some strange woman, and that thy life will be lost; for in this city of Baghdad no one can do anything of this kind, especially on such a day as this; seeing that the Wali of Baghdad is a terrible, sharp sword.—Wo to thee, O wicked old man! I exclaimed, what are these words with which thou addressest me!—And upon this, he kept a long silence.

The time of prayer had now arrived, and the time of the Khutbeh[14] was near, when he had finished shaving my head: So I said to him, Go with this food and drink to thy friends, and I will wait for thee until thou return, and thou shalt accompany me:—and I continued my endeavours to deceive him; that he might go away; but he said to me, Verily thou art deceiving me, and wilt go alone, and pre-cipitate thyself into a calamity from which there will be no escape for thee; by Allah! by Allah! then quit not this spot until I return to thee, and accompany thee, that I may know what will be the result of thine affair.—I replied, Well: prolong not thine absence from me. And he took the food and drink and other things which I had given him, but intrusted them to a porter to convey them to his abode, and concealed himself in one of the by-streets. I then immediately arose. The mueddins on the menarehs had chanted the Selam of Friday; and I put on my clothes, and went forth alone, and, arriving at the by-street, stopped at the door of the house where I had seen the damsel: and lo, the barber was behind me, and I knew it not. I found the door open, and entered; and immediately the master of the house returned from the prayers, and entered the saloon, and closed the door; and I said within myself, How did this devil discover me?

[14] Friday sermon.

Now it happened, just at this time, for the fulfilment of God's purpose to rend the veil of protection before me, that a female slave belonging to the master of the house committed some offence, in consequence of which he beat her, and she cried out; whereupon a male slave came in to him to liberate her; but he beat him also, and he likewise cried out; and the barber concluded that he was beating me; so he cried, and rent his clothes, and sprinkled dust upon his head, shrieking, and calling for assistance. He was surrounded by people, and said to them, My master hath been killed in the house of the Kadi! Then running to my house, crying out all the while, and with a crowd behind him, he gave the news to my family; and I knew not what he had done when they approached, crying, Alas for our master!— the barber all the while being before them, with his clothes rent, and a number of the people of the city with them. They continued shrieking, the barber shrieking at their head, and all of them exclaiming, Alas for our slain!—Thus they advanced to the house in which I was confined; and when the Kadi heard of this occurrence, the event troubled him, and he arose, and opened the door, and seeing a great crowd, he was confounded, and said, O people, what is the news?

The servants replied, Thou hast killed our master.— O people, rejoined he, what hath your master done unto me that I should kill him; and wherefore do I see this barber before you?—Thou hast just now beaten him with mikra‘ahs, said the barber; and I heard his cries.—What hath he done that I should kill him? repeated the Kadi. And whence, he added, came he; and whither would he go? —Be not an old man of malevolence, exclaimed the barber; for I know the story, and the reason of his entering thy house, and the truth of the whole affair; thy daughter is in love with him, and he is in love with her; and thou hast discovered that he had entered thy house, and hast ordered thy young men, and they have beaten him. By Allah, none shall decide between us and thee except the Khalifeh; or thou shalt bring forth to us our master that his family may take him; and oblige me not to enter and take him forth from you: haste then thyself to produce him.

Upon this, the Kadi was withheld from speaking, and
became utterly abashed before the people: but presently he
said to the barber, If thou speak truth, enter thyself, and
bring him forth. So the barber advanced, and entered the
house; and when I saw him do so, I sought for a way to
escape; but I found no place of refuge except a large chest
which I observed in the same apartment in which I then
was; I therefore entered this, and shut down the lid, and
held in my breath. Immediately after, the barber ran into
the saloon, and, without looking in any other direction than
that in which I had concealed myself, came thither: then
turning his eyes to the right and left, and seeing nothing
but the chest, he raised it upon his head; whereupon my
reason forsook me. He quickly descended with it; and
I, being now certain that he would not quit me, opened the
chest, and threw myself upon the ground. My leg was
broken by the fall; and when I came to the door of the
house, I found a multitude of people: I had never seen
such a crowd as was there collected on that day; so I
began to scatter gold among them, to divert them; and
while they were busied in picking it up, I hastened through
the by-streets of Baghdad, followed by this barber; and
wherever I entered, he entered after me, crying, They
would have plunged me into affliction on account of my
master! Praise be to God who aided me against them,
and delivered my master from their hands! Thou con-
tinuedst, O my master, to be excited by haste for the accomplishment of thine evil design until thou broughtest
upon thyself this event; and if God had not blessed thee
with me, thou hadst not escaped from this calamity into
which thou hast fallen; and they might have involved thee
in a calamity from which thou wouldst never have escaped.
Beg, therefore, of God, that I may live for thy sake, to
liberate thee in future. By Allah, thou hast almost destroyed
me by thine evil design, desiring to go alone; but we will
not be angry with thee for thine ignorance, for thou art
endowed with little sense and of a hasty disposition.—Art
thou not satisfied, replied I, with that which thou hast done,
but wilt thou run after me through the market-streets?—And
I desired for death to liberate me from him; but found it

not; and in the excess of my rage I ran from him, and, entering a shop in the midst of the market, implored the protection of its owner; and he drove away the barber from me.

I then seated myself in a magazine belonging to him, and said within myself, I cannot now rid myself of this barber; but he will be with me night and day, and I cannot endure the sight of his face. So I immediately summoned witnesses, and wrote a document, dividing my property among my family, and appointing a guardian over them, and I ordered him to sell the house and all the immovable possessions, charging him with the care of the old and young, and set forth at once on a journey in order to escape from this wretch. I then arrived in your country, where I took up my abode, and have remained a considerable time; and when ye invited me, and I came unto you, I saw this vile wretch among you, seated at the upper end of the room. How, then, can my heart be at ease, or my sitting in your company be pleasant to me, with this fellow, who hath brought these events upon me, and been the cause of the breaking of my leg?

The young man still persevered in his refusal to remain with us; and when we had heard his story, we said to the barber, Is this true which the young man hath said of thee? —By Allah, he answered, it was through my intelligence that I acted thus towards him; and had I not done so, he had perished: myself only was the cause of his escape; and it was through the goodness of God, by my means, that he was afflicted by the breaking of his leg instead of being punished by the loss of his life. Were I a person of many words, I had not done him this kindness; and now I will relate to you an event that happened to me, that ye may believe me to be a man of few words, and less of an impertinent than my brothers; and it was this:—

The Barber's Story of Himself

I was living in Baghdad, in the reign of the Prince of the Faithful El-Muntasir bi-llah,[15] who loved the poor and

15 Great-grandson of Harun Er-Rashid; acceded 861 A. D.

indigent, and associated with the learned and virtuous; and it happened, one day, that he was incensed against ten persons, in consequence of which, he ordered the chief magistrate of Baghdad to bring them to him in a boat. I saw them, and I said within myself, These persons have assembled for nothing but an entertainment, and, I suppose, will pass their day in this boat eating and drinking; and none shall be their companion but myself:—so I embarked, and mixed myself among them; and when they had landed on the opposite bank, the guards of the Wali came with chains, and put them upon their necks, and put a chain upon my neck also.—Now this, O people, is it not a proof of my generosity, and of my paucity of speech? For I determined not to speak.—They took us, therefore, all together, in chains, and placed us before El-Muntasir bi-llah, the Prince of the Faithful; whereupon he gave orders to strike off the heads of the ten; and the executioner struck off the heads of the ten, and I remained. The Khalifeh then turning his eyes, and beholding me, said to the executioner, Wherefore dost thou not strike off the heads of all the ten? He answered, I have beheaded every one of the ten.—I do not think, rejoined the Khalifeh, that thou hast beheaded more than nine; and this who is before me is the tenth. But the executioner replied, By thy beneficence, they are ten.—Count them, said the Khalifeh. And they counted them; and lo, they were ten. The Khalifeh then looked towards me, and said, What hath induced thee to be silent on this occasion; and how hast thou become included among the men of blood?—And when I heard the address of the Prince of the Faithful, I said to him, O Prince of the Faithful, that I am the sheykh Es-Samit (the Silent): I possess, of science, a large stock; and as to the gravity of my understanding, and the quickness of my apprehension, and the paucity of my speech, they are unbounded: my trade is that of a barber; and yesterday, early in the morning, I saw these ten men proceeding to the boat; whereupon I mixed myself with them, and embarked with them, thinking that they had met together for an entertainment; but soon it appeared that they were criminals; and the guards came to them, and put chains upon their necks, and upon my neck also they put a chain; and from the excess of my generosity I was silent, and spoke not: my speech was not heard on that occasion, on account of the excess of my generosity; and they proceeded with us until they stationed us before thee, and thou gavest the order to strike off the heads of the ten, and I remained before the executioner, and acquainted you not with my case. Was not this great generosity which compelled me to accompany them to slaughter? But throughout my life I have acted in this excellent manner.

When the Khalifeh heard my words, and knew that I was of a very generous character, and of few words, and not inclined to impertinence as this young man, whom I delivered from horrors, asserteth, he said, Hast thou brothers? I answered, Yes: six.—And are thy six brothers, said he, like thyself, distinguished by science and knowledge, and paucity of speech? I answered, They lived not so as to be like me: thou hast disparaged me by thy supposition, O Prince of the Faithful, and it is not proper that thou shouldst compare my brothers to me; for through the abundance of their speech, and the smallness of their generous qualities, each of them experienced a defect: the first was lame; the second, deprived of many of his teeth; the third, blind; the fourth, one-eyed; the fifth, cropped of his ears; and the sixth had both his lips cut off: and think not, O Prince of the Faithful, that I am a man of many words: nay, I must prove to thee that I am of a more generous character than they; and each of them met with a particular adventure, in consequence of which he experienced a defect: if thou please, I will relate their stories to thee.

THE BARBER'S STORY OF HIS FIRST BROTHER

KNOW, O Prince of the Faithful, that the first (who was named El-Bakbuk) was the lame one. He practised the art of a tailor in Baghdad, and used to sew in a shop which he hired of a man possessing great wealth, who lived over the shop, and who had, in the lower part of his house, a mill. And as my lame brother was sitting in his shop one day, sewing, he raised his head, and saw a woman like the rising full moon, at a projecting window of the house, looking at the people passing by; and as soon as he beheld her, his heart was entangled by her love. He passed that day gazing at her, and neglecting his occupation, until the evening; and on the following morning he opened his shop, and sat down to sew; but every time that he sewed a stitch, he looked towards the window; and in this state he continued, sewing nothing sufficient to earn a piece of silver.

On the third day he seated himself again in his place, looking towards the woman; and she saw him, and, perceiving that he had become enslaved by her love, laughed in his face, and he, in like manner, laughed in her face. She then disappeared from before him, and sent to him her slave-girl, with a wrapper containing a piece of red flowered silk; and the girl, coming to him, said to him, My mistress saluteth thee, and desireth thee to cut out for her, with the hand of skill, a shirt of this piece, and to sew it beautifully. So he answered, I hear and obey:—and he cut out for her the shirt, and finished the sewing of it on that day; and on the following day the slave-girl came to him again, and said to him, My mistress saluteth thee, and saith to thee, How didst thou pass last night?—for she tasted not sleep, from her passion for thee.—She then placed before him a piece of yellow satin, and said to him, My mistress desireth thee to cut out for her, of this piece, two pairs of trousers, and to make them this day. He replied, I hear and obey. Salute her with abundant salutations, and say to her, Thy slave is submissive to thine order, and command him to do whatsoever thou wilt.—He then busied himself with the cutting out, and used all diligence in sewing the two pairs of trousers; and presently the woman looked out at him from the window, and saluted him by a sign, now casting down her eyes, and now smiling in his face, so that he imagined he should soon obtain possession of her. After this, she disappeared from before him, and the slave-girl came to him; so he delivered to her the two pairs of trousers, and she took them and departed: and when the night came, he threw himself upon his bed, and remained turning himself over in restlessness until the morning.

On the following day, the master of the house came to my brother, bringing some linen, and said to him, Cut out and make this into shirts for me. He replied, I hear and obey:—and ceased not from his work until he had cut out twenty shirts by the time of nightfall, without having tasted food. The man then said to him, How much is thy hire for this?—but my brother answered not; and the damsel made a sign to him that he should receive nothing, though he was absolutely in want of a single copper coin. For three days he continued scarcely eating or drinking anything, in his diligence to accomplish his work, and when he had finished it, he went to deliver the shirts.

Now the young woman had acquainted her husband with the state of my brother's mind, but my brother knew not this; and she planned with her husband to employ him in sewing without remuneration, and moreover to amuse themselves by laughing at him: so, when he had finished all the work that they gave him, they contrived a plot against him, and married him to their slave-girl; and on the night when he desired to introduce himself to her, they said to him, Pass this night in the mill, and to-morrow thou shalt enjoy happiness. My brother, therefore, thinking that their intention was good, passed the night in the mill alone. Meanwhile, the husband of the young woman went to the miller, and instigated him by signs to make my brother turn the mill. The miller, accordingly, went in to him at midnight, and began to exclaim, Verily this bull is lazy, while there is a great quantity of wheat, and the owners of the flour are demanding it: I will therefore yoke him in the mill, that he may finish the grinding of the flour:—and so saying, he yoked my brother, and thus he kept him until near morning, when the owner of the house came, and saw him yoked in the mill, and the miller flogging him with the whip; and he left him, and retired. After this, the slave-girl to whom he had been contracted in marriage came to him early in the morning, and, having unbound him from the mill, said to him, Both I and my mistress have been distressed by this which hath befallen thee, and we have participated in the burden of thy sorrow. But he had no tongue wherewith to answer her, by reason of the severity of the flogging. He then returned to his house; and lo, the sheykh who had performed the marriage-contract came and saluted him, saying, May God prolong thy life! May thy marriage be blessed!—May God not preserve the liar! returned my brother: thou thousandfold villain! By Allah, I went only to turn the mill in the place of the bull until the morning.— Tell me thy story, said the sheykh:—and my brother told him what had happened to him: upon which the sheykh said, Thy star agreeth not with hers: but if thou desire that I should change for thee the mode of the contract, I will change it for another better than it, that thy star may agree with hers.—See then, replied my brother, if thou hast any other contrivance to employ.

My brother then left him, and repaired again to his shop, hoping that somebody might give him some work, with the profit of which he might obtain his food; and lo, the slave-girl came to him. She had conspired with her mistress to play him this trick, and said to him, Verily, my mistress is longing for thee, and she hath gone up to look at thy face from the window. And my brother had scarcely heard these words when she looked out at him from the window, and, weeping, said, Wherefore hast thou cut short the intercourse between us and thee? But he returned her no answer: so she swore to him that all that had happened to him in the mill was not with her consent: and when my brother beheld her beauty and loveliness, the troubles that had befallen him became effaced from his memory, and he accepted her excuse, and rejoiced at the sight of her. He saluted her, therefore, and conversed with her, and then sat a while at his work; after which the slave-girl came to him, and said, My mistress saluteth thee, and informeth thee that her husband hath determined to pass this next night in the house of one of his intimate friends; wherefore, when he hath gone thither, do thou come to her.—Now the husband of the young woman had said to her, How shall we contrive when he cometh to thee that I may take him and drag him before the Wali? She replied, Let me then play him a trick, and involve him in a disgrace for which he shall be paraded throughout this city as an example to others:—and my brother knew nothing of the craftiness of women. Accordingly, at the approach of evening, the slave-girl came to him, and, taking him by the hand, returned with him to her mistress, who said to him, Verily, O my master, I have been longing for thee.—Hasten then, said he, to give me a kiss, first of all. And his words were not finished when the young woman's husband came in from his neighbour's house, and, seizing my brother, exclaimed to him, By Allah, I will not loose thee but in the presence of the chief magistrate of the police. My brother humbled himself before him; but, without listening to him, he took him to the house of the Wali, who flogged him with whips, and mounted him upon a camel, and conveyed him through the streets of the city, the people crying out, This is the recompense of him who breaketh into the harims of others!—and he fell from the camel, and his leg broke: so he became lame. The Wali then banished him from the city; and he went forth, not knowing whither to turn his steps: but I, though enraged, overtook him, and brought him back; and I have taken upon myself to provide him with meat and drink unto the present day.

The Khalifeh laughed at my story, and exclaimed, Thou hast spoken well:—but I replied, I will not accept this honour until thou hast listened to me while I relate to thee what happened to the rest of my brothers; and think me not a man of many words.—Tell me, said the Khalifeh, what happened to all thy brothers, and grace my ears with these nice particulars: I beg thee to employ exuberance of diction in thy relation of these pleasant tales.

The Barber's Story of His Second Brother

So I said, Know, O Prince of the Faithful, that my second brother, whose name was El-Heddar, was going one day to transact some business, when an old woman met him, and said to him, O man, stop a little, that I may propose to thee a thing, which, if it please thee, thou shalt do for me. My brother, therefore, stopped; and she said to him, I will guide thee to a thing, and rightly direct thee to it, on the condition that thy words be not many. So he said, Communicate what thou hast to tell me:—and she proceeded thus:—What sayest thou of a handsome house, with running water, and fruit and wine, and a beautiful face to behold, and a smooth cheek to kiss, and an elegant form to embrace; and to enjoy all these pleasures without interruption? Now, if thou wilt act agreeably with the condition that I have imposed upon thee, thou wilt see prosperity.—When my brother had heard her words, he said to her, O my mistress, how is it that thou hast sought me out in preference to all the rest of the creation for this affair; and what is there in me that hath pleased thee? She replied, Did I not say to thee that thou must not be a person of many words? Be silent then, and come with me.

The old woman then went her way, my brother following her, eager to enjoy the pleasures which she had described to him, until they had entered a spacious house, when she went up with him to an upper story, and my brother perceived that he was in a beautiful palace, in which he beheld four damsels, than whom none more lovely had ever been seen, singing with voices that would charm a heart as insensible as stone. One of these damsels drank a cup of wine; and my brother said to her, May it be attended with health and vigour!—and advanced to wait upon her; but she prevented his doing so, giving him to drink a cup of wine; and as soon as he had drunk it, she slapped him on his neck. When he found that she treated him thus, he went out from the chamber in anger, and with many words; but the old woman, following him, made a sign to him with her eye that he should return: so he returned, and seated himself, without speaking; and upon this, the damsel slapped him again upon the back of his neck until he became senseless; after which, recovering, he withdrew again. The old woman, however, overtook him, and said to him, Wait a little, and thou shalt attain thy wish.—How many times, said he, shall I wait a little before I attain it? The old woman answered, When she hath become exhilarated with wine thou shalt obtain her favour. He therefore returned to his place, and resumed his seat. All the four damsels then arose, and the old woman directed them to divest my brother of his outer clothes, and to sprinkle some rose-water upon his face; and when they had done so, the most

beautiful one among them said to him, May Allah exalt
thee to honour! Thou hast entered my abode, and if thou
have patience to submit to my requisitions, thou wilt attain
thy wish.—O my mistress, he replied, I am thy slave, and
under thy authority.—Know then, said she, that I am
devotedly fond of frolic, and he who complieth with my
demands will obtain my favour. Then she ordered the
other damsels to sing; and they sang so that their hearers
were in an ecstasy; after which the chief lady said to one
of the other damsels, Take thy master, and do what is
required, and bring him back to me immediately.

Accordingly, she took him away, ignorant of that which
she was about to do; and the old woman came to him, and
said, Be patient; for there remaineth but little to do. He
then turned towards the damsel, and the old woman said to
him, Be patient: thou hast almost succeeded, and there
remaineth but one thing, which is, to shave thy beard.—
How, said he, shall I do that which will disgrace me among
the people? The old woman answered, She desireth this
only to make thee like a beardless youth, that there may be
nothing on thy face to prick her; for her heart is affected
with a violent love for thee. Be patient, therefore, and thou
shalt attain thy desire.—So my brother patiently submitted
to the damsel's directions: his beard was shaven, and he
was shorn also of his eyebrows and mustaches, and his face
was painted red, before the damsel took him back to the
chief lady, who, when she saw him, was at first frightened
at him, and then laughed until she fell backwards, and
exclaimed, O my master, thou hast gained me by these
proofs of thine amiable manners! She then conjured him
by her life to arise and dance; and he did so; and there
was not a single cushion in the chamber that she did not
throw at him. In like manner also the other damsels threw
at him various things, such as oranges, and limes, and
citrons, until he fell down senseless from the pelting, while
they slapped him incessantly upon the back of his neck, and
cast things in his face. But at length the old woman said
to him, Now thou hast attained thy wish. Know that there
remaineth to thee no more beating, nor doth there remain
for thee to do more than one thing, namely, this: it is her

custom, when she is under the influence of wine, to suffer no one to come near her until she hath taken off her outer clothes: thou, being prepared in the like manner, must run after her, and she will run before thee as though she were flying from thee; but cease not to follow her from place to place until thou overtake her. He arose, therefore, and did so: the lady ran before, and as he followed her, she passed from chamber to chamber, and he still ran after her. At last he heard her utter a slight sound as she ran before him, and, continuing his pursuit, he suddenly found himself in the midst of the street.

This street was in the market of the leather-sellers, who were then crying skins for sale; and when the people there collected saw him in this condition, almost naked, with shaven beard and eyebrows and mustaches, and with his face painted red, they shouted at him, and raised a loud laugh, and some of them beat him with the skins until he became insensible. They then placed him upon an ass, and conducted him to the Wali, who exclaimed, What is this?—They answered, This descended upon us from the house of the Wezir, in this condition. And the Wali inflicted upon him a hundred lashes, and banished him from the city: but I went out after him, and brought him back privately into the city, and allotted him a maintenance. Had it not been for my generous disposition, I had not borne with such a person.

The Barber's Story of His Third Brother

As to my third brother (the blind man, Bakbak), who was also surnamed Kuffeh, fate and destiny impelled him one day to a large house, and he knocked at the door, hoping that its master would answer him, and that he might beg of him a trifle. The owner called out, Who is at the door?—but my brother answered not; and then heard him call with a loud voice, Who is this? Still, however, he returned him no answer; and he heard the sounds of his footsteps approaching until he came to the door and opened it, when he said to him, What dost thou desire? My brother answered, Something for the sake of God, whose

name be exalted!—Art thou blind? said the man; and my
brother answered, Yes.—Then give me thy hand, rejoined
the master of the house;—so my brother stretched forth to
him his hand, and the man took him into the house, and
led him up from stair-case to stair-case until he had ascended
to the highest platform of the roof: my brother thinking
that he was going to give him some food or money: and
when he had arrived at this highest terrace of his house, the
owner said, What dost thou desire, O blind man?—I desire
something, he answered again, for the sake of God, whose
name be exalted!—May God, replied the man, open to thee
some other way!—What is this! exclaimed my brother:
couldst thou not tell me so when I was below?—Thou
vilest of the vile! retorted the other: why didst thou not
ask of me something for the sake of God when thou heardest
my voice the first time, when thou wast knocking at the
door?—What then, said my brother, dost thou mean to do
to me?—The man of the house answered, I have nothing
to give thee.—Then take me down the stairs, said my
brother. The man replied, The way is before thee. So
my brother made his way to the stairs, and continued
descending until there remained, between him and the door,
twenty steps, when his foot slipped and he fell, and, rolling
down, broke his head.

He went forth, not knowing whither to direct his steps,
and presently there met him two blind men, his companions,
who said to him, What hath happened to thee this day?
My brother, therefore, related to them the event that had
just befallen him; and then said to them, O my brothers, I
desire to take a portion of the money now in our possession,
to expend it upon myself.—Now the owner of the house
which he had just before entered had followed him to
acquaint himself with his proceedings, and without my
brother's knowledge he walked behind him until the latter
entered his abode; when he went in after him, still unknown.
My brother then sat waiting for his companions; and when
they came in to him, he said to them, Shut the door, and
search the room, lest any stranger have followed us. When
the intruder, therefore, heard what he said, he arose, and
clung to a rope that was attached to the ceiling; and the

blind men went feeling about the whole of the chamber, and, finding no one, returned and seated themselves by my brother, and brought forth their money, and counted it; and lo, it was more than ten thousand pieces of silver. Having done this, they laid it in a corner of the room, and each of them took of the surplus of that sum as much as he wanted, and they buried the ten thousand pieces of silver in the earth; after which, they placed before themselves some food, and sat eating; but my brother heard the sound of a stranger by his side, and said to his friends, Is there a stranger among us? Then stretching forth his hand, it grasped the hand of the intruder; whereupon he cried out to his companions, saying, Here is a stranger!—and they fell upon him with blows until they were tired, when they shouted out, O Muslims! a thief hath come in upon us, and desireth to take our property!—and immediately a number of persons collected around them.

Upon this, the stranger whom they accused of being a thief shut his eyes, feigning to be blind like themselves, so that no one who saw him doubted him to be so; and shouted, O Muslims! I demand protection of Allah and the Sultan! I demand protection of Allah and the Wali! I demand protection of Allah and the Emir! for I have important information to give to the Emir!—and before they could collect their thoughts, the officers of the Wali surrounded them and took them all, including my brother, and conducted them before their master. The Wali said, What is your story?—and the stranger replied, Hear my words, O Wali; the truth of our case will not become known to thee but by means of beating; and if thou wilt, begin by beating me before my companions. The Wali therefore said, Throw down this man, and flog him with whips:—and accordingly they threw him down and flogged him; and when the stripes tortured him, he opened one of his eyes; and after they had continued the flogging a little longer, he opened his other eye; upon which the Wali exclaimed, What meaneth this conduct, O thou villain?— Grant me indemnity, replied the man, and I will acquaint thee:—and the Wali having granted his request, he said, We four pretend that we are blind, and. intruding among other people, enter their houses, and see their women, and employ stratagems to corrupt them, and to obtain money from them. We have acquired, by these means, vast gain, amounting to ten thousand pieces of silver; and I said to my companions, Give me my due, two thousand and five hundred; and they rose against me and beat me, and took my property. I beg protection, therefore, of Allah and of thee; and thou art more deserving of my share than they. If thou desire to know the truth of that which I have said, flog each of them more than thou hast flogged me, and he will open his eyes.

So the Wali immediately gave orders to flog them; and the first of them who suffered was my brother. They continued beating him until he almost died; when the Wali said to them, O ye scoundrels! do ye deny the gracious gift of God, feigning yourselves to be blind? My brother exclaimed, Allah! Allah! Allah! there is none among us who seeth!—They then threw him down again, and ceased not to beat him until he became insensible, when the Wali said, Leave him until he shall have recovered, and then give him a third flogging:—and in the meantime, he gave orders to flog his companions, to give each of them more than three hundred stripes; while the seeing man said to them, Open your eyes, or they will flog you again after this time. Then addressing himself to the Wali, he said, Send with me some person to bring thee the property; for these men will not open their eyes, fearing to be disgraced before the spectators. And the Wali sent with him a man, who brought him the money; and he took it, and gave to the informer, out of it, two thousand and five hundred pieces of silver, according to the share which he claimed, in spite of the others (retaining the rest), and banished from the city my brother and the two other men; but I went forth, O Prince of the Faithful, and, having overtaken my brother, asked him respecting his sufferings; and he acquainted me with that which I have related unto thee. I then brought him back secretly into the city, and allotted him a supply of food and drink as long as he lived.

The Khalifeh laughed at my story, and said, Give him a present, and let him go:—but I replied, I will receive nothing until I have declared to the Prince of the Faithful what happened to the rest of my brothers, and made it manifest to him that I am a man of few words:—whereupon the Khalifeh said, Crack our ears, then, with thy ridiculous stories, and continue to us thy disclosure of vices and misdeeds. So I proceeded thus:—

The Barber's Story of His Fourth Brother

My fourth brother, O Prince of the Faithful, was the one-eyed (named El-Kuz el Aswani): he was a butcher in Baghdad, and both sold meat and reared lambs; and the great and the rich had recourse to him to purchase of him their meat, so that he amassed great wealth, and became possessor of cattle and houses. Thus he continued to prosper for a long time; and as he was in his shop, one day, there accosted him an old man with a long beard, who handed to him some money, saying, Give me some meat for it. So he took the money, and gave him the meat; and when the old man had gone away, my brother looked at the money which he had paid him, and, seeing that it was of a brilliant whiteness, put it aside by itself. This old man continued to repair to him during a period of five months, and my brother always threw his money into a chest by itself; after which period he desired to take it out for the purpose of buying some sheep; but on opening the chest, he found all the contents converted into white paper, clipped round; and he slapped his face, and cried out; whereupon a number of people collected around him, and he related to them his story, at which they were astonished.

He then went again, as usual, into his shop, and, having killed a ram and hung it up within the shop, he cut off some of the meat, and suspended it outside, saying within himself, Perhaps now this old man will come again, and if so, I will seize him:—and very soon after, the old man approached with his money; upon which my brother arose, and, laying hold upon him, began to cry out, O Muslims, come to my aid, and hear what this scoundrel hath done unto me! But when the old man heard his words he said to him, Which will be more agreeable to thee—that thou abstain from disgracing me, or that I disgrace thee, before

the people?—For what wilt thou disgrace me? said my
brother. The old man answered, For thy selling human
flesh for mutton.—Thou liest, thou accursed! exclaimed my
brother.—None is accursed, rejoined the old man, but he
who hath a man suspended in his shop. My brother said,
If it be as thou hast asserted, my property and blood shall
be lawful to thee:—and immediately the old man exclaimed,
O ye people here assembled! verily this butcher slaughtereth
human beings, and selleth their flesh for mutton; and if ye
desire to know the truth of my assertion, enter his shop!
So the people rushed upon his shop, and beheld the ram
converted into a man, hung up, and they laid hold upon
my brother, crying out against him, Thou infidel! Thou
scoundrel!—and those who had been his dearest friends
turned upon him and beat him; and the old man gave him
a blow upon his eye, and knocked it out. The people then
carried the carcass, and took with them my brother, to the
chief magistrate of the police; and the old man said to him,
O Emir, this man slaughtereth human beings, and selleth
their flesh for mutton; and we have therefore brought him
to thee: arise, then, and perform the requisition of God,
whose might and glory be extolled! Upon this, the magistrate thrust back my brother from him, and, refusing to
listen to what he would have said, ordered that five hundred
blows of a staff should be inflicted upon him, and took all
his property. Had it not been for the great amount of his
wealth, he had put him to death. He then banished him
from the city.

My brother, therefore, went forth in a state of distraction, not knowing what course to pursue; but he journeyed
onwards until he arrived at a great city, where he thought
fit to settle as a shoemaker: so he opened a shop, and sat
there working for his subsistence. And one day he went
forth on some business, and, hearing the neighing of horses,
he inquired respecting the cause, and was told that the King
was going forth to hunt; whereupon he went to amuse himself with the sight of the procession: but the King happen-
ing to look on one side, his eye met that of my brother, and
immediately he hung down his head, and exclaimed, I seek
refuge with God from the evil of this day! He then turned

aside the bridle of his horse, and rode back, and all his troops returned with him; after which, he ordered his pages to run after my brother, and to beat him; and they did so; giving him so severe a beating that he almost died; and he knew not the cause. He returned to his abode in a miserable plight, and afterwards went and related his misfortune to one of the King's attendants, who laughed at the recital until he fell backwards, and said to him, O my brother, the King cannot endure the sight of a one-eyed person, and especially when the defect is that of the left eye; for in this case, he faileth not to put the person to death.

When my brother heard these words, he determined to fly from that city; and forthwith departed from it, and repaired to another city, where there was no King. Here he remained a long time; and after this, as he was meditating upon his adventure in the former city, he went out one day to amuse himself, and heard again the neighing of horses behind him; upon which he exclaimed, The decree of God hath come to pass!—and ran away, seeking for a place in which to conceal himself; but he found none, until, continuing his search, he saw a door set up as a barricade; so he pushed this, and it fell down; and, entering the doorway, he beheld a long passage, into which he advanced. Suddenly, however, two men laid hold upon him, and exclaimed, Praise be to God who hath enabled us to take thee, O thou enemy of God! For these three nights thou hast suffered us to enjoy neither quiet nor sleep, and we have found no repose: nay, thou hast given us a foretaste of death!—O men, said my brother, what hath happened unto you? They answered, Thou keepest a watch upon us, and desirest to disgrace us, and to disgrace the master of the house! Is it not enough for thee that thou hast reduced him to poverty, thou and thy companions? Produce now the knife wherewith thou threatenest us every night.—And so saying, they searched him, and found upon his waist the knife with which he cut the shoe-leather.—O men, he exclaimed, fear God in your treatment of me, and know that my story is wonderful. They said, What then is thy story? So he related it to them, in the hope that they would liberate him: but they believed not what he said; and, instead of shewing him any regard, they beat him, and tore his clothes; whereupon, his body becoming exposed to their view, they discovered upon his sides the marks of beating with mikra'ahs, and exclaimed, O wretch! these scars bear testimony to thy guilt. They then conducted him before the Wali, while he said within himself, I am undone for my transgressions, and none can deliver me but God, whose name be exalted! And when he was brought before the Wali, the magistrate said to him, O thou scoundrel! nothing but a heinous crime hath occasioned thy having been beaten with mikra'ahs:—and he caused a hundred lashes to be inflicted upon him; after which, they mounted him upon a camel, and proclaimed before him, This is the recompense of him who breaketh into men's houses!—But I had already heard of his misfortunes, and gone forth, and found him; and I accompanied him about the city while they were making this proclamation, until they left him; when I took him, and brought him back secretly into Baghdad, and apportioned him a daily allowance of food and drink.

The Barber's Fifth Brother

My fifth brother (El-Feshshar ["Alnaschar"]) was cropped of his ears, O Prince of the Faithful. He was a pauper, who begged alms by night, and subsisted upon what he thus acquired by day: and our father was a very old man, and he fell sick and died, leaving to us seven hundred pieces of silver, of which each of us took his portion; namely, a hundred pieces. Now my fifth brother, when he had received his share, was perplexed, not knowing what to do with it; but while he was in this state, it occurred to his mind to buy with it all kinds of articles of glass, and to sell them and make profit: so he bought glass with his hundred pieces of silver, and put it in a large tray, and sat upon an elevated place, to sell it, leaning his back against a wall. And as he sat, he meditated, and said within himself, Verily my whole stock consisteth of this glass: I will sell it for two hundred pieces of silver; and with the two hundred I will buy other glass which I will sell for four hundred; and thus I will continue buying and selling until I have acquired great wealth. Then with this I will purchase all kinds of merchandise and essences and jewels, and so obtain vast gain. After that, I will buy a handsome house, and memluks, and horses, and gilded saddles; and I will eat and drink; and I will not leave in the city a single female singer but I will have her brought to my house that I may hear her songs.—All this he calculated with the tray of glass lying before him.—Then, said he, I will send all the female betrothers to seek in marriage for me the daughters of Kings and Wezirs; and I will demand as my wife the daughter of the chief Wezir; for I have heard that she is endowed with perfect beauty and surprising loveliness; and I will give as her dowry a thousand pieces of gold. If her father consent, my wish is attained; and if he consent not, I will take her by force, in spite of him: and when I have come back to my house, I will buy ten young eunuchs, and I will purchase the apparel of Kings and Sultans, and cause to be made for me a saddle of gold set with jewels; after which I will ride every day upon a horse, with slaves behind me and before me, and go about through the streets and markets to amuse myself, while the people will salute me and pray for me. Then I will pay a visit to the Wezir, who is the father of the maiden, with memluks behind me and before me, and on my right hand and on my left; and when he seeth me, he will rise to me, in humility, and seat me in his own place; and he himself will sit down below me, because I am his son-in-law. I will then order one of the servants to bring a purse containing the pieces of gold which compose the dowry; and he will place it before the Wezir; and I will add to it another purse, that he may know my manly spirit and excessive generosity, and that the world is contemptible in my eye; and when he addresseth me with ten words, I will answer him with two. And I will return to my house; and when any person cometh to me from the house of the Wezir, I will clothe him with a rich dress: but if any come with a present, I will return it; I will certainly not accept it. Then, on the night of the bridal display, I will attire myself in the most magnificent of my dresses, and sit upon a mattress covered with silk; and when my wife cometh to me, like the full moon, decked with her ornaments

and apparel, I will command her to stand before me as
stands the timid and the abject; and I will not look at her,
on account of the haughtiness of my spirit and the gravity
of my wisdom; so that the maids will say, O our master
and our lord, may we be thy sacrifice! This thy wife, or
rather thy handmaid, awaiteth thy kind regard, and is standing before thee: then graciously bestow on her one glance;
for the posture hath become painful to her.—Upon this, I
will raise my head, and look at her with one glance, and
again incline my head downwards; and thus I will do until
the ceremony of displaying her is finished; whereupon they
will conduct her to the sleeping-chamber; and I will rise
from my place, and go to another apartment, and put on my
night-dress, and go to the chamber in which she is sitting,
where I will seat myself upon the divan; but I will not look
towards her. The tirewomen will urge me to approach
her; but I will not hear their words, and will order some
of the attendants to bring a purse containing five hundred pieces of gold for them, and command them to
retire from the chamber. And when they have gone, I
will seat myself by the side of the bride; but with averted
countenance, that she may say, Verily this is a man of a
haughty spirit. Then her mother will come to me, and will
kiss my hands, and say to me, O my master, look upon thy
handmaid with the eye of mercy; for she is submissively
standing before thee. But I will return her no answer.
And she will kiss my feet, again and again, and will say, O
my master, my daughter is young and hath seen no man
but thee; and if she experience from thee repugnance, her
heart will break: incline to her, therefore, and speak to
her, and calm her mind. And upon this I will look at her
through the corner of my eye, and command her to remain
standing before me, that she may taste the savour of
humiliation, and know that I am the Sultan of the age.
Then her mother will say to me, O my master, this is thy
handmaid: have compassion upon her, and be gracious to
her:—and she will order her to fill a cup with wine, and to
put it to my mouth. So her daughter will say, O my lord,
I conjure thee by Allah that thou reject not the cup from
thy slave; for verily I am thy slave. But I will make her

no reply; and she will urge me to take it, and will say, It must be drunk; and will put it to my mouth: and upon this, I will shake my hand in her face, and spurn her with my foot, and do thus.—So saying, he kicked the tray of glass, which, being upon a place elevated above the ground, fell, and all that was in it broke: there escaped nothing: and he cried out and said, All this is the result of my pride! And he slapped his face, and tore his clothes; the passengers gazing at him, while he wept, and exclaimed, Ah! O my grief!

The people were now repairing to perform the Friday-prayers; and some merely cast their eyes at him, while others noticed him not; but while he was in this state, deprived of his whole property, and weeping, without intermission, a female approached him, on her way to attend the Friday-prayers: she was of admirable loveliness; the odour of musk was diffused from her; under her was a mule with a stuffed saddle covered with gold-embroidered silk; and with her was a number of servants; and when she saw the broken glass, and my brother's state and his tears, she was moved with pity for him, and asked respecting his case. She was answered, He had a tray of glass, by the sale of which to obtain his subsistence, and it is broken, and he is afflicted as thou seest:—and upon this, she called to one of the servants, saying, Give what thou hast with thee to this poor man. So he gave him a purse, and he took it, and when he had opened it, he found in it five hundred pieces of gold, whereupon he almost died of excessive joy, and offered up prayers for his benefactress.

He returned to his house a rich man, and sat reflecting, and lo, a person knocked at the door: he rose, therefore, and opened it; and beheld an old woman whom he knew not, and she said to him, O my son, know that the time of prayer hath almost expired, and I am not prepared by ablution; wherefore I beg that thou wilt admit me into thy house, that I may perform it. He replied, I hear and obey; —and, retiring within, gave her permission to enter; his mind still wandering from joy on account of the gold; and when she had finished the ablution, she approached the spot where he was sitting, and there performed the prayers of two rek'ahs. She then offered up a supplication for my brother; and he thanked her, and doffed her two pieces of gold; but when she saw this, she exclaimed, Extolled be God's perfection! Verily I wonder at the person who fell in love with thee in thy beggarly condition! Take back thy money from me, and if thou want it not, return it to her who gave it thee when thy glass broke.—O my mother, said he, how can I contrive to obtain access to her? She answered, O my son, she hath an affection for thee; but she is the wife of an affluent man; take then with thee all thy money, and when thou art with her be not deficient in courteousness and agreeable words; so shalt thou obtain of her favours and her wealth whatever thou shalt desire. My brother, therefore, took all the gold, and arose and went with the old woman, hardly believing what she had told him; and she proceeded, and my brother behind her, until they arrived at a great door, at which she knocked; whereupon a Greek damsel came and opened the door, and the old woman entered, ordering my brother to do the same. He did so, and found himself in a large house, where he beheld a great furnished chamber, with curtains hung in it; and, seating himself there, he put down the gold before him, and placed his turban on his knees; and scarcely had he done so, when there came to him a damsel, the like of whom had never been seen, attired in most magnificent apparel. My brother stood up at her approach; and when she beheld him she laughed in his face, and rejoiced at his visit: then going to the door, she locked it; after which she returned to my brother, and took his hand, and both of them went together into a private chamber, carpeted with various kinds of silk, where my brother sat down, and she seated herself by his side, and toyed with him for a considerable time. She then rose, saying to him, Move not, from this place until I return to thee;—and was absent from him for a short period; and as my brother was waiting for her, there came in to him a black slave, of gigantic stature, with a drawn sword, the brightness of which dazzled the sight; and he exclaimed to my brother, Wo to thee! Who brought thee to this place? Thou vilest of men! Thou misbegotten wretch, and nursling of impunity!—My brother was unable to make any reply; his tongue was instantly tied; and the slaves laid hold upon him, and stripped him, and struck him more than eighty blows with the flat of his sword, until he fell sprawling upon the floor; when he retired from him, concluding that he was dead, and uttered a great cry, so that the earth trembled, and the place resounded at his voice, saying, Where is El-Melihah?—upon which a girl came to him, holding a handsome tray containing salt; and with this she forthwith stuffed the flesh-wounds with which my brother's skin was gashed until they gaped open; but he moved not, fearing the slave would discover that he was alive, and kill him. The girl then went away, and the slave uttered another cry, like the first, whereupon the old woman came to my brother, and, dragging him by the feet to a deep and dark vault, threw him into it upon a heap of slain. In this place he remained for two whole days; and God (whose perfection he extolled!) made the salt to be the means of preserving his life, by stanching the flow of blood from his veins; so, when he found that he had strength sufficient to move, he arose, and, opening a shutter in the wall, emerged from the place of the slain; and God (to whom be ascribed all might and glory!) granted him his protection. He therefore proceeded in the darkness, and concealed himself in the passage until the morning, when the old woman went forth to seek another victim, and my brother, going out after her, without her knowledge, returned to his house.

He now occupied himself with the treatment of his wounds until he was restored; and continued to watch for the old woman, and constantly saw her taking men, one after another, and conducting them to the same house. But he uttered not a word on the subject; and when his health returned, and his strength was completely renewed, he took a piece of rag, and made of it a purse, which he filled with pieces of glass: he then tied it to his waist, and disguised himself so that no one would know him, in the dress of a foreigner; and, taking a sword, placed it within his clothes; and as soon as he saw the old woman, he said to her, in the dialect of a foreigner, Old woman, hast thou a pair of scales fit for weighing nine hundred pieces of gold? The old woman answered, I have a young son, a money-changer, and he hath all kinds of scales;

therefore accompany me to him before he go forth from
his abode, that he may weigh for thee thy gold. So my
brother said, Walk on before me:—and she went, and my
brother followed her until she arrived at the door, and
knocked; upon which the girl came out, and laughed in his
face; and the old woman said to her, I have brought you to-
day some fat meat. The girl then took my brother's hand,
and conducted him into the house (the same which he had
entered before), and after she had sat with him a short time,
she rose, saying to him, Quit not this place until I return
to thee:—and she retired; and my brother had remained not
long after when the slave came to him with the drawn
sword, and said to him, Rise, thou unlucky! So my brother
rose, and, as the slave walked before him, he put his hand
to the sword which was concealed beneath his clothes, and
struck the slave with it, and cut off his head; after which
he dragged him by his feet to the vault, and called out,
Where is El-Melihah? The slave-girl, therefore, came,
having in her hand the tray containing the salt; but when she
saw my brother with the sword in his hand, she turned back
and fled: my brother, however, overtook her, and struck
off her head. He then called out, Where is the old woman?
—and she came; and he said to her, Dost thou know me, O
malevolent hag? She answered, No, O my lord.—I am, said
he, the man who had the pieces of gold, and in whose house
thou performedst the ablution, and prayedst; after which,
devising a stratagem against me, thou betrayedst me into
this place.—The old woman exclaimed, Fear God in thy
treatment of me!—but my brother, turning towards her,
struck her with the sword, and clove her in twain. He then
went in search for the chief damsel, and when she saw him,
her reason fled, and she implored his pardon; whereupon he
granted her his pardon, and said to her, What occasioned
thy falling into the hands of this black? She answered, I
was a slave to one of the merchants, and this old woman
used to visit me; and one day she said to me, We are cele-
brating a festivity, the like of which no one hath seen, and
I have a desire that thou shouldst witness it. I replied, I
hear and obey:—and arose, and clad myself in the best of
my attire, and, taking with me a purse containing a hundred

pieces of gold, proceeded with her until she entered this house, when suddenly this black took me, and I have continued with him in this state three years, through the stratagem of the old witch.—My brother then said to her, Is there any property of his in the house?—Abundance, she answered; and if thou canst remove it, do so:—and upon this, he arose and went with her, when she opened to him chests filled with purses, at the sight of which he was confounded; and she said to him, Go now, and leave me here, and bring some person to remove the property. So he want out, and, having hired ten men, returned; but on his arrival at the door, he found it open, and saw neither the damsel nor the purses; he found, however, some little money remaining, and the stuffs. He discovered, therefore, that she had eluded him; and he took the money that remained, and, opening the closets, took all the stuffs which they contained, leaving nothing in the house.

He passed the next night full of happiness; but when the morning came, he found at the door twenty soldiers, and on his going forth to them, they laid hold upon him, saying, The Wali summoneth thee. So they took him, and conducted him to the Wali, who, when he saw him, said to him, Whence obtainedst thou these stuffs?—Grant me indemnity, said my brother:—and the Wali gave him the handkerchief of indemnity; and my brother related to him all that had befallen him with the old woman from first to last, and the flight of the damsel; adding,—and of that which I have taken, take thou what thou wilt; but leave me wherewith to procure my food. The Wali thereupon demanded the whole of the money and the stuffs; but fearing that the Sultan might become acquainted with the matter, he retained a portion only, and gave the rest to my brother, saying to him, Quit this city, or I will hang thee. My brother replied, I hear and obey:—and went forth to one of the surrounding cities. Some robbers, however, came upon him, and stripped and beat him, and cut off his ears; and I, having heard of his situation, went forth to him, taking to him some clothes; and brought him back privily into the city, and supplied him with daily food and drink.

The Barber's Story of His Sixth Brother

My sixth brother (Shakalik), O Prince of the Faithful, had his lips cut off. He was in a state of extreme poverty, possessing nothing of the goods of this perishable world; and he went forth one day to seek for something with which to stay his departing spirit, and on his way he beheld a handsome house, with a wide and lofty vestibule, at the door of which were servants, commanding and forbidding; whereupon he inquired of one of the persons standing there, who answered, This house belongeth to a man of the sons of the Barmekis. My brother, therefore, advanced to the door-keepers, and begged them to give him something; and they said, Enter the door of the house, and thou wilt obtain what thou desirest of its master. So he entered the vestibule, and proceeded through it a while until he arrived at a mansion of the utmost beauty and elegance, having a garden in the midst of it, unsurpassed in beauty by anything that had ever been seen: its floors were paved with marble, and its curtains were hanging around. He knew not in which direction to go; but advanced to the upper extremity; and there he beheld a man of handsome countenance and beard, who, on seeing my brother, rose to him, and welcomed him, inquiring respecting his circumstances. He accordingly informed him that he was in want; and when the master of the house heard his words, he manifested excessive grief, and, taking hold of his own clothes, rent them, and exclaimed, Am I in the city, and thou in it hungry? It is a thing that I cannot endure!—Then promising him every kind of happiness, he said, Thou must stay and partake of my salt. But my brother replied, O my master, I have not patience to wait; for I am in a state of extreme hunger.

Upon this, the master of the house called out, Boy, bring the basin and ewer!—and he said, O my guest, advance, and wash thy hand. He then performed the same motions as if he were washing his hand; and called to his attendants to bring the table; whereupon they began to come and go as though they were preparing it; after which the master of the house took my brother, and sat down with him at this imaginary table, and proceeded to move his hands and lips as if he were eating; saying to my brother, Eat, and be not ashamed, for thou art hungry, and I know how thou art suffering from the violence of thy hunger. My brother, therefore, made the same motions, as if he also were eating, while his host said to him, Eat, and observe this bread and its whiteness. To this, my brother at first made no reply; but observed in his own mind, Verily this is a man who loveth to jest with others:—so he said to him, O my master, in my life I have never seen bread more beautifully white than this, or any of sweeter taste:—on which the host rejoined, This was made by a female slave of mine whom I purchased for five hundred pieces of gold. He then called out, Boy, bring to us the sikbaj,[16] the like of which is not found among the dishes of Kings!—and, addressing my brother, he said, Eat, O my guest; for thou art hungry, vehemently so and in absolute want of food. So my brother began to twist about his mouth, and to chew, as in eating. The master of the house now proceeded to demand different kinds of viands, one after another; and, though nothing was brought, he continued ordering my brother to eat. Next he called out, Boy, place before us the chickens stuffed with pistachio-nuts:—and said to his guest, Eat that of which thou hast never tasted the like.—O my master, replied my brother, verily this dish hath not its equal in sweetness or flavour:—and the host, thereupon, began to put his hand to my brother's mouth as though he were feeding him with morsels; and proceeded to enumerate to him the various different kinds of viands, and to describe their several excellencies; while his hunger so increased that he longed for a cake of barley-bread. The master of the house then said to him, Hast thou tasted anything more delicious than the spices in these dishes?—No, O my master, answered my brother.—Eat more then, resumed the host; and be not ashamed.—I have eaten enough of the meats, replied the guest. So the man of the house called to his attendants to bring the sweets; and they moved their hands about in the air as if they were bringing them; whereupon the host said to my brother, Eat of this dish; for it is

---

[16] A dish composed of meat, wheat-flour, and vinegar.

excellent; and of these kataïf,[17] by my life! and take this
one before the sirup runs from it.—May I never be deprived
of thee, O my master! exclaimed my brother, proceeding
to inquire of him respecting the abundance of musk in the
kataïf.—This, answered the host, is my usual custom in
my house: they always put for me, in each of the kataïf, a
mithkal[18] of musk, and half a mithkal of ambergris.—All
this time my brother was moving his head and mouth, and
rolling about his tongue between his cheeks, as if he were
enjoying the sweets. After this, the master of the house
called out to his attendants, Bring the dried fruits!—and
again they moved about their hands in the air as though
they were doing what he ordered; when he said to my
brother, Eat of these almonds, and of these walnuts, and of
these raisins;—and so on; enumerating the various kinds
of dried fruits; and added again, Eat, and be not ashamed.
—O my master, replied my brother, I have had enough,
and have not power to eat anything more:—but the host
rejoined, If thou desire, O my guest, to eat more, and to
delight thyself with extraordinary dainties, by Allah! by
Allah! remain not hungry.

My brother now reflected upon his situation, and upon
the manner in which this man was jesting with him, and said
within himself, By Allah, I will do to him a deed that shall
make him repent before God of these actions! The man of
the house next said to his attendants, Bring us the wine:—
and, as before, they made the same motions with their hands
in the air as if they were doing what he commanded; after
which he pretended to hand to my brother a cup, saying, Take
this cup, for it will delight thee:—and his guest replied, O
my master, this is of thy bounty:—and he acted with his
hand as though he were drinking it.—Hath it pleased thee?
said the host.—O my master, answered my brother, I have
never seen anything more delicious than this wine.—Drink
then, rejoined the master of the house, and may it be
attended with benefit and health:—and he himself pretended
to drink, and to hand a second cup to my brother, who,
after he had affected to drink it, feigned himself intoxicated,

17 Small pancakes or other sweet pastry.
18 The weight of a dinar.

and, taking his host unawares, raised his hand until the whiteness of his arm-pit appeared, and struck him such a slap upon his neck that the chamber rang at the blow; and this he followed by a second blow; whereupon the man exclaimed, What is this, thou vilest of the creation?—O my master, answered my brother, I am thy slave, whom thou hast graciously admitted into thine abode, and thou hast fed him with thy provisions, and treated him with old wine, and he hath become intoxicated, and committed an outrage upon thee; but thou art of too exalted dignity to be angry with him for his ignorance.

When the master of the house heard these words of my brother, he uttered a loud laugh, and said to him, Verily for a long time have I made game of men, and jested with all persons accustomed to joking and rudeness, but I have not seen among them any who could endure this trick, nor any who had sagacity to conform to all my actions, except thee: now therefore, I pardon thee; and be thou my companion in reality, and never relinquish me. He then gave orders to bring a number of the dishes above mentioned, and he and my brother ate together to satisfaction; after which they removed to the drinking-chamber, where female slaves like so many moons sang all kinds of melodies, and played on all kinds of musical instruments. There they drank until intoxication overcame them: the master of the house treated my brother as a familiar friend, became greatly attached to him, and clad him with a costly dress; and on the following morning they resumed their feasting and drinking. Thus they continued to live for a period of twenty years: the man then died, and the Sultan seized upon his property, and took possession of it.

My brother, upon this, went forth from the city, a fugitive; and upon his way, a party of Arabs came upon him. They made him a captive; and the man who captured him tortured him with beating, and said to him, By Allah, purchase thyself of me by wealth, or I will kill thee:—but my brother, weeping, replied, By Allah, I possess nothing, O Sheykh of the Arabs; nor do I know the means of obtaining any property: I am thy captive; I have fallen into thy hands, and do with me what thou wilt. And immediately the tyrannical Bedawi drew forth from his girdle a broad-bladed knife (such as, if plunged into the neck of a camel, would cut it across from one jugular vein to the other) and, taking it in his right hand, approached my poor brother, and cut off with it his lips; still urging his demand.

Now this Bedawi had a handsome wife, who, when he was absent, used to manifest a strong affection for my brother; though he observed a proper decorum towards her, fearing God (whose name be exalted!), and it happened one day, that she had called him, and seated him with her; but while they were together, lo, her husband came in upon them; and when he beheld my brother, he exclaimed, Wo to thee, thou base wretch! Dost thou desire now to corrupt my wife?—Then drawing his knife, he inflicted upon him another cruel wound; after which he mounted him upon a camel, and having cast him upon a mountain, left him there, and went his way. Some travellers, however, passed by him, and when they discovered him, they gave him food and drink, and acquainted me with his case, so I went forth to him, and conveyed him back into the city, and allotted him a sufficient maintenance.

Now I have come unto thee, O Prince of the Faithful, continued the barber, and feared to return to my house without relating to thee these facts; for to neglect doing so had been an error. Thus thou hast seen that, although having six brothers, I am of a more upright character than they.—But when the Prince of the Faithful had heard my story, and all that I had related to him respecting my brothers, he laughed, and said, Thou hast spoken truth, O Samit (O silent man); thou art a person of few words, and devoid of impertinence; now, however, depart from this city, and take up thine abode in another. So he banished me from Baghdad; and I journeyed through various countries, and traversed many regions, until I heard of his death, and of the succession of another Khalifeh; when returning to my city, I met with this young man, unto whom I did the best of deeds, and who, had it not been for me, had been slain: yet he hath accused me of that which is not in my character; for all that he hath related of me, with respect to impertinence, and loquacity, and dulness, and want of taste, is false, O people,—

The tailor then proceeded thus:—When we heard the story of the barber, and were convinced of his impertinence and loquacity, and that the young man had been treated unjustly by him, we seized hold upon him, and put him in confinement, and, seating ourselves to keep watch over him, ate and drank; and the feast was finished in the most agreeable manner. We remained sitting together until the call to afternoon-prayers, when I went forth, and returned to my house; but my wife looked angrily at me, and said, Thou hast been all the day enjoying thy pleasure while I have been sitting at home sorrowful; now if thou go not forth with me and amuse me for the remainder of the day, thy refusal will be the cause of my separation from thee. So I took her and went out with her, and we amused ourselves until nightfall, when, returning home, we met this humpback, full of drink, and repeating verses; upon which I invited him to come home with us and he consented. I then went forth to buy some fried fish, and having bought it and returned, we sat down to eat; and my wife took a morsel of bread and a piece of fish, and put them into his mouth, and choked him, so that he died; whereupon I took him up, and contrived to throw him into the house of this physician, and he contrived to throw him into the house of the steward, and the steward contrived to throw him in the way of the broker.—This is the story of what happened to me yesterday. Is it not more wonderful than that of the humpback?

When the King had heard this story, he ordered certain of his chamberlains to go with the tailor, and to bring the barber; saying to them, His presence is indispensable, that I may hear his talk, and it may be the cause of the deliverance of you all: then we will bury this humpback decently in the earth, for he hath been dead since yesterday; and we will make him a monument round his grave, since he hath been the occasion of our acquaintance with these wonderful stories.

The chamberlains and the tailor soon came back, after having gone to the place of confinement and brought the barber, whom they placed before the King; and when the King beheld him, he saw him to be an old man, passed his ninetieth year, of dark countenance, and white beard and eyebrows, with small ears, and long nose, and a haughty aspect. The King laughed at the sight of him and said to him, O silent man, I desire that thou relate to me somewhat of thy stories.—O King of the age, replied the barber, what is the occasion of the presence of this Christian and this Jew and this Muslim, and this humpback lying dead among you; and what is the reason of this assembly?—Wherefore dost thou ask this? said the King. The barber answered, I ask it in order that the King may know me to be no impertinent person, nor one who meddleth with that which doth not concern him, and that I am free from the loquacity of which they accuse me: for I am fortunate in my characteristic appellation, since they have surnamed me Es-Samit; and, as the poet hath said,—

Seldom hast thou seen a person honoured with a surname, but thou
    wilt find, if thou search, that his character is expressed by it.

The King therefore said, Explain to the barber the case of this humpback, and what happened to him yesterday evening, and explain to him also what the Christian hath related, and the Jew and the steward and the tailor. So they repeated to him the stories of all these persons.

The barber, thereupon, shook his head, saying, By Allah, this is a wonderful thing! Uncover this humpback that I may examine him.—And they did so. He then seated himself at his head, and, taking it up, placed it upon his lap, and looked at his face, and laughed so violently that he fell backwards, exclaiming, For every death there is a cause; and the death of this humpback is most wonderful: it is worthy of being registered in the records, that posterity may be instructed by this event!—The King, astonished at his words, said, O Samit, explain to us the reason of thy saying this.—O King, replied the barber, by thy beneficence, life is yet in the humpback! He then drew forth from his bosom a pot containing some ointment, and with this he anointed the neck of the humpback; after which he covered it up until it perspired; when he took forth an iron forceps, and put it down his throat, and extracted the piece of fish with its bone, and all the people saw them. The humpback now sprang upon his feet, and sneezed, and, recovering his consciousness, drew his hands over his face, and exclaimed, There is no Deity but God! Mohammad is God's Apostle! God bless and save him!—and all who were present were astonished at the sight and the King laughed until he became insensible; as did also the other spectators. The King exclaimed, By Allah, this accident is wonderful! I have never witnessed anything more strange!—and added, O Muslims! O assembly of soldiers! have ye ever in the course of your lives seen any one die and after that come to life? But had not God blessed him with this barber, the humpback had been to-day numbered among the people of the other world; for the barber hath been the means of restoring him to life.—They replied, This is indeed a wonderful thing!

The King then gave orders to record this event; and when they had done so, he placed the record in the royal library; and he bestowed dresses of honour upon the Jew and the Christian and the steward; upon each of them, a costly dress; the tailor he appointed to be his own tailor, granting him regular allowances, and reconciling him and the humpback with each other: the humpback he honoured with a rich and beautiful dress, and with similar allowances, and appointed him his cup-companion; and upon the barber also he conferred the like favours, rewarding him with a costly dress of honour, regular allowances, and a fixed salary, and appointing him state-barber, and his own cup-companion: so they all lived in the utmost happiness and comfort until they were visited by the terminator of delights and the separator of friends.

THE STORY OF NUR-ED-DIN AND ENIS-EL-JELIS

THERE was, in El-Basrah, a certain King, who loved the poor and indigent, and regarded his subjects with benevolence; he bestowed of his wealth upon him who believed in Mohammad (God bless and save him!) and was such as one of the poets who have written of him hath thus described:—

He used his lances as pens; and the hearts of his enemies, as paper; their blood being his ink;
And hence, I imagine, our forefathers applied to the lance the term Khattiyeh.

The name of this King was Mohammad the son of Suleyman Ez-Zeyni; and he had two Wezirs; one of whom was named El-Mo'in the son of Sawi; and the other, El-Fadl the son of Khakan. El-Fadl the son of Khakan was the most generous of the people of his age, upright in conduct, so that all hearts agreed in loving him, and the wise complied with his counsel, and all the people supplicated for him length of life: for he was a person of auspicious aspect, a preventer of evil and mischief: but the Wezir El-Mo'in the son of Sawi hated others, and loved not good; he was a man of inauspicious aspect; and in the same degree that the people loved Fadl-ed-Din the son of Khakan, so did they abhor El-Mo'in the son of Sawi in accordance with the decree of the Almighty.

Now the King Mohammad the son of Suleyman Ez-Zenyi was sitting one day upon his throne, surrounded by the officers of his court, and he called to his Wezir El-Fadl the son of Khakan, and said to him, I desire a female slave unsurpassed in beauty by any in her age, of perfect loveliness and exquisite symmetry, and endowed with all praiseworthy qualities.—Such as this, replied his courtiers, is not to be found for less than ten thousand pieces of gold. And the Sultan thereupon called out to the treasurer, saying, Carry ten thousand pieces of gold to the house of El-Fadl the son of Khakan. So the treasurer did as he commanded, and the Wezir departed, after the Sultan had ordered him to repair every day to the market, and to commission the brokers to procure what he had described, and had commanded also that no female slave of a greater price than one thousand pieces of gold should be sold without having been shewn to the Wezir.

The brokers, therefore, sold no female slave without shewing her to him, and he complied with the King's command, and thus he continued to do for a considerable time, no slave pleasing him: but on a certain day, one of the brokers came to the mansion of the Wezir El-Fadl, and found that he had mounted to repair to the palace of the King; and he laid hold upon his stirrup, and repeated these two verses:—

O thou who hast reanimated what was rotten in the state! Thou art the Wezir ever aided in Heaven.
Thou hast revived the noble qualities that were extinct among men. May thy conduct never cease to be approved by God!

He then said, O my master, the female slave for the procuring of whom the noble mandate was issued hath arrived. The Wezir replied, Bring her hither to me. So the man returned, and, after a short absence, came again, accompanied by a damsel of elegant stature, high-bosomed, with black eyelashes, and smooth cheek, and slender waist, and large hips, clad in the handsomest apparel; the moisture of her lips was sweeter than syrup; her figure put to shame the branches of the Oriental willow; and her speech was more soft than the zephyr passing over the flowers of the garden; as one of her describers hath thus expressed:—

Her skin is like silk, and her speech is soft, neither redundant nor deficient:
Her eyes, God said to them, Be,—and they were, affecting men's hearts with the potency of wine.
May my love for her grow more warm each night, and cease not until the day of judgment!

The locks on her brow are dark as night, while her forehead shines like the gleam of morning.

When the Wezir beheld her, she pleased him extremely, and he looked towards the broker, and said to him, What is the price of this damsel? The broker answered, The price bidden for her hath amounted to ten thousand pieces of gold, and her owner hath sworn that this sum doth not equal the cost of the chickens which she hath eaten, nor the cost of the dresses which she hath bestowed upon her teachers; for she hath learnt writing and grammar and lexicology, and the interpretation of the Kur'an, and the fundamentals of law and religion, and medicine, and the computation of the calendar, and the art of playing upon musical instruments. The Wezir then said, Bring to me her master:—and the broker immediately brought him; and lo, he was a foreigner, who had lived so long that time had reduced him to bones and skin, as the poet hath said,—

How hath time made me to tremble! For time is powerful and severe.
I used to walk without being weary; but now I am weary and do not walk.

And the Wezir said to him, Art thou content to receive for this damsel ten thousand pieces of gold from the Sultan Mohammad the son of Suleyman Ez-Zeyni? The foreigner answered, As she is for the Sultan, it is incumbent on me to give her as a present to him, without price. So the Wezir, upon this, ordered that the money should be brought, and then weighed the pieces of gold for the foreigner; after which, the slave-broker addressed the Wezir, and said, With the permission of our lord the Wezir, I will speak.—Impart what thou hast to say, replied the Wezir.—It is my opinion then, said the broker, that thou shouldst not take up this damsel to the Sultan to-day; for she hath just arrived from her journey, and the change of air hath affected her, and the journey hath fatigued her; but rather let her remain with thee in thy palace ten days, that she may take rest, and her beauty will improve: then cause her to be taken into the bath, and attire her in clothes of the handsomest description, and go up with her to the Sultan: so shalt thou experience more abundant good-fortune. And the Wezir considered the advice of the slave-broker, and approved it. He therefore took her into his palace, and gave her a private apartment to herself, allotting her every day what she required of food and drink and other supplies, and she continued a while in this state of enjoyment.

Now the Wezir El-Fadl had a son like the shining full moon, with brilliant countenance, and red cheek, marked with a mole like a globule of ambergris, and with grey down. The youth knew not of this damsel, and his father had charged her, saying, Know that I have purchased thee for the King Mohammad the son of Suleyman Ez-Zeyni, and that I have a son who hath not left a girl in the quarter without making love to her: therefore keep thyself concealed from him, and beware of shewing him thy face, or suffering him to hear thy voice. The damsel replied, I hear and obey:—and he left her and departed. And it happened, as fate had ordained, that she went one day into the bath which was in the house, and, after certain of the female slaves had bathed her, she attired herself in rich apparel, and her beauty and loveliness increased in consequence. She then went in to the Wezir's wife, and kissed her hand, and said to her, May it be favourable, O Enis-el-Jelis! How didst thou find this bath?—O my mistress, she answered, I wanted nothing but thy presence there. And upon this, the mistress of the house said to the female slaves, Arise, and let us go into the bath. And they complied with her command, and went, accompanied by their mistress, who first charged two young slave-girls to keep the door of the private apartment in which was Enis-el-Jelis, saying to them, Suffer no one to go in to the damsel;—and they replied, We hear and obey. But while Enis-el-Jelis was sitting in her chamber, lo, the Wezir's son, whose name was 'Ali Nur-ed-Din, came in, and asked after his mother and the family. The two girls answered, They are gone into the bath. Now the damsel Enis-el-Jelis heard the speech of 'Ali Nur-ed-Din as she sat in her chamber, and she said within herself, I wonder what this youth is like, of whom the Wezir hath told me that he hath not left a girl in the quarter without making love to her: by Allah, I have a desire to see him. She then rose upon her feet, fresh as she was from the bath, and, approaching the door of the chamber, looked at 'Ali Nur-ed-Din, and beheld him to be a youth like the full moon. The sight of him occasioned her a thousand sighs; and a look from the youth, at her, affected him also in the same manner. Each was caught in the snare of the other's love, and the youth approached the two slave-girls, and cried out at them; whereupon they fled from before him, and stopped at a distance, looking to see what he would do. He then advanced to the door of the chamber, and, opening it, went in, and said to the damsel, Art thou she whom my father hath purchased for me? She answered, Yes. And upon this, the youth, who was in a state of intoxication, went up to her, and embraced her, while she, in like manner, threw her arms around his neck, and kissed him. But the two slave-girls, having seen their young master enter the chamber of the damsel Enis-el-Jelis, cried out. The youth, therefore, soon ran forth, and fled for safety, fearing the consequence of his intrusion; and when the mistress of the house heard the cry of the two slave-girls, she came out dripping from the bath, saying, What is the cause of this cry in the house? And when she drew near to the two slave-girls whom she had placed at the door of the private chamber, she said to them, Wo to you! What is the matter?—They answered, as soon as they beheld her, Our master 'Ali Nur-ed-Din came to us and beat us, and we fled from him, and he went into the chamber of Enis-el-Jelis, and when we cried out to thee he fled. The mistress of the house then went to Enis-el-Jelis, and said to her, What is the news?—O my mistress, she answered, as I was sitting here, a youth of handsome person came in to me, and said to me, Art thou she whom my father hath purchased for me?—And I answered, Yes.— By Allah, O my mistress, I believed that what he said was true; and he came up to me and embraced me, and kissed me three times, and left me overcome by his love.

Upon this, the mistress of the house wept, and slapped her face, and her female slaves did the like, fearing for 'Ali Nur-ed-Din, lest his father should slay him; and while they were in this state, lo, the Wezir came in, and inquired what had happened. His wife said to him, Swear that thou wilt listen to that which I shall say. He replied, Well? So she told him what his son had done; and he mourned, and rent his clothes, and slapped his face, and plucked his beard. His wife then said to him, Kill not thyself. I will give thee, of my own property, ten thousand pieces of gold, her price.— But upon this, he raised his head towards her, and said to her, Wo to thee! I want not her price; but I fear the loss of my life and my property.—Wherefore, O my master? she asked.—Knowest thou not, said he, that we have this enemy El-Mo'in the son of Sawi? When he heareth of this event, he will repair to the Sultan, and say to him, Thy Wezir whom thou imaginest to love thee hath received from thee ten thousand pieces of gold, and purchased therewith a female slave such as no one hath seen equalled, and when she pleased him, he said to his son, Take her; for thou art more worthy of her than the Sultan:—and he took her; and the damsel is now with him.—Then the King will say, Thou liest. And he will say to the King, With thy permission, I will break in upon him suddenly, and bring her to thee. And he will give him permission to do so: he will therefore make a sudden attack upon the house, and take the damsel, and conduct her into the presence of the Sultan, and he will question her, and she will not be able to deny: he will then say, O my lord, I give thee good counsel, but I am not in favour with thee:—and the Sultan will make an example of me, and all the people will make me a gazing-stock, and my life will be lost.—His wife, however, replied, Acquaint no one; for this thing hath happened privily: commit, therefore, thine affair unto God, in this extremity. And upon this, the heart of the Wezir was quieted, and his mind was relieved.

Such was the case of the Wezir.—Now as to Nur-ed-Din, he feared the result of his conduct, and so passed each day in the gardens, not returning to his mother until towards the close of the night: he then slept in her apartment, and rose before morning without being seen by any one else. Thus he continued to do for the space of a month, not seeing the face of his father; and at length his mother said to his father, O my master, wilt thou lose the damsel and lose the child? For if it long continue thus with the youth, he will flee his country.—And what is to be done? said he. She answered, Sit up this night, and when he cometh, lay hold upon him, and be reconciled to him, and give him the damsel; for she loveth him, and he loveth her; and I will give thee her price. So the Wezir sat up the whole night, and when his son came, he laid hold upon him, and would have cut his throat; but his mother came to his succour, and said to her husband, What dost thou desire to do unto him? He answered her, I desire to slay him. The youth then said to his father, Am I of so small account in thy estimation? And upon this, the eyes of his father filled with tears, and he said to him, O my son, is the loss of my property and my life of small account with thee?—Listen, O my father, rejoined the youth:—and he implored his forgiveness. So the Wezir rose from the breast of his son, and was moved with compassion for him; and the youth rose, and kissed his father's hand; and the Wezir said, O my son, if I knew that thou wouldst act equitably to Enis-el-Jelis, I would give her to thee.—O my father, replied the youth, wherefore should I not act equitably towards her? And his father said, I charge thee, O my son, that thou take not a wife to share her place, and that thou do her no injury, nor sell her. He replied, O my father, I swear to thee that I will neither take a wife to share her place, nor sell her:— and he promised him by oaths to act as he had said, and took up his abode with the damsel, and remained with her a year; and God (whose name be exalted!) caused the King to forget the affair of the female slave; but the matter became known to El-Mo'in the son of Sawi; yet he could not speak of it, on account of the high estimation in which the other Wezir was held by the Sultan.

After this year had expired, the Wezir Fadl-ed-Din the son of Khakan entered the bath, and came out in a state of excessive perspiration, in consequence of which the external air smote him, so that he became confined to his bed, and long remained sleepless; and his malady continued unremittingly; so he called, thereupon, his son, 'Ali Nur-ed-Din, and when he came before him, said to him, O my son, verily the means of life are apportioned, and its period is decreed, and every soul must drink the cup of death. I have nothing with which to charge thee but the fear of God, and forethought with regard to the results of thine actions, and that thou conduct thyself kindly to the damsel Enis-el-Jelis.—O my father, said the youth, who is like unto thee? Thou hast been celebrated for virtuous actions, and the praying of the preachers for thee on the pulpits.—O my son, rejoined the Wezir, I hope for the approbation of God, whose name be exalted! And then he pronounced the two professions of the faith, and uttered a sigh, and was recorded among the company of the blest. And upon this, the palace was filled with shrieking, and the news reached the ears of the Sultan, and the people of the city heard of the death of El-Fadl the son of Khakan, and even the boys in the schools wept for him. His son 'Ali Nur-ed-Din arose, and prepared his funeral, and the Emirs and Wezirs and other officers of the state attended it, and among them was the Wezir El-Mo'in the son of Sawi; and as the procession passed out from the mansion, one of the mourners recited these verses:—

I said to the man who was appointed to wash him,—Would that
    he had yielded obedience to my counsel,—
Put away from him the water, and wash him with the tears of
    honour, shed in lamentation for him:
And remove these fragrant substances collected for his corpse, and
    perfume him rather with the odours of his praise:
And order the noble angels to carry him in honour. Dost thou
    not behold them attending him?
Cause not men's necks to be strained by bearing him: enough are
    they laden already by his benefits.

'Ali Nur-ed-Din for a long time remained in a state of violent grief for the loss of his father; but as he was sitting one day in his father's house, a person knocked at the door, and he rose up and opened it, and lo, there was a man who was one of his father's intimate companions, and he kissed the hand of Nur-ed-Din, and said to him, O my master, he who hath left a son like thee hath not died. This is the destination of the lord of the first and the last among mankind.[1] O my master, cheer up thy heart, and give over

          [1] The Prophet Mohammad.

mourning.—And upon this, 'Ali Nur-ed-Din arose, and went to the guest-chamber, and removed thither all that he required, and his companions came together to him, and he took again his slave. Ten of the sons of the merchants became his associates, and he gave entertainment after entertainment, and began to be lavish with presents. His steward, therefore, came to him, and said to him, O my master Nur-ed-Din, hast thou not heard the saying, He who expendeth and doth not calculate is reduced to poverty? This profuse expenditure, and these magnificent presents, will annihilate the property.—But when 'Ali Nur-ed-Din heard these words of his steward, he looked at him, and replied, Of all that thou hast said to me, I will not attend to one word. How excellent is the saying of the poet:—

If I be possessed of wealth and be not liberal, may my hand never be extended, nor my foot raised !
Shew me the avaricious who hath attained glory by his avarice, and the munificent who hath died through his munificence.

Know, O steward, he continued, that if there remain in thy hands what will suffice for my dinner, thou shalt not burden me with anxiety respecting my supper.—So the steward left him, and went his way; and 'Ali Nur-ed-Din resumed his habits of extravagant generosity: whenever any one of his companions said, Verily this thing is beautiful!—he would reply, It is a present to thee:—and if any said, O my master, verily such a house is delightful!—he would reply, It is a present to thee.

He ceased not to give entertainments to his companions from the commencement of day, one after another, until he had passed in this manner a whole year; after which, as he was sitting with them, he heard the slave-girl recite these two verses:—

Thou thoughtest well of the days when they went well with thee, and fearedst not the evil that destiny was bringing.
Thy nights were peaceful, and thou wast deceived by them: in the midst of their brightness there cometh gloom.

And immediately after, a person knocked at the door; so Nur-ed-Din rose, and one of his companions followed him without his knowledge; and when he opened the door, he beheld his steward, and said to him, What is the news?— O my master, answered the steward, that which I feared on thy account hath happened to thee.—How is that? asked Nur-ed-Din. The steward answered, Know that there remaineth not of thy property in my hands, anything equivalent to a piece of silver, or less than a piece of silver; and these are the accounts of thy expenses, and of thy original property, When 'Ali Nur-ed-Din heard these words, he hung down his head towards the ground, and exclaimed, There is no strength nor power but in God! And the man who had followed him secretly to pry into his case, as soon as he heard what the steward told him, returned to his companions, and said to them, See what ye will do; for 'Ali Nur-ed-Din hath become a bankrupt. So when Nur-ed-Din returned to them, grief appeared to them in his countenance, and immediately one of them rose, and, looking towards him, said to him, O my master, I desire that thou wouldst permit me to depart.— Why thus depart to-day? said Nur-ed-Din. His guest answered, My wife is to give birth to a child this night, and it is impossible for me to be absent from her: I desire, therefore, to go and see her. And he gave him leave. Then another rose, and said to him, O my master Nur-ed-Din, I desire to-day to visit my brother; for he celebrateth the circumcision of his son. Thus each of them asked leave of him deceitfully, and went his way, until all had departed.

So 'Ali Nur-ed-Din remained alone; and he called his slave-girl, and said to her, O Enis-el-Jelis, seest thou not what hath befallen me? And he related to her what the steward had told him. She replied, O my master, for some nights past, I have been anxious to speak to thee of this affair; but I heard thee reciting these two verses:—

When fortune is liberal to thee, be thou liberal to all others before
  she escape from thee:
For liberality will not annihilate thy wealth when she is favourable; nor avarice preserve it when she deserteth thee.

And when I heard thee repeat these words, I was silent, and would not make any remark to thee.—O Enis-el-Jelis, he rejoined, thou knowest that I have not expended my

wealth but on my companions; and I do not think that they
will abandon me without relief.—By Allah, said she, they
will be of no use to thee. But he said, I will immediately
arise and go to them, and knock at their doors; perhaps I
shall obtain from them something which I will employ as
a capital wherewith to trade, and I will cease from diversion
and sport. So he arose instantly, and proceeded without
stopping until he arrived at the by-street in which his ten
companions resided; for they all lived in that same street:
and he advanced to the first door, and knocked; and there
came forth to him a slave-girl, who said to him, Who art
thou? He answered, Say to thy master,—'Ali Nur-ed-Din
is standing at the door, and saith to thee, Thy slave kisseth
thy hands, looking for a favour from thee.—And the girl
entered and acquainted her master; but he called out to her,
saying, Return, and tell him, He is not here.—The girl, therefore, returned to Nur-ed-Din, and said to him, My master,
Sir, is not here. And he went on, saying within himself, If
this is a knave, and hath denied himself, another is not. He
then advanced to the next door, and said as he had before;
and the second also denied himself; and Nur-ed-Din exclaimed,—

They are gone, who, if thou stoodest at their door, would bestow
    upon thee the bounty thou desirest.

By Allah, he added, I must try all of them: perchance one
of them may stand me in the place of all the others. And
he went round to all the ten; but found not that one of them
would open the door, or shew himself, or even order him a
cake or bread; and he recited the following verses:—

A man in prosperity resembleth a tree, around which people flock
    as long as it hath fruit;
But as soon as it hath dropped all that it bore, they disperse from
    beneath it, and seek another.
Perdition to all the people of this age! for I find not one man of
    integrity among ten.

He then returned to his slave: his anxiety had increased,
and she said to him, O my master, said I not unto thee that
they would not profit thee?—By Allah, he replied, not one
of them shewed me his face.—O my master, rejoined she,

sell of the movables of the house a little at a time, and
expend the produce. And he did so until he had sold all
that was in the house, and there remained nothing in his
possession; and upon this he looked towards Enis-el-Jelis,
and said to her, What shall we do now?—It is my advice,
O my master, she answered, that thou arise immediately,
and take me to the market, and sell me; for thou knowest
that thy father purchased me for ten thousand pieces of gold,
and perhaps God may open to thee a way to obtain a part
of this price; and if God have decreed our reunion, we
shall meet again. But he replied, O Enis-el-Jelis, it is not
easy for me to endure thy separation for one hour.—Nor
is the like easy to me, said she: but necessity is imperious.
And upon this, he took Enis-el-Jelis, his tears flowing down
his cheeks, and went and delivered her to the broker, saying
to him, Know the value of that which thou art to cry for
sale.—O my master Nur-ed-Din, replied the broker, noble
qualities are held in remembrance. Is she not Enis-el-Jelis,
whom thy father purchased of me for ten thousand pieces of
gold?—He answered, Yes. And the broker thereupon went
to the merchants; but he found that they had not all yet
assembled; so he waited until the rest had come; and the
market was filled with all varieties of female slaves, Turkish
and Greek and Circassian and Georgian and Abyssinian;
and when he beheld its crowded state, he arose and exclaimed,
O merchants! O possessors of wealth! everything that is
round is not a nut; nor is everything long, a banana; nor
is everything that is red, meat; nor is everything white, fat;
nor is everything that is ruddy, wine; nor is everything
tawny, a date! O merchants! this precious pearl, whose
value no money can equal, with what sum will ye open the
bidding for her?—And one of the merchants answered,
With four thousand and five hundred pieces of gold.

But, lo, the Wezir El-Mo'in the son of Sawi was in the
market, and, seeing 'Ali Nur-ed-Din standing there, he said
within himself, What doth he want here, having nothing left
wherewith to purchase female slaves? Then casting his
eyes around, and hearing the broker as he stood crying in
the market with the merchants around him, he said within
himself, I do not imagine anything else than that he hath

become a bankrupt, and come forth with the slave-girl to sell her; and if this be the case, how pleasant to my heart! He then called the crier, who approached him, and kissed the ground before him; and the Wezir said to him, I desire this female slave whom thou art crying for sale. The broker, therefore, being unable to oppose his wish, brought the slave and placed her before him; and when he beheld her, and considered her charms, her elegant figure and her soft speech, he was delighted with her, and said to the broker. To what has the bidding for her amounted? The broker answered, Four thousand and five hundred pieces of gold. And as soon as the merchants heard this, not one of them could bid another piece of silver or of gold; but all of them drew back, knowing the tyrannical conduct of that Wezir. El-Mo'in the son of Sawi then looked towards the broker, and said to him, Why standest thou still? Take away the slave-girl for me at the price of four thousand and five hundred pieces of gold, and thou wilt have five hundred for thyself.—So the broker went to 'Ali Nur-ed-Din, and said to him, O my master, the slave-girl is lost to thee without price.—How so? said Nur-ed-Din. The broker answered, We opened the bidding for her at four thousand and five hundred pieces of gold; but this tyrant El-Mo'in the son of Sawi came into the market, and when he beheld the damsel she pleased him, and he said to me, Ask her owner if he will agree for four thousand pieces of gold, and five hundred for thee:—and I doubt not but he knoweth that the slave belongeth to thee; and if he give thee her price immediately, it will be through the goodness of God; but I know, from his injustice, that he will write thee an order upon some of his agents for the money, and then send to them and desire them to give thee nothing; and every time that thou shalt go to demand it of them, they will say to thee, To-morrow we will pay thee:—and they will not cease to promise thee, and to defer from day to day, notwithstanding thy pride; and when they are overcome by thy importunity they will say, Give us the written order:—and as soon as they have received the paper from thee they will tear it in pieces: so thou wilt lose the price of the slave.

When Nur-ed-Din, therefore, heard these words of the broker, he said to him, What is to be done? The broker answered, I will give thee a piece of advice, and if thou receive it from me, thou will have better fortune.—What is it? Asked Nur-ed-Din.—That thou come to me immediately, answered the broker, while I am standing in the midst of the market, and take the slave-girl from me, and give her a blow with thy hand, and say to her, Wo to thee! I have expiated my oath that I swore, and brought thee to the market, because I swore to thee that thou shouldst be exposed in the market, and that the broker should cry thee for sale.—If thou do this, perhaps the trick will deceive him and the people, and they will believe that thou tookest her not to the market but to expiate the oath.—This, replied Nur-ed-Din, is the right counsel. So the broker returned into the midst of the market, and, taking hold of the hand of the slave-girl, made a sign to the Wezir El-Mo'in the son of Sawi, saying, O my lord, this is her owner who hath just come. Then 'Ali Nur-ed-Din advanced to the broker, and tore the damsel from him, and struck her with his hand, saying to her, Wo to thee! I have brought thee to the market for the sake of expiating my oath. Go home, and disobey me not again. I want not thy price, that I should sell thee; and if I sold the furniture of the house and everything else of the kind over and over again, their produce would not amount to thy price.—But when El-Mo'in the son of Sawi, beheld Nur-ed-Din, he said to him, Wo to thee! Hast thou anything left to be sold or bought?—And he would have laid violent hands upon him. The merchants then looked towards Nur-ed-Din (and they all loved him), and he said to them, Here am I before you, and ye have all known his tyranny.—By Allah, exclaimed the Wezir, were it not for you, I had killed him! Then all of them made signs, one to another, with the eye, and said, Not one of us will interfere between thee and him. And upon this, 'Ali Nur-ed-Din went up to the Wezir, the son of Sawi (and Nur-ed-Din was a man of courage), and he dragged the Wezir from his saddle, and threw him upon the ground. There was at that spot a kneading-place for mud,[1] and the Wezir fell into the midst of it, and Nur-ed-

[1] By this is meant, a place where mud was kneaded to be employed in building. The mortar generally used in the construction of Arab houses is composed of mud in the proportion of one-half, with a fourth part of lime, and the remaining part of the ashes of straw and rubbish.

Din beat him with his fist, and a blow fell upon his teeth, by which his beard became dyed with his blood. Now there were with the Wezir ten memluks, and when they saw Nur-ed-Din treat their master in this manner, they put their hands upon the hilts of their swords, and would have fallen upon him and cut him in pieces; but the people said to them, This is a Wezir, and this is the son of a Wezir, and perhaps they may make peace with each other, and ye will incur the anger of both of them; or perhaps a blow may fall upon your master, and ye will all of you die the most ignominious of deaths: it is advisable, therefore, that ye interfere not between them.—And when 'Ali Nur-ed-Din had ceased from beating the Wezir, he took his slave-girl and returned to his house.

The Wezir, the son of Sawi, then immediately arose, and his dress, which before was white, was now dyed with three colours, the colour of mud, and the colour of blood, and the colour of ashes; and when he beheld himself in this condition, he took a round mat, and hung it to his neck, and took in his hand two bundles of coarse grass, and went and stood beneath the palace of the Sultan, and cried out, O King of the age! I am oppressed!—So they brought him before the King, who looked at him attentively, and saw that he was his Wezir, El-Mo'in the son of Sawi. He said, therefore, Who hath done thus unto thee?—and the Wezir cried and moaned, and repeated these two verses :—

Shall fortune oppress me while thou existest; and the dogs devour me when thou art a lion?
Shall all else who are dry drink freely from thy tanks, and I thirst in thine asylum when thou art as rain?

—O my lord, he continued, thus is every one who loveth thee and serveth thee: these afflictions always befall him.— And who, said the King again, hath done thus unto thee? —Know, answered the Wezir, that I went forth to-day to the market of the female slaves with the idea of buying a cook-maid, and saw in the market a slave-girl the like of whom I had never in my life beheld, and the broker said that she belonged to 'Ali Nur-ed-Din. Now our lord the Sultan had given his father ten thousand pieces of gold to buy for him with it a beautiful female slave, and he bought that girl, and she pleased him; so he gave her to his son; and when his father died, the son pursued the path of prodigality, until he sold all his houses and gardens and utensils; and when he had become a bankrupt, nothing else remaining in his possession, he took the slave-girl to the market to sell her, and delivered her to the broker: so he cried her for sale, and the merchants continued bidding for her until her price amounted to four thousand pieces of gold; whereupon I said to myself, I will buy this for our lord the Sultan; for her original price was from him. I therefore said, O my son, receive her price, four thousand pieces of gold. But when he heard my words, he looked at me and replied, O ill-omened old man! I will sell her to the Jews and the Christians rather than to thee.—I then said to him, I would not buy her for myself, but for our lord the Sultan, who is our benefactor. As soon, however, as he had heard these words from me, he was filled with rage, and dragged me and threw me down from the horse, notwithstanding my advanced age, and beat me, and ceased not to do so until he left me in the state in which thou seest me. Nothing exposed me to all this ill treatment but my coming to purchase this slave-girl for your majesty.—The Wezir then threw himself upon the ground, and lay weeping and trembling.

Now when the Sultan beheld his condition, and had heard his speech, the vein of anger swelled between his eyes, and he looked towards the members of his court who were attending him; whereupon forty swordsmen stood before him, and he said to them, Descend immediately to the house of 'Ali the son of El-Fadl the son of Khakan, and plunder it and demolish it, and bring hither him and the slave-girl with their hands bound behind them: drag them along upon their faces, and so bring them before me. They replied, we hear and obey:—and went forth to repair to the house of 'Ali Nur-ed-Din. But there was in the court of the Sultan a chamberlain named 'Alam-ed-in Senjer, who had been one of the memluks of El-Fadl the son of Khakan, the father of 'Ali Nur-ed-Din; and when he heard the order of the Sultan, and saw the enemies prepared to slay his master's son, it was insupportable to him; so he mounted his horse, and proceeded to the house of 'Ali Nur-ed-Din, and knocked at the door. Nur-ed-Din came forth to him, and, when he saw him, knew him, and would have saluted him; but he said, O my master, this is not a time for salutation, nor for talking. Nur-ed-Din said, O 'Alam-ed-Din, what is the news? He replied, Save thyself by flight, thou and the slave-girl; for El-Mo'in the son of Sawi hath set up a snare for you, and if ye fall into his hands he will slay you: the Sultan hath sent to you forty swordsmen, and it is my advice that ye fly before the evil fall upon you. Then Senjer stretched forth his hand to Nur-ed-Din with some pieces of gold, and he counted them, and found them to be forty pieces; and he said, O my master, receive these, and if I had with me more, I would give it thee; but this is not a time for ex-postulating. And upon this, Nur-ed-Din went in to the damsel, and acquainted her with the occurrence, and she was confounded.

The two then went forth immediately from the city, and God let down the veil of his protection upon them, and they proceeded to the bank of the river, where they found a vessel ready to sail: the master was standing in the midst of it, and saying, He who hath anything to do, whether leave-taking or procuring provisions, or who hath forgotten aught, let him do what he desireth and return; for we are going. And they all replied, We have nothing remaining to do, O master. So, upon this, the master said to his crew, Quick! Loose the rope's end, and pull up the stake.—And 'Ali Nur-ed-Din exclaimed, Whither, O master? He an-swered, To the abode of Peace, Baghdad. And Nur-ed-Din embarked, and the damsel with him, and they set the vessel afloat, and spread the sails and it shot along like a bird with its pair of wings, carrying them forward with a favour-able wind.

Meanwhile, the forty men whom the Sultan had sent came to the house of 'Ali Nur-ed-Din, and broke open the doors and entered, and searched all the chambers, but with-out success; so they demolished the house, and returned, and acquainted the Sultan, who said, Search for them in every place where they may be:—and they replied, We hear and obey. The Wezir El-Mo'in the son of Sawi then descended to his house, after the Sultan had invested him with a robe of honour, and had said to him, None shall take vengeance for thee but myself. And he greeted the King with a prayer for long life, and his heart was set at ease: and the Sultan gave orders to proclaim throughout the city, O all ye people! our lord the Sultan hath commanded that whoever shall meet with 'Ali Nur-ed-Din, and bring him to the Sultan, shall be invested with a robe of honour, and he will give him a thousand pieces of gold; and he who shall conceal him, or know where he is, and not give information thereof, will merit the exemplary punishment that shall befall him! So all the people began to search for him; but could not trace him.—Such was the case with these people.

Now as to 'Ali Nur-ed-Din and his slave, they arrived in safety at Baghdad, and the master of the vessel said to them, This is Baghdad, and it is a city of security: winter with its cold hath departed from it, and the spring-quarter hath come with its roses, and its trees are in blossom, and its waters are flowing. And upon this, 'Ali Nur-ed-Din landed with his slave-girl, and gave the master five pieces of gold. They then walked a little way, and destiny cast them among the gardens, and they came to a place which they found swept and sprinkled, with long mastabahs, and pots suspended filled with water, and over it was a covering of trellis-work of canes extending along the whole length of a lane, at the upper end of which was the gate of a garden; but this was shut. And Nur-ed-Din said to the damsel, By Allah, this is a pleasant place!—and she replied, O my master, let us sit down a while upon one of these mastabahs. So they mounted and seated themselves there, and they washed their faces and hands, and enjoyed the current of the zephyr, and slept.—Glory be to Him who sleepeth not!

This garden was called the Garden of Delight, and in it was a palace called the Palace of Diversion, and it belonged to the Khalifeh Harun Er-Rashid, who, when his heart was contracted, used to come to this garden, and enter the palace above mentioned, and there sit. The palace had eighty latticed windows, and eighty lamps were suspended in it, and in the midst of it was a great candlestick of gold; and when the Khalifeh entered it, he commanded the female slaves to open the windows, and ordered Ishak, the cup-companion, to sing with them: so his heart became dilated, and his anxiety ceased. There was a superintendent to the garden, an old man, named the sheykh Ibrahim; and it happened that he went forth once to transact some business, and found there persons diverting themselves with women of suspicious character, whereupon he was violently enraged, and having waited until the Khalifeh came thither some days after, he acquainted him with this occurrence, and the Khalifeh said, Whomsoever thou shalt find at the gate of the garden, do with him what thou wilt. Now on this day the sheykh Ibrahim went out to transact an affair of business, and found the two sleeping at the garden-gate, covered with a single izar; and he said, Do not these two persons know that the Khalifeh hath given me permission to kill every one whom I find here? But I will only give these two a slight beating, that no one may again approach the gate of the garden. He then cut a green palm-stick, and went forth to them, and raised his hand until the whiteness of his arm-pit appeared, and was about to beat them; but he reflected in his mind, and said, O Ibrahim, how shouldst thou beat them when thou knowest not their case? They may be two strangers, or of the children of the road,⁶ whom destiny hath cast here. I will therefore uncover their faces, and look at them.—So he lifted up the izar from their faces and said, These are two handsome persons, and it is not proper that I should beat them. And he covered their faces again, and, approaching the foot of 'Ali Nur-ed-Din, began to rub it gently; whereupon Nur-ed-Din opened his eyes, and saw that he was an old man; and he blushed, and drew in his feet, and, sitting up, took the hand of the sheykh Ibrahim and kissed it; and the sheykh said to him, O my son, whence are ye?—O my master, he answered, we are strangers.— And a tear gushed from his eye. The sheykh Ibrahim then said to him, O my son, know that the Prophet (God bless and save him!) hath enjoined generosity to the stranger. Wilt thou not arise, O my son, and enter the garden, and divert thyself in it, that thy heart may be dilated?—O my master, said Nur-ed-Din, to whom doth this garden belong? The

⁶ Wayfarers.

sheykh answered, O my son, this garden I inherited from my family. And his design in saying this was only that they might feel themselves at ease, and enter the garden. And when Nur-ed-Din heard his words, he thanked him, and arose, together with his slave, and, the sheykh Ibrahim preceding them, they entered the garden.

The gate was arched, and over it were vines with grapes of different colours; the red, like rubies; and the black, like ebony. They entered a bower, and found within it fruits growing in clusters and singly, and the birds were warbling their various notes upon the branches: the nightingale was pouring forth its melodious sounds; and the turtle-dove filled the place with its cooing; and the blackbird, in its singing, resembled a human being; and the ring-dove, a person exhilarated by wine. The fruits upon the trees, comprising every description that was good to eat, had ripened; and there were two of each kind: there were the camphor-apricot, and the almond-apricot, and the apricot of Khurasan; the plum of a colour like the complexion of beauties; the cherry delighting the sense of every man; the red, the white, and the green fig, of the most beautiful colours; and flowers like pearls and coral; the rose, whose redness put to shame the cheeks of the lovely; the violet, like sulphur in contact with fire; the myrtle, the gilliflower, the lavender, and the anemone; and their leaves were bespangled with the tears of the clouds; the chamomile smiled, displaying its teeth, and the narcissus looked at the rose with its negroes' eyes; the citrons resembled round cups; the limes were like bullets of gold; the ground was carpeted with flowers of every colour, and the place beamed with the charms of spring; the river murmured by while the birds sang, and the wind whistled among the trees; the season was temperate, and the zephyr was languishing.

The sheykh Ibrahim conducted them into the elevated saloon, and they were charmed with its beauty and the extraordinary elegances which it displayed, and seated themselves in one of the windows; and Nur-ed-Din, reflecting upon his past entertainments, exclaimed, By Allah, this place is most delightful! It hath reminded me of past events, and quenched in me an anguish like the fire of the ghádá.—The sheykh Ibrahim then brought to them some food, and they ate to satisfaction, and washed their hands, and Nur-ed-Din, seating himself again in one of the windows, called to his slave, and she came to him; and they sat gazing at the trees laden with all kinds of fruits; after which, Nur-ed-Din looked towards the sheykh, and said to him, O sheykh Ibrahim, hast thou not any beverage? For people drink after eating.—So the sheykh brought him some sweet and cold water: but Nur-ed-Din said, This is not the beverage I desire.—Dost thou want wine? asked the sheykh.—Yes, answered Nur-ed-Din. The sheykh exclaimed, I seek refuge with Allah from it! Verily, for thirteen years I have done nothing of that kind; for the Prophet (God bless and save him!) cursed its drinker and its presser and its carrier.— Hear from me two words, said Nur-ed-Din. The sheykh replied, Say what thou wilt. So he said, If thou be neither the presser of the wine, nor its drinker, nor its carrier, will aught of the curse fall upon thee? The sheykh answered, No.—Then take this piece of gold, rejoined Nur-ed-Din, and these two pieces of silver, and mount the ass, and halt at a distance from the place, and whatsoever man thou findest to buy it, call to him, and say to him, take these two pieces of silver, and with this piece of gold buy some wine, and place it upon the ass:—so, in this case, thou wilt be neither the carrier nor the presser, nor the buyer; and nothing will befall thee of that which befalleth the rest.

The sheykh Ibrahim, after laughing at his words, replied, By Allah, I have never seen one more witty than thou, nor heard speech more sweet. And Nur-ed-Din said to him, We have become dependent upon thee, and thou hast nothing to do but to comply with our wishes: bring us, therefore, all that we require.—O my son, said the sheykh, my buttery here is before thee (and it was the store-room furnished for the Prince of the Faithful): enter it then, and take from it what thou wilt; for it containeth more than thou desirest. So Nur-ed-Din entered the store-room, and beheld in it vessels of gold and silver and crystal, adorned with a variety of jewels; and he took out such of them as he desired, and poured the wine into the vessels of earthen-ware and bottles of glass; and he and the damsel began to drink, astonished at the beauty of the things which they beheld. The sheykh Ibrahim then brought to them sweet-scented flowers, and seated himself at a distance from them; and they continued drinking, in a state of the utmost delight, until the wine took effect upon them, and their cheeks reddened, and their eyes wantoned like those of the gazelle, and their hair hung down: whereupon the sheykh Ibrahim said, What aileth me that I am sitting at a distance from them? Why should I not sit by them? And when shall I be in the company of such as these two, who are like two moons?—He then advanced, and seated hmself at the edge of the raised portion of the floor; and Nur-ed-Din said to him, O my master, by my life I conjure thee to approach and join us. So he went to them; and Nur-ed-Din filled a cup, and, looking at the sheykh, said to him, Drink, that thou mayest know how delicious is its flavour. But the sheykh Ibrahim exclaimed, I seek refuge with Allah! Verily, for thirteen years I have done nothing of that kind. —And Nur-ed-Din, feigning to pay no attention to him, drank the cup, and threw himself upon the ground, pretending that intoxication had overcome him.

Upon this, Enis-el-Jelis looked towards the sheykh, and said to him, O sheykh Ibrahim, see how this man hath treated me.—O my mistress, said he, what aileth him? She rejoined, Always doth he treat me thus: he drinketh a while, and then sleepeth, and I remain alone, and find no one to keep me company over my cup. If I drink, who will serve me? And if I sing, who will hear me?—The sheykh, moved with tenderness and affection for her by her words, replied, It is not proper that a cup-companion be thus. The damsel then filled a cup, and, looking at the sheykh Ibrahim, said to him, I conjure thee by my life that thou take it and drink it; reject it not, but accept it, and refresh my heart. So he stretched forth his hand, and took the cup, and drank it; and she filled for him a second time, and handed it to him, saying, O my master, this remaineth for thee. He replied, By Allah, I cannot drink it: that which I have drunk is enough for me. But she said, By Allah, it is indispensable:—and he took the cup, and drank it. She then gave him the third; and he took it, and was about to drink it, when lo, Nur-ed-Din, raised himself, and said to him, O sheykh Ibrahim, what is this? Did I not conjure thee a while ago, and thou refusedst, and saidst, Verily, for thirteen years I have not done it?—The sheykh Ibrahim, touched with shame, replied, By Allah, I am not in fault; for she pressed me. And Nur-ed-Din laughed, and they resumed their carousal, and the damsel, turning her eyes towards her master, said to him, O my master, drink thou, and do not urge the sheykh Ibrahim; that I may divert thee with the sight of him. So she began to fill and to hand to her master, and her master filled and gave to her, and thus they continued to do, time after time; till at length the sheykh Ibrahim looked towards them and said, What meaneth this? And what sort of carousal is this? Wherefore do ye not give me to drink, since I have become your cup-companion?—At this they both laughed until they became almost senseless; and then drank, and gave him to drink; and they continued thus until the expiration of a third of the night, when the damsel said, O sheykh Ibrahim, with thy permission shall I rise and light one of the candles which are arranged here?—Rise, he answered; but light not more than one candle. But she sprang upon her feet, and, beginning with the first candle, proceeded until she had lighted eighty. She then sat down again; and presently Nur-ed-Din said, O sheykh Ibrahim, in what favour am I held with thee? Wilt thou not allow me to light one of these lamps?—The sheykh answered, Arise, and light one lamp, and be not thou also troublesome. So he arose, and, beginning with the first lamp, lighted all the eighty; and the saloon seemed to dance. And after this, the sheykh Ibrahim, overcome by intoxication, said to them, Ye are more frolicsome than I:—and he sprang upon his feet, and opened all the windows, and sat down again with them, and they continued carousing and reciting verses; and the place rang with their merriment.

Now God, the All-seeing and All-knowing, who hath appointed a cause to every event, had decreed that the Khalifeh should be sitting that night at one of the windows looking towards the Tigris, by moonlight; and he looked in that direction, and saw the light of lamps and candles reflected in the river, and, turning his eyes up towards the palace in the garden, he beheld it beaming with those candles and lamps, and exclaimed, Bring hither to me Ja'far El-Barmeki! In the twinkling of an eye, Ja'far stood before the Prince of the Faithful; and the Khalifeh said to him, O dog of Wezirs, dost thou serve me and not acquaint me with what happeneth in the city of Baghdad?—What, asked Ja'far, is the occasion of these words? The Khalifeh answered, If the city of Baghdad were not taken from me, the Palace of Diversion were not enlivened with the light of the lamps and candles, and its windows were not opened. Wo to thee! Who could do these things unless the office of Khalifeh were taken from me?—Who, said Ja'far (the muscles of his side quivering from fear), informed thee that the lamps and candles were lighted in the Palace of Diversion, and that its windows were opened? The Khalifeh replied, Advance hither to me, and look. So Ja'far approached the Khalifeh, and, looking towards the garden, beheld the palace as it were a flame of fire, its light surpassing that of the moon. He desired, therefore, to make an excuse for the sheykh Ibrahim, the superintendent, thinking, from what he beheld, that the event might have occurred through his permission: and accordingly he said, O Prince of the Faithful, the sheykh Ibrahim last week said to me, O my master Ja'far, I am desirous of entertaining my children during my life and the life of the Prince of the Faithful.—And what, said I, is thy design in saying this? He answered, It is my wish that thou wouldst obtain for me permission from the Khalifeh that I may celebrate the circumcision of my sons in the palace. So I said, Do what thou wilt with respect to the entertainment of thy sons, and, if God will, I shall have an interview with the Khalifeh, and will acquaint him with it. And he left me thus; and I forgot to acquaint thee.—O Ja'far, said the Khalifeh, thou wast guilty of one offence against me, and then thine offence became two: for thou hast erred in two points: the first, thy not acquainting me with this affair; and the second, thy not accomplishing the desire of the sheykh Ibrahim; for he did not come to thee and address thee with these words but to hint a request for some money by the aid of which to effect his design, and thou neither gavest him anything nor acquaintedst me that I might give him.—O Prince of the Faithful, replied Ja'far, I forgot.

The Khalifeh then said, By my forefathers, I will not pass the remainder of my night but with him, for he is a just man, who frequenteth the sheykhs, and attendeth to the poor, and favoureth the indigent; and I imagine all his acquaintances are with him this night: so I must repair to him: perhaps one of them may offer up for us a prayer productive of good to us in this world and the next; and probably some advantage may accrue to him from my presence, and he will receive pleasure from this, together with his friends.—O Prince of the Faithful, replied Ja'far, the greater part of the night hath passed, and they are now about to disperse. But the Khalifeh said, We must go to them. And Ja'far was silent, and was perplexed in his mind, not knowing what to do. So the Khalifeh rose upon his feet, and Ja'far rose and preceded him, and Mesrur the eunuch went with them. The three walked on reflecting, and, departing from the palace, proceeded through the streets, in the attire of merchants, until they arrived at the gate of the garden above mentioned; and the Khalifeh, approaching it, found it open; and he was surprised, and said, See, O Ja'far, how the sheykh Ibrahim hath left the gate open until this hour, which is not his usual custom. They then entered, and came to the end of the garden, where they stopped beneath the palace; and the Khalifeh said, O Ja'far, I desire to take a view of them secretly before I go up to them, that I may see how the sheykhs are occupied in the dispensing of their blessings and the employment of their miraculous powers; for they have qualities which distinguish them both in their private retirements and in their public exercises; and now we hear not their voices, nor discover any indication of their presence. Having thus said, he looked around, and, seeing a tall walnut-tree, he said, O Ja'far, I would climb this tree (for its branches are near to the windows) and look at them. And accordingly he ascended the tree, and climbed from branch to branch until he came to that which was opposite to one of the windows, and there he sat, and, looking in through this window of the palace, beheld a damsel and a young man, like two moons (extolled be the perfection of Him who created them!); and he saw the sheykh Ibrahim sitting with a cup in his hand, and saying, O mistress of beauties, drinking unaccompanied by merry sounds is not pleasant. Hast thou not heard the saying of the poet?—

Circulate it in the large cup, and in the small; and receive it from the hand of the shining moon;[4]

And drink not without merry sounds; for I have observed that horses drink to the sound of whistling.

When the Khalifeh witnessed this conduct of the sheykh Ibrahim, the vein of anger swelled between his eyes, and he descended, and said, O Ja'far, I have never seen anything of the miraculous performances of the just such as I have beheld this night: ascend, therefore, thyself also, into this tree, and look, lest the blessings of the just escape thee.—On hearing the words of the Prince of the Faithful, Ja'far was perplexed at his situation; and he climbed up into the tree, and looked, and saw Nur-ed-Din and the sheykh Ibrahim and the damsel, and the sheykh Ibrahim had the cup in his hand. As soon as he beheld this, he made sure of destruction; and he descended, and stood before the Prince of the Faithful, and the Khalifeh said, O Ja'far, praise be to God who hath made us to be of the number of those who follow the external ordinances of the holy law, and averted from us the sin of disguising ourselves by the practice of hypocrisy! But Ja'far was unable to reply, from his excessive confusion. The Khalifeh then looked towards him, and said, Who can have brought these persons hither, and admitted them into my palace? But the like of this young man and this damsel, in beauty and loveliness and symmetry of form, mine eye hath never beheld.—Ja'far, now conceiving a hope that the Khalifeh might be propitiated, replied, Thou hast spoken truly, O Prince of the Faithful. And the Khalifeh said, O Ja'far, climb up with us upon this branch which is opposite them, that we may amuse ourselves by observing them. So they both climbed up into the tree, and, looking at them, heard the sheykh Ibrahim say, O my mistress, I have re-

4 The cupbearer.

linquished decorum by the drinking of wine; but the pleasure of this is not complete without the melodious sounds of stringed instruments.—O sheykh Ibrahim, replied Enis-el-Jelis, by Allah, if we had any musical instrument, our happiness were perfect. And when the sheykh Ibrahim heard her words, he rose upon his feet.—The Khalifeh said to Ja'far, What may he be going to do? Ja'far replied, I know not.— And the sheykh Ibrahim went away, and returned with a lute; and the Khalifeh, looking attentively at it, saw that it was the lute of Ishak the cup-companion; and said, By Allah, if this damsel sing not well, I will crucify you all; but if she sing well, I will pardon them, and crucify thee. So Ja'far said, O Allah, let her not sing well!—Why? asked the Khalifeh.—That thou mayest crucify all of us, answered Ja'far; and then we shall cheer one another by conversation. And the Khalifeh laughed: and the damsel took the lute, and tuned its strings, and played upon it in a manner that would melt iron, and inspire an idiot with intellect; after which she sang with such sweetness that the Khalifeh exclaimed, O Ja'far, never in my life have I heard so enchanting a voice as this! —Perhaps, said Ja'far, the anger of the Khalifeh hath departed from him?—Yea, he answered; it hath departed. He then descended with Ja'far from the tree, and, looking towards him, said, I am desirous of going up to them, to sit with them, and to hear the damsel sing before me.—O Prince of the Faithful, replied Ja'far, if thou go up to them, probably they will be troubled by thy presence; and as to the sheykh Ibrahim, he will assuredly die of fear. The Khalifeh therefore said, O Ja'far, thou must acquaint me with some stratagem by means of which I may learn the truth of the affair without their knowing that I have discovered them. And he and Ja'far walked towards the Tigris, reflecting upon this matter; and lo, a fisherman stood beneath the windows of the palace, and he threw his net, hoping to catch something by means of which to obtain his subsistence.—Now the Khalifeh had, on a former occasion, called to the sheykh Ibrahim, and said to him, What was that noise that I heard beneath the windows of the palace?—and he answered, The voices of the fishermen, who are fishing:—so he said, Go down and forbid them from coming to this place. They were therefore forbidden to come thither; but this night there came a fisherman named Kerim, and, seeing the garden-gate open, he said within himself, This is a time of inadvertence, and perhaps I may catch some fish on this occasion:—so he took his net, and threw it into the river, and then recited some verses, contrasting the condition of the poor fisherman, toiling throughout the night, with that of the lord of the palace, who, awaking from a pleasant slumber, findeth the fawn in his possession; and as soon as he had finished his recitation, lo, the Khalifeh, unattended, stood at his head. The Khalifeh knew him, and exclaimed, O Kerim!—and the fisherman, hearing him call him by his name, turned towards him; and when he beheld the Khalifeh, the muscles of his side quivered, and he said, By Allah, O Prince of the Faithful, I did not this in mockery of the mandate; but poverty and the wants of my family impelled me to the act of which thou art witness. The Khalifeh replied, Throw thy net for my luck. And the fisherman advanced, rejoicing exceedingly, and cast the net, and, having waited until it had attained its limit and become steady at the bottom, drew it in again, and there came up in it a variety of fish that could not be numbered.

The Khalifeh was delighted at this, and said, O Kerim, strip off thy clothes:—and he did so. He was clad in a jubbeh⁵ in which were a hundred patches of coarse woollen stuff, containing vermin of the most abominable kind, and among them fleas in such numbers that he might almost have been transported by their means over the face of the earth; and he took from his head a turban which for three years he had never unwound; but when he happened to find a piece of rag he twisted it around it: and when he had taken off the jubbeh and the turban, the Khalifeh pulled off from his own person two vests of silk of Alexandria and Ba'lbekk, and a melwatah⁶ and a farajiyeh, and said to the fisherman, Take these, and put them on. The Khalifeh then put on himself the fisherman's jubbeh and turban, and, having drawn a litham⁷ over his face, said to the fisherman, Go about thy

⁵ A long outer coat with sleeves nearly reaching to the wrist.
⁶ A jubbeh or dress of costly material.
⁷ [The Bedawi muffler, made by the end of the head-kerchief.]

business;—and he kissed the feet of the Khalifeh, and
thanked him, reciting these two verses:—

Thou hast granted me favours beyond my power to acknowledge,
    and completely satisfied all my wants.
I will thank thee, therefore, as long as I live, and when I die my
    bones will thank thee in their grave.

But scarcely had he finished his verses, when the vermin over-
ran the person of the Khalifeh, and he began to seize them
with his right hand and his left from his neck, and to throw
them down; and he exclaimed, O fisherman, wo to thee!
What are these abundant vermin in this jubbeh?—O my lord,
he answered, at present they torment thee; but when a week
shall have passed over thee, thou wilt not feel them, nor think
of them. The Khalifeh laughed, and said to him, How can
I suffer this jubbeh to remain upon me? The fisherman replied, I wish to tell thee something; but I am ashamed,
through my awe of the Khalifeh.—Impart, said the Khalifeh,
what thou hast to tell me. So he said to him, It hath occurred to my mind, O Prince of the Faithful, that thou desirest to learn the art of fishing, in order that thou mayest
be master of a trade that may profit thee; and if such be
thy desire, this jubbeh is suitable to thee. And the Khalifeh
laughed at his words.

The fisherman then went his way, and the Khalifeh took
the basket of fish, and, having put upon it a little grass, went
with it to Ja'far, and stood before him; and Ja'far, thinking
that he was Kerim the fisherman, feared for him, and said,
O Kerim, what brought thee hither? Save thyself by flight;
for the Khalifeh is here this night.—And when the Khalifeh
heard the words of Ja'far, he laughed until he fell down
upon his back. So Ja'far said, Perhaps thou art our lord the
Prince of the Faithful?—Yes, O Ja'far, answered the Khalifeh, and thou art my Wezir, and I came with thee hither,
and thou knowest me not. How then should the sheykh
Ibrahim know me when he is drunk? Remain where thou art
until I return to thee.—Ja'far replied, I hear and obey:—and
the Khalifeh advanced to the door of the palace, and knocked.
The sheykh Ibrahim arose, therefore, and said, Who is at the
door? He answered, I, O sheykh Ibrahim. The sheykh said,
Who art thou?—and the Khalifeh answered, I am Kerim the

fisherman: I heard that there were guests with thee, and have therefore brought thee some fish; for it is excellent.—Now Nur-ed-Din and the damsel were both fond of fish, and when they heard the mention of it they rejoiced exceedingly, and said, O my master, open to him, and let him come in to us with the fish which he hath brought. So the sheykh Ibrahim opened the door, and the Khalifeh, in his fisherman's disguise, entered, and began by salutation; and the sheykh Ibrahim said to him, Welcome to the robber, the thief, the gambler! Come hither, and shew us the fish which thou hast brought. —He therefore shewed it to them; and lo, it was alive, and moving; and the damsel exclaimed, By Allah, O my master, this fish is excellent! I wish it were fried!—By Allah, said the sheykh Ibrahim, thou hast spoken truth. Then, addressing the Khalifeh, he said, O fisherman, I wish thou hadst brought this fish fried. Arise, and fry it for us, and bring it.—On the head be thy commands, replied the Khalifeh: I will fry it, and bring it.—Be quick, said they, in doing it.

The Khalifeh therefore arose and ran back to Ja'far, and said, O Ja'far, they want the fish fried.—O Prince of the Faithful, replied he, give it me, and I will fry it. But the Khalifeh said, By the tombs of my ancestors, none shall fry it but myself: with my own hand will I do it! He then repaired to the hut of the superintendent, and, searching there, found in it everything that he required, the frying-pan, and even the salt, and wild marjoram, and other things. So he approached the fire-place, and put on the frying-pan, and fried it nicely; and when it was done, he put it upon a banana-leaf, and, having taken from the garden some limes, he went up with the fish, and placed it before them. The young man, therefore, and the damsel and the sheykh Ibrahim advanced and ate; and when they had finished, they washed their hands, and Nur-ed-Din said, By Allah, O fisherman, thou hast done us a kindness this night. Then putting his hand into his pocket, he took forth for him three pieces of gold, of those which Senjer had presented to him when he was setting forth on his journey, and said, O fisherman, excuse me; for, by Allah, if I had known thee before the events that have lately happened to me, I would have extracted the bitterness of poverty from thy heart; but take this as accordant with my present circumstances. So saying, he threw the pieces of gold to the Khalifeh, who took them, and kissed them, and put them in his pocket. The object of the Khalifeh in doing this was only that he might hear the damsel sing: so he said to him, Thou hast treated me with benefi-cence, and abundantly recompensed me; but I beg of thy un-bounded indulgence that this damsel may sing an air, that I may hear her. Nur-ed-Din therefore said, O Enis-el-Jelis! She replied, Yes.—By my life, said he, sing to us something for the gratification of this fisherman; for he desireth to hear thee. And when she had heard what her master said, she took the lute, and tried it with her fingers, after she had twisted its pegs, and sang to it these two verses:—

The fingers of many a fawn-like damsel have played upon the lute,
    and the soul hath been ravished by the touch.
She hath made the deaf to hear her songs; and the dumb hath
    exclaimed, Thou hast excelled in thy singing!

Then she played again, in an extraordinary manner, so as to charm the minds of her hearers, and sang the following couplet:—

We are honoured by your visiting our abode, and your splendour
    hath dispelled the darkness of the moonless night:
It is therefore incumbent upon me to perfume my dwelling with
    musk and rosewater and camphor.

Upon this, the Khalifeh was affected with violent emotion, and overcome by ecstasy, so that he was no longer master of himself from excessive delight; and he began to exclaim, Allah approve thee! Allah approve thee! Allah approve thee! So Nur-ed-Din said to him, O fisherman, have the damsel and her art in striking the chords pleased thee?— Yea, by Allah! exclaimed the Khalifeh. And Nur-ed-Din immediately said, She is bestowed upon thee as a present from me, the present of a generous man who will not revoke his gift. And he rose upon his feet, and took a melwatah, and threw it upon the Khalifeh in the fisherman's disguise, ordering him to depart with the damsel. But she looked towards him, and said, O my master, wilt thou part from me without bidding me farewell? If we must be separated, pause while I take leave of thee.—And she recited the following couplet :—

If you depart from me, still your abode will be in my heart, in the
recess of my bosom.
I implore the Compassionate to grant our reunion ; and a boon such
as this, God will grant to whom He pleaseth.

And when she had finished, Nur-ed-Din thus replied to
her :—

She bade me farewell on the day of separation, saying, while she
wept from the pain that it occasioned,
What wilt thou do after my departure ?—Say this, I replied, unto
him who will survive it.

The Khalifeh, when he heard this, was distressed at the
thought of separating them, and, looking towards the young
man, he said to him, O my master, art thou in fear on account
of any crime, or art thou in debt to any one ? Nur-ed-Din
answered, By Allah, O fisherman, a wonderful event, and an
extraordinary adventure, happened to me and this damsel :
if it were engraved on the understanding, it would be a lesson
to him who would be admonished.—Wilt thou not, rejoined
the Khalifeh, relate to us thy story, and acquaint us with thy
case ? Perhaps thy doing so may be productive of relief ; for
the relief of God is near.—So Nur-ed-Din said, Wilt thou
hear our story in poetry or in prose ?—Prose, answered the
Khalifeh, is mere talk ; and verse, words put together like
pearls. And Nur-ed-Din hung down his head towards the
ground, and then related his story in a series of verses ; but
when he had finished, the Khalifeh begged him to explain his
case more fully. He therefore acquainted him with the whole
of his circumstances from beginning to end ; and when the
Khalifeh understood the affair, he said to him, Whither
wouldst thou now repair ? He answered, God's earth is wide.
The Khalifeh then said to him, I will write for thee a letter
which thou shalt convey to the Sultan Mohammad the son
of Suleyman Ez-Zeyni, and when he shall have read it, he
will do thee no injury.—Is there in the world, said Nur-ed-
Din, a fisherman who correspondeth with Kings ? Verily this
is a thing that can never be.—Thou hast spoken truly, re-

joined the Khalifeh; but I will acquaint thee with the cause. Know that I read in the same school with him, under a master, and I was his monitor; and after that, prosperity was his lot, and he became a Sultan, while God made me to be a fisherman: yet I have never sent to request anything of him, but he hath performed my wish; and if I sent to him every day to request a thousand things of him, he would do what I asked. When Nur-ed-Din, therefore, heard his words, he said to him, Write, that I may see. And he took an ink-horn and a pen, and wrote (after the phrase, In the name of God, the Compassionate, the Merciful).—To proceed.—This letter is from Harun Er-Rashid the son of El-Mahdi, to his highness Mohammad the son of Suleyman Ez-Zeyni, who hath been encompassed by my beneficence, and whom I constituted my viceroy of a portion of my dominions. I acquaint thee that the bearer of this letter is Nur-ed-Din the son of El-Fadl the son of Khakan the Wezir, and on his arrival in thy presence thou shalt divest thyself of the regal authority, and seat him in thy place; for I have appointed him to the office to which I formerly appointed thee: so disobey not my commands: and peace be on thee.—He then gave the letter to 'Ali Nur-ed-Din, who took it and kissed it and put it in his turban, and immediately set forth on his journey.

The sheykh Ibrahim now looked towards the Khalifeh in his fisherman's disguise, and said to him, O most contemptible of fishermen, thou hast brought us two fish worth twenty half-dirhems, and received three pieces of gold, and desirest to take the slave also. But when the Khalifeh heard these words, he cried out at him, and made a sign to Mesrur, who immediately discovered himself, and rushed in upon him. Ja'far, meanwhile, had sent one of the attendants of the garden to the porter of the palace to demand a suit of clothing of him for the Prince of the Faithful; and the man went, and brought the dress, and kissed the ground before the Khalifeh, who took off and gave to him that with which he was then clad, and put on this suit. The sheykh Ibrahim was sitting on a chair: the Khalifeh paused to see the result: and the sheykh was astounded, and began to bite the ends of his fingers through his confusion, saying, Am I asleep or awake? The Khalifeh then looked at him, and said, O sheykh

Ibrahim, what is this predicament in which thou art placed? And upon this, the sheykh recovered from his intoxication, and, throwing himself upon the ground, implored forgiveness: and the Khalifeh pardoned him; after which he gave orders that the damsel should be conveyed to the palace where he resided; and when she had arrived there, he appropriated to her a separate lodging, and appointed persons to wait upon her, and said to her, Know that I have sent thy master as Sultan of El-Basrah, and, if God please, I will despatch to him a dress of honour, and send thee also to him with it.

As to Nur-ed-Din, he continued his journey until he entered El-Basrah, and went up to the palace of the Sultan, when he uttered a loud cry, whereupon the Sultan desired him to approach; and when he came into the presence of the King, he kissed the ground before him, and produced the letter, and handed it to him. And as soon as the Sultan saw the superscription in the handwriting of the Prince of the Faithful, he rose upon his feet, and, having kissed it three times, said, I hear and pay obedience to God (whose name be exalted!) and to the Prince of the Faithful. He then summoned before him the four Kadis,[8] and the Emirs, and was about to divest himself of the regal office: but, lo, the Wezir El-Mo'in the son of Sawi was before him, and the Sultan gave him the letter of the Prince of the Faithful, and when he saw it, he rent it in pieces, and put it into his mouth, and chewed it, and threw it down. The Sultan, enraged, cried, Wo to thee! What hath induced thee to act thus?—He answered, This man hath had no interview with the Khalifeh nor with his Wezir; but is a young wretch, an artful devil, who, having met with a paper containing the handwriting of the Khalifeh, hath counterfeited it, and written what he desired: wherefore then shouldst thou abdicate the sovereignty, when the Khalifeh hath not sent to thee an envoy with a royal autographical mandate; for if this affair were true, he had sent with him a Chamberlain or a Wezir; but he came alone.—What then is to be done? said the Sultan. The Wezir answered, Send away this young man with me, and I will take charge of him, and despatch him in company with a Chamberlain to the city of Baghdad; and if his words be true, he will bring us a royal

8 Of the four orthodox sects.

autographical mandate and diploma of investiture; and if not true, they will send him back to us with the Chamberlain, and I will take my revenge upon my offender.

When the Sultan heard what the Wezir said, it pleased him; and the Wezir took him away, and cried out to the pages, who threw down Nur-ed-Din, and beat him until he became insensible. He then ordered to put a chain upon his feet, and called to the jailer; and when he came, he kissed the ground before him. This jailer was named Kuteyt; and the Wezir said to him, O Kuteyt, I desire that thou take this person, and cast him into one of the subterranean cells which are in thy prison, and torture him night and day. The jailer replied, I hear and obey:—and he put Nur-ed-Din into the prison, and locked the door upon him; but after having done this, he gave orders to sweep a mastabah within the door, and furnished it with a prayer-carpet and a pillow, and seated Nur-ed-Din upon it, and loosed his chain, and treated him with kindness. The Wezir every day sent to him, commanding him to beat him; and the jailer pretended that he tortured him, while, on the contrary, he treated him with benignity.

Thus he continued to do for forty days; and on the forty-first day, there came a present from the Khalifeh, and when the Sultan saw it, it pleased him, and he conferred with the Wezirs upon the subject; but one said, Perhaps this present was designed for the new Sultan. Upon this, the Wezir El-Mo'in the son of Sawi remarked, It were proper to have slain him on his arrival:—and the Sultan exclaimed, Now thou hast reminded me of him, go down and bring him, and I will strike off his head. The Wezir replied, I hear and obey:—and arose, saying, I desire to proclaim throughout the city, He who wisheth to witness the decapitation of Nur-ed-Din 'Ali the son of El-Fadl the son of Khakan, let him come to the palace:—so that all the people may come to behold it, and I may gratify my heart, and mortify my enviers. The Sultan said, Do what thou wilt. So the Wezir descended, full of joy and happiness, and went to the Wali, and ordered him to make this proclamation; and when the people heard the crier, they all grieved and wept, even the boys in the schools, and the tradesmen in their shops; and numbers of the people strove together to take for themselves places where they might behold the spectacle, while others repaired to the prison, to accompany him thence. The Wezir then went forth, attended by ten memluks, to the prison: and Kuteyt the jailer said to him, What dost thou desire, O our lord the Wezir?—Bring forth to me, said the Wezir, this young wretch. The jailer replied, He is in a most miserable state from the excessive beating that I have inflicted upon him. And he entered, and found him reciting some verses, commencing thus:—

Who is there to aid me in my affliction? For my pain hath become intense, and my remedy is scarce procurable!

And the jailer pulled off from him his clean clothes, and, having clad him in two dirty garments, brought him out to the Wezir. Nur-ed-Din then looked at him, and saw that he was his enemy who had incessantly desired his destruction; and when he beheld him, he wept, and said to him, Art thou secure from misfortune? Hast thou not heard the saying of the poet?—

They made use of their power, and used it tyrannically; and soon it became as though it never had existed.

O Wezir, know that God (whose perfection be extolled, and whose name be exalted!) is the doer of whatsoever He willeth.—O 'Ali, replied the Wezir, wouldst thou frighten me by these words? I am now going to strike off thy head, in spite of the people of El-Basrah; and I will pay no regard to thy counsel; but I will rather attend to the saying of the poet:—

Let fortune do whatever it willeth, and bear with cheerful mind the effects of fate.

How excellent also is the saying of another poet:—

He who liveth after his enemy a single day, hath attained his desire.

The Wezir then ordered his pages to convey him on the back of a mule; whereupon they said to him (being distressed to obey), Suffer us to stone him and cut him in pieces, though our lives should be sacrificed in consequence. But he replied, Never do it. Have ye not heard what the poet hath said:—

A decreed term is my inevitable lot; and as soon as its days have
    expired, I die.
If the lions dragged me into their forest, they could not close it
    while aught of it remained.

So they proceeded to proclaim before Nur-ed-Din, This is the smallest recompense of him who forgeth a letter from the Khalifeh to the Sultan. And they continued to parade him throughout El-Basrah until they stationed him beneath the window of the palace, and in the place of blood, when the executioner approached him, and said to him, I am a slave under command; and if thou hast any want, acquaint me with it, that I may perform it for thee; for there remaineth not of thy life any more than the period until the Sultan shall put forth his face from the window. And upon this, Nur-ed-Din looked to the right and left, and recited these verses:—

Is there among you a merciful friend, who will aid me? I conjure
    you by Allah to answer me!
My life hath passed, and my death is at hand! Is there any who
    will pity me, to obtain my recompense,
And consider my state, and relieve my anguish, by a draught of
    water that my torment may be lightened?

And the people were excited to tears for him; and the executioner took some water to hand it to him; but the Wezir arose from his place, and struck the kulleh[9] of water with his hand, and broke it, and called to the executioner, commanding him to strike off his head; whereupon he bound Nur-ed-Din's eyes. The people, however, called out against the Wezir, and raised a tumultuous cry against him, and many words passed between them; and while they were in this state, lo, a dust rose, and filled the sky and the open tracts; and when the Sultan beheld it, as he sat in the palace, he said to his attendants, See what is the news. The Wezir said, After thou shalt first have beheaded this man. But the Sultan replied, Wait thou until we see what is the news.

   Now this dust was the dust of Ja'far, the Wezir of the

---

[9] A small porous earthen bottle with a wide mouth.

Khalifeh, and of his attendants; and the cause of their coming was this:—The Khalifeh had passed thirty days without remembering the affair of 'Ali the son of El-Fadl the son of Khakan, and no one mentioned it to him, until he came one night to the private apartment of Enis-el-Jelis, and heard her lamenting, as she recited, with a soft voice, the saying of the poet:—

Thine image [is before me] whether distant or near, and my tongue never ceaseth to mention thee.

Her lamentation increased, and lo, the Khalifeh opened the door, and entered the chamber, and saw Enis-el-Jelis weeping. On beholding the Khalifeh, she fell at his feet, and, having kissed them three times, recited these two verses:—

O thou of pure origin, and of excellent birth; of ripe-fruitful branch, and of unsullied race!
I remind thee of the promise thy beneficence granted, and far be it from thee that thou shouldst forget it.

The Khalifeh said to her, Who art thou? She answered, I am the present given to thee by 'Ali the son of El-Fadl the son of Khakan; and I request the fulfilment of the promise which thou gavest me, that thou wouldst send me to him with the honorary gift; for I have now been here thirty days and have not tasted sleep. And upon this, the Khalifeh summoned Ja'far El-Barmeki, and said to him, For thirty days I have heard no news of 'Ali the son of El-Fadl the son of Khakan, and I imagine nothing less than that the Sultan hath killed him: but, by my head! by the tombs of my ancestors! if any evil event have happened to him, I will destroy him who hath been the cause of it, though he be the dearest of men in my estimation! I desire, therefore, that thou journey immediately to El-Basrah, and bring me an account of the conduct of the King Mohammad the son of Suleyman Ez-Zeyni to 'Ali the son of El-Fadl the son of Khakan.

So Ja'far obeyed his commands, and set forth on his journey, and when he approached, and saw this tumult and crowd, he said, What is the occasion of this crowd? They related to him, therefore, the situation in which they were with regard to Nur-ed-Din; and when he heard their words, he hastened to go up to the Sultan, and, having saluted him, acquainted him with the cause of his coming, and told him, that if any evil event had happened to 'Ali Nur-ed-Din, the Khalifeh would destroy him who was the cause of it. He then arrested the Sultan, and the Wezir El-Mo'in the son of Sawi, and gave orders to liberate 'Ali Nur-ed-Din, and enthroned him as Sultan in the place of the Sultan Moham-mad the son of Suleyman Ez-Zeyni; after which he remained in El-Basrah three days, the usual period of entertainment; and on the morning of the fourth day, 'Ali Nur-ed-Din said to Ja'far, I have a longing desire to see the Prince of the Faithful. So Ja'far said to the King Mohammad the son of Suleyman, Prepare thyself for travelling; for we will perform the morning-prayers, and depart to Baghdad. He replied, I hear and obey:—and they performed the morning-prayers, and mounted all together, with the Wezir El-Mo'in the son of Sawi, who now repented of what he had done. As to 'Ali Nur-ed-Din, he rode by the side of Ja'far: and they continued their journey until they arrived at Baghdad, the Abode of Peace.

They then presented themselves before the Khalifeh and related to him the case of Nur-ed-Din; whereupon the Kha-lifeh addressed him, saying, Take this sword, and strike off with it the head of thine enemy. And he took it, and ap-proached El-Mo'in the son of Sawi; but he looked at him, and said to him, I did according to my nature, and do thou according to thine. And Nur-ed-Din threw down the sword from his hand, and, looking towards the Khalifeh, said, O Prince of the Faithful, he hath beguiled me. So the Khalifeh said, Do thou leave him:—and he said to Mesrur, O Mesrur, advance thou, and strike off his head. Mesrur, therefore, did so: and upon this, the Khalifeh said to 'Ali the son of El-Fadl the son of Khakan, Request of me what thou wilt. He replied, O my lord, I have no want of the sovereignty of El-Basrah, and desire nothing but to have the honour of serving thee.—Most willingly I assent, said the Khalifeh:— and he summoned the damsel, and when she had come before him, he bestowed favours upon them both: he gave to them one of the palaces of Baghdad, and assigned to them regular allowances, and made Nur-ed-Din one of his companions at the table; and he remained with him until death overtook him.

THE STORY OF ES-SINDIBAD OF THE SEA AND ES-SINDIBAD OF THE LAND

THERE was, in the time of Khalifeh, the Prince of the Faithful, Harun Er-Rashid, in the city of Baghdad, a man called Es-Sindibad the Porter. He was a man in poor circumstances, who bore burdens for hire upon his head. And it happened to him that he bore one day a heavy burden, and that day was excessively hot; so he was wearied by the load, and perspired profusely, the heat violently oppressing him. In this state he passed by the door of a merchant, the ground before which was swept and sprinkled, and there the air was temperate; and by the side of the door was a wide mastabah. The porter therefore put down his burden upon that mastabah, to rest himself, and to scent the air; and when he had done so, there came forth upon him, from the door, a pleasant, gentle gale, and an exquisite odour, wherewith the porter was delighted. He seated himself upon the edge of the mastabah, and heard in that place the melodious sounds of stringed instruments, with the lute among them, and mirth-exciting voices, and varieties of distinct recitations. He heard also the voices of birds, warbling, and praising God (whose name be exalted!) with diverse tones and with all dialects; consisting of turtle-doves and hezars and blackbirds and nightingales and ring-doves and kirawans;[1] whereupon he wondered in his mind, and was moved with great delight. He then advanced to that door, and found within the house a great garden, wherein he beheld pages and slaves and servants and other dependants, and such things as existed not elsewhere save in the abodes of Kings and Sultans; and after that, there blew upon him the odour of delicious, exquisite viands, of all different kinds, and of delicious wine.

[1] Or karawan: stone-curlew.

Upon this he raised his eyes towards heaven, and said,
Extolled be thy perfection, O Lord! O Creator! O Supplier
of the conveniences of life! Thou suppliest whom Thou
wilt without reckoning! O Allah, I implore thy forgiveness
of all offences, and turn to Thee repenting of all faults! O
Lord, there is no animadverting upon Thee with respect to
thy judgment, and thy power; for Thou art not to be questioned regarding that which Thou doest, and Thou art able
to do whatsoever Thou wilt! Extolled be thy perfection!
Thou enrichest whom Thou wilt, and whom Thou wilt Thou
impoverishest! Thou magnifiest whom Thou wilt, and whom
Thou wilt Thou abasest! There is no deity but Thou!
How great is thy dignity! and how mighty is thy dominion! and how excellent is thy government! Thou hast bestowed favours upon him whom Thou choosest among thy
servants, and the owner of this place is in the utmost
affluence, delighting himself with pleasant odours and
delicious meats and exquisite beverages of all descriptions.
And Thou hast appointed unto thy creatures what Thou
wilt, and what Thou hast predestined for them; so that
among them one is weary, and another is at ease; and
one of them is prosperous, and another is like me, in the
extreme of fatigue and abjection!—And he recited thus:—

How many wretched persons are destitute of ease! and how many
    are in luxury, reposing in the shade!
I find myself afflicted by trouble beyond measure; and strange is
    my condition, and heavy is my load!
Others are in prosperity, and from wretchedness are free, and never
    for a single day have borne a load like mine;
Incessantly and amply blest, throughout the course of life, with
    happiness and grandeur, as well as drink and meat.
All men whom God hath made are in origin alike; and I resemble
    this man, and he resembleth me;
But otherwise, between us is a difference as great as the difference
    that we find between wine and vinegar.
Yet in saying this, I utter no falsehood against Thee, [O my Lord;]
    art wise, and with justice Thou hast judged.

And when Es-Sindibad the Porter had finished the recitation of his verses, he desired to take up his burden and
to depart. But, lo, there came forth to him from that
door a young page, handsome in countenance, comely in

stature, magnificent in apparel; and he laid hold upon the porter's hand, saying to him, Enter: answer the summons of my master; for he calleth for thee. And the porter would have refused to enter with the page; but he could not. He therefore deposited his burden with the door-keeper in the entrance-passage, and, entering the house with the page, he found it to be a handsome mansion, presenting an appearance of joy and majesty. And he looked towards a grand chamber, in which he beheld noblemen and great lords; and in it were all kinds of flowers, and all kinds of sweet scents, and varieties of dried and fresh fruits, together with abundance of various kinds of exquisite viands, and beverage prepared from the fruit of the choicest grape-vines. In it were also instruments of music and mirth, and varieties of beautiful slave-girls, all ranged in proper order. And at the upper end of that chamber was a great and venerable man, in the sides of whose beard grey hairs had begun to appear. He was of handsome form, comely in countenance, with an aspect of gravity and dignity and majesty and state-liness. So, upon this, Es-Sindibad the Porter was con-founded, and he said within himself, By Allah, this place is a portion of Paradise, or it is the palace of a King or Sultan! Then, putting himself in a respectful posture, he saluted the assembly, prayed for them, and kissed the ground before them; after which he stood, hanging down his head in humility. But the master of the house gave him permission to seat himself. He therefore sat. And the master of the house had caused him to draw near unto him, and now began to cheer him with conversation, and to welcome him; and he put before him some of the various excellent, delicious, exquisite viands. So Es-Sindibad the Porter ad-vanced, and, having said, In the name of God, the Com-passionate, the Merciful,—ate until he was satisfied and satiated, when he said, Praise be to God in every case!—and washed his hands, and thanked them for this.

The master of the house then said, Thou art welcome, and thy day is blessed. What is thy name, and what trade dost thou follow?—O my master, he answered, my name is Es-Sindibad the Porter, and I bear upon my head men's merchandise for hire. And at this, the master of the house smiled, and he said to him, Know, O porter, that thy name is like mine; for I am Es-Sindibad of the Sea: but, O porter, I desire that thou let me hear the verses that thou wast reciting when thou wast at the door. The porter therefore was ashamed, and said to him, I conjure thee by Allah that thou be not angry with me; for fatigue and trouble, and paucity of what the hand possesseth, teach a man ill manners, and impertinence. His host, however, replied, Be not ashamed; for thou hast become my brother; recite then the verses, since they pleased me when I heard them from thee as thou recitedst them at the door. So upon this the porter recited to him those verses, and they pleased him, and he was moved with delight on hearing them. He then said to him, O porter, know that my story is wonderful, and I will inform thee of all that happened to me and befell me before I attained this prosperity and sat in this place wherein thou seest me. For I attained not this prosperity and this place save after severe fatigue and great trouble and many terrors. How often have I endured fatigue and toil in my early years! I have performed seven voyages, and connected with each voyage is a wonderful tale, that would confound the mind. All that which I endured happened by fate and destiny, and from that which is written there is no escape nor flight.

The First Voyage of Es-Sindibad of the Sea

Know, O masters, O noble persons, that I had a father; a merchant, who was one of the first in rank among the people and the merchants, and who possessed abundant wealth and ample fortune. He died when I was a young child, leaving to me wealth and buildings and fields; and when I grew up, I put my hand upon the whole of the property, ate well and drank well, associated with the young men, wore handsome apparel, and passed my life with my friends and companions, feeling confident that this course would continue and profit me; and I ceased not to live in this manner for a length of time. I then returned to my reason, and recovered from my heedlessness, and found that my wealth had passed away, and my condition had changed, and all [the money] that I had possessed had gone. I recovered not to see my situation but in a state of fear and confusion of mind, and remembered a tale that I had heard before, the tale of our lord Suleyman the son of Da'ud (on both of whom be peace!), respecting his saying, Three things are better than three: the day of death is better than the day of birth; and a living dog is better than a dead lion; and the grave is better than the palace.[2] Then I arose, and collected what I had, of effects and apparel, and sold them; after which I sold my buildings and all that my hand possessed, and amassed three thousand pieces of silver; and it occurred to my mind to travel to the countries of other people; and I remembered one of the sayings of the poets, which was this:—

In proportion to one's labour, eminences are gained; and he who
    seeketh eminence passeth sleepless nights.
He diveth in the sea who seeketh for pearls, and succeedeth in
    acquiring lordship and good fortune.
Whoso seeketh eminence without labouring for it loseth his life
    in the search of vanity.

Upon this, I resolved, and arose, and bought for myself goods and commodities and merchandise, with such other things as were required for travel; and my mind had consented to my performing a sea-voyage. So I embarked in a ship, and it descended to the city of El-Basrah, with a company of merchants; and we traversed the sea for many days and nights. We had passed by island after island, and from sea to sea, and from land to land, and in every place by which we passed we sold and bought, and exchanged merchandise. We continued our voyage until we arrived at an island like one of the gardens of Paradise, and at that island the master of the ship brought her to anchor with us. He cast the anchor, and put forth the landing-plank, and all who were in the ship landed upon that island. They had prepared for themselves fire-pots, and they lighted the fires in them; and their occupations were various: some cooked; others washed; and others amused themselves. I was

[2] Eccles., vii. 1; ix. 4.

among those who were amusing themselves upon the shores
of the island, and the passengers were assembled to eat and
drink and play and sport. But while we were thus engaged,
lo, the master of the ship, standing upon its side, called out
with his loudest voice, O ye passengers, whom may God
preserve! come up quickly in to the ship, hasten to embark,
and leave your merchandise, and flee with your lives, and
save yourselves from destruction; for this apparent island,
upon which ye are, is not really an island, but it is a great
fish that hath become stationary in the midst of the sea, and
the sand hath accumulated upon it, so that it hath become
like an island, and trees have grown upon it since times of
old; and when ye lighted the fire upon it, the fish felt the heat,
and put itself in motion, and now it will descend with you
into the sea, and ye will all be drowned: then seek for yourselves escape before destruction, and leave the merchandise.
—The passengers, therefore, hearing the words of the
master of the ship, hastened to go up into the vessel, leaving
the merchandise, and their other goods, and their copper
cooking-pots, and their fire-pots; and some reached the
ship, and others reached it not. The island had moved,
and descended to the bottom of the sea, with all that were
upon it, and the roaring sea, agitated with waves, closed
over it.

I was among the number of those who remained behind
upon the island; so I sank in the sea with the rest who
sank. But God (whose name be exalted!) delivered me
and saved me from drowning and supplied me with a great
wooden bowl, of the bowls in which the passengers had
been washing, and I laid hold upon it and got into it, induced by the sweetness of life, and beat the water with my
feet as with oars, while the waves sported with me, tossing
me to the right and left. The master of the vessel had
caused her sails to be spread, and pursued his voyage with
those who had embarked, not regarding such as had been
submerged; and I ceased not to look at that vessel until it
was concealed from my eye. I made sure of destruction,
and night came upon me while I was in this state; but
I remained so a day and a night, and the wind and the
waves aided me until the bowl came to a stoppage with me

under a high island, whereon were trees overhanging the sea. So I laid hold upon a branch of a lofty tree, and clung to it, after I had been at the point of destruction; and I kept hold upon it until I landed on the island, when I found my legs benumbed, and saw marks of the nibbling of fish upon their hams, of which I had been insensible by reason of the violence of the anguish and fatigue that I was suffering.

I threw myself upon the island like one dead, and was unconscious of my existence, and drowned in my stupefaction; and I ceased not to remain in this condition until the next day. The sun having then risen upon me, I awoke upon the island, and found that my feet were swollen, and that I had become reduced to the state in which I then was. Awhile I dragged myself along in a sitting posture, and then I crawled upon my knees. And there were in the island fruits in abundance, and springs of sweet water: therefore I ate of those fruits; and I ceased not to continue in this state for many days and nights. My spirit had then revived, my soul had returned to me, and my power of motion was renewed; and I began to meditate, and to walk along the shore of the island, amusing myself among the trees with the sight of the things that God (whose name be exalted!) had created; and I had made for myself a staff from those trees, to lean upon it. Thus I remained until I walked, one day, upon the shore of the island, and there appeared unto me an indistinct object in the distance. I imagined that it was a wild beast, or one of the beasts of the sea; and I walked towards it, ceasing not to gaze at it; and, lo, it was a mare, of superb appearance, tethered in a part of the island by the sea-shore. I approached her; but she cried out against me with a great cry, and I trembled with fear of her, and was about to return, when, behold, a man came forth from beneath the earth, and he called to me and pursued me, saying to me, Who art thou, and whence hast thou come, and what is the cause of thine arrival in this place? So I answered him, O my master, know that I am a stranger, and I was in a ship, and was submerged in the sea with certain others of the passengers; but God supplied me with a wooden bowl, and I got into it, and it bore me along until the waves cast me upon this island. And when he heard my words, he laid hold of my hand and said to me, Come with me. I therefore went with him, and he descended with me into a grotto beneath the earth, and conducted me into a large subterranean chamber, and, having seated me at the upper end of that chamber, brought me some food. I was hungry; so I ate until I was satiated and contented, and my soul became at ease. Then he asked me respecting my case, and what had happened to me; wherefore I acquainted him with my whole affair from beginning to end; and he wondered at my story.

And when I had finished my tale, I said, I conjure thee by Allah, O my master, that thou be not displeased with me: I have acquainted thee with the truth of my case and of what hath happened to me, and I desire of thee that thou inform me who thou art, and what is the cause of thy dwelling in this chamber that is beneath the earth, and what is the reason of thy tethering this mare by the sea-side. So he replied, Know that we are a party dispersed in this island, upon its shores, and we are the grooms of the King El-Mihraj, having under our care all his horses; and every month, when moonlight commenceth, we bring the swift mares, and tether them in this island, every mare that has not foaled, and conceal ourselves in this chamber beneath the earth, that they may attract the sea-horses. This is the time of the coming forth of the sea-horse; and afterwards, if it be the will of God (whose name be exalted!), I will take thee with me to the King El-Mihraj, and divert thee with the sight of our country. Know, moreover, that if thou hadst not met with us, thou hadst not seen any one in this place, and wouldst have died in misery, none knowing of thee. But I will be the means of the preservation of thy life, and of thy return to thy country.—I therefore prayed for him, and thanked him for his kindness and beneficence; and while we were thus talking, the horse came forth from the sea, as he had said. And shortly after, his companions came each leading a mare; and, seeing me with him, they inquired of me my story, and I told them what I had related to him. They then drew near to me, and spread the table, and ate, and invited me: so I ate with them; after which, they arose, and mounted the horses, taking me with them, having mounted me on a mare.

We commenced our journey, and proceeded without ceasing until we arrived at the city of the King El-Mihraj, and they went in to him and acquainted him with my story. He therefore desired my presence, and they took me in to him, and stationed me before him; whereupon I saluted him, and he returned my salutation, and welcomed me, greeting me in an honourable manner, and inquired of me respecting my case. So I informed him of all that had happened to me, and of all that I had seen, from beginning to end; and he wondered at that which had befallen me and happened to me, and said to me, O my son, by Allah thou hast experienced an extraordinary preservation, and had it not been for the predestined length of thy life, thou hadst not escaped from these difficulties; but praise be to God for thy safety! Then he treated me with beneficence and honour, caused me to draw near to him, and began to cheer me with conversation and courtesy; and he made me his superintendent of the sea-port, and registrar of every vessel that came to the coast. I stood in his presence to transact his affairs, and he favoured me and benefited me in every respect; he invested me with a handsome and costly dress, and I became a person high in credit with him in intercessions, and in accomplishing the affairs of the people. I ceased not to remain in his service for a long time; and whenever I went to the shore of the sea, I used to inquire of the merchants and travellers and sailors respecting the direction of the city of Baghdad, that perchance some one might inform me of it, and I might go with him thither and return to my country; but none knew it, nor knew any one who went to it. At this I was perplexed, and I was weary of the length of my absence from home; and in this state I continued for a length of time, until I went in one day to the King El-Mihraj, and found with him a party of Indians. I saluted them, and they returned my salutation, and welcomed me, and asked me respecting my country; after which, I questioned them as to their country, and they told me that they consisted of various races. Among them are the Shakiriyeh, who are the most noble of their races, who oppress no one, nor offer violence to any. And among them are a class called the Brahmans, a people who never drink wine; but they are persons of pleasure and joy and sport and merriment, and possessed of camels and horses and cattle. They informed me also that the Indians are divided into seventy-two classes; and I wondered at this extremely. And I saw, in the dominions of the King El-Mihraj, an island, among others, which is called Kasil, in which is heard the beating of tambourines and drums throughout the night, and the islanders and travellers informed us that Ed-Dejjal[8] is in it. I saw too, in the sea in which is that island, a fish two hundred cubits long, and the fishermen fear it; wherefore they knock some pieces of wood, and it fleeth from them; and I saw a fish whose face was like that of the owl. I likewise saw during that voyage many wonderful and strange things, such that, if I related them to you, the description would be too long.

I continued to amuse myself with the sight of those islands and the things that they contained, until I stood one day upon the shore of the sea, with a staff in my hand, as was my custom, and lo, a great vessel approached, wherein were many merchants; and when it arrived at the harbour of the city and its place of anchoring, the master furled its sails, brought it to an anchor by the shore, and put forth the landing-plank; and the sailors brought out every thing that was in that vessel to the shore. They were slow in taking forth the goods, while I stood writing their account, and I said to the master of the ship, Doth aught remain in thy vessel? He answered, Yes, O my master; I have some goods in the hold of the ship; but their owner was drowned in the sea at one of the islands during our voyage hither, and his goods are in our charge; so we desire to sell them, and to take a note of their price, in order to convey it to his family in the city of Baghdad, the Abode of Peace. I therefore said to the master, What was the name of that man, the owner of the goods? He answered, His name was Es-Sindibad of the Sea, and he was drowned on his voyage with us in the sea. And when I heard his words, I looked at him with a scrutinizing eye, and recognized him; and I

[8] Antichrist of the Muslims.

cried out at him with a great cry, and said, O master, know that I am the owner of the goods which thou hast mentioned, and I am Es-Sindibad of the Sea, who descended upon the island from the ship, with the other merchants who descended; and when the fish that we were upon moved, and thou calledst out to us, some got into the vessel, and the rest sank, and I was among those who sank. But God (whose name be exalted!) preserved me and saved me from drowning by means of a large wooden bowl, of those in which passengers were washing, and I got into it, and began to beat the water with my feet, and the wind and the waves aided me until I arrived at this island, when I landed on it, and God (whose name be exalted!) assisted me, and I met the grooms of the King El-Mihraj, who took me with them and brought me to this city. They then led me into the King El-Mihraj, and I acquainted him with my story; whereupon he bestowed benefits upon me, and appointed me clerk of the harbour of this city, and I obtained profit in his service, and favour with him. Therefore these goods that thou hast are my goods and my portion.

But the master said, There is no strength nor power but in God, the High, the Great! There is no longer faith nor conscience in any one!—Wherefore, O master, said I, when thou hast heard me tell thee my story? He answered, Because thou heardest me say that I had goods whose owner was drowned: therefore thou desirest to take them without price; and this is unlawful to thee; for we saw him when he sank, and there were with him many of the passengers, not one of whom escaped. How then dost thou pretend that thou art the owner of the goods?—So I said to him, O master, hear my story, and understand my words, and my veracity will become manifest to thee; for falsehood is a characteristic of the hypocrites. Then I related to him all that I had done from the time that I went forth with him from the city of Baghdad until we arrived at that island upon which we were submerged in the sea, and I mentioned to him some circumstances that had occurred between me and him. Upon this, therefore, the master and the merchants were convinced of my veracity, and recognized me; and they congratulated me on my safety, all of them saying, By

Allah, we believed not that thou hadst escaped drowning; but God hath granted thee a new life. They then gave me the goods, and I found my name written upon them, and nought of them was missing. So I opened them, and took forth from them something precious and costly; the sailors of the ship carried it with me, and I went up with it to the King to offer it as a present, and inform him that this ship was the one in which I was a passenger. I told him also that my goods had arrived all entire, and that this present was a part of them. And the King wondered at this affair extremely; my veracity in all that I had said became manifest to him, and he loved me greatly, and treated me with exceeding honour, giving me a large present in return for mine.

Then I sold my bales, as well as the other goods that I had, and gained upon them abundantly; and I purchased other goods and merchandise and commodities of that city. And when the merchants of the ship desired to set forth on their voyage, I stowed all that I had in the vessel, and, going in to the King, thanked him for his beneficence and kindness; after which I begged him to grant me permission to depart on my voyage to my country and my family. So he bade me farewell, and gave me an abundance of things at my departure, of the commodities of that city; and when I had taken leave of him, I embarked in the ship, and we set sail by the permission of God, whose name be exalted! Fortune served us, and destiny aided us, and we ceased not to prosecute our voyage night and day until we arrived in safety at the city of El-Basrah. There we landed, and remained a short time; and I rejoiced at my safety, and my return to my country; and after that, I repaired to the city of Baghdad, the Abode of Peace, with abundance of bales and goods and merchandise of great value. Then I went to my quarter, and entered my house, and all my family and companions came to me. I procured for myself servants and other dependants, and memluks and concubines and male black slaves, so that I had a large establishment; and I purchased houses and other immovable possessions, more than I had at first. I enjoyed the society of my companions and friends, exceeding my former habits, and forgot all that

I had suffered from fatigue, and absence from my native country, and difficulty, and the terrors of travel. I occupied myself with delights and pleasures, and delicious meats and exquisite drinks, and continued in this state. Such were the events of the first cf my voyages; and to-morrow, if it be the will of God (whose name be exalted!), I will relate to you the tale of the second of the seven voyages.

Es-Sindibad of the Sea then made Es-Sindibad of the Land to sup with him; after which he gave orders to present him with a hundred pieces of gold, and said to him, Thou hast cheered us by thy company this day. So the porter thanked him, and took from him what he had given him, and went his way, meditating upon the events that befell and happened to mankind, and wondering extremely. He slept that night in his abode; and when the morning came, he repaired to the house of Es-Sindibad of the Sea, and went in to him; and he welcomed him, and treated him with honour, seating him by him. And after the rest of his companions had come, the food and drink were set before them, and the time was pleasant to them, and they were merry. Then Es-Sindibad of the Sea began his narrative thus:—[4]

The Second Voyage of Es-Sindibad of the Sea

KNOW, O my brothers, that I was enjoying a most comfortable life, and the most pure happiness, as ye were told yesterday, until it occurred to my mind, one day, to travel again to the lands of other people, and I felt a longing for the occupation of traffic, and the pleasure of seeing the countries and islands of the world, and gaining my subsistence. I resolved upon that affair, and, having taken forth from my money a large sum, I purchased with it goods and merchandise suitable for travel, and packed them up. Then I went to the bank of the river, and found a handsome, new vessel, with sails of comely canvas, and it had a numerous crew, and was superfluously equipped. So I

[4] [A paragraph similar to the preceding occurs at the end of the narrative of each of Es-Sindibad's voyages, but, as in the case of Shahrazad's repetitions each night, it is not here repeated.]

embarked my bales in it, as did also a party of merchants besides, and we set sail that day. The voyage was pleasant to us, and we ceased not to pass from sea to sea, and from island to island; and at every place where we cast anchor, we met the merchants and the grandees, and the sellers and buyers, and we sold and bought, and exchanged goods. Thus we continued to do until destiny conveyed us to a beautiful island, abounding with trees bearing ripe fruits, where flowers diffused their fragrance, with birds warbling, and pure rivers: but there was not in it an inhabitant, nor a blower of a fire. The master anchored our vessel at that island and the merchants with the other passengers landed there, to amuse themselves with the sight of its trees, and to extol the perfection of God, the One, the Omnipotent, and to wonder at the power of the Almighty King. I also landed upon the island with the rest, and sat by a spring of pure water among the trees. I had with me some food, and I sat in that place eating what God (whose name be exalted!) had allotted me. The zephyr was sweet to us in that place, and the time was pleasant to me; so slumber overcame me, and I reposed there, and became immersed in sleep, enjoying that sweet zephyr, and the fragrant gales. I then arose, and found not in the place a human being nor a Jinni. The vessel had gone with the passengers, and not one of them remembered me, neither any of the merchants nor any of the sailors: so they left me in the island.

I looked about it to the right and left, and found not in it any one save myself. I was therefore affected with violent vexation, not to be exceeded, and my gall-bladder almost burst by reason of the severity of my grief and mourning and fatigue. I had not with me aught of worldly goods, neither food nor drink, and I had become desolate, weary in my soul, and despairing of life; and I said, Not every time doth the jar escape unbroken; and if I escaped the first time, and found him who took me with him from the shore of the island to the inhabited part, far, far from me this time is the prospect of my finding him who will convey me to inhabited lands! Then I began to weep and wail for myself until vexation overpowered me; and I

blamed myself for that which I had done, and for my
having undertaken this voyage and fatigue after I had been
reposing at ease in my abode and my country, in ample
happiness, and enjoying good food and good drink and
good apparel, and had not been in want of any thing, either
of money or goods or merchandise. I repented of my
having gone forth from the city of Baghdad, and set out on
a voyage over the sea, after the fatigue that I had suffered
during my first voyage, and I felt at the point of destruction,
and said, Verily to God we belong, and verily unto Him we
return! And I was in the predicament of the mad. After
that, I rose and stood up, and walked about the island to
the right and left, unable to sit in one place. Then I
climbed up a lofty tree; and began to look from it to the
right and left; but saw nought save sky and water, and
trees and birds, and islands and sands. Looking, however,
with a scrutinizing eye, there appeared to me on the island
a white object, indistinctly seen in the distance, of enormous
size: so I descended from the tree, and went towards it,
and proceeded in that direction without stopping until I
arrived at it; and, lo, it was a huge white dome, of great
height and large circumference. I drew near to it, and
walked round it; but perceived no door to it; and I found
that I had not strength nor activity to climb it, on account
of its exceeding smoothness. I made a mark at the place
where I stood, and went round the dome measuring its
circumference; and, lo, it was fifty full paces; and I meditated upon some means of gaining an entrance into it.

The close of the day, and the setting of the sun, had
now drawn near; and, behold, the sun was hidden, and
the sky became dark, and the sun was veiled from me.
I therefore imagined that a cloud had come over it; but
this was in the season of summer: so I wondered; and I
raised my head, and, contemplating that object attentively,
I saw that it was a bird, of enormous size, bulky body, and
wide wings, flying in the air; and this it was that concealed the body of the sun, and veiled it from view upon the
island. At this my wonder increased, and I remembered
a story which travellers and voyagers had told me long
before, that there is, in certain of the islands, a bird of

enormous size, called the rukh, that feedeth its young ones with elephants. I was convinced, therefore, that the dome which I had seen was one of the eggs of the rukh. I wondered at the works of God (whose name be exalted!); and while I was in this state, lo, that bird alighted upon the dome, and brooded over it with its wings, stretching out its legs behind upon the ground; and it slept over it. —Extolled be the perfection of Him who sleepeth not!— Thereupon I arose, and unwound my turban from my head, and folded it and twisted it so that it became like a rope; and I girded myself with it, binding it tightly round my waist, and tied myself by it to one of the feet of that bird, and made the knot fast, saying within myself, Perhaps this bird will convey me to a land of cities and inhabitants, and that will be better than my remaining in this island. I passed the night sleepless, fearing that if I slept, the bird would fly away with me when I was not aware; and when the dawn came, and morn appeared, the bird rose from its egg, and uttered a great cry, and drew me up into the sky. It ascended and soared up so high that I imagined it had reached the highest region of the sky, and after that, it descended with me gradually until it alighted with me upon the earth, and rested upon a lofty spot. So when I reached the earth, I hastily untied the bond from its foot, fearing it, though it knew not of me nor was sensible of me; and after I had loosed my turban from it, and disengaged it from its foot, shaking as I did so, I walked away. Then it took something from the face of the earth in its talons, and soared to the upper region of the sky; and I looked attentively at that thing, and, lo, it was a serpent, of enormous size, of great body, which it had taken and carried off towards the sea; and I wondered at that event.

After this I walked about that place, and found myself upon an eminence, beneath which was a large, wide, deep valley; and by its side, a great mountain, very high; no one could see its summit by reason of its excessive height, and no one had power to ascend it. I therefore blamed myself for that which I had done, and said, Would that I had remained in the island, since it is better than this desert place; for in the island are found, among various fruits, what I might have eaten, and I might have drunk of its rivers; but in this place are neither trees nor fruits nor rivers: and there is no strength nor power but in God, the High, the Great! Verily every time that I escape from a calamity, I fall into another that is greater and more severe! —Then I arose, and emboldened myself, and walked in that valley; and I beheld its ground to be composed of diamonds, with which they perforate minerals and jewels, and with which also they perforate porcelain and the onyx; and it is a stone so hard that neither iron nor rock have any effect upon it, nor can any one cut off aught from it, or break it, unless by means of the lead-stone. All that valley was likewise occupied by serpents and venomous snakes, every one of them like a palm-tree; and by reason of its enormous size, if an elephant came to it, it would swallow it. Those serpents appeared in the night, and hid themselves in the day, fearing lest the rukh and the vulture should carry them off, and after that tear them in pieces; and the cause of that I know not. I remained in that valley, repenting of what I had done, and said within myself, By Allah, I have hastened my own destruction! The day departed from me, and I began to walk along that valley, looking for a place in which to pass the night, fearing those serpents, and forgetting my food and drink and subsistence, occupied only by care for my life. And there appeared to me a cave near by; so I walked thither, and I found its entrance narrow. I therefore entered it and, seeing a large stone by its mouth, I pushed it, and stopped with it the mouth of the cave while I was within it; and I said within myself, I am safe now that I have entered this place; and when daylight shineth upon me, I will go forth, and see what destiny will do. Then I looked within the cave, and beheld a huge serpent sleeping at the upper end of it over its eggs. At this my flesh quaked, and I raised my head, and committed my case to fate and destiny; and I passed all the night sleepless, until the dawn rose and shone, when I removed the stone with which I had closed the entrance of the cave, and went forth from it, like one intoxicated, giddy from excessive sleeplessness and hunger and fear.

I then walked along the valley; and while I was thus
occupied, lo, a great slaughtered animal fell before me, and
I found no one. So I wondered thereat extremely; and I
remembered a story that I heard long before from certain of the merchants and travellers, and persons in the habit
of journeying about,—that in the mountains of the diamonds
are experienced great terrors, and that no one can gain
access to the diamonds, but that the merchants who import
them know a stratagem by means of which to obtain them:
that they take a sheep, and slaughter it, and skin it, and cut
up its flesh, which they throw down from the mountain to
the bottom of the valley: so, descending fresh and moist,
some of these stones stick to it. Then the merchants leave
it until midday, and birds of the large kind of vulture and
the aquiline vulture descend to that meat, and, taking it in
their talons, fly up to the top of the mountain; whereupon
the merchants come to them, and cry out at them, and they
fly way from the meat. The merchants then advance to
that meat, and take from it the stones sticking to it; after
which they leave the meat for the birds and the wild beasts,
and carry the stones to their countries. And no one can
procure the diamonds but by means of this stratagem.—
Therefore when I beheld that slaughtered animal, and remembered this story, I arose and went to the slaughtered
beast. I then selected a great number of these stones, and
put them into my pocket, and within my clothes; and I
proceeded to select, and put into my pockets and my
girdle and my turban, and within my clothes. And while I
was doing thus, lo, another great slaughtered animal. So I
bound myself to it with my turban, and, laying myself down
on my back, placed it upon my bosom, and grasped it firmly.
Thus it was raised high above the ground; and, behold, a
vulture descended upon it, seized it with its talons, and flew
up with it into the air, with me attached to it; and it ceased
not to soar up until it had ascended with it to the summit
of the mountain, when it alighted with it, and was about to
tear off some of it. And thereupon a great and loud cry
arose from behind that vulture, and something made a
clattering with a piece of wood upon the mountain; whereat
the vulture flew away in fear, and soared into the sky.

I therefore disengaged myself from the slaughtered animal, with the blood of which my clothes were polluted; and I stood by its side. And, lo, the merchant who had cried out at the vulture advanced to the slaughtered animal, and saw me standing there. He spoke not to me; for he was frightened at me, and terrified; but he came to the slaughtered beast, and turned it over; and, not finding anything upon it, he uttered a loud cry, and said, Oh, my disappointment! There is no strength nor power but in God! We seek refuge with God from Satan the accursed!— He repented, and struck hand upon hand, and said, Oh, my grief! What is this affair?—So I advanced to him, and he said to me, Who art thou, and what is the reason of thy coming to this place? I answered him, Fear not, nor be alarmed; for I am a human being, of the best of mankind; and I was a merchant, and my tale is marvellous, and my story extraordinary, and the cause of my coming to this mountain and this valley is wondrous to relate. Fear not; for thou shalt receive of me what will rejoice thee: I have with me abundance of diamonds, of which I will give thee as much as will suffice thee, and every piece that I have is better than all that would come to thee by other means: therefore be not timorous nor afraid.—And upon this the man thanked me, and prayed for me, and conversed with me; and, lo, the other merchants heard me talking with their companion; so they came to me. Each merchant had thrown down a slaughtered animal; and when they came to us, they saluted me, and congratulated me on my safety, and took me with them; and I acquainted them with my whole story, relating to them what I had suffered on my voyage, and telling them the cause of my arrival in this valley. Then I gave to the owner of the slaughtered animal to which I had attached myself an abundance of what I had brought with me; and he was delighted with me, and prayed for me, and thanked me for that; and the other merchants said to me, By Allah, a new life hath been decreed thee; for no one ever arrived at this place before thee and escaped from it; but praise be to God for thy safety—They passed the next night in a pleasant and safe place, and I passed the night with them, full of the utmost joy at my safety and my escape from the valley of serpents, and my arrival in an inhabited country.

And when day came, we arose and journeyed over that great mountain, beholding in that valley numerous serpents; and we continued to advance until we arrived at a garden in a great and beautiful island, wherein were camphor-trees, under each of which trees a hundred men might shade themselves. When any one desireth to obtain some camphor from one of these trees, he maketh a perforation in the upper part of it with something long, and catcheth what descendeth from it. The liquid camphor floweth from it, and concreteth like gum. It is the juice of that tree; and after this operation, the tree drieth, and becometh firewood. In that island too is a kind of wild beast called the rhinoceros which pastureth there like oxen and buffaloes in our country; but the bulk of that wild beast is greater than the bulk of the camel, and it eateth the tender leaves of trees. It is a huge beast, with a single horn, thick, in the middle of its head, a cubit in length, wherein is the figure of a man. And in that island are some animals of the ox-kind. Moreover, the sailors, and travellers, and persons in the habit of journeying about in the mountains and the lands, have told us, that this wild beast which is named the rhinoceros lifteth the great elephant upon its horn, and pastureth with it upon the island and the shores, without being sensible of it; and the elephant dieth upon its horn; and its fat, melting by the heat of the sun, and flowing upon its head entereth its eyes, so that it becometh blind. Then it lieth down upon the shore, and the rukh cometh to it, and carrieth it off [with the elephant] in its talons to its young ones, and feedeth them with it and with that which is upon its horn, [namely the elephant]. I saw also in that island abundance of the buffalo-kind, the like of which existeth not among us.

The valley before mentioned containeth a great quantity of diamonds such as I carried off and hid in my pockets. For these the people gave me in exchange goods and commodities belonging to them; and they conveyed them for me, giving me likewise pieces of silver and pieces of gold; and I ceased not to proceed with them, amusing myself with the sight of different countries, and of what God hath created, from valley to valley and from city to city, we, in our way, selling and buying, until we arrived at the city of El-Basrah. We remained there a few days, and then I came to the city of Baghdad, the Abode of Peace, and came to my quarter, and entered my house, bringing with me a great quantity of diamonds, and money and commodities and goods in abundance. I met my family and relations, bestowed alms and gifts, made presents to all my family and companions, and began to eat well and drink well and wear handsome apparel. I associated with friends, and companions, forgot all that I had suffered, and ceased not to enjoy a pleasant life and joyful heart and dilated bosom, with sport and merriment. Every one who heard of my arrival came to me, and inquired of me respecting my voyage, and the states of the different countries: so I informed him, relating to him what I had experienced and suffered; and he wondered at the severity of my sufferings, and congratulated me on my safety.—This is the end of the account of the events that befell me and happened to me during the second voyage; and to-morrow, if it be the will of God (whose name be exalted), I will relate to you the events of the third voyage.

The Third Voyage of Es-Sindibad of the Sea

Know, O my brothers (and hear from me the story of the third voyage, for it is more wonderful than the preceding stories, hitherto related—and God is all-knowing with respect to the things which He hideth, and omniscient), that, in the times past, when I returned from the second voyage, and was in a state of the utmost joy and happiness, rejoicing in my safety, having gained great wealth, as I related to you yesterday, God having compensated me for all that I had lost, I resided in the city of Baghdad for a length of time in the most perfect prosperity and delight, and joy and happiness. Then my soul became desirous of travel and diversion, and I longed for commerce and gain and profits; the soul being prone to evil. So I meditated, and bought an abundance of goods suited for a sea-

voyage, and packed them up, and departed with them from
the city of Baghdad to the city of El-Basrah. There,
coming to the bank of the river, I beheld a great vessel, in
which were many merchants and other passengers, people
of worth, and comely and good persons, people of religion
and kindness and probity. I therefore embarked with them
in that vessel, and we departed in reliance on the blessing
of God (whose name be exalted!), and his aid and favour,
rejoicing in expectation of good-fortune and safety. We
ceased not to proceed from sea to sea, and from island to
island, and from city to city; at every place by which we
passed diverting ourselves, and selling and buying, in the
utmost joy and happiness. Thus we did until we were, one
day, pursuing our course in the midst of the roaring sea,
agitated with waves, when, lo, the master standing at the
side of the vessel, looked at the different quarters of the
sea, and then slapped his face, furled the sails of the ship,
cast its anchors, plucked his beard, rent his clothes, and
uttered a great cry. So we said to him, O master, what is
the news? And he answered, Know, O passengers, whom
may God preserve! that the wind hath prevailed against us,
and driven us out of our course in the midst of the sea, and
destiny hath cast us, through our evil fortune, towards the
Mountain of Apes. No one hath ever arrived at this place
and escaped, and my heart is impressed with the conviction
of the destruction of us all.—And the words of the master
were not ended before the apes had come to us and surrounded the vessel on every side, numerous as locusts,
dispersed about the vessel and on the shore. We feared
that, if we killed one of them, or struck him, or drove him
away, they would kill us, on account of their excessive
number; for numbers prevail against courage; and we
feared them lest they should plunder our goods and our
commodities. They are the most hideous of beasts, and
covered with hair like black felt, their aspect striking
terror. No one understandeth their language or their state,
they shun the society of men, have yellow eyes, and black
faces, and are of small size, the height of each one of them
being four spans. They climbed up the cables, and severed
them with their teeth, and they severed all the ropes of

the vessel in every part: so the vessel inclined with the wind, and stopped at their mountain, and on their coast. Then, having seized all the merchants and the other passengers, and landed upon the island, they took the vessel with the whole of its contents, and went their way with it.

They left us upon the island, the vessel became concealed from us, and we knew not whither they went with it. And while we were upon that island, eating of its fruits and its herbs, and drinking of the rivers that were there, lo, there appeared to us an inhabited house in the midst of the island. We therefore went towards it, and walked to it; and, behold, it was a pavilion, with lofty angles, with high walls, having an entrance with folding doors, which were open; and the doors were of ebony. We entered this pavilion, and found in it a wide, open space, like a wide, large court, around which were many lofty doors, and at its upper end was a high and great mastabah. There were also in it utensils for cooking, hung over the fire-pots, and around them were many bones. But we saw not there any person; and we wondered at that extremely. We sat in the open space in that pavilion a little while, after which we slept; and we ceased not to sleep from near the mid-time between sunrise and moon until sunset. And, lo, the earth trembled beneath us, and we heard a confused noise from the upper air, and there descended upon us, from the summit of the pavilion, a person of enormous size, in human form, and he was of black complexion, of lofty stature, like a great palm-tree: he had two eyes like two blazes of fire, and tusks like the tusks of swine, and a mouth of prodigious size, like the mouth of a well, and lips like the lips of a camel, hanging down upon his bosom, and he had ears like two mortars, hanging down upon his shoulders, and the nails of his hands were like the claws of the lion. So when we beheld him thus, we became unconscious of our existence, our fear was vehement, and our terror was violent, and through the violence of our fear and dread and terror we became as dead men. And after he had descended upon the ground, he sat a little while upon the mastabah. Then he arose and came to us, and, seizing me by my hands from among my companions the merchants, lifted me up from the ground in his hand, and felt me and turned me over; and I was in his hand like a little mouthful. He continued to feel me as the butcher feeleth the sheep that he is about to slaughter; but he found me infirm from excessive affliction, and lean from excessive fatigue and from the voyage; having no flesh. He therefore let me go from his hand, and took another, from among my companions; and he turned him over, as he had turned me over, and felt him as he had felt me, and let him go. He ceased not to feel us and turn us over, one after another, until he came to the master of our ship, who was a fat, stout, broad-shouldered man; a person of strength and vigour: so he pleased him, and he seized him as the butcher seizeth the animal that he is about to slaughter, and, having thrown him on the ground, put his foot upon his neck, which he thus broke. Then he brought a long spit, and thrust it into his throat, and spitted him; after which he lighted a fierce fire, and placed over it that spit upon which the master was spitted, and ceased not to turn him round over the burning coals until his flesh was thoroughly roasted; when he took him off from the fire, put him before him, and separated his joints as a man separates the joints of a chicken, and proceeded to tear in pieces his flesh with his nails, and to eat of it. Thus he continued to do until he had eaten his flesh, and gnawed his bones, and there remained of him nothing but some bones, which he threw by the side of the pavilion. He then sat a little, and threw himself down, and slept upon that mastabah, making a noise with his throat like that which is made by a lamb or other beast when slaughtered; and he slept uninterruptedly until the morning, when he went his way.

As soon, therefore, as we were sure that he was far from us, we conversed together, and wept for ourselves, saying, Would that we had been drowned in the sea, or that the apes had eaten us; for it were better than the roasting of a man upon burning coals! By Allah, this death is a vile one! But what God willeth cometh to pass, and there is no strength nor power but in God, the High, the Great! We die in sorrow, and no one knoweth of us; and there is no escape for us from this place!—We then arose and went forth upon the island, to see for us a place in which to hide ourselves, or to flee; and it had become a light matter to us to die, rather than that our flesh should be roasted with fire. But we found not for us a place in which to hide ourselves; and the evening overtook us. So we returned to the pavilion, by reason of the violence of our fear, and sat there a little while; and, lo, the earth trembled beneath us, and that black approached us, and, coming among us, began to turn us over, one after another, as on the former occasion, and to feel us, until one pleased him; whereupon he seized him, and did with him as he did with the master of the ship the day before. He roasted him, and ate him upon that mastabah, and ceased not to sleep that night, making a noise with his throat like a slaughtered animal; and when the day came, he arose and went his way, leaving us as usual. Upon this we assembled together and conversed, and said, one to another, By Allah, if we cast ourselves into the sea and die drowned, it will be better than our dying burnt; for this mode of being put to death is abominable! And one of us said, Hear my words. Verily we will contrive a stratagem against him and kill him, and be at ease from apprehension of his purpose, and relieve the Muslims from his oppression and tyranny.—So I said to them, Hear, O my brothers. If we must kill him, we will transport this wood, and remove some of this firewood, and make for ourselves rafts, each to bear three men, after which we will contrive a stratagem to kill him, and embark on the rafts, and proceed over the sea to whatsoever place God shall desire. Or we will remain in this place until a ship shall pass by, when we will embark in it. And if we be not able to kill him, we will embark [on our rafts], and put out to sea; and if we be drowned, we shall be preserved from being roasted over the fire, and from being slaughtered. If we escape, we escape; and if we be drowned, we die martyrs. —To this they all replied, By Allah, this is a right opinion and a wise proceeding. And we agreed upon this matter, and commenced the work. We removed the pieces of wood out of the pavilion, and constructed rafts, attached them to the sea-shore, and stowed upon them some provisions; after which we returned to the pavilion.

And when it was evening, lo, the earth trembled with us, and the black came in to us, like the biting dog. He turned us over and felt us, one after another, and, having taken one of us, did with him as he had done with the others before him. He ate him, and slept upon the mastabah, and the noise from his throat was like thunder. So thereupon we arose, and took two iron spits, of those which were set up, and put them in the fierce fire until they were red-hot, and became like burning coals; when we grasped them firmly, and went with them to that black while he lay asleep snoring, and we thrust them into his eyes, all of us pressing upon them with our united strength and force. Thus we pushed them into his eyes as he slept, and his eyes were destroyed, and he uttered a great cry, whereat our hearts were terrified. Then he arose resolutely from that mastabah, and began to search for us, while we fled from him to the right and left, and he saw us not; for his sight was blinded; but we feared him with a violent fear, and made sure, in that time, of destruction, and despaired of safety. And upon this he sought the door, feeling for it, and went forth from it, crying out, while we were in the utmost fear of him; and lo, the earth shook beneath us, by reason of the vehemence of his cry. So when he went forth from the pavilion, we followed him, and he went his way, searching for us. Then he returned, accompanied by a female, greater than he, and more hideous in form; and when we beheld him, and her who was with him, more horrible than he in appearance, we were in the utmost fear. As soon as the female saw us, we hastily loosed the rafts that we had constructed, and embarked on them, and pushed them forth into the sea. But each of the two blacks had a mass of rock, and they cast at us until the greater number of us died from the casting, there remaining of us only three persons, I and two others; and the raft conveyed us to another island.

We walked forward upon that island until the close of the day, and the night overtook us in this state; so we slept a little; and we awoke from our sleep, and, lo, a serpent of enormous size, of large body and wide belly, had surrounded us. It approached one of us, and swallowed him to his shoulders: then it swallowed the rest of him, and we heard his ribs break in pieces in its belly; after which it went its way. At this we wondered extremely, and we mourned for our companion, and were in the utmost fear for ourselves, saying, By Allah, this is a wonderful thing! Every death that we witness is more horrible than the preceding one! We were rejoiced at our escape from the black; but our joy is not complete! There is no strength nor power but in God! By Allah, we have escaped from the black and from drowning; but how shall we escape from this unlucky serpent?—Then we arose and walked on over the island, eating of its fruits, and drinking of its rivers, and we ceased not to proceed till morning, when we found a great, lofty tree. So we climbed up it, and slept upon it; I having ascended to the highest of its branches. But when the night arrived, and it was dark, the serpent came, looking to the right and left, and, advancing to the tree upon which we were, came up to my companion, and swallowed him to his shoulders; and it wound itself round the tree with him, and I heard his bones break in pieces in its belly: then it swallowed him entirely, while I looked on; after which it descended from the tree, and went its way.—I remained upon that tree the rest of the night; and when the day came, and the light appeared, I descended from the tree, like one dead, by reason of excessive fear and terror, and desired to cast myself into the sea, that I might be at rest from the world; but it was not a light matter to me to do so; for life is dear. So I tied a wide piece of wood upon the soles of my feet, crosswise, and I tied one like it upon my left side, and a similar one upon my right side, and a similar one upon the front of my body, and I tied one long and wide upon the top of my head, crosswise, like that which was under the soles of my feet. Thus I was in the midst of these pieces of wood, and they enclosed me on every side. I bound them tightly, and threw myself with the whole upon the ground; so I lay in the midst of the pieces of wood, which enclosed me like a closet. And when the evening arrived, the serpent approached as it was wont, and saw me, and drew towards me; but it could not swallow me when I was in that state, with the pieces of wood round me on every side. It went round me; but could not come at me: and I looked at it, being like a dead man, by reason of the violence of my fear and terror. The serpent retired from me, and returned to me; and thus it ceased not to do: every time that it desired to get at me to swallow me, the pieces of wood tied upon me on every side prevented it. It continued to do thus from sunset until daybreak arrived and the light appeared and the sun rose, when it went its way, in the utmost vexation and rage. Upon this, therefore, I stretched forth my hands and loosed myself from those pieces of wood, in a state like that of the dead, through the severity of that which I had suffered from that serpent.

I then arose, and walked along the island until I came to the extremity of it; when I cast a glance towards the sea, and beheld a ship at a distance, in the midst of the deep. So I took a great branch of a tree, and made a sign with it to the passengers, calling out to them; and when they saw me, they said, We must see what this is. Perhaps it is a man.—Then they approached me, and heard my cries to them. They therefore came to me, and took me with them in the ship, and asked me respecting my state: so I informed them of all that had happened to me from beginning to end, and of the troubles that I had suffered; whereat they wondered extremely. They clad me with some of their clothes, attiring me decently; and after that, they put before me some provisions, and I ate until I was satisfied. They also gave me to drink some cool and sweet water, and my heart was revived, my soul became at ease, and I experienced great comfort. God (whose name be exalted!) had raised me to life after my death: so I praised Him (exalted be his name!) for His abundant favours, and thanked Him. My courage was strengthened after I had made sure of destruction, so that it seemed to me that all which I then experienced was a dream.—We proceeded on our voyage, and the wind was fair to us by the permission of God (whose name be exalted!) until we came in sight of an island called the Island of Es-Selahit, where sandal-wood is abundant, and there the master anchored the ship, and the merchants and other passengers landed, and took forth their goods to sell and buy. The owner of the ship

then looked towards me, and said to me, Hear my words,
Thou art a stranger and poor, and hast informed us that
thou hast suffered many horrors: I therefore desire to
benefit thee with something that will aid thee to reach thy
country, and thou wilt pray for me.—I replied, So be it, and
thou shalt have my prayers. And he rejoined, Know that
there was with us a man voyaging, whom we lost, and we
know not whether he be living or dead, having heard no
tidings of him. I desire to commit to thee his bales that
thou mayest sell them in this island. Thou shalt take
charge of them, and we will give thee something propor-
tionate to thy trouble and thy service; and what remaineth
of them we will take and keep until we return to the city of
Baghdad, when we will inquire for the owner's family, and
give to them the remainder, together with the price of that
which shall be sold of them. Wilt thou then take charge of
them, and land with them upon this island, and sell them as
do the merchants?—I answered, I hear and obey thee, O
my master; and thou art beneficent and kind. And I prayed
for him and thanked him for that.

He thereupon ordered the porters and sailors to land
those goods upon the island, and to deliver them to me.
And the clerk of the ship said, O master, what are these
bales which the sailors and porters have brought out, and
with the name of which of the merchants shall I mark them?
He answered, Write upon them the name of Es-Sindibad of
the Sea, who was with us, and was drowned [or left behind]
at the island [of the rukh], and of whom no tidings have
come to us; wherefore we desire that this stranger sell them,
and take charge of the price of them, and we will give him
somewhat of it in requital of his trouble and his sale of them.
What shall remain we will take with us until we return to the
city of Baghdad, when, if we find him, we will give it to
him; and if we find him not, we will give it to his family in
Baghdad.—So the clerk replied, Thy words are good, and
thy notion is excellent. And when I heard the words of
the master, mentioning that the bales were to be inscribed
with my name, I said within myself, By Allah, I am Es-
Sindibad of the Sea. Then I fortified myself, and waited
till the merchants had landed and had assembled conversing

and consulting upon affairs of selling and buying, when I advanced to the owner of the ship, and said to him, O my master, dost thou know what manner of man was the owner of the bales which thou hast committed to me that I may sell them? He answered me, I know not his condition; but he was a man of the city of Baghdad, called Es-Sindibad of the Sea; and we had cast anchor at one of the islands, where he was lost, and we have had no tidings of him to the present time. So upon this I uttered a great cry, and said to him, O master (whom may God preserve!), know that I am Es-Sindibad of the Sea. I was not drowned; but when thou anchoredst at the island, and the merchants and other passengers landed, I also landed with the party, taking with me something to eat on the shore of the island. Then I enjoyed myself in sitting in that place, and slumber over-taking me, I slept, and became immersed in sleep; after which I arose and found not the ship, nor found I any one with me. Therefore this wealth is my wealth, and these goods are my goods. All the merchants also who transport diamonds saw me when I was upon the mountain of the diamonds, and they will bear witness for me that I am Es-Sindibad of the Sea, as I informed them of my story and of the events that befell me with you in the ship. I informed them that ye had forgotten me upon the island, asleep, and that I arose and found not any one, and that what had befallen me befell me.

And when the merchants and other passengers heard my words, they assembled around me; and some of them believed me, and others disbelieved me. But while we were thus talking, lo, one of the merchants, on his hearing me mention the valley of diamonds arose and advanced to me, and said to them, Hear, O company, my words. When I related to you the most wonderful thing that I had seen in my travels, I told you that, when we cast down the slaughtered animals into the valley of diamonds, I casting down mine with the rest, as I was accustomed to do, there came up with my slaughtered beast a man attached to it, and ye believed me not, but accused me of falsehood.—They replied, Yes: thou didst relate to us this thing, and we believed thee not. And the merchant said to them, This is the man who attached himself to my slaughtered animal, and he gave me some diamonds of high price, the like of which exist not, rewarding me with more than would have come up with my slaughtered animal; and I took him as my companion until we arrived at the city of El-Basrah, whence he proceeded to his country, having bidden us farewell, and we returned to our own countries. This is he, and he informed us that his name was Es-Sindibad of the Sea: he told us likewise of the departure of the ship, and of his sitting in that island. And know ye that this man came not to us here but in order that ye might believe my words respecting the matter which I told you; and all these goods are his property; for he informed us of them at the time of his meeting with us, and the truth of his assertion hath become manifest.—So when the master heard the words of that merchant, he arose and came to me, and, having looked at me awhile with a scrutinizing eye, said, What is the mark of thy goods? I answered him, Know that the mark of my goods is of such and such a kind. And I related to him a circumstance that had occurred between me and him when I embarked with him in the vessel from El-Basrah. He therefore was convinced that I was Es-Sindibad of the Sea, and he embraced me and saluted me, and congratulated me on my safety, saying to me, By Allah, O my master, thy story is wonderful and thy case is extraordinary! But praise be to God who hath brought us together, and restored thy goods and thy wealth to thee!

Upon this, I disposed of my goods according to the knowledge I possessed and they procured me, during that voyage, great gain, whereat I rejoiced exceedingly, congratulating myself on my safety, and on the restoration of my wealth to me. And we ceased not to sell and buy at the islands until we arrived at the country of Es-Sind,[5] where likewise we sold and bought. And I beheld in that sea [which we navigated, namely the Sea of India,] many wonders and strange things that cannot be numbered nor calculated. Among the things that I saw there were a fish in the form of the cow, and a creature in the form of the ass; and I saw a bird that cometh forth from a sea-shell,

[5] Western India.

and layeth its eggs and hatcheth them upon the surface of the water, and never cometh forth from the sea upon the face of the earth.—After this we continued our voyage, by permission of God (whose name be exalted!), and the wind and voyage were pleasant to us, until we arrived at El-Basrah, where I remained a few days. Then I came to the city of Baghdad, and repaired to my quarter, entered my house, and saluted my family and companions and friends. I rejoiced at my safety and my return to my country and my family and city and district, and I gave alms and presents, and clad the widows and the orphans, and collected my companions and friends. And I ceased not to live thus, eating and drinking, and sporting and making merry, eating well and drinking well, associating familiarly and mingling in society; and I forgot all that had happened to me, and the distresses and horrors that I had suffered. And I gained during that voyage what could not be numbered nor calculated.—Such were the most wonderful of the things that I beheld during that voyage; and to-morrow, if it be the will of God (whose name be exalted!), thou shalt come. [O Sindibad of the Land,] and I will relate to thee the story of the fourth voyage; for it is more wonderful than the stories of the preceding voyages.

The Fourth Voyage of Es-Sindibad of the Sea

KNOW, O my brothers, that when I returned to the city of Baghdad, and met my companions and my family and my friends, and was enjoying the utmost pleasure and happiness and ease, and had forgotten all that I had experienced, by reason of the abundance of my gains, and had become immersed in sport and mirth, and the society of friends and companions, leading the most delightful life, my wicked soul suggested to me to travel again to the countries of other people, and I felt a longing for associating with the different races of men, and for selling and gains. So I resolved upon this, and purchased precious goods, suitable to a sea-voyage, and, having packed up many bales, more than usual, I went from the city of Baghdad to the city of El-Basrah, where I embarked my bales in a ship, and joined myself to a party of the chief men of El-Basrah, and we set forth on our voyage. The vessel proceeded with us, confiding in the blessing of God (whose name be exalted!), over the roaring sea agitated with waves, and the voyage was pleasant to us; and we ceased not to proceed in this manner for a period of nights and days, from island to island and from sea to sea, until a contrary wind rose against us one day. The master therefore cast the anchors, and stayed the ship in the midst of the sea, fearing that she would sink in the midst of the deep. And while we were in this state, supplicating, and humbling ourselves to God (whose name be exalted!), there rose against us a great tempest, which rent the sails in strips, and the people were submerged with all their bales and their commodities and wealth. I was submerged among the rest, and I swam in the sea for half a day, after which I abandoned myself; but God (whose name be exalted!) aided me to lay hold upon a piece of one of the planks of the ship, and I and a party of the merchants got upon it. We continued sitting upon this plank, striking the sea with our feet, and the waves and the wind helping us; and we remained in this state a day and a night. And on the following day, shortly before the mid-time between sunrise and noon, a wind rose against us, the sea became boisterous, the waves and the wind were violent, and the water cast us upon an island; and we were like dead men, from excess of sleeplessness and fatigue, and cold and hunger, and fear and thirst.

We walked along the shores of that island, and found upon it abundant herbs; so we ate some of them to stay our departing spirits, and to sustain us; and passed the next night upon the shore of the island. And when the morning came, and diffused its light and shone, we rose and walked about the island to the right and left, and there appeared to us a building in the distance. We therefore proceeded over the island in the direction of that building which we had seen from a distance, and ceased not to proceed until we stood at its door. And while we were standing there, lo, there came forth to us from that door a party of naked men, who, without speaking to us, seized us, and took us to their King, and he commanded us to sit. So we sat; and they brought to us some food, such as we knew not, nor in our lives had we seen the like of it; wherefore my stomach consented not to it, and I ate none of it in comparison with my companions, and my eating so little of it was owing to the grace of God (whose name be exalted!), in consequence of which I have lived to the present time. For when my companions ate of that food, their minds became stupefied, and they ate like madmen, and their states became changed. Then the people brought to them cocoa-nut-oil, and gave them to drink of it, and anointed them with it; and when my companions drank of that oil, their eyes became turned in their faces, and they proceeded to eat of that food contrary to their usual manner. Upon this, therefore, I was confounded respecting their case, and grieved for them, and became extremely anxious by reason of the violence of my fear for myself with regard to these naked men. I observed them attentively, and, lo, they were a Magian people, and the King of their city was a ghul; and every one who arrived at their country, or whom they saw or met in the valley or the roads, they brought to their King, and they fed him with that food, and anointed him with that oil, in consequence of which his body became expanded, in order that he might eat largely; and his mind was stupefied, his faculty of reflection was destroyed, and he became like an idiot. Then they gave him to eat and drink in abundance of that food and oil, until he became fat and stout, when they slaughtered him and roasted him, and served him as meat to their King. But as to the companions of the King, they ate the flesh of men without roasting or otherwise cooking it. So when I saw them do thus, I was in the utmost anguish on my own account and on account of my companions. The latter, by reason of the excessive stupefaction of their minds, knew not what was done unto them, and the people committed them to a person who took them every day and went forth to pasture them on that island like cattle.

But as for myself, I became, through the violence of fear and hunger, infirm and wasted in body, and my flesh dried upon my bones. So when they saw me in this state, they left me and forgot me, and not one of them remembered me, nor did I occur to their minds, until I contrived a stratagem one day, and, going forth from that place, walked along the island to a distance. And I saw a herdsman sitting upon something elevated in the midst of the sea; and I certified myself of him, and, lo, he was the man to whom they had committed my companions that he might pasture them; and he had with him many like them. As soon, therefore, as that man beheld me, he knew that I was in possession of my reason, and that nought of that which had afflicted my companions had afflicted me. So he made a sign to me from a distance, and said to me, Turn back, and go along the road that is on thy right hand; thou wilt so reach the King's highway. Accordingly I turned back, as this man directed me, and, seeing a road on my right hand, I proceeded along it, and ceased not to go on, sometimes running by reason of fear, and sometimes walking at my leisure until I had taken rest. Thus I continued to do until I was hidden from the eyes of the man who directed me to the way, and I saw him not nor did he see me. The sun had disappeared from me, and darkness approached; wherefore I sat to rest, and desired to sleep; but sleep came not to me that night on account of the violence of my fear and hunger and fatigue. And when it was midnight, I arose and walked on over the island, and I ceased not to proceed until day arrived, and the morning came and diffused its light and shone, and the sun rose over the tops of the high hills and over the low gravelly plains. I was tired and hungry and thirsty: so I began to eat of the herbs and vegetables that were upon the island, and continued to eat of them till I was satiated, and my departing spirit was stayed; after which I arose and walked on again over the island; and thus I ceased not to do all the day and the next night; whenever I was hungry, eating of the vegetables.

In this manner I proceeded for the space of seven days with their nights: and on the morning of the eighth day, I cast a glance, and beheld a faint object in the distance. So I went towards it, and ceased not to proceed until I came up to it, after sunset; and I looked at it with a scrutinizing eye, while I was yet distant from it, and with a fearful heart in consequence of what I had suffered first and after, and, lo, it was a party of men gathering pepper. And when I approached them, and they saw me, they hastened to me, and came to me and surrounded me on every side, saying to me, Who art thou, and whence hast thou come? I answered them, Know ye, O people, that I am a poor foreigner. And I informed them of my whole case, and of the horrors and distresses that had befallen me, and what I had suffered; whereupon they said, By Allah, this is a wonderful thing! But how didst thou escape from the blacks, and how didst thou pass by them in this island, when they are a numerous people, and eat men, and no one is safe from them, nor can any pass by them?—So I acquainted them with that which had befallen me among them, and with the manner in which they had taken my companions, and fed them with food of which I did not eat. And they congratulated me on my safety, and wondered at that which had befallen me. Then they made me sit among them until they had finished their work, and they brought me some nice food. I therefore ate of it, being hungry, and rested with them a while; after which they took me and embarked with me in a vessel, and went to their island and their abodes. They then took me to their King, and I saluted him, and he welcomed me and treated me with honour, and inquired of me my story. So I related to him what I had experienced, and what had befallen me and happened to me from the day of my going forth from the city of Baghdad until I had come unto him. And the King wondered extremely at my story, and at the events that had happened to me; he, and all who were present in his assembly. After that, he ordered me to sit with him. Therefore I sat; and he gave orders to bring the food, which accordingly they brought, and I ate of it as much as sufficed me, and washed my hands, and offered up thanks for the favour of God (whose name be exalted!), praising Him and glorifying Him. I then rose from the presence of the King, and diverted myself with a sight of his city; and, lo, it was a flourishing city, abounding with inhabitants and wealth, and with food and markets and goods, and sellers and buyers.

So I rejoiced at my arrival at that city, and my heart was at ease; I became familiar with its inhabitants, and was magnified and honoured by them and by their King above the people of his dominions and the great men of his city. And I saw that all its great men and its small rode excellent and fine horses without saddles; whereat I wondered; and I said to the King, Wherefore, O my lord, dost thou not ride on a saddle; for therein is ease to the rider, and additional power? He said, What kind of thing is a saddle? This is a thing that in our lives we have never seen, nor have we ever ridden upon it.—And I said to him, Wilt thou permit me to make for thee a saddle to ride upon and to experience the pleasure of it? He answered me, Do so. I therefore said to him, Furnish me with some wood. And he gave orders to bring me all that I required. Then I asked for a clever carpenter, and sat with him, and taught him the construction of the saddle, and how he should make it. Afterwards I took some wool, and teased it, and made felt of it; and I caused some leather to be brought, and covered the saddle with it, and polished it. I then attached its straps, and its girth: after which I brought the blacksmith, and described to him the form of the stirrups, and he forged an excellent pair of stirrups; and I filed them, and tinned them. Then I attached fringes of silk. Having done this, I arose and brought one of the best of the King's horses, girded upon him that saddle, attached to it the stirrups, bridled him, and brought him forward to the King; and it pleased him, and was agreeable to him. He thanked me, and seated himself upon it, and was greatly delighted with that saddle; and he gave me a large present as a reward for that which I had done for him. And when his Wezir saw that I had made that saddle, he desired of me one like it. So I made for him a saddle like it. The grandees and dignitaries likewise desired of me saddles, and I made for them. I taught the carpenter the construction of the saddle; and the blacksmith, the mode of making stirrups; and we employed ourselves in making these things, and sold them to the great men and masters. Thus I collected abundant wealth, and became in high estimation with them, and they loved me exceedingly.

I continued to enjoy a high rank with the King and his attendants and the great men of the country and the lords of the state, until I sat one day with the King, in the utmost happiness and honour; and while I was sitting, the King said to me, Know, O thou, that thou hast become magnified and honoured among us, and hast become one of us, and we cannot part with thee, nor can we suffer thee to depart from our city; and I desire of thee that thou obey me in an affair, and reject not that which I shall say. So I said to him, And what dost thou desire of me, O King? For I will not reject that which thou shalt say, since thou hast shewn favour and kindness and beneficence to me, and (praise be to God!) I have become one of thy servants.—And he answered, I desire to marry thee among us to a beautiful, lovely, elegant wife, possessed of wealth and loveliness, and thou shalt become a dweller with us, and I will lodge thee by me in my palace: therefore oppose me not, nor reject what I say. And when I heard the words of the King, I was abashed at him, and was silent, returning him no answer, by reason of the exceeding bashfulness with which I regarded him. So he said, Wherefore dost thou not reply to me, O my son? And I answered him, O my master, it is thine to command, O King of the age! And upon this he sent immediately and caused the Kadi and the witnesses to come, and married me forthwith to a woman of noble rank, of high lineage, possessing abundant wealth and fortune, of great origin, of surprising loveliness and beauty, owner of dwellings and possessions and buildings. Then he gave me a great, handsome house, standing alone, and he gave me servants and other dependents, and assigned me supplies and salaries. Thus I became in a state of the utmost ease and joy and happiness, forgetting all the fatigue and affliction and adversity that had happened to me; and I said within myself, When I set forth on my voyage to my country, I will take her with me. But every event that is predestined to happen to man must inevitably take place, and no one knoweth what will befall him. I loved her and she loved me with a great affection, concord existed between me and her, and we lived in a most delightful manner, and most comfortable abode, and ceased not to enjoy this state for a length of time.

Then God (whose name be exalted!) caused to die the wife of my neighbour, and he was a companion of mine. So I went in to him to console him for the loss of his wife, and beheld him in a most evil state, anxious, weary in soul and heart; and upon this I consoled him and comforted him, saying to him, Mourn not for thy wife. God will happily compensate thee by giving thee one better than she, and thy life will be long if it be the will of God, whose name be exalted!—But he wept violently, and said to me, O my companion, how can I marry another after her, or how can God compensate me by giving me a better than she, when but one day remaineth of my life? So I replied, O my brother, return to thy reason, and do not announce thine own death; for thou art well, in prosperity and health. But he said to me, O my companion, by thy life, to-morrow thou wilt lose me, and never in thy life wilt thou see me again.—And how so? said I. He answered me, This day they will bury my wife, and they will bury me with her in the sepulchre; for it is our custom in our country, when the wife dieth, to bury with her her husband alive; and when the husband dieth, they bury with him his wife alive; that neither of them may enjoy life after the other. I therefore said to him, By Allah, this custom is exceedingly vile, and none can endure it!—And while we were thus conversing, lo, most of the people of the city came, and proceeded to console my companion for the loss of his wife and for himself. They began to prepare her body for burial according to their custom, brought a bier, and carried the woman in it, with all her apparel and ornaments and wealth, taking the husband with them; and they went forth with them to the outside of the city, and came to a place in the side of a mountain by the sea. They advanced to a spot there, and lifted up from it a great stone, and there appeared, beneath the place of this, a margin of stone, like the margin of a well. Into this they threw down that woman; and, lo, it was a great pit beneath the mountain. Then they brought the man, tied him beneath his bosom by a rope of fibres of the palm-tree, and let him down into the pit. They also let down to him a great jug of sweet water, and seven cakes of bread; and when they had let him down, he loosed himself from the rope, and they drew it up, and covered the mouth of the pit with that great stone as it was before, and went their ways, leaving my companion with his wife in the pit.—So I said within myself, By Allah, this death is more grievous than the first death! I then went to their King, and said to him, O my lord, how is it that ye bury the living with the dead in your country? And he answered me, Know that this is our custom in our country: when the husband dieth, we bury with him his wife; and when the wife dieth, we bury with her her husband alive; that we may not separate them in life nor in death; and this custom we have received from our forefathers. And I said, O King of the age, and in like manner the foreigner like me, when his wife dieth among you do ye with him as ye have done with this man? He answered me, Yes: we bury him with her, and do with him as thou hast seen. And when I heard these words from him, my gall-bladder almost burst by reason of the violence of my grief and mourning for myself; my mind was stupefied, and I became fearful lest my wife should die before me and they should bury me alive with her. Afterwards, however, I comforted myself, and said, Perhaps I shall die before her: and no one knoweth which will precede and which will follow. And I proceeded to beguile myself with occupations.

And but a short time had elapsed after that when my wife fell sick, and she remained so a few days, and died. So the greater number of the people assembled to console me, and to console her family for her death; and the King also came to console me for the loss of her, as was their custom. Then they brought for her a woman to wash her, and they washed her, and decked her with the richest of her apparel, and ornaments of gold, and necklaces and jewels. And when they had attired my wife, and put her in the bier, and carried her and gone with her to that mountain, and lifted up the stone from the mouth of the pit, and cast her into it, all my companions, and the family of my wife, advanced to bid me farewell and to console me for the loss of my life. I was crying out among them, I am a foreigner, and am unable to endure your custom! But they would not hear what I said, nor pay any regard to my words. They laid hold upon me and bound me by force, tying with me seven cakes of bread and a jug of sweet water, according to their custom, and let me down into that pit. And, lo, it was a great cavern beneath that mountain. They said to me, Loose thyself from the ropes. But I would not loose myself. So they threw the ropes down upon me, and covered the mouth of the pit with the great stone that was upon it, and went their ways. I beheld in that cavern many dead bodies, and their smell was putrid and abominable; and I blamed myself for that which I had done, saying, By Allah, I deserve all that happeneth to me and befalleth me! I knew not night from day; and I sustained myself with little food, not eating until hunger almost killed me, nor drinking until my thirst became violent, fearing the exhaustion of the food and water that I had with me. I said, There is no strength nor power but in God, the High, the Great! What tempted me to marry in this city? And every time that I say, I have escaped from a calamity, I fall into a calamity that is more mighty than the preceding one! By Allah, my dying this death is unfortunate! Would that I had been drowned in the sea, or had died upon the mountains! It had been better for me than this evil death!—And I continued in this manner, blaming myself. I laid myself down upon the bones of the dead, begging aid of God (whose name be exalted!), and wished for death, but I found it not, by reason of the severity of my sufferings. Thus I remained until hunger burned my stomach, and thirst inflamed me; when I sat, and felt for the bread, and ate a little of it, and I swallowed after it a little water. Then I rose and stood up, and walked about the sides of the cavern, and I found that it was spacious sideways, and with vacant cavities; but upon its bottom were numerous dead bodies, and rotten bones, that had lain there from old times. And upon this I made for myself a place in the side of the cavern, remote from the fresh corpses, and there I slept.

At length my provision became greatly diminished, little remaining with me. During each day, or in more than a day, I had eaten but once, and drunk one draught, fearing the exhaustion of the water and food that was with me before my death; and I ceased not to do this until I was sitting one day, and while I sat, meditating upon my case, thinking what I should do when my food and water were exhausted, lo, the mass of rock was removed from its place, and the light beamed down upon me. So I said, What can be the matter? And, behold, the people were standing at the top of the pit, and they let down a dead man with his wife with him alive, and she was weeping and crying out for herself; and they let down with her a large quantity of food and water. I saw the woman; but she saw not me; and they covered the mouth of the pit with the stone, and went their ways. Then I arose, and, taking in my hand a long bone of a dead man, I went to the woman, and struck her upon the middle of the head; whereupon she fell down senseless; and I struck her a second and a third time, and she died. So I took her bread and what else she had, and I found upon her abundance of ornaments and apparel, necklaces and jewels and minerals. And having taken the water and food that was with her, I sat in a place that I had prepared in a side of the cavern, wherein to sleep, and proceeded to eat a little of that food, as much only as would sustain me, lest it should be exhausted quickly, and I should die of hunger and thirst.

I remained in that cavern a length of time; and whenever they buried a corpse, I killed the person who was buried with it alive, and took that person's food and drink, to subsist upon it, until I was sleeping one day, and I awoke from my sleep, and heard something make a noise in a side of the cavern. So I said, What can this be? I then arose and walked towards it, taking with me a long bone of a dead man; and when it was sensible of my presence, it ran away, and fled from me; and, lo, it was a wild beast. But I followed it to the upper part of the cavern, and thereupon a light appeared to me from a small spot, like a star. Sometimes it appeared to me, and sometimes it was concealed from me. Therefore when I saw it, I advanced towards it; and the nearer I approached to it, the larger did the light from it appear to me. So upon this I was convinced that it was a hole in that cavern, communicating with the open country; and I said within myself, There must be some cause for this: either it is a second mouth, like that from which they let me down, or it is a fissure in this place. I meditated in my mind a while, and advanced towards the light; and, lo, it was a perforation in the back of that mountain, which the wild beasts had made, and through which they entered this place; and they ate of the dead bodies until they were satiated, and went forth through this perforation. When I saw it, therefore, my mind was quieted, my soul was tranquillized, and my heart was at ease; I made sure of life after death, and became as in a dream. Then I managed to force my way through that perforation, and found myself on the shore of the sea, upon a great mountain, which formed a barrier between the sea on the one side, and the island and city on the other, and to which no one could gain access. So I praised God (whose name be exalted!), and thanked Him, and rejoiced exceedingly, and my heart was strengthened. I then returned through that perforation into the cavern, and removed all the food and water that was in it, that I had spared. I also took the clothes of the dead, and clad myself in some of them, in addition to those I had on me; and I took abundance of the things that were on the dead, consisting of varieties of necklaces and jewels, long necklaces of pearls, ornaments of silver and gold set with various minerals, and rarities; and, having tied up some clothes of the dead in apparel of my own, I went forth from the perforation to the back of the mountain, and stood upon the shore of the sea. Every day I entered the cavern, and explored it; and whenever they buried a person alive, I took the food and water, and killed that person, whether male or female; after which I went forth from the perforation, and sat upon the shore of the sea, to wait for relief from God (whose name be exalted!), by means of a ship passing by me. And I removed from that cavern all the ornaments that I found, and tied them up in the clothes of the dead.

I ceased not to remain in this state for a length of time; and afterwards, as I was sitting one day, upon the shore of the sea, meditating upon my case, lo, a vessel passed along in the midst of the roaring sea agitated with waves. So I took in my hand a white garment, of the clothes of the dead, and tied it to a staff, and ran with it along the sea-shore, making a sign to the people with that garment, until they happened to look, and saw me upon the summit of the mountain. They therefore approached me, and heard my voice, and sent to me a boat in which was a party of men from the ship; and when they drew near to me they said to me, Who art thou, and what is the reason of thy sitting in this place, and how didst thou arrive at this mountain; for in our lives we have never seen any one who hath come unto it? So I answered them, I am a merchant. The vessel that I was in was wrecked, and I got upon a plank, together with my things, and God facilitated my landing at this place, with my things, by means of my exertion and my skill, after severe toil. They therefore took me with them in the boat, and embarked all that I had taken from the cavern, tied up in the garments and grave-clothes, and they proceeded with me until they took me up into the ship, to the master, and all my things with me. And the master said to me, O man, how didst thou arrive at this place, which is a great mountain, with a great city behind it? All my life I have been accustomed to navigate this sea, and to pass by this mountain; but have never seen any thing there except the wild beasts and the birds.—I answered him, I am a merchant. I was in a great ship, and it was wrecked, and all my merchandise, consisting of these stuffs and clothes which thou seest, was submerged; but I placed it upon a great plank, one of the planks of the ship, and destiny and fortune aided me, so that I landed upon this mountain, where I waited for some one to pass by and take me with him.

And I acquainted them not with the events that had befallen me in the city, or in the cavern; fearing that there might be with them in the ship some one from that city. Then I took forth and presented to the owner of the ship a considerable portion of my property, saying to him, O my master, thou hast been the means of my escape from this mountain: therefore receive from me this as a recompense for the favour which thou hast done to me. But he would not accept it from me; and he said to me, We take nothing from any one; and when we behold a shipwrecked person on the shore of the sea or on an island, we take him with us, and feed him and give him to drink; and if he be naked, we clothe him; and when we arrive at the port of safety, we give him something of our property as a present, and act towards him with kindness and favour for the sake of God, whose name be exalted!—So upon this I offered up prayers for the prolongation of his life.

We ceased not to proceed on our voyage from island to island and from sea to sea. I hoped to escape, and was rejoiced at my safety; but every time that I reflected upon my abode in the cavern with my wife, my reason left me. We pursued our course until we arrived at the Island of the Bell, when we proceeded to the island of Kela in six days. Then we came to the kingdom of Kela, which is adjacent to India, and in it are a mine of lead, and places where the Indian cane groweth, and excellent camphor; and its King is a King of great dignity, whose dominion extendeth over the Island of the Bell. In it is a city called the City of the Bell, which is two days' journey in extent. —At length, by the providence of God, we arrived in safety at the city of El-Basrah, where I landed, and remained a few days; after which I came to the city of Baghdad, and to my quarter, and entered my house, met my family and my companions, and made inquiries respecting them; and they rejoiced at my safety, and congratulated me. I stored all the commodities that I had brought with me in my magazines, gave alms and presents, and clad the orphans and the widows; and I became in a state of the utmost joy and happiness, and returned to my former habit of associating with familiars and companions and brothers, and indulging in sport and merriment.—Such were the most wonderful of the events that happened to me in the course of the fourth voyage. But, O my brother, [O Sindibad of the Land,] sup thou with me, and observe thy custom by coming to me to-morrow, when I will inform thee what happened to me and what befell me during the fifth voyage; for it was more wonderful and extraordinary than the preceding voyages.

The Fifth Voyage of Es-Sindibad of the Sea

Know, O my brothers, that when I returned from the fourth voyage, and became immersed in sport and merriment and joy, and had forgotten all that I had experienced, and what had befallen me, and what I had suffered, by reason of my excessive joy at the gain and profit and benefits that I had obtained, my mind again suggested to me to travel, and to divert myself with the sight of the countries of other people, and the islands. So I arose and meditated upon that subject, and bought precious goods, suited for a sea-voyage. I packed up the bales, and departed from the city of Baghdad to the city of El-Basrah; and, walking along the bank of the river, I saw a great, handsome, lofty vessel, and it pleased me; wherefore I purchased it. Its apparatus was new, and I hired for it a master and sailors, over whom I set my black slaves and my pages as superintendents, and I embarked in it my bales. And there came to me a company of merchants, who also embarked their bales in it, and paid me hire. We set sail in the utmost joy and happiness, and rejoicing in the prospect of safety and gain, and ceased not to pursue our voyage from island to island and from sea to sea, diverting ourselves with viewing the islands and towns, and landing at them and selling and buying. Thus we continued to do until we arrived one day at a large island, destitute of inhabitants. There was no person upon it: it was deserted and desolate; but on it was an enormous white dome, of great bulk; and we landed to amuse ourselves with a sight of it, and, lo, it was a great egg of a rukh. Now when the merchants had landed, and were diverting themselves with viewing it, not knowing that it was the egg of a rukh, they struck it with stones; whereupon it broke, and there poured down from it a great quantity of liquid, and the young rukh appeared within it. So they pulled it and drew it forth from the shell, and killed it, and took from it abundance of meat. I was then in the ship, and knew not of it, and they acquainted me not with that which they did. But in the mean time one of the passengers said to me, O my master, arise and divert thyself with the sight of this egg which we imagined to be a dome. I therefore arose to take a view of it, and found the merchants striking the egg. I called out to them, Do not this deed; for the rukh will come and demolish our ship, and destroy us. But they would not hear my words.

And while they were doing as above related, behold, the sun became concealed from us, and the day grew dark, and there came over us a cloud by which the sky was obscured. So we raised our heads to see what had intervened between us and the sun, and saw that the wings of the rukh were what veiled from us the sun's light, so that the sky was darkened. And when the rukh came, and beheld its egg broken, it cried out at us; whereupon its mate, the female bird, came to it, and they flew in circles over the ship, crying out at us with a voice more vehement than thunder. So I called out to the master and the sailors, and said to them, Push off the vessel, and seek safety before we perish. The master therefore hastened, and, the merchants having embarked, he loosed the ship, and we departed from that island. And when the rukhs saw that we had put forth to sea, they absented themselves from us for a while. We proceeded, and made speed, desiring to escape from them, and to quit their country; but, lo, they had followed us, and they now approached us, each of them having in its claws a huge mass of rock from a mountain; and the male bird threw the rock that he had brought upon us. The master, however, steered away the ship, and the mass of rock missed her by a little space. It descended into the sea by the ship, and the ship went up with us, and down, by reason of the mighty plunging of the rock, and we beheld the bottom of the sea in consequence of its vehement force. Then the mate of the male rukh threw upon us the rock that she had brought, which was smaller than the former one, and, as destiny had ordained, it fell upon the stern of the ship, and crushed it, making the rudder fly into twenty pieces, and all that was in the ship became submerged in the sea.

I strove to save myself, impelled by the sweetness of life, and God (whose name be exalted!) placed within my reach one of the planks of the ship; so I caught hold of it, and, having got upon it, began to row upon it with my feet, and the wind and the waves helped me forward. The vessel had sunk near an island in the midst of the sea, and destiny cast me, by permission of God (whose name be exalted!), to that island. I therefore landed upon it; but I was at my last breath, and in the state of the dead, from the violence of the fatigue and distress and hunger and thirst that I had suffered. I then threw myself down upon the shore of the sea, and remained lying there a while, until my soul felt at ease, and my heart was tranquillized, when I walked along the island, and saw that it resembled one of the gardens of Paradise. Its trees bore ripe fruits, its rivers were flowing, and its birds were warbling the praises of Him to whom belongeth might and permanence. Upon that island was an abundance of trees and fruits, with varieties of flowers. So I ate of the fruits until I was satiated, and I drank of those rivers until I was satisfied with drink; and I praised God (whose name be exalted!) for this, and glorified Him. I then remained sitting upon the island till evening came, and night approached; whereupon I rose; but I was like a slain man, by reason of the fatigue and fear that I had experienced; and I heard not in that island a voice, nor did I see in it any person.

I slept there without interruption until the morning, and then rose and stood up, and walked among the trees; and I saw a streamlet, by which sat an old man, a comely person, who was clad from the waist downwards with a covering made of the leaves of trees. So I said within myself, Perhaps this old man hath landed upon this island and is one of the shipwrecked persons with whom the vessel fell to pieces. I then approached him and saluted him, and he returned the salutation by a sign, without speaking; and I said to him, O sheykh, what is the reason of thy sitting in this place? Whereupon he shook his head, and sighed, and made a sign to me with his hand, as though he would say, Carry me upon thy neck, and transport me from this place to the other side of the streamlet. I therefore said within myself, I will act kindly with this person, and transport him to this place to which he desireth to go: perhaps I shall obtain for it a reward [in heaven]. Accordingly I advanced to him, and took him upon my shoulders, and conveyed him to the place that he had indicated to me; when I said to him, Descend at thine ease. But he descended not from my shoulders. He had twisted his legs round my neck, and I looked at them, and I saw that they were like the hide of the buffalo in blackness and roughness. So I was frightened at him, and desired to throw him down from my shoulders; but he pressed upon my neck with his feet, and squeezed my throat, so that the world became black before my face, and I was unconscious of my existence, falling upon the ground in a fit, like one dead. He then raised his legs, and beat me upon my back and my shoulders; and I suffered violent pain; wherefore I rose with him. He still kept his seat upon my shoulders, and I had become fatigued with bearing him; and he made a sign to me that I should go in among the trees, to the best of the fruits. When I disobeyed him, he inflicted upon me, with his feet, blows more violent than those of whips; and he ceased not to direct me with his hand to every place to which he desired to go, and to that place I went with him. If I loitered, or went leisurely, he beat me; and I was as a captive to him. We went into the midst of the island, among the trees, and he descended not from my shoulders by night nor by day: when he desired to sleep, he would wind his legs round my neck, and sleep a little, and then he would arise and beat me, whereupon I would arise with him quickly, unable to disobey him, by reason of the severity of that which I suffered from him; and I blamed myself for having taken him up, and having had pity on him. I continued with him in this condition, enduring the most violent fatigue, and said within myself, I did a good act unto this person, and it hath become an evil to myself! By Allah, I will never more do good unto any one as long as I live!—I begged of God (whose name be exalted!), at every period and in every hour, that I might die, in consequence of the excessive fatigue and distress that I suffered.

Thus I remained for a length of time, until I carried him one day to a place in the island where I found an abundance of pumpkins, many of which were dry. Upon this I took a large one that was dry, and, having opened its upper extremity, and cleansed it, I went with it to a grape-vine, and filled it with the juice of the grapes. I then stopped up the aperture, and put it in the sun, and left it for some days, until it had become pure wine; and every day I used to drink of it, to help myself to endure the fatigue that I underwent with that obstinate devil; for whenever I was intoxicated by it, my energy was strengthened. So, seeing me one day drinking, he made a sign to me with his hand, as though he would say, What is this? And I answered him, This is something agreeable, that invigorateth the heart, and dilateth the mind. Then I ran with him, and danced among

the trees; I was exhilarated by intoxication, and clapped
my hands, and sang, and was joyful. Therefore when he
beheld me in this state, he made a sign to me to hand him
the pumpkin, that he might drink from it; and I feared him,
and gave it to him; whereupon he drank what remained in
it, and threw it upon the ground, and, being moved with
merriment, began to shake upon my shoulders. He then
became intoxicated, and drowned in intoxication; all his
limbs, and the muscles of his sides, became relaxed, and he
began to lean from side to side upon my shoulders. So
when I knew that he was drunk, and that he was unconscious
of existence, I put my hand to his feet, and loosed them
from my neck. Then I stooped with him, and sat down,
and threw him upon the ground. I scarcely believed that I
had liberated myself and escaped from the state in which I
had been; but I feared him, lest he should arise from his
intoxication, and torment me. I therefore took a great mass
of stone from among the trees, and, coming to him, struck
him upon his head as he lay asleep, so that his flesh became
mingled with his blood, and he was killed. May no mercy
of God be on him!

After that, I walked about the island, with a happy mind,
and came to the place where I was before, on the shore of
the sea. And I remained upon that island eating of its
fruits, and drinking of the water of its rivers, for a length of
time, and watching to see some vessel passing by me, until
I was sitting one day, reflecting upon the events that had
befallen me and happened to me, and I said within myself,
I wonder if God will preserve me in safety, and if I shall
return to my country, and meet my family and my companions. And, lo, a vessel approached from the midst of
the roaring sea agitated with waves, and it ceased not in
its course until it anchored at that island; whereupon the
passengers landed there. So I walked towards them; and
when they beheld me, they all quickly approached me and
assembled around me, inquiring respecting my state, and the
cause of my coming to that island. I therefore acquainted
them with my case, and with the events that had befallen
me; whereat they wondered extremely. And they said to
me, This man who rode upon thy shoulders is called the

Old Man of the Sea, and no one ever was beneath his limbs and escaped from him except thee; and praise be to God for thy safety! Then they brought me some food, and I ate until I was satisfied; and they gave me some clothing, which I put on, covering myself decently. After this, they took me with them in the ship; and when we had proceeded days and nights, destiny drove us to a city of lofty buildings, all the houses of which overlooked the sea. That city is called the City of the Apes; and when the night cometh, the people who reside in it go forth from the doors that open upon the sea, and, embarking in boats and ships, pass the night upon the sea, in their fear of the apes, lest they should come down upon them in the night from the mountains.

I landed to divert myself in this city, and the ship set sail without my knowledge. So I repented of my having landed there, remembering my companions, and what had befallen them from the apes, first and afterwards; and I sat weeping and mourning. And thereupon a man of the inhabitants of the city advanced to me and said to me, O my master, it seemeth that thou art a stranger in this country. I therefore replied, Yes: I am a stranger, and a poor man. I was in a ship which anchored at this city, and I landed from it to divert myself in the city, and returned, but saw not the ship.—And he said, Arise and come with us, and embark in the boat; for if thou remain in the city during the night, the apes will destroy thee. So I replied, I hear and obey. I arose immediately, and embarked with the people in the boat, and they pushed it off from the land until they had propelled it from the shore of the sea to the distance of a mile. They passed the night, and I with them; and when the morning came, they returned in the boat to the city, and landed, and each of them went to his occupation. Such hath been always their custom, every night; and to every one of them who remaineth behind in the city during the night, the apes come, and they destroy him. In the day, the apes go forth from the city, and eat of the fruits in the gardens, and sleep in the mountains until the evening, when they return to the city. And this city is in the furthest parts of the country of the blacks.—Among the most won-

derful of the events that happened to me in the treatment
that I met with from its inhabitants, was this. A person of
the party with whom I passed the night said to me, O my
master, thou art a stranger in this country. Art thou skilled
in any art with which thou mayest occupy thyself?—And I
answered him, No, by Allah, O my brother: I am acquainted
with no art, nor do I know how to make any thing. I was
a merchant, a person of wealth and fortune, and I had a
ship, my own property, laden with abundant wealth and
goods; but it was wrecked in the sea, and all that was in it
sank, and I escaped not drowning but by the permission of
God; for He provided me with a piece of a plank, upon
which I placed myself; and it was the means of my escape
from drowning.—And upon this the man arose and brought
me a cotton bag, and said to me, Take this bag, and fill it
with pebbles from this city, and go forth with a party of the
inhabitants. I will associate thee with them, and give them
a charge respecting thee, and do thou as they shall do. Perhaps thou wilt accomplish that by means of which thou
wilt be assisted to make thy voyage, and to return to thy
country.

Then that man took me and led me forth from the city,
and I picked up small pebbles, with which I filled that bag.
And, lo, a party of men came out from the city, and he
associated me with them, giving them a charge respecting
me, and saying to them, This is a stranger; so take him
with you, and teach him the mode of gathering. Perhaps
he may gain the means of subsistence, and ye will obtain
[from God] a reward and recompense.—And they replied,
We hear and obey. They welcomed me, and took me with
them, and proceeded, each of them having a bag like mine,
filled with pebbles; and we ceased not to pursue our way
until we arrived at a wide valley, wherein were many lofty
trees, which no one could climb. In that valley were also
many apes, which, when they saw us, fled from us, and
ascended those trees. Then the men began to pelt the
apes with the stones that they had with them in the bags;
upon which the apes began to pluck off the fruits of those
trees, and to throw them at the men; and I looked at the
fruits which the apes threw down, and, lo, they were cocoa-

nuts. Therefore when I beheld the party do thus, I chose
a great tree, upon which were many apes, and, advancing to
it, proceeded to pelt those apes with stones; and they broke
off nuts from the tree and threw them at me. So I collected
them as the rest of the party did, and the stones were not
exhausted from my bag until I had collected a great quantity. And when the party had ended this work, they gathered
together all that was with them, and each of them carried
off as many of the nuts as he could. We then returned to
the city during the remainder of the day, and I went to the
man, my companion, who had associated me with the party,
and gave him all that I had collected, thanking him for his
kindness. But he said to me, Take these and sell them,
and make use of the price. And afterwards he gave me the
key of a place in his house, and said to me, Put here these
nuts that thou hast remaining with thee, and go forth every
day with the party as thou hast done this day; and of what
thou bringest, separate the bad, and sell them, and make use
of their price; and the rest keep in thy possession in this
place. Perhaps thou wilt accumulate of them what will aid
thee to make thy voyage.—So I replied, Thy reward is due
from God, whose name be exalted! I did as he told me,
and continued every day to fill the bag with stones, and to
go forth with the people, and do as they did. They used to
commend me, one to another, and to guide me to the tree
upon which was abundance of fruit; and I ceased not to
lead this life for a length of time, so that I collected a great
quantity of good cocoa-nuts, and I sold a great quantity, the
price of which became a large sum in my possession. I
bought every thing that I saw and that pleased me, my time
was pleasant, and my good fortune increased throughout the
whole city.

I remained in this state for some time; after which, as I
was standing by the seaside, lo, a vessel arrived at that city,
and cast anchor by the shore. In it were merchants, with
their goods, and they proceeded to sell and buy, and to
exchange their goods for cocoa-nuts and other things. So I
went to my companion, informed him of the ship that had
arrived, and told him that I desired to make the voyage to
my country. And he replied, It is thine to determine. I

therefore bade him farewell, and thanked him for his kindness to me. Then I went to the ship, and, accosting the master, engaged with him for my passage, and embarked in that ship the cocoa-nuts and other things that I had with me, after which they set sail that same day. We continued our course from island to island and from sea to sea, and at every island at which we cast anchor I sold some of those cocoa-nuts, and exchanged; and God compensated me with more than I had before possessed and lost. We passed by an island in which are cinnamon and pepper, and some persons told us that they had seen, upon every bunch of pepper, a large leaf that shadeth it and wardeth from it the rain whenever it raineth; and when the rain ceaseth to fall upon it, the leaf turneth over from the bunch, and hangeth down by its side. From that island I took with me a large quantity of pepper and cinnamon, in exchange for cocoa-nuts. We passed also by the Island of El-'Asirat, which is that wherein is the Kamari aloes-wood. And after that, we passed by another island, the extent of which is five days' journey, and in it is the Sanfi aloes-wood, which is superior to the Kamari; but the inhabitants of this island are worse in condition and religion than the inhabitants of the island of the Kamari aloes-wood; for they love depravity and the drinking of wines, and know not the call to prayer, nor the act of prayer. And we came after that to the pearl-fisheries; whereupon I gave to the divers some cocoa-nuts, and said to them, Dive for my luck and lot. Accordingly they dived in the bay there, and brought up a great number of large and valuable pearls; and they said to me, O my master, by Allah, thy fortune is good! So I took up into the ship what they had brought up for me, and we proceeded, relying on the blessing of God (whose name be exalted!), and continued our voyage until we arrived at El-Basrah, where I landed, and remained a short time. I then went thence to the city of Baghdad, entered my quarter, came to my house, and saluted my family and companions, who congratulated me on my safety. I stored all the goods and commodities that I had brought with me, clothed the orphans and the widows, bestowed alms and gifts, and made presents to my family and my companions and my friends. God had compensated me with four times as much as I had lost, and I forgot what had happened to me, and the fatigue that I had suffered, by reason of the abundance of my gain and profits, and resumed my first habits of familiar intercourse and fellowship.—Such were the most wonderful things that happened to me in the course of the fifth voyage: but sup ye, and to-morrow come again, and I will relate to you the events of the sixth voyage; for it was more wonderful than this.

The Sixth Voyage of Es-Sindibad of the Sea

KNOW, O my brothers and my friends and my companions, that when I returned from that fifth voyage, and forgot what I had suffered, by reason of sport and merriment and enjoyment and gayety, and was in a state of the utmost joy and happiness, I continued thus until I was sitting one day in exceeding delight and happiness and gayety; and while I sat, lo, a party of merchants came to me, bearing the marks of travel. And upon this I remembered the days of my return from travel, and my joy at meeting my family and companions and friends, and at entering my country; and my soul longed again for travel and commerce. So I determined to set forth. I bought for myself precious, sumptuous goods, suitable for the sea, packed up my bales, and went from the city of Baghdad to the city of El-Basrah, where I beheld a large vessel, in which were merchants and great men, and with them were precious goods. I therefore embarked my bales with them in this ship, and we departed in safety from the city of El-Basrah. We continued our voyage from place to place and from city to city, selling and buying, and diverting ourselves with viewing different countries. Fortune and the voyage were pleasant to us, and we gained our subsistence, until we were proceeding one day, and, lo, the master of the ship vociferated and called out, threw down his turban, slapped his face, plucked his beard, and fell down in the hold of the ship by reason of the violence of his grief and rage. So all the merchants and other passengers came together to him and said to him, O master, what is the matter? And he answered them, Know, O company, that we have wandered from our course, having passed forth from the sea in which we were, and entered a sea of which we know not the routes; and if God appoint not for us some means of effecting our escape from this sea, we all perish: therefore pray to God (whose name be exalted!) that He may save us from this case. Then the master arose and ascended the mast, and desired to loose the sails; but the wind became violent upon the ship, and drove her back, and her rudder broke near a lofty mountain; whereupon the master descended from the mast, and said, There is no strength nor power but in God, the High, the Great! No one is able to prevent what is predestined! By Allah, we have fallen into a great peril, and there remaineth to us no way of safety or escape from it!—So all the passengers wept for themselves: they bade one another farewell, because of the expiration of their lives, and their hope was cut off. The vessel drove upon that mountain, and went to pieces; its planks were scattered, and all that was in it was submerged; the merchants fell into the sea, and some of them were drowned, and some caught hold upon that mountain, and landed upon it.

I was of the number of those who landed upon the mountain; and, lo, within it was a large island. By it were many vessels broken in pieces, and upon it were numerous goods, on the shore of the sea, of the things thrown up by the sea from the ships that had been wrecked, and the passengers of which had been drowned. Upon it was an abundance, that confounded the reason and the mind, of commodities and wealth that the sea cast upon its shores. I ascended to the upper part of the island, and walked about it, and I beheld in the midst of it a stream of sweet water, flowing forth from beneath the nearest part of the mountain, and entering at the furthest part of it, on the opposite side [of the valley]. Then all the other passengers went over that mountain to [the interior of] the island, and dispersed themselves about it, and their reason was confounded at that which they beheld. They became like madmen in consequence of what they saw upon the island, of commodities and wealth lying on the shore of the sea. I beheld also in the midst of the above-mentioned stream an abundance of various kinds of jewels and minerals, with jacinths and large pearls, suitable to Kings. They were like gravel in the channels of the water which flowed through the fields; and all the bed of that stream glittered by reason of the great number of minerals and other things that it contained. We likewise saw on that island an abundance of the best kind of Sanfi aloes-wood, and Kamari aloes-wood. And in that island is a gushing spring of crude ambergris, which floweth like wax over the side of that spring through the violence of the heat of the sun, and spreadeth upon the sea-shore, and the monsters of the deep come up from the sea and swallow it, and descend with it into the sea; but it becometh hot in their stomachs, therefore they eject it from their mouths into the sea, and it congealeth on the surface of the water. Upon this, its colour and its qualities become changed, and the waves cast it up on the shore of the sea: so the travellers and merchants who know it take it and smell it. But as to the crude ambergris that is not swallowed, it floweth over the side of that mountain, and congealeth upon the ground; and when the sun shineth upon it, it melteth, and from it the odour of the whole of that valley becometh like the odour of musk. Then, when the sun withdraweth from it, it congealeth again. The place wherein is this crude ambergris no one can enter: no one can gain access to it: for the mountain surroundeth that island.

We continued to wander about the island, diverting ourselves with the view of the good things which God (whose name be exalted!) had created upon it, and perplexed at our case, and at the things that we beheld, and affected with violent fear. We had collected upon the shore of the sea a small quantity of provisions, and we used it sparingly, eating of it every day, or two days, only one meal, dreading the exhaustion of our stock, and our dying in sorrow, from the violence of hunger and fear. Each one of us that died we washed, and shrouded in some of the clothes and linen which the sea cast upon the shore of the island; and thus we did until a great number of us had died, and there remained of us but a small party, who were weakened by a colic occasioned by the sea. After this, we remained a short period, and all my associates and companions died, one after another, and each of them who died we buried.

Then I was alone on that island, and there remained with me but little of the provisions, after there had been much. So I wept for myself, and said, Would that I had died before my companions, and that they had washed me and buried me! There is no strength nor power but in God, the High, the Great!—And I remained a short time longer; after which I arose and dug for myself a deep grave on the shore of the island, and said within myself, When I fall sick, and know that death hath come to me, I will lie down in this grave, and die in it, and the wind will blow the sand upon me, and cover me; so I shall become buried in it. I blamed myself for my little sense, and my going forth from my country and my city, and my voyaging to foreign countries, after what I had suffered in the first instance, and the second and the third and the fourth and the fifth; and when I had not performed one of my voyages without suffering in it horrors and distresses more troublesome and more difficult than the horrors preceding. I believed not that I could escape and save myself, and repented of undertaking sea-voyages, and of my returning to this life when I was not in want of wealth, but had abundance, so that I could not consume what I had, nor spend half of it during the rest of my life; having enough for me, and more than enough.

Then I meditated in my mind, and said, This river must have a beginning and an end, and it must have a place of egress into an inhabited country. The right plan in my opinion will be for me to construct for myself a small raft, of sufficient size for me to sit upon it, and I will go down and cast it upon this river, and depart on it. If I find safety, I am safe, and escape, by permission of God (whose name be exalted!); and if I find no way of saving myself, it will be better for me to die in this river than in this place.—And I sighed for myself. Then I arose and went and collected pieces of wood that were upon that island, of Sanfi and Kamari aloes-wood, and bound them upon the shore of the sea with some of the ropes of the ships that had been wrecked; and I brought some straight planks, of the planks of the ships, and placed them upon those pieces of wood. I made the raft to suit the width of the river, less wide than the latter, and bound it well and firmly; and having taken with me some of those minerals and jewels and goods, and of the large pearls that were like gravel, as well as other things that were upon the island, and some of the crude, pure, excellent ambergris, I put them upon that raft, with all that I had collected upon the island, and took with me what remained of the provisions. I then launched the raft upon the river, made for it two pieces of wood like oars, and acted in accordance with the following saying of one of the poets:—

Depart from a place wherein is oppression, and leave the house to
    tell its builder's fate;
For thou wilt find, for the land that thou quittest, another; but
    no soul wilt thou find to replace thine own.
Grieve not on account of nocturnal calamities; since every afflic-
    tion will have its end;
And he whose death is decreed to take place in one land will not
    die in any land but that.
Send not thy messenger on an errand of importance; for the soul
    hath no faithful minister save itself.

I departed upon the raft along the river, meditating upon what might be the result of my case, and proceeded to the place where the river entered beneath the mountain. I propelled the raft into that place, and became in intense darkness within it, and the raft continued to carry me in with the current to a narrow place beneath the mountain, where the sides of the raft rubbed against the sides of the channel of the river, and my head rubbed against the roof of the channel. I was unable to return thence, and I blamed myself for that which I had done, and said, If this place become narrower to the raft, it will scarcely pass through it, and it cannot return: so I shall perish in this place in sorrow, inevitably! I threw myself upon my face on the raft, on account of the narrowness of the channel of the river, and ceased not to proceed, without knowing night from day, by reason of the darkness in which I was involved beneath that mountain, together with my terror and fear for myself lest I should perish. In this state I continued my course along the river, which sometimes widened and at other times contracted; but the intensity of the darkness

wearied me excessively, and slumber overcame me in consequence of the violence of my distress. So I lay upon
my face on the raft, which ceased not to bear me along
while I slept, and knew not whether the time was long or
short.

At length I awoke, and found myself in the light; and,
opening my eyes, I beheld an extensive tract, and the raft
tied to the shore of an island, and around me a company of
Indians, and [people like] Abyssinians. When they saw
that I had risen, they rose and came to me, and spoke to
me in their language; but I knew not what they said, and
imagined that it was a dream, and that this occurred in
sleep, by reason of the violence of my distress and vexation.
And when they spoke to me and I understood not their
speech, and returned them not an answer, a man among
them advanced to me, and said to me, in the Arabic
language, Peace be on thee, O our brother! What art thou,
and whence hast thou come, and what is the cause of thy
coming to this place? We are people of the sown lands
and the fields, and we came to irrigate our fields and our
sown lands, and found thee asleep on the raft: so we laid
hold upon it, and tied it here by us, waiting for thee to
rise at thy leisure. Tell us then what is the cause of thy
coming to this place.—I replied, I conjure thee by Allah,
O my master, that thou bring me some food; for I am
hungry; and after that, ask of me concerning what thou
wilt. And thereupon he hastened, and brought me food,
and I ate until I was satiated and was at ease, and my fear
subsided, my satiety was abundant, and my soul returned to
me. I therefore praised God (whose name be exalted!)
for all that had occurred, rejoiced at my having passed
forth from that river, and having come to these people;
and I told them of all that had happened to me from beginning to end, and of what I had experienced upon that river,
and of its narrowness. They then talked together, and said,
We must take him with us and present him to our King,
that he may acquaint him with what hath happened to him.
Accordingly they took me with them, and conveyed with me
the raft, together with all that was upon it, of riches and
goods, and jewels and minerals, and ornaments of gold, and

they took me in to their King, who was the King of
Sarandib,[6] and acquainted him with what had happened;
whereupon he saluted me and welcomed me, and asked me
respecting my state, and respecting the events that had
happened to me. I therefore acquainted him with all my
story, and what I had experienced, from the first to last; and
the King wondered at this narrative extremely, and congratulated me on my safety. Then I arose and took forth
from the raft a quantity of the minerals and jewels, and
aloes-wood and crude ambergris, and gave it to the King;
and he accepted it from me, and treated me with exceeding
honour, lodging me in a place in his abode. I associated
with the best and the greatest of the people, who paid me
great respect, and I quitted not the abode of the King.

The island of Sarandib is under the equinoctial line;
its night being always twelve hours, and its day also twelve
hours. Its length is eighty leagues; and its breadth, thirty;
and it extendeth largely between a lofty mountain and a
deep valley. This mountain is seen from a distance of three
days, and it containeth varieties of jacinths, and different
kinds of minerals, and trees of all sorts of spices, and its
surface is covered with emery, wherewith jewels are cut into
shape: in its rivers also are diamonds, and pearls are in its
valleys. I ascended to the summit of the mountain, and
diverted myself with a view of its wonders, which are not
to be described; and afterwards I went back to the King,
and begged him to give me permission to return to my
country. He gave me permission after great pressing, and
bestowed upon me an abundant present from his treasuries;
and he gave me a present and a sealed letter, saying to me,
Convey these to the Khalifeh Harun Er-Rashid, and give
him many salutations from us. So I replied, I hear and
obey. Then he wrote for me a letter on skin of the khawi,
which is finer than parchment, of yellowish colour; and
the writing was in ultramarine. And the form of what he
wrote to the Khalifeh was this:—Peace be on thee, from
the King of India, before whom are a thousand elephants,
and on the battlements of whose palace are a thousand
jewels. To proceed: we have sent to thee a trifling present:

[6] Ceylon.

accept it then from us. Thou art to us a brother and
sincere friend, and the affection for you that is in our
hearts is great: therefore favour us by a reply. The
present is not suited to thy dignity; but we beg of thee,
O brother, to accept it graciously. And peace be on thee!
—And the present was a cup of ruby, a span high, the
inside of which was embellished with precious pearls; and
a bed covered with the skin of the serpent that swalloweth
the elephant, which skin hath spots, each like a piece of
gold, and whosoever sitteth upon it never becometh diseased,
and a hundred thousand mithkals of Indian aloes-wood;
and a slave-girl like the shining full moon. Then he bade
me farewell, and gave a charge respecting me to the merchants and the master of the ship.

So I departed thence, and we continued our voyage
from island to island and from country to country until
we arrived at Baghdad, whereupon I entered my house, and
met my family and my brethren; after which I took the
present, with a token of service from myself for the Khalifeh.
On entering his presence, I kissed his hand, and placed
before him the whole, giving him the letter; and he read
it, and took the present, with which he was greatly rejoiced,
and he treated me with the utmost honour. He then said
to me, O Sindibad, is that true which this King hath stated
in his letter? And I kissed the ground, and answered,
O my lord, I witnessed in his kingdom much more than
he hath mentioned in his letter. On the day of his public
appearance, a throne is set for him upon a huge elephant,
eleven cubits high, and he sitteth upon it, having with
him his chief officers and pages and guests, standing in two
ranks, on his right and on his left. At his head standeth
a man having in his hand a golden javelin, and behind him
a man in whose hand is a great mace of gold, at the top
of which is an emerald a span in length, and of the thick-
ness of a thumb. And when he mounteth, there mount at
the same time with him a thousand horsemen clad in gold
and silk; and as the King proceedeth, a man before him
proclaimeth, saying, This is the King of great dignity, of
high authority! And he proceedeth to repeat his praises
in terms that I remember not, at the end of his panegyric

saying, This is the King the owner of the crown the like of which neither Suleyman nor the Mihraj possessed! Then he is silent; and one behind him proclaimeth, saying, He will die! Again I say, He will die! Again I say, He will die!—And the other saith, Extolled be the perfection of the Living who dieth not!—Moreover, by reason of his justice and good government and intelligence, there is no Kadi in his city; and all the people of his country distinguish the truth from falsity.—And the Khalifeh wondered at my words, and said, How great is this King! His letter hath shewn me this; and as to the greatness of his dominion, thou hast told us what thou hast witnessed. By Allah, he hath been endowed with wisdom and dominion!—Then the Khalifeh conferred favours upon me, and commanded me to depart to my abode. So I came to my house, and gave the legal and other alms, and continued to live in the same pleasant circumstances as at present. I forgot the arduous troubles that I had experienced, discarded from my heart the anxieties of travel, rejected from my mind distress, and betook myself to eating and drinking, and pleasures and joy.

The Seventh Voyage of Es-Sindibad of the Sea

When I relinquished voyaging, and the affairs of commerce, I said within myself, What hath happened to me sufficeth me. And my time was spent in joy and pleasures. But while I was sitting one day, the door was knocked: so the door-keeper opened, and a page of the Khalifeh entered and said, The Khalifeh summoneth thee. I therefore went with him to his majesty, and kissed the ground before him and saluted him, whereupon he welcomed me and treated me with honour; and he said to me, O Sindibad, I have an affair for thee to perform. Wilt thou do it?—So I kissed his hand, and said to him, O my lord, what affair hath the master for the slave to perform? And he answered me, I desire that thou go to the King of Sarandib, and convey to him our letter and our present; for he sent to us a present and a letter. And I trembled thereat, and replied, By Allah the Great, O my lord, I have taken a hatred to voyaging; and when a voyage on the sea, or any other travel, is mentioned to me, my joints tremble, in consequence of what hath befallen me and what I have experienced of troubles and horrors, and I have no desire for that whatever. Moreover I have bound myself by an oath not to go forth from Baghdad.—Then I informed the Khalifeh of all that had befallen me from the first to last; and he wondered exceedingly, and said, By Allah the Great, O Sindibad, it hath not been heard from times of old that such events have befallen any one as have befallen thee, and it is incumbent on thee that thou never mention the subject of travel. But for my sake thou wilt go this time, and convey our present and our letter to the King of Sarandib; and thou shalt return quickly if it be the will of God (whose name be exalted!), that we may no longer have a debt of favour and courtesy to the King.—So I replied that I heard and obeyed, being unable to oppose his command. He then gave me the present and the letter, with money for my expenses, and I kissed his hand and departed from him.

I went from Baghdad to the sea, and embarked in a ship, and we proceeded days and nights, by the aid of God (whose name be exalted!), until we arrived at the island of Sarandib, and with us were many merchants. As soon as we arrived, we landed at the city, and I took the present and the letter, and went in with them to the King, and kissed the ground before him. And when he saw me, he said, A friendly welcome to thee, O Sindibad! By Allah the Great, we have longed to see thee, and praise be to God who hath shewn us thy face a second time!—Then he took me by the hand, and seated me by his side, welcoming me, and treating me with familiar kindness, and he rejoiced greatly. He began to converse with me, and addressed me with courtesy, and said, What was the cause of thy coming to us, O Sindibad? So I kissed his hand, and thanked him, and answered him, O my lord, I have brought thee a present and a letter from my master the Khalifeh Harun Er-Rashid. I then offered to him the present and the letter, and he read the letter, and rejoiced at it greatly. The present was a horse worth ten thousand pieces of gold, with its saddle adorned with gold set with jewels; and a book, and a sumptuous dress, and a hundred different kinds of white cloths of Egypt, and silks of Es-Suweys[7] and El-Kufeh and Alexandria, and Greek carpets, and a hundred menns of silk and flax, and a wonderful extraordinary cup of crystal, in the midst of which was represented the figure of a lion with a man kneeling before him and having drawn an arrow in his bow with his utmost force, and also the table of Suleyman the son of Da'ud, on whom be peace! And the contents of the letter were as follows:—Peace from the King Er-Rashid, strengthened by God (who hath given to him and to his ancestors the rank of the noble, and wide-spread glory), on the fortunate Sultan. To proceed: thy letter hath reached us, and we rejoiced at it; and we have sent the book [entitled] the Delight of the Intelligent, and the Rare Present for Friends; together with varieties of royal rarities; therefore do us the favour to accept them: and peace be on thee!—Then the King conferred upon me abundant presents, and treated me with the utmost honour; so I prayed for him, and thanked him for his beneficence; and some days after that, I begged his permission to depart; but he permitted me not save after great pressing. Thereupon I took leave of him, and went forth from his city, with merchants and other companions, to return to my country, without any desire for travel or commerce.

We continued our voyage until we had passed many islands; but in the midst of our course over the sea, there appeared to us a number of boats, which surrounded us, and in them were men like devils, having, in their hands, swords and daggers, and equipped with coats of mail, and arms and bows. They smote us, and wounded and slew those of us who opposed them, and, having taken the ship with its contents, conveyed us to an island, where they sold us as slaves, for the smallest price. But a rich man purchased me, and took me into his house, fed me and gave me to drink, and clad me and treated me in a friendly manner. So my soul was tranquillized, and I rested a little. Then, one day, he said to me, Dost thou not know any art or trade? I answered him, O my lord, I am a merchant: I

7 Suez.

know nothing but traffic. And he said, Dost thou know the art of shooting with the bow and arrow?—Yes, I answered: I know that. And thereupon he brought me a bow and arrows, and mounted me behind him upon an elephant: then he departed at the close of night, and, conveying me among some great trees, came to a lofty and firm tree, upon which he made me climb; and he gave me the bow and arrows, saying to me, Sit here now, and when the elephants come in the daytime to this place, shoot at them with the arrows: perhaps thou wilt strike one of them; and if one of them fall, come to me and inform me. He then left me and departed; and I was terrified and frightened. I remained concealed in the tree until the sun rose; when the elephants came forth wandering about among the trees, and I ceased not to discharge my arrows till I shot one of them. I therefore went in the evening to my master, and informed him; and he was delighted with me, and treated me with honour; and he went and removed the slain elephant.

In this manner I continued, every day shooting one, and my master coming and removing it, until one day, I was sitting in the tree, concealed, and suddenly elephants innumerable came forth, and I heard the sounds of their roaring and growling, which were such that I imagined the earth trembled beneath them. They all surrounded the tree in which I was sitting, their circuit being fifty cubits, and a huge elephant, enormously great, advanced and came to the tree, and, having wound his trunk around it, pulled it up by the roots, and cast it upon the ground. I fell down senseless among the elephants, and the great elephant, approaching me, wound his trunk around me, raised me on his back, and went away with me, the other elephants accompanying. And he ceased not to proceed with me, while I was absent from the world, until he had taken me into a place, and thrown me from his back, when he departed, and the other elephants followed him. So I rested a little, and my terror subsided; and I found myself among the bones of elephants. I knew therefore that this was the burial-place of the elephants, and that that elephant had conducted me to it on account of the teeth.

I then arose, and journeyed a day and a night until I

arrived at the house of my master, who saw me changed in complexion by fright and hunger. And he was rejoiced at my return, and said, By Allah, thou hast pained our heart; for I went and found the tree torn up, and I imagined that the elephants had destroyed thee. Tell me, then, how it happened with thee.—So I informed him of that which had befallen me; whereat he wondered greatly, and rejoiced; and he said to me, Dost thou know that place? I answered, Yes, O my master. And he took me, and we went out, mounted on an elephant, and proceeded until we came to that place; and when my master beheld those numerous teeth, he rejoiced greatly at the sight of them; and he carried away as much as he desired, and we returned to the house. He then treated me with increased favour, and said to me, O my son, thou hast directed us to a means of very great gain. May God then recompense thee well! Thou art freed for the sake of God, whose name be exalted! These elephants used to destroy many of us on account of [our seeking] these teeth; but God hath preserved thee from them, and thou hast profited us by these teeth to which thou hast directed us.—I replied, O my master, may God free thy neck from the fire [of Hell]! And I request of thee, O my master, that thou give me permission to depart to my country.—Yes, said he: thou shalt have that permission: but we have a fair, on the occasion of which the merchants come to us and purchase the teeth of these elephants of us. The time of the fair is now near; and when they have come to us, I will send thee with them, and will give thee what will convey thee to thy country.—So I prayed for him and thanked him; and I remained with him treated with respect and honour.

Then, some days after this, the merchants came as he had said, and bought and sold and exchanged; and when they were about to depart, my master came to me, and said, The merchants are going: therefore arise that thou mayest depart with them to thy country. Accordingly I arose, determined to go with them. They had bought a great quantity of those teeth, and packed up their loads, and embarked them in the ship; and my master sent me with them. He paid for me the money for my passage in the ship, together with all that was required of me, and gave me a large quantity of goods. And we pursued our voyage from island to island until we had crossed the sea and landed on the shore, when the merchants took forth what was with them, and sold. I also sold what I had at an excellent rate; and I purchased some of the most elegant of things suited for presents, and beautiful rarities, with every thing that I desired. I likewise bought for myself a beast to ride, and we went forth, and crossed the deserts from country to country until I arrived at Baghdad; when I went in to the Khalifeh, and, having given the salutation, and kissed his hand, I informed him of what had happened and what had befallen me; whereupon he rejoiced at my safety, and thanked God (whose name be exalted!); and he caused my story to be written in letters of gold. I then entered my house, and met my family and my brethren.—This is the end of the history of the events that happened to me during my voyages; and praise be to God, the One, the Creator, the Maker!

And when Es-Sindibad of the Sea had finished his story, he ordered his servant to give to Es-Sindibad of the Land a hundred pieces of gold, and said to him, How now, O my brother? Hast thou heard of the like of these afflictions and calamities and distresses, or have such troubles as have befallen me befallen any one else, or hath any one else suffered such hardships as I have suffered? Know then that these pleasures are a compensation for the toil and humiliations that I have experienced.—And upon this, Es-Sindibad of the Land advanced, and kissed his hands, and said to him, O my lord, by Allah, thou hast undergone great horrors, and hast deserved these abundant favours: continue then, O my lord, in joy and security; for God hath removed from thee the evils of fortune; and I beg of God that He may continue to thee thy pleasures, and bless thy days.— And upon this, Es-Sindibad of the Sea bestowed favours upon him, and made him his boon-companion; and he quitted him not by night nor by day as long as they both lived.

Praise be to God, the Mighty, the Omnipotent, the Strong, the Eminent in power, the Creator of the heaven and the earth, and of the land and the seas!

THE STORY OF THE CITY OF BRASS

THERE was, in olden time, and in an ancient age and period, in Damascus of Syria, a King, one of the Khalifehs, named 'Abd-El-Melik the son of Marwan; and he was sitting, one day, having with him the great men of his empire, consisting of Kings and Sultans, when a discussion took place among them, respecting the traditions of former nations. They called to mind the stories of our lord Suleyman the son of Da'ud (on both of whom be peace!), and the dominion and authority which God (whose name be exalted!) had bestowed upon him over mankind and the Jinn and the birds and the wild beasts and other things; and they said, We have heard from those who were before us that God (whose perfection be extolled, and whose name be exalted!) bestowed not upon any one the like of that which He bestowed upon our lord Suleyman, and that he attained to that to which none other attained, so that he used to imprison the Jinn and the Marids and the Devils in bottles of brass, and pour molten lead over them, and seal this cover over them with a signet.

Then Talib [the son of Sahl] related, that a man embarked in a ship with a company of others, and they voyaged to the island of Sicily, and ceased not in their course until there arose against them a wind which bore them away to one of the lands of God, whose name be exalted! This happened during the black darkness of night, and when the day shone forth, there came out to them, from caves in that land, people of black complexion and with naked bodies, like wild beasts, not understanding speech. They had a King of their own race, and none of them knew Arabic save their King. So when they saw the ship and those who were in her, he came forth to them attended by a party of his companions, and saluted them and welcomed them, and inquired of them respecting their religion. They therefore acquainted him with their state; and he said to them, No harm shall befall you. And when he asked them respecting their religion, each of them was of some one of the religions prevailing before the manifestation of El-Islam, and before the mission of Mohammad, may God bless and save him!— wherefore the people of the ship said, We know not what thou sayest. Then the King said to them, There hath not come to us any one of the sons of Adam before you. And he entertained them with a banquet of the flesh of birds and of wild beasts and of fish, beside which they had no food. And after this, the people of the ship went down to divert themselves in the city, and they found one of the fishermen who had cast his net in the sea to catch fish, and he drew it up, and lo, in it was a bottle of brass, stopped with lead, which was sealed with the signet of Suleyman the son of Da'ud, on both of whom be peace! And the fisherman came forth and broke it; whereupon there proceeded from it a blue smoke, which united with the clouds of heaven; and they heard a horrible voice, saying, Repentance! re-pentance! O Prophet of God!—Then, of that smoke there was formed a person of terrible aspect, of terrific make, whose head would reach [as high as] a mountain; and he disappeared from before their eyes. As to the people of the ship, their hearts were almost eradicated; but the blacks thought nothing of the event. And a man returned to the King, and asked him respecting this; and the King answered him, Know that this is one of the Jinn whom Suleyman the son of Da'ud, when he was incensed against them, imprisoned in these bottles, and he poured lead over them, and threw them into the sea. When the fisherman casteth his net, it generally bringeth up these bottles; and when they are broken, there cometh forth from them a Jinni, who imagineth that Suleyman is still living; wherefore he repenteth, and saith, Repentance! O Prophet of God!

And the Prince of the Faithful, 'Abd-El-Melik the son of Marwan, wondered at these words, and said, Extolled be the perfection of God! Suleyman was endowed with a mighty dominion!—And among those who were present in that assembly was En-Nabighah Edh-Dhubyani;[1] and he said, Talib hath spoken truth in that which he hath related, and the proof of his veracity is the saying of the Wise, the First, [thus versified]—

And [consider] Suleyman, when the Deity said to him, Perform
    the office of Khalifeh, and govern with diligence;
And whoso obeyeth thee, honour him for doing so; and whoso
    disobeyeth thee, imprison him for ever.

He used to put them into bottles of brass, and to cast them into the sea.—And the Prince of the Faithful approved of these words, and said, By Allah, I desire to see some of these bottles! So Talib the son of Sahl replied, O Prince of the Faithful, thou art able to do so, and yet remain in thy country. Send to thy brother 'Abd-El-'Aziz, the son of Marwan, desiring him to bring them to thee from the Western country,[2] that he may write orders to Musa[3] to journey from the Western Country to this mountain which we have mentioned, and to bring thee what thou desirest of these bottles; for the furthest tract of his province is adjacent to this mountain.—And the Prince of the Faithful approved of his advice, and said, O Talib, thou hast spoken truth in that which thou hast said, and I desire that thou be my messenger to Musa the son of Nuseyr for this purpose, and thou shalt have a white ensign, together with what thou shalt desire of wealth or dignity or other things, and I will be thy substitute to take care of thy family. To this, Talib replied, Most willingly, O Prince of the Faithful. And the Khalifeh said to him, Go in dependence on the blessing of God, and his aid. Then he gave orders that they should write for him a letter to his brother 'Abd-El-'Aziz, his viceroy in Egypt, and another letter to Musa, his viceroy in the Western Country, commanding him to journey, himself, in search of the bottles of Suleyman, to leave his son to govern the country in his stead, and to take with him guides, to expand wealth, and to collect a large number of men, and not to be remiss in accomplishing that object, nor to use any pretext to excuse himself. He sealed the two

[1] An Arab poet, who, however, died before Islam.
[2] El-Maghrib, North Africa.
[3] [The Arab general who conquered North Africa and Spain.]

letters, and delivered them to Talib the son of Sahl, commanding him to hasten, and to elevate the ensigns over
his head; and he gave him riches and riders and footmen
to aid him in his way: he gave orders also to supply his
house with every thing requisite.

So Talib went forth on his way to Egypt. He proceeded
with his companions, traversing the districts from Syria,
until they entered Misr;[4] when the Governor of Egypt met
him, and lodged him with him; and he treated him with
the utmost honour during the period of his stay with
him. Then he sent with him a guide who accompanied him
to Upper Egypt until they came to the Emir Musa the
son of Nuseyr; and when he knew of his approach, he went
forth to him and met him, and rejoiced at his arrival;
and Talib handed to him the letter. So he took it and
read it and understood its meaning; and he put it upon
his head saying, I hear and obey the command of the
Prince of the Faithful. He determined to summon the
great men; and they presented themselves; and he inquired of them respecting that which had been made known
to him by the letter; whereupon they said, O Emir, if thou
desire him who will guide thee to that place, have recourse
to the sheykh 'Abd-Es-Samad the son of 'Abd-El-Kuddus El-
Masmudi; for he is a knowing man, and hath travelled
much, and he is acquainted with the deserts and wastes and
the seas, and their inhabitants and their wonders, and the
countries and their districts. Have recourse therefore to
him, and he will direct thee to the object of thy desire.
Accordingly he gave orders to bring him, and he came before
him; and, lo, he was a very old man, whom the vicissitudes
of years and times had rendered decrepit. The Emir Musa
saluted him, and said to him, O sheykh 'Abd-Es-Samad, our
lord the Prince of the Faithful, 'Abd-El-Melik the son of
Marwan, hath commanded us thus and thus, and I possess
little knowledge of that land, and it hath been told me that
thou art acquainted with that country and the routes. Hast
thou then a wish to accomplish the affair of the Prince of
the Faithful?—The sheykh replied, Know, O Emir, that
this route is difficult, far extending, with few tracks. The

I. e., El-Fustat, "Old Cairo."

Emir said to him, How long a period doth it require? He answered, It is a journey of two years and some months going, and the like returning; and on the way are difficulties and horrors, and extraordinary and wonderful things. Moreover, thou art a warrior for the defence of the faith, and our country is near unto the enemy; so perhaps the Christians may come forth during our absence: it is expedient therefore that thou leave in thy province one to govern it.— He replied, Well. And he left his son Harun as his substitute in his province, exacted an oath of fidelity to him, and commanded the troops that they should not oppose him, but obey him in all that he should order them to do. And they heard his words, and obeyed him. His son Harun was of great courage, an illustrious hero, and a bold champion; and the sheykh 'Abd-Es-Samad pretended to him that the place in which were the things that the Prince of the Faithful desired was four months' journey distant, on the shore of the sea, and that throughout the whole route were halting-places adjacent one to another, and grass and springs. And he said, God will assuredly make this affair easy to us through the blessing attendant upon thee, O Viceroy of the Prince of the Faithful. Then the Emir Musa said, Knowest thou if any one of the Kings have trodden this land before us? He answered him, Yes, O Emir: this land belonged to the King of Alexandria, Darius the Greek.

After this they departed, and they continued their journey until they arrived at a palace; whereupon the sheykh said, Advance with us to this palace, which presenteth a lesson to him who will be admonished. So the Emir Musa advanced thither, together with the sheykh 'Abd-Es-Samad and his chief companions, till they came to its entrance. And they found it open, and having lofty angles, and steps, among which were two wide steps of coloured marbles, the like of which hath not been seen: the ceilings and walls were decorated with gold and silver and minerals, and over the entrance was a slab, whereon was an inscription in ancient Greek; and the sheykh 'Abd-Es-Samad said, Shall I read it, O Emir? The Emir answered, Advance and read. May God bless thee! for nought hath happened to us during this journey but what hath been the result of the blessing attend-

ant upon thee.—So he read it; and, lo, it was poetry; and
it was this:—

Here was a people whom, after their works, thou shalt see wept
    over for their lost dominion;
And in this palace is the last information respecting lords collected
    in the dust.
Death hath destroyed them and disunited them, and in the dust
    they have lost what they amassed;
As though they had only put down their loads to rest a while:
    quickly have they departed!

And the Emir Musa wept until he became insensible, and he
said, There is no deity but God, the Living, the Enduring
without failure! He then entered the palace, and was confounded by its beauty and its construction; and he looked
at the figures and images that it contained. And, lo, over
the second door were inscribed some verses. So the Emir
Musa said, Advance, O sheykh, and read. Accordingly he
advanced and read; and the verses were these:—

How many companies have alighted in the tabernacles since times
    of old, and taken their departure!
Consider thou then what the accidents of fortune have done with
    others when they have befallen them.
They have shared together what they collected, and they have left
    the pleasure thereof, and departed.
What enjoyments they had! and what food did they eat! and then
    in the dust they themselves were eaten!

And again the Emir Musa wept violently: the world became
yellow before his face; and he said, We have been created
for a great object!
    Then they attentively viewed the palace; and, lo, it was
devoid of inhabitants, destitute of household and occupants:
its courts were desolate, and its apartments were deserted;
and in the midst of it was a chamber covered with a
lofty dome, rising high into the air, around which were
four hundred tombs. To these tombs the Emir Musa drew
near, and, behold, among them was a tomb constructed of
marble, whereupon were engraved these verses:—

How often have I stood [in fight]! and how often slain! and to
    how many things have I been a witness!
And how often have I eaten! and how often drunk! and how
    often have I heard the songs of beauteous damsels!

And how often have I ordered! and how often forbidden! and
   how many strong fortresses are seen,
Which I have besieged and searched, and from which I have taken
   the lovely females' ornaments!
But in my ignorance I transgressed to obtain things wished for,
   which proved at last to be frail.
Then consider attentively thy case, O man, before thou shalt drink
   the cup of death;
For after a little while shall the dust be poured upon thee, and
   thou wilt be lifeless.

And the Emir Musa, and those who were with him, wept.
Then he drew near to the dome-crowned chamber, and, lo,
it had eight doors of sandal-wood, with nails of gold, ornamented with stars of silver set with various jewels. And over
the first door were inscribed these verses:—

What I have left, I left not from generosity; but through the
   sentence and decree operating upon man.
Long time I lived, happy and enraged, defending my asylum like
   a fierce lion.
I was never quiet, nor would I bestow a mustard-seed, by reason
   of my avarice, though I were cast into the fire.
Thus did I until I was smitten by the decree of the glorious Deity,
   the Creator, the Maker.
When my death was appointed soon to take place, I could not
   prevent it by my numerous stratagems;
My troops that I had collected availed not, and none of my friends
   aided me, nor my neighbour.
Throughout my whole life was I wearied in my journey to the
   grave, now in ease, and now in difficulty.
So, when the purses have become laden, shouldst thou accumulate
   dinar upon dinar,
It will pass before the morning to another, and they will have
   brought thee a camel-driver and a grave-digger;
And on the day of thy judgment, lone shalt thou meet God, laden
   with sin and crimes and heavy burdens.
Then let not the world deceive thee with its beauty; but see what
   it hath done to thy family and neighbour.

And when the Emir Musa heard these verses, he wept again
so violently that he became insensible; and after he had
recovered, he entered the chamber covered with the dome,
and beheld in it a long tomb, of terrible appearance, whereon
was a tablet of iron of China; and the sheykh 'Abd-Es-Samad
drew near to it, and read its inscription; and, lo, on it was
written,—

In the name of God, the Eternal, the Everlasting throughout all ages: in the name of God, who begetteth not, and who is not begotten, and unto whom there is none like: in the name of God, the Mighty and Powerful: in the name of the Living who dieth not.— To proceed:—O thou who arrivest at this place, be admonished by the misfortunes and calamities that thou beholdest, and be not deceived by the world and its beauty, and its falsity and calumny, and its fallacy and finery; for it is a flatterer, a cheat, a traitor. Its things are borrowed, and it will take the loan from the borrower: and it is like the confused visions of the sleeper, and the dream of the dreamer, as though it were the sarab[5] of the plain, which the thirsty imagineth to be water: the Devil adorneth it for man until death. These are the characteristics of the world: confide not therefore in it, nor incline to it; for it will betray him who dependeth upon it, and who in his affairs relieth upon it. Fall not in its snares, nor cling to its skirts. For I possessed four thousand bay horses in a stable; and I married a thousand damsels, of the daughters of Kings, high-bosomed virgins, like moons; and I was blessed with a thousand children, like stern lions; and I lived a thousand years, happy in mind and heart; and I amassed riches such as the Kings of the regions of the earth were unable to procure, and I imagined that my enjoyments would continue without failure. But I was not aware when there alighted among us the terminator of delights and the separator of companies, the desolator of abodes and the ravager of inhabited mansions, the destroyer of the great and the small and the infants and the children and the mothers. We had resided in this palace in security until the event decreed by the Lord of all creatures, the Lord of the heavens and the Lord of the earths, befell us, and the thunder of the Manifest Truth assailed us, and there died of us every day two, till a great company of us had perished. So when I saw that destruction had entered our dwellings, and had alighted among us, and drowned us in the sea of deaths, I summoned a writer, and ordered him to write these verses and admonitions and lessons, and caused them to be engraved upon these doors and tablets and tombs. I had an army comprising a thousand thousand bridles, composed of hardy men, with spears, and coats of mail, and sharp swords, and strong arms; and I ordered them to clothe themselves with the long coats of mail, and to hang on the keen swords, and to place in rest the terrible lances, and mount the high-blooded horses. Then, when the event appointed by the Lord of all creatures, the Lord of the earth and the heavens, befell us, I said, O companies of troops and soldiers, can ye prevent that which hath befallen me from the Mighty King? But the soldiers and troops were unable to do so, and they said, How shall we contend against Him from whom none hath secluded, the Lord of the door that hath no door-keeper? So I said, Bring to me the wealth. (And it was contained in a thousand pits, in

---

[5] Mirage.

each of which were a thousand hundred-weights of red gold, and in them were varieties of pearls and jewels, and there was the like quantity of white silver, with treasures such as the Kings of the earth were unable to procure.)   And they did so; and when they had brought the wealth before me, I said to them, Can ye deliver me by means of all these riches, and purchase for me therewith one day during which I may remain alive?   But they could not do so. They resigned themselves to fate and destiny, and I submitted to God with patient endurance of fate and affliction until He took my soul, and made me to dwell in my grave.   And if thou ask concerning my name, I am Kush the son of Sheddad the son of 'Ad the Greater.

And upon the same tablet were also inscribed these verses:—

Shouldst thou think upon me after the length of my age, and the vicissitudes of days and circumstances,
I am the son of Sheddad, who held dominion over mankind and each tract of the whole earth.
All the stubborn troops became abject unto me, and Esh-Sham from Misr unto 'Adnan.
In glory I reigned, abasing their Kings, the people of the earth fearing my dominion;
And I beheld the tribes and armies in my power, and saw the countries and their inhabitants dread me.
When I mounted, I beheld my army comprising a million bridles upon neighing steeds;
And I possessed wealth that could not be calculated, which I treasured up against misfortunes,
Determining to devote the whole of my property for the purpose of extending the term of my life.
But the Deity would nought save the execution of his purpose; and thus I became separated from my brethren.
Death, the disuniter of mankind, came to me, and I was removed from grandeur to the mansion of contempt;
And I found [the recompense of] all my past actions, for which I am pledged: for I was sinful!
Then raise thyself, lest thou be upon a brink; and beware of calamities!   Mayest thou be led aright!

And again the Emir Musa wept until he became insensible, in considering the fates of the people; after which, as they were going about through the different apartments of the palace, and viewing attentively its chambers and its places of diversion, they came to a table upon four legs of alabaster, whereon was inscribed,—

Upon this table have eaten a thousand one-eyed Kings, and a thousand Kings each sound in both eyes. All of them have quitted the world, and taken up their abode in the burial-grounds and the graves.

And the Emir Musa wrote all this. Then he went forth, and took not with him from the palace aught save the table.

The soldiers proceeded, with the sheykh 'Abd-Es-Samad before them shewing them the way, until all the first day had passed, and the second, and the third. They then came to a high hill, at which they looked, and, lo, upon it was a horseman of brass, on the top of whose spear was a wide and glistening head that almost deprived the beholder of sight, and on it was inscribed, O thou who comest up to me, if thou know not the way that leadeth to the City of Brass, rub the hand of the horseman, and he will turn, and then will stop, and in whatsoever direction he stoppeth, thither proceed, without fear and without difficulty; for it will lead thee to the City of Brass.—And when the Emir Musa had rubbed the hand of the horseman, it turned like the blinding lightning, and faced a different direction from that in which they were travelling.

The party therefore turned thither and journeyed on, and it was the right way. They took that route, and continued their course the same day and the next night until they had traversed a wide tract of country. And as they were proceeding, one day, they came to a pillar of black stone, wherein was a person sunk to his arm-pits, and he had two huge wings, and four arms; two of them like those of the sons of Adam, and two like the fore-legs of lions, with claws. He had hair upon his head like the tails of horses, and two eyes like two burning coals, and he had a third eye, in his forehead, like the eye of the lynx, from which there appeared sparks of fire. He was black and tall; and he was crying out, Extolled be the perfection of my Lord, who hath appointed me this severe affliction and painful torture until the day of resurrection! When the party beheld him, their reason fled from them, and they were stupefied at the sight of his form, and retreated in flight; and the Emir Musa said to the sheykh 'Abd-Es-Samad, What is this? He answered, I know not what he is. And the Emir said, Draw near to him and investigate his case: perhaps he will discover it, and perhaps thou wilt learn his history. The sheykh 'Abd-Es-Samad replied, May God amend the state of the Emir! Verily we fear him.—Fear ye not, rejoined the Emir; for he is withheld from injuring you and others by the state in which he is. So the sheykh 'Abd-Es-Samad drew near to him, and said to him, O thou person, what is thy name, and what is thy nature, and what hath placed thee here in this manner? And he answered him, As to me, I am an 'Efrit of the Jinn, and my name is Dahish the son of El-A'mash, and I am restrained here by the majesty, confined by the power, [of God,] tormented as long as God (to whom be ascribed might and glory!) willeth. Then the Emir Musa said, O sheykh 'Abd-Es-Samad, ask him what is the cause of his confinement in this pillar. He therefore asked respecting that, and the 'Efrit answered him, Verily my story is wonderful; and it is this:—

There belonged to one of the sons of Iblis an idol of red carnelian, of which I was made guardian; and there used to worship it one of the Kings of the sea, of illustrious dignity, of great glory, leading, among his troops of the Jann, a million warriors who smote with swords before him, and who answered his prayer in cases of difficulty. These Jann who obeyed him were under my command and authority, following my words when I ordered them: all of them were in rebellion against Suleyman the son of Da'ud (on both of whom be peace!); and I used to enter the body of the idol, and command them and forbid them. Now the daughter of that King was a frequent adorer of the idol, assiduous in the worship of it, and she was the handsomest of the people of her age, endowed with beauty and loveliness, and elegance and perfection; and I described her to Suleyman, on whom be peace!

So he sent to her father, saying to him, Marry to me thy daughter and break thy carnelian-idol, and bear witness that there is no deity but God, and that Suleyman is the Prophet of God. If thou do so, thy due shall be the same as our due, and thy debt as our debt. But if thou refuse, I bring against thee forces with which thou hast not power to contend: therefore prepare an answer to the ques-

tion,[6] and put on the garment of death; for I will come
to thee with forces that shall fill the vacant region, and leave
thee like yesterday that hath passed.—And when the messenger of Suleyman (on whom be peace!) came to him, he
was insolent and contumacious, and magnified himself and
was proud. Then he said to his wezirs, What say ye respecting the affair of Suleyman the son of Da'ud? For he
hath sent demanding my daughter, and commanding me to
break my carnelian-idol, and to adopt his faith.—And they
replied, O great King, can Suleyman do unto thee that, when
thou art in the midst of this vast sea? If he come unto
thee, he cannot prevail against thee; since the Marids of the
Jinn will fight on thy side; and thou shalt seek aid against
him of thine idol that thou worshippest; for he will aid thee
against him and will defend thee. The right opinion is, that
thou consult thy lord (and they meant by him the red
carnelian-idol), and hear what will be his reply: if he counsel thee to fight him, fight him; but otherwise, do not.—And
upon this the King went immediately, and, going in to his
idol, after he had offered a sacrifice and slain victims, fell
down before it prostrate, and began to weep, and to recite
these verses:—

O my lord, verily I know thy dignity; and, behold, Suleyman
    desireth to break thee.
O my lord, verily I seek thy defence: command then; for I am
    obedient to thy command.

(Then that 'Efrit, the half of whom was in the pillar, said
to the sheykh 'Abd-Es-Samad, while those around him
listened,) And thereupon I entered the body of the idol, by
reason of my ignorance, and the paucity of my sense, and
my solicitude respecting the affair of Suleyman, and recited
this couplet:—

As for me, I am not in fear of him; for I am acquainted with
    every thing.
If he wish to wage war with me, I will go forth, and I will snatch
    his soul from him.

So when the King heard my reply to him, his heart was
strengthened, and he determined to wage war with Suleyman

[6] On the day of judgment.

the Prophet of God (on whom be peace!) and to fight against him. Accordingly, when the messenger of Suleyman came, he inflicted upon him a painful beating, and returned him a shameful reply; and he sent to threaten Suleyman, saying to him, by the messenger, Thy mind hath suggested to thee desires. Dost thou threaten me with false words? Either come thou to me, or I will go to thee.

Then the messenger returned to Suleyman, and acquainted him with all that had occurred and happened to him. And when the Prophet of God, Suleyman, heard that, [it was as though] his resurrection took place;[7] his resolution was roused, and he prepared his forces, consisting of Jinn and men, and wild beasts, and birds and reptiles. He commanded his Wezir Ed-Dimiryat, the King of the Jinn, to collect the Marids of the Jinn from every place: so he collected for him, of the Devils, six hundred millions. He also commanded Asaf the son of Barkhiya [his Wezir of men] to collect his soldiers of mankind; and their number was one million or more. He made ready the accoutrements and weapons, and mounted, with his forces of the Jinn and of mankind, upon the carpet, with the birds flying over his head, and the wild beasts beneath the carpet marching, until he alighted upon his enemy's coast, and surrounded his island, having filled the land with the forces. He then sent to our King, saying to him, Behold, I have arrived: therefore repel from thee that which hath come down, or else submit thyself to my authority, and acknowledge my mission, and break thine idol, and worship the One, the Adored God, and marry to me thy daughter according to law, and say thou, and those who are with thee, I testify that there is no deity but God, and I testify that Suleyman is the Prophet of God. If thou say that, peace and safety shall be thy lot. But if thou refuse, thy defending thyself from me in this island shall not prevent thee: for God (whose name be blessed and exalted!) hath commanded the wind to obey me, and I will order it to convey me unto thee on the carpet, and will make thee an example to restrain others.—So the messenger came to him, and communicated to him the message of the Prophet of God, Suleyman, on

[7] *I. e.*, his passion rose.

whom be peace! But the King said to him, There is no
way for the accomplishment of this thing that he requireth
of me: therefore inform him that I am coming forth unto
him. Accordingly the messenger returned to Suleyman, and
gave him the reply. The King then sent to the people of his
country, and collected for himself, of the Jinn that were
under his authority, a million; and to these he added others,
of the Marids and Devils that were in the islands of the
seas and on the tops of the mountains; after which he made
ready his forces, and opened the armouries, and distributed
to them the weapons. And as the Prophet of God, Suleyman (on whom be peace!), he disposed his troops, commanding the wild beasts to form themselves into two
divisions, on the right of the people and on their left,
and commanding the birds to be upon the islands.   He
ordered them also, when the assault should be made, to
tear out the eyes of their antagonists with their beaks, and
to beat their faces with their wings; and he ordered the
wild beasts to tear in pieces their horses; and they replied,
We hear and obey God and thee, O Prophet of God! Then
Suleyman, the Prophet of God, set for himself a couch of
alabaster adorned with jewels, and plated with plates of red
gold, and he placed his Wezir Asaf the son of Barkhiya on
the right side, and his Wezir Ed-Dimiryat on the left side,
and the Kings of mankind on his right, and the Kings of
the Jinn on his left, and the wild beasts and the vipers and
serpents before him.

After this, they came upon us all together, and we contended with him in a wide tract for a period of two days;
and calamity befell us on the third day, and the decree of
God (whose name be exalted!) was executed among us. The
first who charged upon Suleyman were I and my troops; and
I said to my companions, Keep in your places in the battle-
field while I go forth to them and challenge Ed-Dimiryat.
And, lo, he came forth, like a great mountain, his fires flaming, and his smoke ascending; and he approached, and smote
me with a flaming fire; and his arrow prevailed over my fire.
He cried out at me with a prodigious cry, so that I imagined
the heaven had fallen and closed over me, and the mountains
shook at his voice. Then he commanded his companions, and

they charged upon us all together: we also charged upon them, and we cried out, one to another: the fires rose and the smoke ascended, the hearts of the combatants were almost cleft asunder, and the battle raged. The birds fought in the air; and the wild beasts in the dust; and I contended with Ed-Dimiryat until he wearied me and I wearied him; after which I became weak, and my companions and troops were enervated, and my tribes were routed. The Prophet of God, Suleyman, cried out, Take ye this great tyrant, the ill-omened, the infamous! And the men charged upon the men, and the Jinn upon the Jinn; defeat befell our King, and we became unto Suleyman a spoil. His troops charged upon our forces, with the wild beasts on their right and left, and the birds were over our heads, tearing out the eyes of the people, sometimes with their talons and sometimes with their beaks, and sometimes they beat with their wings upon the faces of the combatants, while the wild beasts bit the horses and tore in pieces the men, until the greater portion of the party lay upon the face of the earth like the trunks of palm-trees. As to me, I flew from before Ed-Dimiryat; but he followed me a journey of three months, until he overtook me. I had fallen down through fatigue, and he rushed upon me, and made me a prisoner. So I said to him, By Him who hath exalted thee and abased me, pity me, and take me before Suleyman, on whom be peace! But when I came before Suleyman, he met me in a most evil manner: he caused this pillar to be brought, and hollowed it, and put me in it, and sealed me with his signet; after which, he chained me, and Ed-Dimiryat conveyed me to this place, where he set me down as thou seest me; and this pillar is my prison until the day of resurrection. He charged a great king to guard me in this prison, and I am in this condition tortured as thou seest me.

The party therefore wondered at him, and at the horrible nature of his form; and the Emir Musa said, There is no deity but God! Suleyman was endowed with a mighty dominion!—And the sheykh 'Abd-Es-Samad said to the 'Efrit, O thou, I ask thee concerning a thing of which do thou inform us. The 'Efrit replied, Ask concerning what thou wilt. And the sheykh said, Are there in this place any of the 'Efrits confined in bottles of brass from the time of Suley-

man, on whom be peace? He answered, Yes, in the Sea of
El-Karkar, where are a people of the descendants of Nuh
(on whom be peace!), whose country the deluge reached not,
and they are separated there from [the rest of] the sons of
Adam.—And where, said the sheykh, is the way to the City
of Brass, and the place wherein are the bottles? What distance is there between us and it?—The 'Efrit answered, It
is near. So the party left him, and proceeded; and there appeared to them a great black object, with two [seeming] fires
corresponding with each other in position, in the distance, in
that black object; whereupon the Emir Musa said to the
sheykh, What is this great black object, and what are these
two corresponding fires? The guide answered him, Be rejoiced, O Emir; for this is the City of Brass, and this is the
appearance of it that I find described in the Book of Hidden
Treasures; that its wall is of black stones, and it hath two
towers of brass of El-Andalus,[8] which the beholder seeth
resembling two corresponding fires; and thence it is named
the City of Brass.—They ceased not to proceed until they arrived at it; and, lo, it was lofty, strongly fortified, rising high
into the air, impenetrable: the height of its walls was eighty
cubits, and it had five and twenty gates, none of which would
open but by means of some artifice; and there was not one
gate to it that had not, within the city, one like it: such was
the beauty of the construction and architecture of the city.
They stopped before it, and endeavoured to discover one of
its gates; but they could not; and the Emir Musa said to the
sheykh 'Abd-Es-Samad, O sheykh, I see not to this city any
gate. The sheykh replied, O Emir, thus do I find it described
in the Book of Hidden Treasures; that it hath five and twenty
gates, and that none of its gates may be opened but from
within the city.—And how, said the Emir, can we contrive to
enter it, and divert ourselves with a view of its wonders?

Then the Emir Musa ordered one of his young men to
mount a camel, and ride round the city, in the hope that he
might discover a trace of a gate, or a place lower than that
to which they were opposite. So one of his young men
mounted, and proceeded around it for two days with their
nights, prosecuting his journey with diligence, and not rest-

[8] Spain; not merely Andalusia.

ing; and when the third day arrived, he came in sight of his companions, and he was astounded at that which he beheld of the extent of the city, and its height. Then he said, O Emir, the easiest place in it is this place at which ye have alighted. And thereupon the Emir Musa took Talib the son of Sahl, and the sheykh 'Abd-Es-Samad, and they ascended a mountain opposite the city, and overlooking it; and when they had ascended that mountain, they saw a city than which eyes had not beheld any greater. Its pavilions were lofty, and its domes were shining; its mansions were in good condition, and its rivers were running; its trees were fruitful, and its gardens bore ripe produce. It was a city with impenetrable gates, empty, still, without a voice or a cheering inhabitant, but the owl hooting in its quarters, and birds skimming in circles in its areas, and the raven croaking in its districts and its great thoroughfare-streets, and bewailing those who had been in it. The Emir Musa paused, sorrowing for its being devoid of inhabitants, and its being despoiled of people and dwellers; and he said, Extolled be the perfection of Him whom ages and times change not, the Creator of the creation by his power! And while he was extolling the perfection of God (to whom be ascribed might and glory!), he happened to look aside, and, lo, there were seven tablets of white marble, appearing from a distance. So he approached them, and, behold, they were sculptured and inscribed; and he ordered that their writing should be read; therefore the sheykh 'Abd-Es-Samad advanced and examined them and read them; and they contained admonition, and matter for example and restraint, unto those endowed with faculties of discernment. Upon the first tablet was inscribed, in the ancient Greek character,—

O son of Adam, how heedless art thou of the case of him who hath been before thee! Thy years and age have diverted thee from considering him. Knowest thou not that the cup of death will be filled for thee, and that in a short time thou wilt drink it? Look then to thyself before entering thy grave. Where are those who possessed the countries and abased the servants of God and led armies? Death hath come upon them; and God is the terminator of delights and the separator of companions and the devastator of flourishing dwellings; so He hath transported them from the amplitude of palaces to the straitness of the graves.

And in the lower part of the tablet were inscribed these verses:—

Where are the Kings and the peoplers of the earth? They have
    quitted that which they have built and peopled;
And in the grave they are pledged for their past actions: there,
    after destruction, they have become putrid corpses.
Where are the troops? They repelled not, nor profited. And
    where is that which they collected and hoarded?
The decree of the Lord of the Throne surprised them. Neither
    riches nor refuge saved them from it.

And the Emir Musa fainted; his tears ran down upon his cheeks, and he said, By Allah, indifference to the world is the most appropriate and the most sure course! Then he caused an inkhorn and a paper to be brought, and he wrote the inscription of the first tablet; after which he drew near to the second tablet, and the third, and the fourth; and, having copied what was inscribed on them, he descended from the mountain; and the world had been pictured before his eyes.

And when he came back to the troops, they passed the day devising means of entering the city; and the Emir Musa said to his Wezir, Talib the son of Sahl, and to those of his chief officers, who were around him, How shall we contrive to enter the city, that we may see its wonders? Perhaps we shall find in it something by which we may ingratiate ourselves with the Prince of the Faithful.—Talib the son of Sahl replied, May God continue the prosperity of the Emir! Let us make a ladder, and mount upon it, and perhaps we shall gain access to the gate from within.—And the Emir said, This is what occurred to my mind, and excellent is the advice. Then he called to the carpenters and blacksmiths, and ordered them to make straight some pieces of wood, and to construct a ladder covered with plates of iron. And they did so, and made it strong. They employed themselves in constructing it a whole month, and many men were occupied in making it. And they set it up and fixed it against the wall, and it proved to be equal to the wall in height, as though it had been made for it before that day. So the Emir Musa wondered at it, and said, God bless you! It seemeth, from the excellence of your work, as though ye had adapted it by measurement to the wall.—

He then said to the people, Which of you will ascend this
ladder, and mount upon the wall, and walk along it, and contrive means of descending into the city, that he may see how
the case is, and then inform us of the mode of opening the
gate? And one of them answered, I will ascend it, O Emir,
and descend and open the gate. The Emir therefore replied,
Mount. God bless thee!—Accordingly, the man ascended the
ladder until he reached the top of it; when he stood, and fixed
his eyes towards the city, clapped his hands, and cried out
with his loudest voice, saying, Thou art beautiful! Then he
cast himself down into the city, and his flesh became mashed
with his bones. So the Emir Musa said, This is the action of
the rational. How then will the insane act? If we do thus
with all our companions, there will not remain of them one;
and we shall be unable to accomplish our affair, and the affair
of the Prince of the Faithful. Depart ye; for we have no
concern with this city.—But one of them said, Perhaps another than this may be more steady than he. And a second
ascended, and a third, and a fourth, and a fifth; and they
ceased not to ascend by that ladder to the top of the wall,
one after another, until twelve men of them had gone, acting
as acted the first. Therefore the sheykh 'Abd-Es-Samad said,
There is none for this affair but myself, and the experienced is
not like the inexperienced. But the Emir Musa said to him,
Thou shalt not do that, nor will I allow thee to ascend to
the top of this wall; for shouldst thou die, thou wouldst be
the cause of the death of us all, and there would not remain
of us one; since thou art the guide of the party. The sheykh
however replied, Perhaps the object will be accomplished by
my means, through the will of God (whose name be exalted!)
And thereupon all the people agreed to his ascending.

Then the sheykh 'Abd-Es-Samad arose, and encouraged
himself, and, having said, In the name of God, the Compassionate, the Merciful!—he ascended the ladder, repeating
the praises of God (whose name be exalted!), and reciting
the Verses of Safety, until he reached the top of the wall;
when he clapped his hands, and fixed his eyes. The people
therefore all called out to him, and said, O sheykh 'Abd-
Es-Samad, do it not, and cast not thyself down! And they
said, Verily to God we belong, and verily unto Him we

return! If the sheykh 'Abd-Es-Samad fall, we all perish!—
Then the sheykh 'Abd-Es-Samad laughed immoderately, and
sat a long time repeating the praises of God (whose name be
exalted!), and reciting the Verses of Safety; after which he
rose with energy, and called out with his loudest voice, O
Emir, no harm shall befall you; for God (to whom be ascribed might and glory!) hath averted from me the effect of
the artifice and fraudulence of the Devil, through the blessing
resulting from the utterance of the words, In the name of
God, the Compassionate, the Merciful.—So the Emir said to
him, What hast thou seen, O sheykh? He answered, When I
reached the top of the wall, I beheld ten damsels, like moons,
who made a sign with their hands, as though they would say,
Come to us. And it seemed to me that beneath me was a
sea (or great river) of water; whereupon I desired to cast
myself down, as our companions did: but I beheld them dead;
so I withheld myself from them, and recited some words of
the book of God (whose name be exalted!), whereupon God
averted from me the influence of those damsels' artifice, and
they departed from me; therefore I cast not myself down,
and God repelled from me the effect of their artifice and
enchantment. There is no doubt that this is an enchantment
and an artifice which the people of this city contrived in order
to repel from it every one who should desire to look down
upon it, and wish to obtain access to it; and these our companions are laid dead.

He then walked along the wall till he came to the two
towers of brass, when he saw that they had two gates of
gold, without locks upon them, or any sign of the means of
opening them. Therefore the sheykh paused as long as God
willed, and, looking attentively, he saw in the middle of one
of the gates a figure of a horseman of brass, having one hand
extended, as though he were pointing with it, and on it was
an inscription, which the sheykh read, and, lo, it contained
these words:—Turn the pin that is in the middle of the front
of the horseman's body twelve times, and then the gate will
open. So he examined the horseman, and in the middle of the
front of his body was a pin, strong, firm, well fixed; and he
turned it twelve times; whereupon the gate opened immediately, with a noise like thunder; and the sheykh 'Abd-Es-

Samad entered. He was a learned man, acquainted with all languages and characters. And he walked on until he entered a long passage, whence he descended some steps, and he found a place with handsome wooden benches, on which were people dead, and over their heads were elegant shields, and keen swords, and strung bows, and notched arrows. And behind the [next] gate were a bar of iron, and barricades of wood, and locks of delicate fabric, and strong apparatus. Upon this, the sheykh said within himself, Perhaps the keys are with these people. Then he looked, and, lo, there was a sheykh who appeared to be the oldest of them, and he was upon a high wooden bench among the dead men. So the sheykh 'Abd-Es-Samad said, May not the keys of the city be with this sheykh! Perhaps he was the gate-keeper of the city, and these were under his authority.—He therefore drew near to him, and lifted up his garments, and, lo, the keys were hung to his waist. At the sight of them, the sheykh 'Abd-Es-Samad rejoiced exceedingly; his reason almost fled from him in consequence of his joy; and he took the keys, approached the gate, opened the locks, and pulled the gate and the barricades and other apparatus, which opened, and the gate also opened, with a noise like thunder, by reason of its greatness and terribleness, and the enormousness of its apparatus. Upon this, the sheykh exclaimed, God is most great!—and the people made the same exclamation with him, rejoicing at the event. The Emir Musa also rejoiced at the safety of the sheykh 'Abd-Es-Samad, and at the opening of the gate of the city; the people thanked the sheykh for that which he had done, and all the troops hastened to enter the gate. But the Emir Musa cried out to them, O people, if all of us enter, we shall not be secure from some accident that may happen. Half shall enter, and half shall remain behind.

The Emir Musa then entered the gate, and with him half of the people, who bore their weapons of war. And the party saw their companions lying dead: so they buried them. They saw also the gate-keepers and servants and chamberlains and lieutenants lying upon beds of silk, all of them dead. And they entered the market of the city, and beheld a great market, with lofty buildings, none of which projected beyond another: the shops were open, and the scales hung up, and the utensils of brass ranged in order, and the khans were full of all kinds of goods. And they saw the merchants dead in their shops: their skins were dried, and their bones were carious, and they had become examples of him who would be admonished. They saw likewise four markets of particular shops filled with wealth. And they left this place, and passed on to the silk-market, in which were silks and brocades interwoven with red gold and white silver upon various colours, and the owners were dead, lying upon skins, and appearing almost as though they would speak. Leaving these, they went on to the market of jewels and pearls and jacinths; and they left it, and passed on to the market of the money-changers, whom they found dead, with varieties of silks beneath them, and their shops were filled with gold and silver. These they left, and they proceeded to the market of the perfumers; and, lo, their shops were filled with varieties of perfumes, and bags of musk, and ambergris, and aloes-wood, and nedd, and camphor, and other things; and the owners were all dead, not having with them any food. And when they went forth from the market of the perfumers, they found near unto it a palace, decorated, and strongly constructed; and they entered it, and found banners unfurled, and drawn swords, and strung bows, and shields hung up by chains of gold and silver, and helmets gilded with red gold. And in the passages of that palace were benches of ivory, ornamented with plates of brilliant gold, and with silk, on which were men whose skins had dried upon the bones: the ignorant would imagine them to be sleeping; but, from the want of food, they had died, and tasted mortality. Upon this, the Emir Musa paused, extolling the perfection of God (whose name be exalted!), and his holiness, and contemplating the beauty of that palace, and its strong construction, and its wonderful fabrication in the most beautiful form and with the firmest architecture; and most of its decoration was in ultramarine. Around it were inscribed these verses:—

Consider what thou beholdest, O man; and be on thy guard before thou departest;
And prepare good provision, that thou mayest enjoy it; for every dweller in a house shall depart.

Consider a people who decorated their abodes, and in the dust have
    become pledged for their actions.
They built; but their buildings availed not: and treasured; but
    their wealth did not save them when the term had expired.
How often they hoped for what was not decreed them! But they
    passed to the graves, and hope did not profit them;
And from their high and glorious state they were removed to the
    narrowness of the sepulchre. Evil is their abode!
Then there came to them a crier, after they were buried, saying,
    Where are the thrones and the crowns and the apparel?
Where are the faces which were veiled and curtained, and on which,
    for their beauty, proverbs were composed?—
And the grave plainly answered the inquirer for them, As to the
    cheeks, the rose is gone from them.
Long time they ate and drank; but now, after pleasant eating,
    they themselves have been eaten.

And the Emir Músa wept until he became senseless; and
afterwards, having given orders to write these verses, he went
on into the interior of the palace. There he beheld a great
hall, and four large and lofty chambers, each one fronting
another, wide, decorated with gold and silver and with various
colours. In the midst of the hall was a great fountain of
alabaster, over which was a canopy of brocade; and in those
chambers were places [one in each chamber] containing decorated fountains, and tanks lined with marble; and channels of
water flowed along the floors of those chambers, the four
streams meeting together in a great tank lined with marbles
of various colours.—The Emir Musa then said to the sheykh
'Abd-Es-Samad, Enter these chambers with us. So they entered the first chamber; and they found it filled with gold
and with white silver, and pearls and jewels, and jacinths and
precious minerals. They found in it also chests full of red
and yellow and white brocades. And they went thence to the
second chamber, and opened a closet in it, and, lo, it was
filled with arms and weapons of war, consisting of gilded
helmets, and Davidean coats of mail, and Indian swords, and
lances of Khatt Hejer, and maces of Khuwarezm, and other
instruments of war and battle. Then they passed thence to
the third chamber, in which they found closets having upon
their doors closed locks, and over them were curtains worked
with various kinds of embroidery. They opened one of these
closets, and found it filled with weapons decorated with varie-

ties of gold and silver and jewels. And they went thence to the fourth chamber, where also they found closets, one of which they opened, and they found it full of utensils for food and drink, consisting of various vessels of gold and silver, and saucers of crystal, and cups set with brilliant pearls, and cups of carnelian, and other things. So they began to take what suited them of those things, and each of the soldiers carried off what he could. And when they determined to go forth from those chambers, they saw there a door of saj inlaid with ivory and ebony, and adorned with plates of brilliant gold, in the midst of that palace. Over it was hung a curtain of silk worked with various kinds of embroidery, and upon it were locks of white silver, to be opened by artifice, without a key. The sheykh 'Abd-Es-Samad therefore advanced to those locks, and he opened them by his knowledge and boldness and excellent skill. And the party entered a passage paved with marble, upon the sides of which were curtains whereon were figured various wild beasts and birds, all these being worked with red gold and white silver, and their eyes were of pearls and jacinths: whosoever beheld them was confounded. Next they came to a saloon, on beholding which the Emir Musa and the sheykh 'Abd-Es-Samad were amazed at its construction.

They then passed on, and found a saloon constructed of polished marble adorned with jewels. The beholder imagined that upon its floor was running water, and if any one walked upon it he would slip. The Emir Musa therefore ordered the sheykh 'Abd-Es-Samad to throw upon it something that they might be enabled to walk on it; and he did this, and contrived so that they passed on. And they found in it a great dome constructed of stones gilded with red gold. The party had not beheld, in all that they had seen, any thing more beautiful than it. And in the midst of that dome was a great dome-crowned structure of alabaster, around which were lattice-windows, decorated, and adorned with oblong emeralds, such as none of the Kings could procure. In it was a pavilion of brocade, raised upon columns of red gold, and within this were birds, the feet of which were of emeralds; beneath each bird was a net of brilliant pearls, spread over a fountain; and by the brink of the fountain was placed a couch adorned with pearls and jewels and jacinths, whereon was a damsel resembling the shining sun. Eyes had not beheld one more beautiful. Upon her was a garment of brilliant pearls, on her head was a crown of red gold, with a fillet of jewels, on her neck was a necklace of jewels in the middle of which were refulgent gems, and upon her forehead were two jewels the light of which was like that of the sun; and she seemed as though she were looking at the people, and observing them to the right and left. When the Emir Musa beheld this damsel, he wondered extremely at her loveliness, and was confounded by her beauty and the redness of her cheeks and the blackness of her hair. Any beholder would imagine that she was alive, and not dead. And they said to her, Peace be on thee, O damsel! But Talib the son of Sahl said to the Emir, May God amend thy state. Know that this damsel is dead. There is no life in her. How then can she return the salutation?—And he added, O Emir, she is skilfully embalmed; and her eyes have been taken out after her death, and quicksilver hath been put beneath them, after which they have been restored to their places; so they gleam; and whenever the air putteth them in motion, the beholder imagineth that she twinkleth her eyes, though she is dead.— Upon this the Emir Musa said, Extolled be the perfection of God, who hath subdued his servants by death!—And as to the couch upon which was the damsel, it had steps, and upon the steps were two slaves, one of them white and the other black; and in the hand of one of them was a weapon of steel, and in the hand of the other a jewelled sword that blinded the eyes; and before the two slaves was a tablet of gold, whereon was read an inscription, which was this:—

In the name of God, the Compassionate, the Merciful. Praise be to God, the Creator of man; and He is the Lord of lords, and the Cause of causes. In the name of God, the Everlasting, the Eternal: in the name of God, the Ordainer of fate and destiny. O son of Adam, how ignorant art thou in the long indulgence of hope! and how unmindful art thou of the arrival of the predestined period! Knowest thou not that death hath called for thee, and hath advanced to seize thy soul? Be ready then for departure, and make provision in the world; for thou wilt quit it soon. Where is Adam, the father of mankind? Where are Nuh and his offspring? Where are the sovereign Kisras and Cæsars? Where are the Kings of India and El-'Irak? Where are the Kings of the regions of the earth? Where are the Amalekites? Where are the mighty monarchs? The mansions are void of their presence, and they have quitted their families and homes. Where are the Kings of the foreigners and the Arabs? They have all died, and become rotten bones. Where are the lords of high degree? They have all died. Where are Karun and Haman?[9] Where is Sheddad the son of 'Ad? Where are Ken'an and the Lord of the Stakes?[10] God hath cut them off, and it is He who cutteth short the lives of mankind, and He hath made the mansions to be void of their presence. Did they prepare provision for the day of resurrection, and make themselves ready to reply to the Lord of men?—O thou, if thou know me not, I will acquaint thee with my name and my descent. I am Tedmur, the daughter of the King of the Amalekites, of those who ruled the countries with equity. I possessed what none of the Kings possessed, and ruled with justice, and acted impartially towards my subjects: I gave and bestowed, and I lived a long time in the enjoyment of happiness and an easy life, and possessing emancipated female and male slaves. Thus I did until the summoner of death came to my abode, and disasters occurred before me. And the case was this:—Seven years in succession came upon us, during which no water descended on us from heaven, nor did any grass grow for us on the face of the earth. So we ate what food we had in our dwellings, and after that we fell upon the beasts and ate them, and there remained nothing. Upon this, therefore, I caused the wealth to be brought, and meted it with a measure, and sent it by trusty men, who went about with it through all the districts, not leaving unvisited a single large city, to seek for some food. But they found it not; and they returned to us with the wealth, after a long absence. So thereupon we exposed to view our riches and our treasures, locked the gates of the fortresses in our city, and submitted ourselves to the decree of our Lord, committing our case to our Master; and thus we all died, as thou beholdest, and left what we had built and what we had treasured. This is the story: and after the substance there remaineth not aught save the vestige.

And they looked at the lower part of the tablet, and saw inscribed upon it these verses:—

Child of Adam, let not hope make game of thee. From all that thy hands have treasured thou shalt be removed.
I see thee desirous of the world and its embellishments; and the past generations have pursued the same course.
They acquired wealth, both lawful and forbidden; but it repelled not fate when the term expired:

[9] Korah; Haman the chief minister of the Pharaoh of the oppression. See Kur'an, xxviii.
[10] Canaan and the Pharaoh of the oppression.

They led troops in multitudes, and collected riches; and they left
    their wealth and buildings, and departed
To the narrow graves, and lay down in the dust; and there they
    have remained, pledged for their actions;
As if the company of travellers had put down their baggage during
    night in a house where was no food for guests.
And its owner had said to them, O people, there is not any lodging
    for you in it. So they packed after alighting:
And they all thereupon became fearful and timid: neither halting
    nor journeying was pleasant unto them.
Then prepare good provision that will rejoice thee to-morrow; and
    act not save agreeably with the fear of thy Lord.

And upon the tablet were also inscribed these words:—

Whoso arriveth at our city, and entereth it, God facilitating his
entrance into it, let him take of the wealth what he can, but not
touch any thing that is on my body; for it is the covering of my
person, and the attire with which I am fitted forth from the world.
Therefore let him fear God, and not seize aught of it; for he would
destroy himself. I have caused this to be an admonition from me
unto him, and a charge which I give him in confidence. And peace
be on you! I beg God, moreover, to save you from the evil of
trials and sickness.

The Emir Musa, when he heard these words, again wept
so violently that he became insensible; and after he had recovered, he wrote all that he saw, and was admonished by
what he witnessed. He then said to his companions, Bring
the sacks, and fill them with part of these riches and these
vessels and rarities and jewels. And thereupon, Talib the son
of Sahl said to the Emir Musa, O Emir, shall we leave this
damsel with the things that are upon her? They are things
that have no equal, nor is the like of them at any time found,
and they are more than the riches thou hast taken, and will
be the best present by which thou mayest ingratiate thyself
with the Prince of the Faithful.—But the Emir replied, O
thou, heardest thou not that which the damsel hath given as
a charge, in the inscription upon this tablet? Moreover, and
especially, she hath given it as a charge offered in confidence,
and we are not of the people of treachery.—The Wezir Talib,
however, said, And on account of these words wilt thou leave
these riches and these jewels, when she is dead? What then
should she do with these things, which are the ornaments of

the world, and the decoration of the living? With a garment of cotton might this damsel be covered, and we are more worthy of the things than she.—Then he drew near to the steps, and ascended them until he reached the spot between the two men [the slaves before mentioned], when, lo, one of these two smote him upon his back, and the other smote him with the sword that was in his hand, and struck off his head, and he fell down dead. So the Emir Musa said, May God not regard with mercy thy resting-place! There was, in these riches, a sufficiency; and covetousness doth doubtlessly dishonour the person in whom it existeth!—He thereupon gave orders for the entry of the troops, who accordingly entered, and they loaded the camels with part of those riches and minerals; after which the Emir Musa commanded them to close the gate as it was before.

They then proceeded along the sea-coast until they came in sight of a high mountain overlooking the sea. In it were many caves, and, lo, in these was a people of the blacks, clad in hides, and with burnuses of hides upon their heads, whose language was not known. And when they saw the troops, they ran from them, and fled to those caves, while their women and their children stood at the entrances of the caves. So the Emir Musa said, O sheykh 'Abd-Es-Samad, what are these people? And he answered, These are the objects of the inquiry of the Prince of the Faithful. They therefore alighted, and the tents were pitched, and the riches were put down; and they had not rested when the King of the blacks came down from the mountain, and drew near to the troops. He was acquainted with the Arabic language; therefore, when he came to the Emir Musa, he saluted him; and the Emir returned his salutation, and treated him with honour. Then the King of the blacks said to the Emir, Are ye of mankind, or the Jinn? The Emir answered, As to us, we are of mankind; and as to you, there is no doubt but that ye are of the Jinn, because of your seclusion in this mountain that is separated from the world, and because of the greatness of your make. But the King of the blacks replied, Nay, we are a people of the race of Adam, of the sons of Ham the son of Nuh, on whom be peace! And as to this sea, it is known by the name of El-Karkar.—So the Emir Musa said to him,

And whence obtained ye knowledge, when there hath not come unto you any prophet divinely inspired in such a country as this? He answered, Know, O Emir, that there appeareth unto us, from this sea, a person diffusing a light whereby the surrounding tracts are illuminated; and he proclaimeth, with a voice which the distant and the near hear, O sons of Ham, be abashed at Him who seeth and is not seen; and say, There is no deity but God: Mohammad is the Apostle of God. And I am Abu-l-'Abbas El-Khidr.—Before that, we used to worship one another; but he called us to the worship of the Lord of mankind.—Then he said to the Emir Musa, He hath also taught us some words to say.—And what, asked the Emir, are those words? He answered, They are these:—There is no deity but God alone: He hath no partner: to Him belongeth dominion, and to Him belongeth praise: He giveth life and killeth: and He is able to accomplish every thing. And we seek not access to God (to whom be ascribed might and glory!) save by these words, nor know we any others. Also, every night of Friday we see a light upon the face of the earth, and we hear a voice saying, Perfect! Holy! Lord of the Angels and the Spirit! Whatsoever God willeth cometh to pass, and what He willeth not cometh not to pass! Every benefit from God is a gratuitous favour! And there is no strength nor power but in God, the High, the Great!

The Emir Musa then said to him, We are the associates of the King of El-Islam, 'Abd-El-Melik the son of Marwan; and we have come on account of the bottles of brass that are here in your sea, and wherein are the devils imprisoned from the time of Suleyman the son of Da'ud (on both of whom be peace!). He hath commanded us to bring him some of them, that he may see them, and divert himself by the view of them.—And the King of the blacks replied, Most willingly. Then he feasted him with fish, and ordered the divers to bring up from the sea some of the bottles of Suleyman; and they brought up for them twelve bottles; wherewith the Emir Musa was delighted, and the sheykh 'Abd-Es-Samad also, and the soldiers, on account of the accomplishment of the affair of the Prince of the Faithful. The Emir Musa thereupon presented to the King of the blacks many presents, and gave

him large gifts. In like manner too the King of the blacks
gave to the Emir Musa a present consisting of wonders of
the sea, in the form of human beings, and said to him, Your
entertainment for these three days shall be of these fish. And
the Emir replied, We must carry with us some of them, that
the Prince of the Faithful may see them; for thereby will
his heart be pleased more than by the bottles of Suleyman.

Then they bade him farewell, and they journeyed back
until they came to the land of Syria, and went in to the
Prince of the Faithful; whereupon the Emir Musa acquainted
him with all that he had seen, and all that had occurred to
him with respect to the verses and histories and admonitions,
and told him of the case of Talib the son of Sahl. And the
Prince of the Faithful; whereupon the Emir Musa acquainted
with you, that I might have beheld what ye beheld! He
then took the bottles, and proceeded to open one after another, and the devils came forth from them, saying, Repentance, O Prophet of God! We will not return to the like
conduct ever!—And 'Abd-El-Melik the son of Marwan wondered at this. But as to the damsels of the sea, with the
like of which the King of the blacks feasted them, they made
for them troughs of wood, which they filled with water, and
into these they put them. They died, however, in consequence of the intensity of the heat. After this, the Prince of
the Faithful caused the riches to be brought before him, and
divided them among the Muslims. And he said, God hath not
bestowed upon any one the like of what He bestowed upon
Suleyman the son of Da'ud. Then the Emir Musa begged
the Prince of the Faithful that he might appoint his son in
his place as Governor of the province, and that he might himself go to the noble Jerusalem, there to worship God. So the
Prince of the Faithful appointed his son to the government,
and he himself went to the noble Jerusalem, and he died there.

This is the end of that which hath come down to us,
of the history of the City of Brass, entire. And God is
all-knowing.

THE STORY OF JULLANAR OF THE SEA

THERE was, in olden time, and in an ancient age and period, in the land of the Persians, a King named Shah-Zeman, and the place of his residence was Khurasan. He had a hundred concubines; but he had not been blest, during his whole life, with a male child by any of them, nor a female; and he reflected upon this, one day, and lamented that the greater portion of his life had passed, and he had not been blessed with a male child to inherit the kingdom after him as he had inherited it from his fathers and forefathers. So the utmost grief, and violent vexation, befell him on this account.

Now while he was sitting one day, one of his memluks came in to him, and said to him, O my lord, at the door is a slave-girl with a merchant: none more beautiful than she hath been seen. And he replied, Bring to me the merchant and the slave-girl. The merchant and the slave-girl therefore came to him; and when he saw her, he found her to resemble the Rudeyni[1] lance. She was wrapped in an izar of silk embroidered with gold, and the merchant uncovered her face, whereupon the place was illuminated by her beauty, and there hung down from her forehead seven locks of hair reaching to her anklets, like the tails of horses. She had eyes bordered with kohl, and heavy hips, and slender waist: she was such as would cure the malady of the sick, and extinguish the fire of the thirsty, and was as the poet hath said in these verses:—

I am enamoured of her: she is perfect in beauty, and perfect also
    in gravity and in dignity.
She is neither tall nor short; but her hips are such that the izar is
    too narrow for them.

[1] Rudeyneh and her husband Semher, of Khatt Hejer, were famous for making straight spear-shafts.

Her stature is a mean between the small and the large: so there is
    neither tallness nor shortness to find fault with.
Her hair reacheth to her anklets, [and is black as night,] but her
    face is ever like the day.

The King, therefore wondered at the sight of her, and at her
beauty and loveliness, and her stature and justness of form;
and he said to the merchant, O sheykh, for how much is this
damsel to be sold? The merchant answered, O my lord, I
purchased her for two thousand pieces of gold of the merchant who owned her before me, and I have been for three
years travelling with her, and she hath cost, to the period of
her arrival at this place, three thousand pieces of gold; and
she is a present from me unto thee. Upon this, the King conferred upon him a magnificent robe of honour, and gave
orders to present him with ten thousand pieces of gold. So
he took them, and kissed the hands of the King, thanking him
for his bounty and beneficence, and departed. Then the King
committed the damsel to the tirewomen, saying to them,
Amend the state of this damsel, and deck her, and furnish
for her a private chamber, and take her into it. He also
gave orders to his chamberlains that every thing which she
required should be conveyed to her. The seat of government
where he resided was on the shore of the sea, and his city
was called the White City. And they conducted the damsel
into a private chamber, which chamber had windows overlooking the sea; and the King commanded his chamberlains
to close all the doors upon her after taking to her all that
she required.

The King then went in to visit the damsel; but she rose
not to him, nor took any notice of him. So the King said, It
seemeth that she hath been with people who have not taught
her good manners. And looking at the damsel, he saw her
to be a person surpassing in beauty and loveliness, and in
stature and justness of form; her face was like the disk of
the moon at the full, or the shining sun in the clear sky; and
he wondered at her beauty and loveliness, and stature and
justness of form, extolling the perfection of God, the Creator:
lauded be his power! Then the King advanced to the damsel,
and seated himself by her side, pressed her to his bosom, and
seated her upon his thigh; and he kissed her lips, which he

found to be sweeter than honey. After this, he gave orders to bring tables of the richest viands, comprising dishes of every kind; and the King ate, and put morsels into her mouth until she was satisfied, but she spoke not a single word. The King talked to her, and inquired of her her name; but she was silent, not uttering a word, nor returning him an answer, ceasing not to hang down her head towards the ground; and what protected her from the anger of the King was the excess of her beauty and loveliness, and her tenderness of manner. So the King said within himself, Extolled be the perfection of God, the Creator of this damsel! How elegant is she, saving that she doth not speak! But perfection belongeth unto God, whose name be exalted!—Then the King asked the female slaves whether she had spoken; and they answered him, From the time of her arrival to the present moment she hath not spoken one word, and we have not heard her talk. The King therefore caused some of the female slaves and concubines to come, and ordered them to sing to her, and to make merry with her, thinking that then she might perhaps speak. Accordingly the female slaves and concubines played before her with all kinds of musical instruments, and enacted sports and other performances, and they sang so that every one who was present was moved with delight, except the damsel, who looked at them and was silent, neither laughing nor speaking. So the heart of the King was contracted. He however inclined to her entirely, paying no regard to others, but relinquishing all the rest of his concubines and favourites.

He remained with her a whole year, which seemed as one day, and still she spoke not; and he said to her one day, when his love of her, and his passion, were excessive, O desire of souls, verily the love that I have for thee is great, and I have relinquished for thy sake all my female slaves, and the concubines and the women and the favourites, and made thee my worldly portion, and been patient with thee a whole year. I beg God (whose name be exalted!) that He will, in his grace, soften thy heart towards me, and that thou mayest speak to me. Or, if thou be dumb, inform me by a sign, that I may give up hope of thy speaking. I also beg of God (whose perfection be extolled!) that He will bless me by thee with a male child that may inherit my kingdom after me;

for I am single and solitary, having none to be my heir, and my age hath become great. I conjure thee then by Allah, if thou love me, that thou return me a reply.—And upon this, the damsel hung down her head towards the ground, meditating. Then she raised her head, and smiled in the face of the King, whereat it appeared to the King that lightning filled the private chamber; and she said, O magnanimous King, and bold lion, God hath answered thy prayer; for I am about to bear thee issue, and the time is [almost] come. But I know not whether the child is male or female. And were it not for my being in this state, I had not spoken to thee one word.—And when the King heard what she said, his face brightened up with joy and happiness, and he kissed her head and her hands by reason of the violence of his joy, and said, Praise be to God who hath favoured me with things that I desired; the first, thy speaking; and the second, thy information that thou art about to bear me issue. Then the King arose and went forth from her, and seated himself upon the throne of his kingdom in a state of exceeding happiness; and he ordered the Wezir to give out to the poor and the needy and the widows and others a hundred thousand pieces of gold as a thank-offering to God (whose name be exalted!) and an alms on his part. So the Wezir did as the King had commanded him. And after that, the King went in to the damsel, and sat with her, and embraced her and pressed her to his bosom, saying to her, O my mistress, who ownest me as thy slave, wherefore hath been this silence, seeing that thou hast been with me a whole year, night and day, awake and asleep, yet hast not spoken to me during this year except on this day? What then hath been the cause of thy silence?

The damsel answered, Hear, O King of the age, and know that I am a poor person, a stranger, broken-hearted: I have become separated from my mother and my family and my brother. And when the King heard her words, he knew her desire, and he replied, As to thy saying that thou art poor, there is no occasion for such an assertion; for all my kingdom and my goods and possessions are at thy service, and I also have become thy memluk: and as to thy saying, I have become separated from my mother and my family and my brother—inform me in what place they are, and I will send to them, and bring them to thee. So she said to him, Know, O fortunate King, that my name is Jullanar of the Sea. My father was one of the Kings of the Sea, and he died, and left to us the kingdom; but while we were enjoying it, one of the Kings came upon us, and took the kingdom from our hands. I have also a brother named Salih, and my mother is of the women of the sea; and I quarrelled with my brother, and swore that I would throw myself into the hands of a man of the inhabitants of the land. Accordingly I came forth from the sea, and sat upon the shore of an island in the moonlight, and there passed by me a man who took me and conducted me to his abode, and desired to make me his concubine; but I smote him upon his head, and he almost died; wherefore he went and sold me to this man from whom thou tookest me, and he was an excellent, virtuous man, a person of religion and fidelity and kindness. But had not thy heart loved me, and hadst thou not preferred me above all thy concubines, I had not remained with thee one hour; for I should have cast myself into the sea from this window, and gone to my mother and my people. I was ashamed, however, to go to them in the state in which I am; for they would imagine evil of me, and would not believe me, even though I should swear to them, were I to tell them that a King had purchased me with his money, and had made me his worldly portion, and chosen me in preference to his wives and all that his right hand possessed. This is my story, and peace be on thee!—And when he heard her words, he thanked her, and kissed her between her eyes, and said to her, By Allah, O my mistress, and light of my eyes, I cannot endure thy separation for one hour; and if thou quit me, I shall die instantly. How then shall the affair be?—She answered, O my master, the time of the birth is near, and my family must come.—And how, said the King, do they walk in the sea without being wetted? She answered, We walk in the sea as ye walk upon the land, through the influence of the names engraved upon the seal of Suleyman the son of Da'ud, upon both of whom be peace! But, O King, when my family and my brethren come, I will inform them that thou boughtest me with thy money, and hast treated me with kindness and beneficence, and it will be meet that thou con-

firm my assertion to them. They will also see thy state with
their eyes, and will know that thou art a King, the son of
a King.—And thereupon the King said, O my mistress, do
what seemeth fit to thee, and what thou wishest; for I will
comply with thy desire in all that thou wilt do. And the
damsel said, Know, O King of the age, that we walk in
the sea with our eyes open, and see what is in it, and we
see the sun and the moon and the stars and the sky as on
the face of the earth, and this hurteth us not.[2] Know also,
that in the sea are many peoples and various forms of all the
kinds that are on the land; and know, moreover, that all
that is on the land, in comparison with what is in the sea, is
a very small matter.—And the King wondered at her words.

Then the damsel took forth from her shoulders two pieces
of Kamari aloes-wood, and took a bit of them, and, having
lighted a fire in a perfuming-vessel, threw into it that bit,
and she uttered a loud whistle, and proceeded to speak
words which no one understood; whereupon a great smoke
arose, while the King looked on. After this, she said to
the King, O my lord, arise and conceal thyself in a closet,
that I may shew thee my brother and my mother and my
family without their seeing thee; for I desire to bring them,
and thou shalt see in this place, at this time, a wonder, and
shalt wonder at the various shapes and strange forms that
God (whose name be exalted!) hath created. So the King
arose immediately, and entered a closet, and looked to see
what she would do. And she proceeded to burn perfume
and repeat spells until the sea foamed and was agitated, and
there came forth from it a young man of comely form, of
beautiful countenance, like the moon at the full, with shining
forehead, and red cheek, and hair resembling pearls and
jewels; he was, of all the creation, the most like to his
sister, and the tongue of the case itself seemed to recite in
his praise these verses:—

The moon becometh perfect once in each month; but the loveliness
       of thy face is perfect every day.
Its abode is in the heart of one sign at a time; but thine abode is
       in all hearts at once.

[2] These people are perhaps the Ghawwasah, or Divers and Plungers, an
inferior class of the Jinn.

Afterwards, there came forth from the sea a grizzly-haired old woman, and with her five damsels, resembling moons, and bearing a likeness to the damsel whose name was Jullanar. Then the King saw the young man and the old woman and the damsels walk upon the surface of the water until they came to the damsel Jullanar; and when they drew near to the window, and Jullanar beheld them, she rose to them and met them with joy and happiness. On their seeing her, they knew her, and they went in to her and embraced her, weeping violently; and they said to her, O Jullanar, how is it that thou leavest us for four years, and we know not the place in which thou art? By Allah, the world was contracted unto us, by reason of the distress occasioned by thy separation, and we had no delight in food nor in drink a single day, weeping night and day on account of the excess of our longing to see thee.—Then the damsel began to kiss the hand of the young man her brother, and the hand of her mother, and so also the hands of the daughters of her uncle, and they sat with her a while, asking her respecting her state, and the things that had happened to her, and her present condition.

So she said to them, Know ye, that when I quitted you, and came forth from the sea, I sat upon the shore of an island, and a man took me, and sold me to a merchant, and the merchant brought me to this city, and sold me to its King for ten thousand pieces of gold. Then he treated me with attention, and forsook all his concubines and his women and his favourites for my sake, and was diverted by his regard for me from every thing that he possessed and what was in his city.—And when her brother heard her words, he said, Praise be to God who hath reunited us with thee! But it is my desire, O my sister, that thou wouldst arise and go with us to our country and our family.—So when the King heard the words of her brother, his reason fled in consequence of his fear lest the damsel should accept the proposal of her brother, and he could not prevent her, though he was inflamed with love of her; wherefore he became perplexed, in violent fear of her separation. But as to the damsel Jullanar, on hearing the words of her brother, she said, By Allah, O my brother, the man who

purchased me is the King of this city, and he is a great
King, and a man of wisdom, generous, of the utmost
liberality. He hath treated me with honour, and he is a
person of kindness, and of great wealth, but hath no male
child nor a female. He hath shewn favour to me, and
acted well to me in every respect; and from the day when
I came to him to the present time, I have not heard from
him a bad word to grieve my heart; but he hath not ceased
to treat me with courtesy, and hath done nothing without
consulting me, and I am living with him in the best of
states, and the most perfect of enjoyments. Moreover, if I
quitted him, he would perish: for he can never endure my
separation even for a single hour. I also, if I quitted him,
should die, by reason of the violence of my love for him in
consequence of the excess of his kindness to me during the
period of my residence with him; for if my father were
living, my condition with him would not be like my condition
with this great, glorious King. Ye have seen, too, that I am
about to bear him issue; and praise be to God who hath
made me to be a daughter of a King of the Sea, and my
husband the greatest of the Kings of the Land. God (whose
name be exalted!) afflicted me not, but compensated me
well; and as the King hath not a male child nor a female,
I beg God (whose name be exalted!) to bless me with a
male child that may inherit of this great King these buildings
and palaces and possessions of which God hath made him
owner.—And when her brother and the daughters of her
uncle heard her words, their eyes became cheerful thereat,
and they said to her, O Jullanar, thou knowest the place
which thou hast in our estimation, and art acquainted with
our affection for thee, and thou art assured that thou art the
dearest of all persons to us, and art certain that we desire
for thee comfort, without trouble or toil. Therefore if thou
be not in a state of comfort, arise and accompany us to our
country and our family; but if thou be comfortable here, in
honour and happiness, this is our desire and wish; for we
desire not aught save thy comfort in every respect.—And
Jullanar replied, By Allah, I am in a state of the utmost
comfort and enjoyment, in honour and desirable happiness.
So when the King heard these words from her, he rejoiced,

and his heart became tranquillized, and he thanked her for them; his love for her increased, and penetrated to his heart's core, and he knew that she loved him as he loved her, and that she desired to remain with him to see his child which she was to bear him.

Then the damsel Jullanar of the Sea gave orders to the female slaves to bring forward the tables and the viands of all kinds; and Jullanar herself was the person who superintended the preparation of the viands in the kitchen. So the female slaves brought to them the viands and the sweetmeats and the fruits; and she ate with her family. But afterwards they said to her, O Jullanar, thy master is a man who is a stranger to us, and we have entered his abode without his permission and without his knowledge of us, and thou praisest to us his excellence, and hast also brought to us his food, and we have eaten, but have not had an interview with him, nor seen him, nor hath he seen us, nor come into our presence, nor eaten with us, that the bond of bread and salt might be established between us. And they all desisted from eating, and were enraged at her, and fire began to issue from their mouths as from cressets. So when the King beheld this, his reason fled, in consequence of the violence of his fear of them. Then Jullanar rose to them, and soothed their hearts; after which she walked along until she entered the closet in which was the King her master; and she said to him, O my master, didst thou see, and didst thou hear my thanks to thee, and my praise of thee in the presence of my family; and didst thou hear what they said to me, that they desired to take me with them to our family and our country? The King answered her, I heard and saw. May God recompense thee for us well! By Allah, I knew not the extent of the love that thou feelest for me until this blessed hour, and I doubt not of thy love for me.—She replied, O my master, is the recompense of beneficence aught but beneficence? Thou hast treated me with beneficence, and bestowed upon me great favours, and I see that thou lovest me with the utmost love, and thou hast shewn me every kindness, and preferred me above all whom thou lovest and desirest. How then could my heart be happy to quit thee, and to depart from thee; and how could that be when thou bestowest benefits and favours upon me? Now I desire of thy goodness that thou come and salute my family, and see them, and that they may see thee, and that pleasure and mutual friendship may ensue. But know, O King of the age, that my brother and my mother and the daughters of my uncle have conceived a great love for thee in consequence of my praising thee to them, and they have said, We will not depart from thee to our country until we have an interview with the King, and salute him. So they desire to behold thee, and to become familiar with thee.—And the King said to her, I hear and obey; for this is what I desire. He then rose from his place, and went to them, and saluted them with the best salutation; and they hastened to rise to him; they met him in the most polite manner, and he sat with them in the pavilion, ate with them at the table, and remained with them for a period of thirty days. Then they desired to return to their country and abode. So they took leave of the King, and the Queen Jullanar of the Sea, and departed from them, after the King had treated them with the utmost honour.

After this, Jullanar fulfilled her period, and she gave birth to a boy, resembling the moon at the full, whereat the King experienced the utmost happiness, because he had not before been blest with a son nor a daughter during his life. They continued the rejoicings, and the decorations [of the city], for a period of seven days, in the utmost happiness and enjoyment; and on the seventh day, the mother of the Queen Jullanar, and her brother, and the daughters of her uncle, all came, when they knew that Jullanar had given birth to her child. The King met them, rejoicing at their arrival, and said to them, I said I would not name my son until ye should come, and that ye should name him according to your knowledge. And they named him Bedr Basim; all of them agreeing as to this name. They then presented the boy to his maternal uncle, Salih, who took him upon his hands, and, rising with him from among them, walked about the palace to the right and left; after which, he went forth with him from the palace, descended with him to the sea, and walked on until he became concealed from the eye of the King. So when the King saw that he had taken his son, and disappeared from him at the bottom of the sea, he despaired of him, and began to weep and wail. But Jullanar, seeing him in this state, said to him, O King of the age, fear not nor grieve for thy son; for I love my child more than thou, and my child is with my brother; therefore care not for the sea, nor fear his being drowned. If my brother knew that any injury would betide the little one, he had not done what he hath done; and presently he will bring thee thy son safe, if it be the will of God, whose name be exalted!—And but a short time had elapsed when the sea was agitated and disturbed, and the uncle of the little one came forth from it, having with him the King's son safe, and he flew from the sea until he came to them, with the little one on his arms, silent, and his face resembling the moon in the night of its fulness. Then the uncle of the little one looked towards the King, and said to him, Perhaps thou fearedst some injury to thy son when I descended into the sea, having him with me. So he replied, Yes, O my master, I feared for him, and I did not imagine that he would ever come forth from it safe. And Salih said to him, O King of the Land, we applied to his eyes a collyrium that we know, and repeated over him the names engraved upon the seal of Suleyman the son of Da'ud (on both of whom be peace!); for when a child is born among us, we do to him as I have told thee. Fear not therefore, on his account, drowning, nor suffocation, nor all the seas if he descend unto them. Like as ye walk upon the land, we walk in the sea.

He then took forth from his pocket a case, written upon, and sealed; and he broke its seal, and scattered its contents, whereupon there fell from it strung jewels, consisting of all kinds of jacinths and other gems, together with three hundred oblong emeralds, and three hundred oblong large jewels, of the size of the eggs of the ostrich, the light of which was more resplendent than the light of the sun and the moon. And he said, O King of the age, these jewels and jacinths are a present from me unto thee; for we never brought thee a present, because we knew not the place of Jullanar's abode, nor were acquainted with any trace or

tidings of her. So when we saw thee to have become
united to her, and that we all had become one, we brought
thee this present; and after every period of a few days, we
will bring thee the like of it, if it be the will of God, whose
name be exalted! For these jewels and jacinths with us
are more plentiful than the gravel upon the land, and we
know the excellent among them, and the bad, and all the
ways to them, and the places where they are found, and
they are easy of access to us.—And when the King looked
at those jewels and jacinths, his reason was confounded and
his mind was bewildered, and he said, By Allah, one of
these jewels is worth my kingdom! Then the King thanked
Salih of the Sea for his generosity, and, looking towards the
Queen Jullanar, he said to her, I am abashed at thy brother;
for he hath shewn favour to me, and presented me with this
magnificent present, which the people of the earth would
fail to procure. So Jullanar thanked her brother for that
which he had done; but her brother said, O King of the
age, thou hadst a prior claim upon us, and to thank thee
hath been incumbent on us; for thou hast treated my sister
with beneficence, and we have entered thine abode, and
eaten of thy provision; and the poet hath said,—

Had *I* wept before *she* did, in my passion for So'da, I had healed
    my soul before repentance came.
But *she* wept before *I* did: her tears drew mine; and I said, The
    merit belongs to the precedent.

Then Salih said, If we stood serving thee, O King of the
age, a thousand years, regarding nothing else, we could not
requite thee, and our doing so would be but a small thing
in comparison with thy desert.—The King therefore thanked
him eloquently. And Salih remained with the King, he
and his mother and the daughters of his uncle, forty days;
after which he arose and kissed the ground before the King,
the husband of his sister. So the King said to him, What
dost thou desire, O Salih? And he answered, O King of
the age, thou hast conferred favours upon us, and we desire
of thy goodness that thou wouldst grant us a boon, and give
us permission to depart; for we have become desirous of
seeing again our family and our country and our relations
and our homes. We will not, however, relinquish the

service of thee, nor that of my sister nor the son of my sister; and by Allah, O King of the age, to quit you is not pleasant to my heart; but how can we act, when we have been reared in the sea, and the land is not agreeable to us? —So when the King heard his words, he rose upon his feet, and bade farewell to Salih of the Sea and his mother and the daughters of his uncle, and they wept together on account of the separation. Then they said to the King, In a short time we shall be with you, and we will never relinquish you, but after every period of a few days we will visit you. And after this, they flew towards the sea, and descended into it, and disappeared.

· The King treated Jullanar with beneficence, and honoured her exceedingly, and the little one grew up well; and his maternal uncle, with his grandmother and the daughters of his uncle, after every period of a few days used to come to the residence of the King, and to remain with him a month, and two months, and then return to their places. The boy ceased not, with increase of age, to increase in beauty and loveliness until his age became fifteen years; and he was incomparable in his perfect beauty, and his stature and his justness of form. He had learned writing and reading, and history and grammar and philology, and archery; and he learned to play with the spear; and he also learned horsemanship, and all that the sons of the Kings required. There was not one of the children of the inhabitants of the city, men and women, that talked not of the charms of that young man; for he was of surpassing loveliness and perfection; and the King loved him greatly. Then the King summoned the Wezir and the emirs, and the lords of the empire, and the great men of the kingdom, and made them swear by binding oaths that they would make Bedr Basim King over them after his father; so they swore to him by binding oaths, and rejoiced thereat; and the King himself was beneficent to the people, courteous in speech, of auspicious aspect, saying nothing but what was for the good of the people. And on the following day, the King mounted, together with the lords of the empire and all the emirs, and all the soldiers walked with him through the city and returned; and when they drew near to the palace, the King dismounted to wait upon his son, and he and all the emirs and the lords of the empire bore the ghashiyeh before him. Each one of the emirs and the lords of the empire bore the ghashiyeh a while; and they ceased not to proceed until they arrived at the vestibule of the palace; the King's son riding. Thereupon he alighted, and his father embraced him, he and the emirs, and they seated him upon the throne of the kingdom, while his father stood, as also did the emirs, before him. Then Bedr Basim judged the people, displaced the tyrannical and invested the just, and continued to give judgment until near midday, when he rose from the throne of the kingdom, and went in to his mother Jullanar of the Sea, having upon his head the crown, and resembling the moon. So when his mother saw him, and the King before him, she rose to him and kissed him, and congratulated him on his elevation to the dignity of Sultan; and she offered up a prayer in favour of him and his father for length of life, and victory over their enemies. He then sat with his mother and rested; and when the time of afternoon-prayers arrived, he rode with the emirs before him until he came to the horse-course, where he played with arms till the time of nightfall, together with his father and the lords of his empire; after which he returned to the palace, with all the people before him. Every day he used to ride to the horse-course; and when he returned, he sat to judge the people, and administered justice between the emir and the poor man. He ceased not to do thus for a whole year; and after that, he used to ride to the chase, and to go about through the cities and provinces that were under his rule, making proclamation of safety and security, and doing as do the Kings; and he was incomparable among the people of his age in glory and courage, and in justice to the people.

Now it came to pass that the old King, the father of Bedr Basim, fell sick one day, whereupon his heart throbbed, and he felt that he was about to be removed to the mansion of eternity. Then his malady increased so that he was at the point of death. He therefore summoned his son, and charged him to take care of his subjects and his mother and all the lords of his empire and all the dependants. He also made them swear, and covenanted with them, that they

would obey his son, a second time; and he confided in
their oaths. And after this, he remained a few days, and
was admitted to the mercy of God, whose name be exalted!
His son Bedr Basim, and his wife Jullanar, and the emirs
and wezirs and the lords of the empire, mourned over him;
and they made for him a tomb, and buried him in it, and
continued the ceremonies of mourning for him a whole
month. Salih, the brother of Jullanar, and her mother, and
the daughters of her uncle, also came, and consoled them
for the loss of the King; and they said, O Jullanar, if the
King hath died, he hath left this ingenuous youth, and he
who hath left such as he is hath not died. This is he who
hath not an equal, the crushing lion, and the splendid moon.
—Then the lords of the empire, and the grandees, went in
to the King Bedr Basim, and said to him, O King, there is
no harm in mourning for the King; but mourning becometh
not any save women; therefore trouble not thy heart and
ours by mourning for thy father, for he hath died and left
thee, and he who hath left such as thou art hath not died.
They proceeded to address him with soft words, and to
console him, and after that they conducted him into the
bath; and when he came forth from the bath, he put on a
magnificent suit woven of gold, adorned with jewels and
jacinths, and he put the royal crown upon his head, seated
himself upon the throne of his kingdom, and performed the
affairs of the people, deciding equitably between the strong
and the weak, and exacting for the poor man his due from
the emir; wherefore the people loved him exceedingly.
Thus he continued to do so for the space of a whole year;
and after every short period, his family of the sea visited
him; so his life was pleasant, and his eye was cheerful: and
he ceased not to live in this state for a length of time.

I HAVE heard, O King of the Age, that there dwelt in a
city of China a poor tailor who had a son named 'Ala-ed-
Din. Now this boy had been a scatter-brained scapegrace
from his birth. And when he had come to his tenth year his
father wished to teach him a handicraft; and being too poor
to afford to spend money on him for learning an art or craft
or business, he took him into his own shop to learn his trade
of tailoring. But 'Ala-ed-Din, being a careless boy, and
always given to playing with the urchins of the street, would
not stay in the shop a single day, but used to watch till his
father went out on business or to meet a customer, and then
would run off to the gardens along with his fellow-raga-
muffins. Such was his case. He would neither obey his
parents nor learn a trade; till his father, for very sorrow and
grief over his son's misdoing, fell sick and died. But 'Ala-ed-
Din went on in the same way. And when his mother perceived that her husband was dead, and that her son was an
idler of no use whatever, she sold the shop and all its contents, and took to spinning cotton to support herself and her
good-for-nothing son. Meanwhile, 'Ala-ed-Din, freed from
the control of his father, grew more idle and disreputable,
and would not stay at home except for meals, while his
poor unfortunate mother subsisted by the spinning of her
hands; and so it was, until he had come to his fifteenth
year.

One day, as 'Ala-ed-Din was sitting in the street playing
with the gutter-boys, a Moorish Darwish came along, and
stood looking at them, and began to scrutinise 'Ala-ed-Din
and closely examine his appearance, apart from his com-

panions. Now this Darwish was from the interior of Barbary, and was a sorcerer who could heap mountain upon mountain by his spells, and who knew astrology. And when he had narrowly scrutinised 'Ala-ed-Din, he said within himself: "Verily this is the youth I need, and in quest of whom I left my native land." And he took one of the boys aside and asked him concerning 'Ala-ed-Din, whose son he was, and wanted to know all about him. After which, he went up to 'Ala-ed-Din, and took him aside, and said: "Boy, art thou not the son of such a one, the tailor?" And he answered: "Yes, O my master; but as to my father, he has long been dead." When the Moorish sorcerer heard this, he fell upon 'Ala-ed-Din, and embraced him and kissed him and wept till the tears ran down his cheeks. And when 'Ala-ed Din saw the state of the Moor, wonder seized upon him, and he asked him and said: "Why dost thou weep, O my master? and how knowest thou my father?" And the Moor replied in a low and broken voice: "My boy, how dost thou ask me this question after thou hast told me that thy father, my brother is dead? For thy father was my brother, and I have journeyed from my country, and I rejoiced greatly in the hope of seeing him again, after my long exile, and cheering him; and now thou hast told me he is dead. But our blood hideth not from me that thou art my brother's son, and I recognised thee amongst all the boys, although thy father was not yet married when I parted from him. And now, O my son, 'Ala-ed-Din, I have missed the obsequies, and been deprived of the delight of meeting thy father, my brother, whom I had looked to see again, after my long absence, before I die. Separation caused me this grief, and created man hath no remedy or subterfuge against the decrees of God the most High." And he took 'Ala-ed-Din and said to him: "O my son, there remaineth no comfort to me but in thee; thou standest in thy father's place, since thou art his successor, and ' whoso leaveth issue doth not die,' O my son." And the sorcerer stretched forth his hand and took ten gold pieces, and gave them to 'Ala-ed-Din, saying to him: "O my son, where is thy house, and where is thy mother, my brother's widow?" So ' Ala-ed-Din shewed him the way to their house, and the sorcerer

said to him: "O my son, take this money, and give it to
thy mother, and salute her from me, and tell her that thy
uncle hath returned from his exile, and, God willing, will
visit her to-morrow to greet her and to see the house where
my brother lived and the place where he is buried." So
'Ala-ed-Din kissed the hand of the Moor, and went, running
in his joy, to his mother's, and entered, contrary to his
custom, for he was not wont to come home save at meal
times. And when he was come in he cried out in his joy:
"O my mother, I bring thee good news of my uncle, who
hath returned from his exile, and saluteth thee." And she
said: "O my son, dost thou móck me? Who is this uncle
of thine, and how hast thou an uncle at all?" And 'Ala-
ed-Din answered: "O my mother, how canst thou say that
I have no uncles or kinsmen living, when this man is my
uncle on my father's side, and he hath embraced and kissed
me and wept over me, and told me to make this known to
thee!" And she said: "O my son, I know indeed that
thou didst have an uncle, but he is dead, and I know not
any other that thou hast."

On the morrow the Moorish sorcerer went out to seek
'Ala-ed-Din, for his heart could not bear parting from him;
and as he wandered in the streets of the city, he met him
disporting himself as usual along with the other vagabonds,
and, approaching, he took him by the hand and embraced
and kissed him, and took from his purse ten gold pieces,
and said: "Haste thee to thy mother and give her these
gold pieces, and tell her, 'My uncle would fain sup with us;
so take these pieces and make ready for us a good supper.'
But first of all, shew me again the way to your home." And
'Ala-ed-Din replied: "On the head and eye, O my uncle."
And he went before him and shewed him the way home.
So the Moor left him and went his way; while 'Ala-ed-Din
went home and told his mother, and gave her the gold
pieces, and said his uncle would fain take supper with them.
So she arose forthwith and went to the market and bought
what she needed, and returning home she set about making
ready for the supper. And she borrowed from her neighbours
what she needed of dishes and the rest, and when the time
came for supper she said to her son: "Supper is ready, but

perhaps thy uncle doth not know the way to the house; go therefore, and meet him on the road." And he answered, "I hear and obey." And whilst they were talking, a knock came at the door, and when 'Ala-ed-Din opened, behold, there was the Moorish wizard, with a eunuch carrying wine and fruit. And 'Ala-ed-Din brought them in, and the eunuch departed; but the Moor entered and saluted the mother, and began weeping and asking her questions, as, "Where is the place where my brother sat?" And when she shewed him her husband's seat, he went to it and prostrated himself and kissed the ground, and cried: "Ah, how small is my satisfaction and how cruel my fate, since I have lost thee, O my brother, O apple of my eye!" And he went on in this manner, weeping and wailing, until 'Ala-ed-Din's mother was assured that it was true, for verily he had swooned from the violence of his grief. And she raised him up from the ground and said: "What benefit is there in killing thyself?" And she comforted him, and seated him. And after he was seated and before the supper-tray was served, the Moor began talking with her, and said: "O wife of my brother, let it not amaze thee that in all thy life thou hast neither seen me nor heard of me in the days of my departed brother; for it is forty years since I left this city and banished myself from my birthplace and wandered throughout the countries of India and China and Arabia, and came to Egypt and abode in its glorious capital, which is one of the wonders of the world, until at length I journeyed to the interior of the West and abode there for the space of thirty years. One day, O wife of my brother, I was sitting thinking of my native land and my birthplace and my blessed brother, and my longing to see him grew stronger, and I wept and wailed over my separation and distance from him. And at last my yearning made me determine to journey to this country, which is the pillow of my head and my birthplace, for to see my brother. For I said to myself: 'O man, how long wilt thou abandon thy country and thy native place, when thou hast but one brother and no more? So rise and journey and see him ere thou die; for who can tell the calamities of this world and the chances of life? And it would be a sore grief to die without seeing thy brother.

Moreover, God (praised be his name!) hath given thee abundant wealth, and perchance thy brother may be in distress and poverty, and thou canst succour him as well as look upon him.' Therefore I arose and made ready for the journey, and recited the Fatihah, and when the Friday prayers were over, I departed and came to this city, after many troubles and difficulties, which I endured by the help of God. So I arrived here, and the day before yesterday, as I roamed about the streets, I perceived thy son 'Ala-ed-Din playing with the boys, and by Almighty God, O wife of my brother, hardly had I seen him, when my heart went out to him (for blood is loving to its like), and my heart told me that he was my brother's son. And I forgot my troubles and anxieties as soon as I saw him, and could have flown for joy, until he told me of the death of him who is gathered to the mercy of God most High; whereat I swooned for heaviness of grief and regret. But 'Ala-ed-Din hath doubt-less informed thee of my tribulation. Yet am I comforted in part by this child, who hath been bequeathed to us by the departed. Verily, 'he who leaveth issue doth not die.' "

And when he saw that she wept at his words, he turned to 'Ala-ed-Din, to divert her from the thought of her hus-band; and to console her and perfect his deception, he said, "O my son 'Ala-ed-Din, what crafts has thou learned and what is thy trade? Hast thou learned a craft to support thee withal, thyself and thy mother?" And 'Ala-ed-Din was ashamed and hung down his head in confusion, and bent it toward the ground. But his mother cried: "What then! By Allah, he knoweth nothing at all; I never saw so heed-less a child as this. All the day he idleth about with the boys of the street, vagabonds like himself, and his father (O my grief!) died only of grieving over him. And I am now in woeful plight; I toil, and spin night and day to gain a couple of loaves of bread for us to eat together. This is his state, O brother-in-law; and by thy life he cometh not home save to meals, and never else. And as for me, I am minded to lock the door of my house and open not to him, but let him go and seek his own living. I am an old woman, and I have not strength to work and struggle for a livelihood like this. By Allah, I have to support him with food, when

it is I who ought to be supported." And the Moor turned
to 'Ala-ed-Din and said: "O son of my brother, why dost
thou continue in such gracelessness? It is shame upon thee
and befitteth not men like thee. Thou art a person of sense,
my boy, and the son of decent folk. It is a reproach to thee
that thy mother, an aged woman, should toil for thy maintenance. And now that thou hast reached manhood, it behooveth thee to devise some way whereby thou mayest be able
to support thyself. Look about, for God be praised, in this
our city there are plenty of teachers of handicrafts; nowhere
more. So choose a craft that pleaseth thee, for me to set
thee up therein, so that as thou waxest older, my son, thy
trade shall bring thee maintenance. If so be thy father's
calling liketh thee not, choose another that thou preferrest.
Tell me, and I will help thee as best I can, my son." And
when he saw that 'Ala-ed-Din was silent and answered him
never a word, he knew that he did not wish any calling at
all, save idling, so he said: "O son of my brother, let not
my advice be irksome to thee; for if, after all, thou like not
to learn a trade, I will open for thee a merchant's shop of
the richest stuffs, and thou shalt be known among the people,
and take and give and buy and sell and become a man of
repute in the city." And when 'Ala-ed-Din heard his uncle's
words, that he would make him a merchant trader, he rejoiced greatly, for he knew that merchants are well dressed
and well fed. So he looked smilingly at the Moor and inclined his head to signify his content.

And when the Moorish wizard saw 'Ala-ed-Din smiling,
he perceived that he was content to be made a merchant,
and he said to him: "Since thou art satisfied that I make
thee a merchant and open a shop for thee, O son of my
brother, be a man, and, God willing, to-morrow I will take
thee to the market to begin with, and get cut for thee an
elegant dress such as merchants wear, and then find for thee
a shop, and keep my promise to thee." Now 'Ala-ed-Din's
mother had been in doubt whether the Moor were indeed
her brother-in-law; but when she heard his promise to her
son to open a merchant's shop for him and furnish him with
goods and wares and the rest, the woman decided in her
mind that this Moor was verily her brother-in-law, since no

stranger would have acted thus to her son. And she began to direct her son and bade him banish ignorance from his head and become a man, and ever obey his uncle like a son, and retrieve the time he had squandered in idling with his mates. Then she arose, and spread the table and served the supper, and they all sat down, and began to eat and drink; and the Moor discoursed to ‘Ala-ed-Din on the affairs of business and the like, so that the boy did not sleep that night for joy. And when he perceived that the night had fallen, the Moor arose and went to his abode and promised them to return on the morrow to take ‘Ala-ed-Din to have his merchant's clothes made.

The next day the Moor rapped at the door, and the mother of ‘Ala-ed-Din arose and opened to him, but he would not enter, but only desired to take her son with him to the market. So ‘Ala-ed-Din came forth to him and wished him good-day, and kissed his hand; and the Moor took him by the hand and went with him to the market, and entered a clothes-shop of all sorts of stuffs, and demanded a sumptuous suit of merchant's style. So the dealer brought out what he required ready made. And the Moor said to ‘Ala-ed-Din: “ Choose what pleaseth thee, my son.” The boy rejoiced greatly when he understood that his uncle had given him his choice, and he picked out the suit he preferred; and the Moor paid the dealer the price on the spot. Then he took ‘Ala-ed-Din to the Hammam, and they bathed, and came forth, and drank sherbet. And ‘Ala-ed-Din arose and put on his new dress, rejoicing and preening; and he approached his uncle and thanked him, and kissed his hand, and acknowledged his kindness.

After the Moor had come forth from the bath with ‘Ala-ed-Din and taken him to the market of the merchants, and delighted him with the buying and selling therein, he said to him: “ O son of my brother, it behooveth thee to become acquainted with the people, above all with the merchants, in order to learn their business, since it is now thy profession.” And he took him and shewed him about the city and the mosques and all the sights of the place; and then led him to a cook-shop, where dinner was served to them on **silver dishes; and** they dined and ate **and drank until** they were satisfied, and then they went their way. And the Moor pointed out the pleasure-grounds, and great buildings, and entered the Sultan's palace, and shewed him all the beautiful large rooms. Then he took him to the Khan of the foreign merchants, where he had his lodging; and he invited some of the merchants in the Khan to supper; and when they sat down, he informed them that this was his brother's son, whose name was 'Ala-ed-Din. And when they had eaten and drunk and night had fallen, he arose and took 'Ala-ed-Din back to his mother. And when she saw her son, that he was one of the merchants, her reason departed for very joy, and she began to thank her brother-in-law for his goodness, saying: "O my brother-in-law, I could not satisfy myself if I thanked thee all my life, and praised thee for the favour thou hast done to my son." And the Moor replied: "O wife of my brother, it is no favour at all, for this is my son, and it is my duty to fill the place of my brother, his father. So let it suffice thee." And she said: "I pray God, by his favoured ones, the saints of old and of latter days, to keep thee and prolong thy life to me, O my brother-in-law, so that thou mayest be a shield for this orphan youth, and he be ever obedient to thy command and do nothing save what thou orderest him to do." And the Moor replied: "O wife of my brother, 'Ala-ed-Din is of man's estate and intelligent and of an honest stock, and please God he will follow his father's way and refresh thine eye. I am sorry, however, that, to-morrow being Friday the day of worship, I shall not be able to open his shop for him, because on that day all the merchants after service repair to the gardens and walks. But on Saturday, God willing, we will accomplish our affair. And to-morrow I will come here and take 'Ala-ed-Din, and shew him the gardens and walks outside the city, which he may not perhaps have seen before, and point out to him the merchant folk and people of note who walk about and amuse themselves there, so that he may become acquainted with them and they with him."

So the Moor slept that night at his abode, and in the morning he came to the tailor's house and rapped at the door. Now 'Ala-ed-Din, from excess of delight in his new dress, and what with the bathing and eating and drinking and sightseeing of the day before, and the expectation of his uncle's coming on the morrow to take him to the gardens, had not slept that night, nor closed his eyes, nor scarcely believed the morning had come. So as soon as he heard the rap at the door he ran out like a flash of fire and opened the door and met his uncle, who embraced and kissed him, and took him by the hand. And as they went along he said: "O son of my brother, to-day I will shew thee such a sight as thou never didst see in all thy life." And he made the boy laugh and entertained him with his talk. And they went out of the gate of the city and began meandering among the gardens: and the Moor pointed out the splendid pleasure-grounds and wondrous tall palaces. And so often as they looked upon a garden or mansion or palace, the Moor would pause and say: "Doth this astonish thee, O son of my brother?" And 'Ala-ed-Din well nigh flew with delight at seeing things he had never imagined in all his born days. And they ceased not to wander about and amuse themselves till they were weary. Then they entered a large garden hard by, whereat the heart became light and the eye bright, for its brooks trickled amid flowers, and fountains gushed from the jaws of brazen lions, which shone like gold. So they sat down by a lake and rested awhile; and 'Ala-ed-Din was full of happiness and began to make merry and jest with his uncle as though he were of a truth his father's brother. Then the Moor arose, and loosening his girdle, took forth a wallet of food and fruit and so forth, saying: "O son of my brother, thou art hungry; come then and eat thy fill." So 'Ala-ed-Din fell to eating and the Moor ate with him, and their souls were refreshed and made glad, and they reposed. And the Moor said: "O son of my brother, if thou art rested, let us walk a spell and finish our stroll." So 'Ala-ed-Din arose, and the Moor led him from garden to garden till they had quitted all the gardens and come to a lofty hill. But 'Ala-ed-Din, who all his life had never gone beyond the city gates, or taken such a walk, said to the Moor: "O my uncle, whither do we go? We have left all the gardens behind us, and come to the mountain, and if the way be far, I have not strength to walk longer; nay, I am all but fainting from tiredness. There are no more gardens ahead, so let us turn and go back to the city." But the Moor replied: "Nay, my son; this is the road, and it is not yet an end of the gardens; for we are just going to look at one such as is not to be seen among Kings' gardens, and all those thou hast seen are naught compared with it. So pluck up thy courage, for, God be praised, thou art now a grown man." And the Moor set to cheering 'Ala-ed-Din with encouraging words, and related wonderful tales, both true and false, until they came to the place which this Moorish sorcerer had fixed upon, and the which to find he had journeyed from the lands of the West to the countries of China. And when they arrived, he said to 'Ala-ed-Din: "O son of my brother, sit down and rest, for this is the place we are seeking, and if it please God I will shew thee wonders the like of which no one in the world ever saw before, nor hath any one rejoiced in looking upon what thou art to see. When thou art rested, arise and find some faggots of wood and thin dry sticks to make a fire. Then will I shew thee, O son of my brother, a thing beyond description." And when 'Ala-ed-Din heard this, he longed to see what his uncle would do, and forgot his weariness and straightway arose and began to collect small faggots and dry sticks and gathered them together till the Moor cried, "Enough, O son of my brother!" Then the Moor drew from his pocket a box, and opened it, and took from it what incense he required, and he burnt it and muttered adjurations and said mysterious words. And straightway, amid murk and quaking and thunder, the earth opened, and 'Ala-ed-Din was alarmed and terrified at this, and would have fled. But when the sorcerer perceived his intention, he was wroth and furiously enraged thereat, for without 'Ala-ed-Din his design would come to naught, and the treasure he sought to unearth could not be obtained save by means of the boy. And so when he saw him thinking of flight he made for him, and raising his hand, he smote him on the head, so that his teeth were almost knocked out, and he swooned and fell to the ground. And after a while he came to, by the spells of the Moor, and fell a-crying, and said: "O my uncle, what have I done to deserve such a blow from thee?" So the Moor began to mollify him, and said: "O my son, it is my intention to make a man of thee; so thwart me not, who am thine uncle, and, as it were, thy father. Obey me, rather, in all I tell thee, and shortly thou shalt forget all this toil and trouble when thou lookest upon marvellous things." Thereupon, when the earth had opened in front of the wizard, there appeared a marble slab, wherein was a ring of brass. And drawing geometric figures, the Moor said to 'Ala-ed-Din: "If thou dost what I tell thee, thou wilt become richer than all the Kings put together; and for this cause struck I thee, O my son, because there is buried here a treasure which is deposited in thy name, and yet thou wast about to abandon it and flee. And now pull thy wits together and behold how I have cloven the earth by my spells and incantations.

"Under that stone with the ring," he continued, "is the Treasury whereof I told thee. Put forth thy hand to the ring and raise the stone, for no one in the world but thyself hath the power to open it, nor can any save thee set foot in this Treasury, which hath been reserved for thee alone. Wherefore thou must hearken to all that I bid thee, and not gainsay my words a jot. All this, O my son, is for thy good, since this treasure is immense. The Kings of the earth have never seen the like, and it is all for thee and for me."

So poor 'Ala-ed-Din forgot his tiredness and the beating and the tears, and was dazzled at the words of the Moor, and rejoiced to think that he would become so rich that Kings would not be wealthier than he. And he said: "O my uncle, command me what thou wilt, and I will obey thy behest." And the Moor said to him: "O son of my brother, thou art like my own child, and more, since thou art my brother's son, and I have none of kin save thee; and thou art my heir and successor, O my son." And he approached 'Ala-ed-Din and kissed him, saying: "For whom should I design all these labours of mine, my child, except for thee, that I may leave thee a rich man, as rich as can be! Wherefore thwart me not in anything I tell thee, but go to that ring and lift it as I bade thee." And 'Ala-ed-

Din said: "O my uncle, this ring is too heavy for me; I cannot lift it alone; come and help me to raise it, for I am little in years." But the Moor replied: "O my brother's son, we can accomplish nothing if I aid thee, and our labours would be vain; put then thy hand to the ring and lift it, and the stone will come up immediately. Did I not tell thee that none can move it but thyself? Repeat thy name and the names of thy father and mother, whilst thou pullest, and it will come up at once, and thou wilt not feel its weight." So 'Ala-ed-Din summoned his strength and plucked up his courage, and set to work as his uncle had bidden him, and lifted the stone with perfect ease, after saying the names of himself and his father and mother as the Moor had counselled him. So he lifted the slab and cast it on one side.

And when he had lifted the slab from the door of the Treasury, before him lay a passage entered by a descent of twelve steps. And the Moor said to him: "'Ala-ed-Din, pull thy wits together, and do exactly what I tell thee to the uttermost, and fail not a little from it. Descend carefully into yonder passage until thou reachest the end, and there shalt thou find a place divided into four chambers, and in each of these thou shalt see four golden jars and others of virgin gold and silver. Beware that thou touch them not nor take anything out of them, but leave them and go on to the fourth chamber, without even brushing them with thy clothes or loitering a single moment; for if thou do contrary to this thou wilt straightway be transformed and become a black stone. And when thou comest to the fourth chamber thou wilt find a door; then open the door, and repeating the names thou saidst over the slab, enter, and verily thou wilt pass thence into a garden full of fruit trees, whence thou wilt proceed by a path which thou wilt see in front of thee about fifty cubits long, and come upon an alcove[1] in which is a ladder of about fifty steps, and thou shalt see, moreover, a Lamp suspended above the alcove. Take thou the Lamp, and pour out the oil therein, and put it in thy breast, and be not afraid for thy clothes, since it is but common oil. And on thy return thou mayest pluck what thou pleasest from the

[1] Liwan.

trees, for all is thine so long as the Lamp continue in thy hand." And when he had ended, the Moor took a signet ring from his finger and put it on 'Ala-ed-Din's finger, and said: "My son, this ring will guard thee from all peril and fear that may behest thee, so long as thou obeyest all that I have told thee. Arise, therefore, forthwith and descend and pluck up thy courage, and strengthen thy resolve and fear not, for thou art a man now, and no longer a child. And after this, my boy, thou shalt speedily become possessed of riches galore, till thou art the richest man in the world."

So 'Ala-ed-Din arose and went down into the cavern and found the four chambers and the four golden jars therein, and these he passed by with all care and precaution, as the Moor had told him, and he came to the garden and went through it till he found the alcove, and climbing the ladder, he took the Lamp and poured out the oil and put it in his bosom, and went down into the garden, where he began to marvel at the trees with the birds on their branches singing the praises of their glorious Creator. And though he had not noticed it when he entered, these trees were all covered with precious stones instead of fruit, and each tree was of a different kind and had different jewels, of all colours, green and white and yellow and red and other colours, and the brilliance of these jewels paled the sun's rays at noontide. And the size of each stone surpassed description, so that none of the Kings of the world possessed any like the largest or half the size of the least of them. And 'Ala-ed-Din walked among the trees and gazed upon them and on these things which dazzled the sight and bewildered the mind, and as he examined them he perceived that instead of ordinary fruit the yield was of big jewels, emeralds and diamonds, and rubies and pearls, and other precious stones, such as to bewilder the understanding. But as he had never seen such things in his life, and had not reached mature years so as to know the value of such jewels (for he was still a little boy), he imagined that these jewels were all of glass or crystal. And he gathered pockets full of them, and began to examine whether they were ordinary fruit, like figs or grapes and other like eatables; but when he saw that they were of glass (knowing nothing of precious stones), he put some of each kind that grew on the trees into his pockets, and finding them of no use for food, he said in his mind: "I will gather these glass fruits and play with them at home." So he began plucking them and stuffing them into his pockets until they were full; and then, when he had picked more and put them in his girdle, and girded it on, he carried off all he could, intending to use them for ornaments at home, since he imagined, as has been said, that they were only glass. Then he hastened his steps, for fear of his uncle, the Moor, and passed through the four chambers, and came to the cavern, without as much as looking at the jars of gold, notwithstanding that on his way back he was permitted to take of them. And when he came to the steps, and ascended them till none remained but the last one, which was higher than the others, he was unable to climb it by himself, without help, seeing that he was weighted. And he called to the Moor: "O my uncle, give me thy hand and help me to get up." And the sorcerer replied: "O my son, give me the Lamp, and lighten thyself; perhaps it is that which weigheth thee down." But he answered: "O my uncle, the Lamp doth not weigh me down at all; give me only thy hand, and when I am up I will give thee the Lamp." But since the wizard wanted only the Lamp, and nought beside, he began to urge 'Ala-ed-Din to give it him, which, since it was at the bottom of his dress and the bags of precious stones bulged over it, he could not reach to give it him; so the Moor pressed him to give what he could not, and raged furiously, and persisted in demanding the Lamp, when 'Ala-ed-Din could not get at it to give it him.

And when 'Ala-ed-Din could not get at the Lamp to give it to his uncle, the Moor, the impostor, he became frantic at not gaining his desire, though 'Ala-ed-Din had promised to give it him without guile or deceit as soon as he got out of the cave. But when the Moor saw that 'Ala-ed-Din would not give him the Lamp, he was furiously enraged and gave up all hope of getting it. So he muttered incantations and threw incense into the fire, and immediately the slab shut of itself and by the power of magic became closed, the earth buried the stone as heretofore, and 'Ala-ed-Din remained under the ground unable to come forth. For this sorcerer, as we have related, was a stranger and no uncle of 'Ala-ed-Din's; but he misrepresented himself and asserted a lie, in order to gain possession of this Lamp by means of the youth.

So the accursed Moor heaped the earth over him and left him, for whose sake this treasure had been preserved, to die of hunger. For this damnable Moorish sorcerer was from the land of Africa, from the inner Westland, and from his youth he had practised sorcery and all magic arts (the City of Africa [in Barbary] is well known for all these mysteries), and he ceased not to study and learn from his childhood in the City of Africa until he had mastered all the sciences. And one day, by his accomplished skill in sciences and knowledge, acquired in the course of forty years of sorcery and incantation, he discovered that in a remote city of China, called El-Kal'as, there was buried a vast treasure the like of which not one of the Kings of this world had ever amassed, and among this treasure was a Wonderful Lamp, which whoso possessed, mortal man could not excel him in estate or in riches, nor could the mightiest King upon earth attain to the opulence of this Lamp and its power and its potency. And when he discovered by his science and perceived that this treasure could only be obtained by means of a boy of the name of 'Ala-ed-Din, of poor family, and belonging to that city, and understood how it could thus be taken easily and without trouble, he straightway and without hesitation prepared to journey to China, as we have said, and did with 'Ala-ed-Din what he did, and imagined that he would gain possession of the Lamp. But his design and his hopes were frustrated and his labour was in vain. So he resolved to do 'Ala-ed-Din to death, and heaped the earth over him to the end that he might die, for "the living hath no murderer." Moreover, he resolved upon this, in order that 'Ala-ed-Din, as he could not get out, should not be able to bring up the Lamp from below ground. Then he went his way and returned to the regions of Africa, dejected in spirit and disappointed of his aim. Thus was it with the sorcerer.

But as for 'Ala-ed-Din, when the earth was heaped over

him, he began to call to his uncle, the Moor, whom he believed to be such, to stretch out his hand, that he might come forth from the vault to the face of the earth; and he shouted, and no one answered him. Then he understood the trick which the Moor had played upon him, and that he was no uncle at all, but a lying magician. So 'Ala-ed-Din despaired of his life, and perceived to his grief that there remained to him no escape to the earth's surface, and he began to weep and bewail that which had befallen him. But after awhile he arose and descended to see if God Most High would provide him a door of escape. And he went, turning to right and left, and found nothing but darkness, and four doors shut against him; for the sorcerer by his magic had closed all the doors, and had even shut that of the garden through which 'Ala-ed-Din had passed, so that he might not find there a door by which to escape to the surface of the earth, and thus to hasten his death. And 'Ala-ed-Din's weeping increased and his wailing grew louder when he saw the doors all shut, and the garden also, where he had intended to console himself awhile; but he found everything closed, and he gave himself up to weeping and lamenting, like him who hath abandoned hope, and he returned and sat on the steps of the vault where he had first entered.

Thus he sat weeping and wailing and hopeless. But a small thing is it to God (extolled and exalted be he!) if he willeth a thing to say to it, "Be," and it is. Thus doth he create joy in the midst of woe; and thus was it with 'Ala-ed-Din. When the Moorish sorcerer sent him to the vault, he gave him a ring and put it on his finger, saying, "Verily this ring will guard thee from all danger if thou be in trouble and difficulties, and take away from thee all evils, and be thy helper wheresoever thou art." And this was by the decree of God Most High, that it should be the means of 'Ala-ed-Din's escape. For whilst he sat weeping and lamenting his case and abandoning his hope of life, overwhelmed with his misfortune, in his exceeding tribulation be began wringing his hands as the sorrowful are wont to do. And he raised his hands supplicating God, and saying: 'I testify that there is no God but thee alone, the mighty, the omnipotent, the all-conquering, the quickener of the dead, creator of needs and fulfiller thereof, who dispellest troubles and anxieties and turnest them into joy. Thou sufficest me, and thou art the best of protectors; and I testify that Mohammad is thy servant and apostle. O my God, by his favour with thee, release me from this calamity." And whilst he was supplicating God and wringing his hands from heaviness of grief at the calamity which had overtaken him, his hand happened to rub the ring, and, behold, immediately the Slave of the Ring appeared before him and cried: "Here I am, thy slave, between thy hands. Ask what thou wilt, for I am the slave of him on whose hand is the ring, the ring of my master." And 'Ala-ed-Din looked up and saw a Marid like the Jinn of our Lord Suleyman, standing before him; and he was affrighted at the awful apparition, until he heard the Slave of the Ring say: "Ask what thou wilt, for verily am I thy servant, because the ring of my master is on thy hand." So he recovered his spirit and called to mind the words of the Moor when he gave him the ring. And he rejoiced exceedingly and plucked up heart and said to him: "O Slave of the Ring, I wish thee to convey me to the surface of the earth." And hardly had he spoken when, behold, the earth gaped open and he found himself at the door of the Treasury, outside, in face of the world. And when 'Ala-ed-Din saw himself thus in face of the world, after being three days under ground sitting in the dark Treasury, and the light of day and the sunshine smote his face and he could not open his eyes for it, he began to open his eyelids little by little till his eyes were stronger and became accustomed to the light and recovered from the gloom.

Then he perceived that he was on the surface of the earth, whereat he rejoiced greatly, and it astonished him that he should be outside the door of the Treasury which he had entered when the Moorish sorcerer opened it, and yet that the door should be shut and the earth made level so that there was no trace of an entrance at all. And he wondered more and more, and could not believe he was in the same place, till he saw the spot where they had lighted the fire of sticks and faggots, and the place where the sorcerer had muttered his incantations. Then turning right and left, he saw the gardens at a distance, and perceived the road, and he knew it was the same by which he had come. So he gave thanks to God Most High, who had brought him back to the earth's surface and saved him from death after the hope of life had abandoned him. So he arose and walked on the road which he recognized till he came to the city, and entered, and repaired to his home, and went to his mother. And when he saw her, he swooned on the ground before her from exceeding joy at his escape and the recollection of the terror and toil and hunger he had endured. And his mother had been sorrowful since his departure, and had sat sobbing and weeping for him; so when she saw him come in she rejoiced over him with great joy, though grief seized her when she saw him fall swooning to the ground. But she did not give way to her anxiety in the predicament, but poured water on his face and borrowed from her neighbours aromatics for him to sniff. And when he was somewhat restored, he begged her to give him something to eat, saying to her: "O my mother, it is now three days since I ate anything at all." And his mother arose and prepared for him what she had ready by her, and set it before him, saying: "Come, my son, eat and refresh thyself, and when thou art restored, tell me what hath happened to thee and befallen thee, O my child; but I will not ask thee now, because thou art weary." So 'Ala-ed-Din ate and drank and became restored, and when he was better and had regained his spirits, he said to his mother: "Ah, my mother, I have a heavy reckoning against thee for abandoning me to that devilish man who sought my ruin and desired to kill me. Know that I looked death in the face on account of the accursed reprobate whom thou didst acknowledge as my uncle; and had not God Most High delivered me from him, both I and thou, my mother, would have been imposed upon by the plenitude of this villain's promises of the good he would do me, and the zeal of the love he displayed for me. But know, O mother, that this man is a sorcerer, a Moor, a liar, accursed, impostor, cheat, hypocrite. I hold the devils beneath the earth are not his match. May God condemn every record of his

deeds! Listen, then, my mother, to what this devil did—
for all I tell thee is really true. See how this accursed one
brake every promise he made me to work me good; and
look at the love he shewed me and how he acted; and all
to attain his own ambition! And he would have killed
me—God be thanked for my deliverance. Consider and
hearken, O my mother, how this Man of the curse acted."
Then 'Ala-ed-Din informed his mother all that had befallen
him—weeping for excess of joy—telling her how, after he
had left her, the Moor had led him to a mountain wherein
was a treasure, and how he had muttered incantations and
spells. And he added: "After that, O my mother, he beat
me till I fainted from soreness, and a great horror gat hold
of me, when the mountain split asunder and the earth
opened before me by his sorcery, and I trembled and was
afeared at the roaring of the thunder which I heard and
the darkness which fell around as he muttered his spells.
And I would fain have fled from fear when I saw these
awful sights. So when he saw that I was bent upon flight
he reviled me and beat me. But, since the Treasure could
not be unearthed save by me, as it was in my name, and
not his, and because this ill-omened sorcerer knew that it
could only be opened by my means, and this was what he
wanted me for; therefore, after beating me, he thought it
better to mollify me in order to send me to open the
Treasure and obtain his desire. And when he sent me, he
gave me a ring and put it on my finger, after it had been
on his own. So I descended into the Treasury, and found
four chambers all full of gold and silver and the like, and
all this was as nought, for that Devil's own hand commanded
me to touch nothing of it. Then I entered a great garden
full of lofty trees, whose fruits confounded the reason, for all
were of glass of delightful colours; and I came to the hall
in which was this Lamp, and I took it forthwith and emptied
it." And 'Ala-ed-Din took out the Lamp from his bosom,
and shewed it to his mother, and in like manner the
precious stones which he had brought from the garden, of
which there were two large pockets full, of such as not one
was to be met with among the Kings of the world. But
'Ala-ed-Din knew not their worth, but deemed them glass

or crystal. And he continued: "After getting the Lamp, O my mother, and arriving at the door of the Treasury, I called to the accursed Moor, who passed himself off as my uncle, to give me his hand and help me up, as I was overburdened with things and could not get up alone. But he would not give me his hand, but said: 'Hand up the Lamp that is with thee, and then I will give thee my hand and help thee out.' But I had put the Lamp at the bottom of my pocket, and the bags stuck out above it, and I could not get it out to give it him, and I said: 'O my uncle, I cannot give thee the Lamp, but when I am up I will give it thee.' But he did not mean to help me out, for he only wanted the Lamp; and his intention was to take it from me and heap the earth over me and destroy me, as he did his best to do. And this is what happened, O my mother, from this ill-omened sorcerer." And 'Ala-ed-Din told her all the story to the end thereof, and fell to cursing the Moor with all his might from out of his raging soul, saying: "O my mother, woe to this damnable sorcerer, this ill-omened, vile, inhuman cheat and hypocrite, who contemneth all human kindness, and spurneth mercy and compassion!"

When his mother heard her son's story and what the Moorish sorcerer had done to him, she said: "Yea, my son, of a truth he is a miscreant and a hypocrite, a hypocrite who slays folk by his magic; and it was only the grace of God Most High, my son, that delivered thee from the wiles and spells of this accursed, whom I believed to be in truth thine uncle." And 'Ala-ed-Din, since he had not slept a wink for three days, and found himself nodding, sought his repose and went to sleep, and his mother likewise slept afterwards; and he did not wake up till near noon on the second day. As soon as he was awake he wanted something to eat, for he was hungry. And she said to him: "O my son, I have nought to give thee, because thou didst eat yesterday all that there was in the house; but wait awhile; I have spun yarn which I will take to the market and sell and buy thee something to eat with the proceeds." To which 'Ala-ed-Din replied: "Mother, keep thy yarn; sell it not, but give me the Lamp I brought, that I may go sell it, and buy therewith something to eat, for I think the Lamp will fetch more than the yarn." So she arose and brought the Lamp to her son, and she found it very dirty, and said: "O my son, here is the Lamp, but verily it is dirty, and when we have cleaned and polished it it will sell for a greater price." So she went and took a handful of sand, and fell to rubbing the Lamp therewith; but she had hardly begun to rub when there appeared before her one of the Jann, of terrible aspect and vast stature, as it were of the giants. And he said to her: "Tell me what thou dost want of me; here am I, thy slave, and the slave of him who holdeth the Lamp; not I only, but all the slaves of the Wonderful Lamp which is in thy hand." But she trembled, and fear gat hold of her, and her tongue clave as she gazed upon that terrible form; and she could not answer, because she was not accustomed to seeing apparitions like that. So in her terror she could not make any reply to the Marid, but fell down overcome with alarm. But 'Ala-ed-Din her son was waiting hard by, and had seen the 'Efrit of the Ring which he had rubbed when in the Treasury; and hearing the speech of the Jinni to his mother, he hastened forward and seized the Lamp from her hand, saying: "O Slave of the Lamp, I am hungry; and I wish thee to bring me something to eat, and let it be something good beyond imagination." So the Jinni vanished for a moment and brought him a magnificent tray of great price, made of pure silver, on which were twelve dishes of various foods and delicious dainties, and two cups of silver and flagons of clear old wine, and bread whiter than snow; and he set them before 'Ala-ed-Din and vanished. And 'Ala-ed-Din arose and sprinkled water on his mother's face and made her smell pungent perfumes, and she revived. Then he said: "O my mother, come and eat of this food which God Most High hath provided for us." And when his mother saw the beautiful table, that it was of silver, she marvelled at this affair, and said: "O my son, who is this generous benefactor that hath satisfied our hunger and lightened our poverty? Verily we are in his debt, and I am thinking that the Sultan, seeing our case and our poverty, sent this tray of food to us himself." "O my mother," he answered, "this is not a time for speculation; come, let us eat, for we are anhungered." So they went and sat down to the tray and fell to eating, and 'Ala-ed-Din's mother tasted viands such as never in all her life had she eaten the like thereof. So they ate heartily with the utmost appetite from the violence of their hunger; moreover, the food was fit for Kings. But they knew not if the tray were precious or not, for they had never seen its like in their born days. And when they had done eating (but they left enough for supper and to last for the next day), they arose and washed their hands and sat down to talk, and 'Ala-ed-Din's mother turned to her son and said: "O my son, tell me what took place with the Slave, the Jinni, now that God be praised, we have eaten and satisfied ourselves from his good things, and thou hast no excuse for saying to me, 'I am hungry.'" So, 'Ala-ed-Din told her all that had taken place between him and the Slave, while she was fallen in a swoon from affright. And sore amazement took hold upon her, and she said to him: "It is true, for the Jinn do appear before the son of Adam, though I, O my child, in all my days have never seen them; and I am thinking that this is the same that appeared to thee in the Treasury." But he replied: "It is not he, O my mother; this slave who appeared before thee is the Slave of the Lamp." And when she heard these words she said: "How is that, my son?" And he answered her: "This slave is different in aspect from that; and that one was the Slave of the Ring, and this which thou sawest is the Slave of the Lamp which was in thy hand."

And when she heard this she said: "Aha! that accursed, who appeared to me and nearly killed me with fright, belonged to the Lamp!" "Yes," he said, and she continued: "I adjure thee, O my son, by the milk which thou didst suck from me cast away this Lamp and Ring, since they will cause us great fear, and as for me, I cannot bide a second time to look at them. And it is forbidden us to deal with them, since the Prophet (God bless and save him!) hath warned us against them." And he said to her; "O my mother, thy behests be on my head and my eye! Yet as to this behest which thou hast spoken, it is not possible for me to abandon either the Lamp or the Ring. Thyself hast

seen what good they did us when we were anhungered; and
know, O my mother, that the Moor, the liar, the sorcerer,
when I was sent down to the Treasury, wanted nought of
the gold and silver of which the four chambers were full,
but commanded me only to bring him the Lamp, and nought
besides, because he knew its great value, and unless he had
known that this was immense, he had not toiled and laboured
and journeyed from his own country to ours in search of it,
nor would he have imprisoned me in the Treasury when he
despaired of the Lamp, when I would not give it to him.
Therefore, O my mother, it behooveth us to hold fast by this
Lamp and take care of it, for it is our sustenance, and shall
make us rich, and we must not publish it abroad to anyone.
And as touching the Ring, in like manner I may not take
it off my finger, since but for this ring thou hadst not seen
me again alive, but I should have lain dead within the
Treasury under the ground. Then how can I take it off
my hand? And who knoweth what may befall me in life
of troubles and perils and sore calamities, from which this
Ring may deliver me? Only in deference to thy wishes I
will conceal the Lamp, and never again constrain thee to
look upon it." And when his mother had heard his words
and had well weighed them, she perceived they were right,
and said to him: "O my son, do as thou wilt; for myself,
I wish never to see them again, nor would I willingly witness once more the terrible sight which I have seen."

'Ala-ed-Din and his mother continued eating of the
viands which the Jinni had brought them, two days, and
then they were done. So perceiving that nothing remained
to them to eat, he arose, and took one of the plates which
the slave had brought on the tray, which were of pure gold,
though he knew it not; and he went with it to the market.
And there met him a Jew, viler than the devils, and to him
he offered the plate. And when the Jew saw it, he took
'Ala-ed-Din aside so that none should see, and examined
the plate carefully and assured himself that it was of fine
gold; and not knowing whether 'Ala-ed-Din was acquainted
with its worth or was inexperienced in such things, he said
to him: "How much, O my master, is this dish?" And
'Ala-ed-Din answered, "Thou knowest its value." And the

Jew considered how much he should bid for it, since 'Ala-ed-Din had answered him a business-like answer; so he thought to offer him a small price, and yet he feared that 'Ala-ed-Din might know the value of it and expect to receive a high price. So he said within himself: "Perchance he is ignorant of it and knoweth not the value." Then he took from his pocket a dinar of gold and gave it him. And when 'Ala-ed-Din had looked at the piece of gold in his hand, he took it and quickly went away. So the Jew knew that the youth did not understand the value of the plate, so he repented with abject repentance that he had given him a dinar instead of a carat of a sixtieth. 'Ala-ed-Din meanwhile did not tarry, but went to the baker's and bought of him bread and changed the dinar and took and went to his mother and gave her the bread and the change of the gold, and said to her: "O my mother, go and buy for us what we need." And she arose and went to the market and bought all they required, and they ate and were merry. And every time the price of a plate was exhausted, 'Ala-ed-Din took another and went with it to the Jew, and the accursed Hebrew bought it of him for a pitiful price; and he would have reduced the price further, but he was afraid, as he had given him a dinar the first time, that if he reduced it the youth would go away and sell to some one else, and he would thus lose his usurious gains. And 'Ala-ed-Din ceased not to sell plate after plate till all were sold, and there remained only the tray on which the plates were set; and as this was large and heavy, he went and brought the Jew to his house, and shewed him the tray, and when he saw its size he gave him ten dinars, which 'Ala-ed-Din took, and the Jew departed. And 'Ala-ed-Din and his mother subsisted on the ten dinars till they were done.

Then 'Ala-ed-Din arose and fetched the Lamp, and rubbed it, and there appeared before him the Slave who had appeared to him before. And the Jinni said to him: "Command what thou wilt, O my master, for I am thy slave and the slave of him who possesseth the Lamp." And 'Ala-ed-Din answered: "My desire is that thou bring me a tray of food like unto that which thou didst bring me before, for I am starving." Then, in the twinkling of an eye, the

Slave brought him a tray, like the one he came with before; and on it were twelve plates of the richest, and on them the proper viands; and on the tray were also bottles of clear wine and white bread. Now 'Ala-ed-Din's mother had gone forth when she knew that her son intended to rub the Lamp, that she might not look a second time upon the Jinni; and presently she came home and perceived this tray, covered with dishes of silver, and the odour of rich viands permeating her house; and she wondered and rejoiced. And 'Ala-ed-Din said to her: "See, O my mother, thou didst tell me to cast away the Lamp; behold now its advantages!" And she answered: "O my son, God multiply his weal! but I would not look upon him." Then 'Ala-ed-Din and his mother sat down to the tray, and ate and drank till they were satisfied; and they put aside what was left for the morrow. And when the food they had was finished, 'Ala-ed-Din arose and took a plate of the plates of the tray under his garment and sallied forth in quest of the Jew to sell it to him; but by the decrees of destiny he passed by the shop of a jeweller, who was a just man and feared God. And when the jeweller sheykh saw 'Ala-ed-Din he questioned him, saying: "O my son, what dost thou want? for I have seen thee often passing by, and thou wast dealing with a Jewish man, and I have seen thee making over to him various things, and I am thinking that thou hast something with thee now, and thou seekest him to buy it. But thou dost not know, O my son, that the property of the Muslims, who profess the Unity of God Most High, is fair spoil to the Jews, who always defraud them, and worst of all this damned Jew with whom thou hast dealt and into whose hands thou hast fallen. So if thou hast with thee, O my son, anything thou wishest to sell, shew it me, and fear not at all, for I will give thee its value by the truth of the Most High God." So 'Ala-ed-Din produced the plate before the sheykh, who when he had looked upon it, took it and weighed it in his balance, and questioned 'Ala-ed-Din and said: "Didst thou sell the like of this to the Jew?" And he answered, "Yes, its like and its brother." And the other said: "How much did he give thee for its price?" And he answered, "He gave me a dinar." And when the sheykh heard from 'Ala-ed-Din that the Jew had given him only a single dinar for the price of the plate, he exclaimed: "Woe to this accursed who cheats the servants of the Most High God!" And looking at 'Ala-ed-Din he said: "O my son, verily this rascally Jew hath cheated thee and mocked at thee; for thy plate is of fine virgin silver; and I have weighed it and found its value to be seventy dinars. So if thou wilt take its price, take it." And the jeweller sheykh counted out to him seventy dinars, and 'Ala-ed Din took them, and thanked him for his kindness in shewing him the Jew's fraud. And whenever the price of a plate was gone, he went and brought another, so that he and his mother became well to do, though they ceased not to live as of old, as middle-class people, without excess or waste.

'Ala-ed-Din had cast aside his gracelessness and shunned vagabonds, and chose for his companions upright men, and went every day to the market of the merchants and sat with the great and the small of them, and asked them concerning matters of business and the price of investments and the rest. And he would visit the market of the goldsmiths and jewellers; and there he would sit and divert himself with looking at the jewels and how they were bought and sold there. And thus he learned that the pockets full of fruit which he had gathered in the Treasury were not of glass or crystal, but were precious stones. And he knew that he had become possessed of vast riches such as Kings could never amass. And he examined all the stones that were in the market of the jewellers and found that their very biggest was not equal to his smallest. And he ceased not each day to saunter to the Bazar of the Jewellers and make acquaintance with the people, and obtain their good-will, and inquire of them concerning buying and selling and taking and giving and the dear and the cheap; till one day, after rising betimes and putting on his dress, he went as was his wont to the Bazar of the Jewellers, and as he passed he heard the herald calling thus: "By command of the gracious patron, King of the Time, Lord of the Age and the Season: now let all the people close their stores and shops and enter in unto their houses, because Bedr-el-Budur, the daughter of the Sultan, intendeth to visit the bath; and whoso disobeyeth the order, death is his penalty, and his blood be on his own head." And when 'Ala-ed-Din heard this proclamation, he longed to look upon the Sultan's daughter, and said within himself: "Verily all the folk talk of her beauty and loveliness, and the summit of my ambition is to behold her."

So 'Ala-ed-Din set himself to seek a way whereby he might attain to a sight of the daughter of the Sultan, the Lady Bedr-el-Budur; and it seemed best to him to stand behind the door of the Hammam, so as to see her face when she came in. Accordingly, without any delay, he went to the bath before she was expected and stood behind the door, a place where no one could see him; and when the daughter of the Sultan drew near, after going about the city and its quarters and diverting herself thereby, she came to the bath, and on entering, lifted her veil and displayed her face, as it were a radiant sun or a pearl of great price; for she was as the poet sang:

> Borders of kohl enhance the witchery of her glance,
> Gardens of roses are her damask cheeks,
> Black are her tresses as the gloomy night,
> Illumined by the glory of her brow.

When the princess raised her veil from her face and 'Ala-ed-Din looked upon her, he said: "Of a surety her make magnifieth the Mighty Maker, and extolled be he who made her and adorned her with such beauty and loveliness!" His vigour became weak at the sight of her, and his thoughts became distraught, and his sight bewildered, and love of her got hold of his whole soul; and he went home and returned to his mother like one in a dream. And his mother spake to him, but he replied not yea or nay; and she set before him breakfast, but he remained in the same state. So she said to him: "O my son, what hath befallen thee? Doth anything distress thee? Tell me what hath happened to thee, for thou, contrary to thy wont, repliest not when I speak to thee." Then 'Ala-ed-Din,—who had believed that all women were like his mother, and though he had heard of the beauty of Bedr-el-Budur, the daughter of the Sultan, yet knew not what this beauty and loveliness might mean,—turned to his mother and said to her, "Let me alone." But she urged him to come and eat; so he came and ate a little, and then lay on his bed pondering till morning dawned. And he ceased not from this state the next day, so that his mother was perplexed for her son's condition and could not find out what had come over him. And she believed he was seriously sick, and came and asked him, saying: "O my son, if thou feel pain or anything of the kind, tell me, that I may go and bring thee a physician; and this very day there is in this city a doctor from the land of the Arabs whom the Sultan sent for, and the rumour goeth that he is very skilful. So if thou be sick, let me go and call him in."

When 'Ala-ed-Din heard that his mother wished to bring him a physician, he said to her: "O my mother, I am well, and not sick at all. But I always believed that all women resembled thee, until yesterday I saw the Lady Bedr-el-Budur, the daughter of the Sultan, going in to the bath." And he told her all that had betided him, and said: "Perhaps thou didst also hear the herald calling: 'Let no man open his shop or stay in the streets, that the Lady Bedr-el-Budur may go to the Bath.' But I did look upon her, even as she is, because she lifted her veil at the entering of the bath. And when I gazed on her form and saw that noble shape, there seized me, O my mother, a violent ecstasy of love for her, and a fixed resolve to win her possesseth every part of me; nor can I possibly rest until I gain her. And I intend, therefore, to demand her of the Sultan, her father, in lawful wedlock." And when his mother heard his words she feared for his reason, and said: "O my son, God's name be on thee! for it is plain thou hast lost thy reason, my son. But be guided, and be not as the insane." And he answered: "O my mother, I have not lost my reason, nor am I mad, nor can thy words alter what is in my mind, for peace is impossible to me till I win the beloved of my heart, the lovely Lady Bedr-el-Budur. And I am determined to demand her of her father, the Sultan." And she said to him: "O my son, by my life, say not so, lest any one hear thee and say thou art mad. Put away from thee this folly; for who should do a thing like this, to ask it of the Sultan? And I know not how thou wilt set to work to ask this favour of the Sultan, even if thy speech be true, or through whom thou wilt ask it." And he answered: "Through whom, O my mother, should I make this request, when I have thee? And whom have I more trusty than thee? It is my wish that thou thyself ask this request." And she said: "O my son, God preserve me from this! Have I lost my reason like thee? Cast away this thought from thy soul, and think whose son thou art, my son, the child of a tailor, of the poorest and meanest of the tailors to be found in this city; and I, too, thy mother, come of very poor folk. So how dost thou presume to ask in marriage a daughter of the Sultan, who would not deign to marry her to any of the Kings and Sultans, unless they were his equals in grandeur and honour and majesty; and were they less than he but a single degree he would not give them his daughter.

'Ala-ed-Din waited patiently till his mother had ended her speech, and then said: "O my mother, all that thou recallest I know, and it is familiar to me that I am the son of the poor; but all these thy words cannot change my purpose in the least, nor do I the less expect of thee, as I am thy son and thou lovest me, to do me this kindness; otherwise thou wilt undo me, and speedy death is upon me; unless I obtain my desire of the darling of my heart; and in any case, O my mother, I am thy child." And when she heard his words she wept in her grief for him, and said: "O my son, yea verily I am thy mother, nor have I child or blood of my blood save thee; and the height of my desire is to rejoice in thee and wed thee to a wife; but if I seek to ask for thee a bride of our equals and peers, they will ask at once if thou hast trade or merchandise or land or garden, to live on. And what can I answer them? And if I cannot answer the poor people, our likes, how shall I venture upon this hazard and dare this impertinence, O my son, and by what means shall I ask for thee of the Sultan his daughter, and howsoever shall I compass access to the Sultan's presence? And if they question me, what shall I answer? And probably they will take me for a mad woman. And supposing I gain access to the presence, what shall I take him as an offering to his Majesty?"

And she went on: "O my child, the Sultan indeed is
clement, and never rejecteth him who approacheth him to
ask of him equity or mercy or protection. Ask him for
a gift, for he is generous, and granteth grace far and near.
But he granteth his favour to those who deserve it, either
having done something before him in battle or otherwise
served their country. Then as for thee, tell me what hast
thou done before the Sultan's eyes or publicly, that thou
shouldst merit this grace? And again, this grace which
thou askest becometh not our rank, and it is not possible
that the King should give thee the favour which thou
wouldst ask. And whoso approacheth the Sultan to ask
favours, it behooveth him to take with him something befitting his majesty, as I said to thee; and how canst thou
possibly present thyself before the Sultan, and stand before
him and ask his daughter of him when thou hast nothing
with thee to offer him suitable to his rank?" And 'Ala-ed-
Din replied: "O my mother, thou speakest aright and
thinkest well, and it behooveth me to consider all that thou
hast brought to mind. But, my mother, the love of the
Sultan's daughter, the Lady Bedr-el-Budur, hath penetrated
into the core of my heart, and peace is impossible to me
unless I win her. But thou hast reminded me of something
I had forgotten, and this very thing doth embolden me to
ask of him his daughter. Thou sayest, O my mother, that
I have no offering to make to the Sultan, as is the custom
of the folk, yet as a fact I have a gift to present the equal
of which I think doth not exist among the Kings anywhere,
nor anything approaching it; for verily what I thought to
be glass or crystal is nothing but precious stones; and
I believe that all the Kings of the world have never owned
aught to equal the least of them. For by visiting the
jewellers I learned that these are the costliest jewels which
I brought in my pockets from the Treasury. Therefore be
tranquil. In the house is a china bowl; arise, therefore,
and fetch it, that I may fill it with these jewels, and we
will see how they look in it." And his mother arose and
went for the china bowl, and said within herself: "Let me
see if the words of my son concerning these jewels be true
or not." And she set the bowl before 'Ala-ed-Din, and he

drew from his pockets the bags of jewels, and began to
arrange them in the bowl, and ceased not to set them in
order until it was full; and when it was quite full his mother
looked into it, and could not see into it without blinking,
for her eyes were dazzled by the sheen of the jewels and
their radiance and the excess of their flashing. And her
reason was confounded, though she was not certain whether
or not their value was so vastly great; but she considered
that her son's speech might possibly be true—that their
equals could not be found among the King's. Then 'Ala-
ed-Din turned to her and said: "Thou hast seen, O my
mother, that this gift for the Sultan is splendid, and I am
convinced that it will procure thee great favour from him,
and he will receive thee with all honour. So now, O my
mother, thou hast no excuse; collect, therefore, thy faculties
and arise; take this bowl and go with it to the palace."
And his mother replied: "O my son, certainly the present is
exceeding precious, and none, as thou sayest, possesseth its
equal. But who would dare to approach and ask of the
Sultan his daughter, the Lady Bedr-el-Budur? As for me, I
dare not to say to him, 'I want thy daughter' when he asketh
me 'What is thy want?' But I know, O my son, that my
tongue will be tied. And suppose that, by God's help, I pluck
up my courage and say to him: 'It is my desire to become
related to thee by thy daughter, the Lady Bedr-el-Budur
and my son 'Ala-ed-Din,' they will conclude forthwith that
I am possessed, and will cast me forth in shame and disgrace, till I tell thee not only that I shall run in danger of
death, but thou wilt likewise. Yet, in spite of all this, O
my son, in deference to thy wish, I needs must pluck up
heart and go. But if the King welcome me and honour
me on account of the gift, and I should ask of him what
thou wishest, how shall I reply when he asketh me, as is
usual, What is thy condition and thy income? Haply, O
my son, he will ask me this before he asketh me who thou
art." And 'Ala-ed-Din answered: "It is impossible that
the Sultan should thus question thee after looking at the
precious stones and their splendor; nor doth it boot to
consider things which may not happen. Do thou only arise
and ask him for his daughter for me, and offer him the

jewels, and do not sit there inventing obstacles. Hast thou not already learned, O my mother, that this Lamp of mine is now a firm maintenance for us, and that all I demand of it is brought to me? And this is my hope, that by its means I shall know how to make answer to the Sultan if he ask me thus."

And 'Ala-ed-Din and his mother kept talking over the matter all that night. And when morning dawned his mother arose and plucked up courage, the more as her son had explained to her somewhat of the properties of the Lamp and its virtues—that it would supply them with all they wanted. 'Ala-ed-Din, however, when he saw that his mother had plucked up courage on his explaining to her the effects of the Lamp, feared lest she should gossip about it to the people, and said to her: " O my mother, take heed how thou tellest any one about the Lamp and its virtues, for this is our own benefit. Restrain thy thought, lest thou babble to any one about it, for fear we lose it and lose the benefit which we possess from it." And his mother answered, " Fear not for that, O my son." And she arose and took the bowl of precious stones and passed forth early, that she might reach the audience before it was crowded. And she covered the bowl with a kerchief, and went to the palace, and when she arrived the audience was not full ; and she saw the ministers and sundry of the magnates of the state entering to the presence of the Sultan. And presently the levée was completed by the wezirs and lords of the state and grandees and princes and nobles. Then the Sultan appeared, and the ministers bowed down before him, and in like manner the rest of the grandees and nobles. And the Sultan seated himself on the divan on the kingly throne, and all who attended the levée stood before him with crossed arms awaiting his command to be seated. And he ordered them to sit, and every one of them sat down in his order. Then the petitioners presented themselves before the Sultan, and he decided everything, as usual, until the audience was over ; when the King arose and went in to the palace, and every soul departed his own way. And when 'Ala-ed-Din's mother saw the Sultan had risen from his throne and gone into the Harim, she too took her departure and went her way to her house. And when 'Ala-ed-Din perceived her, and saw the bowl in her hand, he thought that probably some accident had befallen her, but he did not wish to question her until she was come in and had set down the bowl. Then she related to him what had happened, and ended by saying: "Praise be to God, my son, that boldness came to me, and I found a place in the levée this day, although it did not fall to my lot to address the Sultan. Probably, if it please God Most High, to-morrow I will speak to him. Indeed, to-day many of the people could not address the Sultan, like me. But to-morrow, my son, be of good cheer, since I must speak to him for the sake of thy desire, and how shall what happened happen again?" And when 'Ala-ed-Din heard his parent's words he rejoiced with exceeding joy; and though he expected the affair from hour to hour, from the violence of his love and yearning for the Lady Bedr-el-Budur, for all that he practised patience. So they slept that night, and in the morning his mother arose and went with the bowl to the audience of the Sultan; but she found it closed. So she asked the bystanders, and they told her that the Sultan did not hold an audience continually, but only thrice a week.

So she resolved to return home that day. And every day she went, and when she saw the audience begin she would stand before the Sultan till it was over, and then she would return; and next day she would go to see if the court were closed; and in this manner she went for a whole month. Now the Sultan had perceived her at every levée, and when she came on the last day and stood before the presence, as was her wont, until it was over, without having courage to come forward or address him a word, and the Sultan had risen and gone to his Harim, and his Grand Wezir with him, the Sultan turned to him and said: "O Wezir, six or seven days at each audience have I seen that old woman presenting herself here; and I see she always carries something under her cloak. Tell me, O Wezir, knowest thou aught of her and her business?" And the Wezir answered: "O our lord the Sultan, verily women are wanting in sense; probably this woman hath come to complain to thee of her husband or one of her people." But the Sultan was not satisfied with the Wezir's reply, but commanded him, if the woman came again to the levée, to bring her before him. So the Wezir put his hand on his head and said: "I hear and obey, O our lord the Sultan."

Now the mother of 'Ala-ed-Din was wont to set forth every day to the audience and stand in the presence before the Sultan, although she was sad and very weary; yet for the sake of her son's desire she made light of her trouble. And one day she came to the levée, as usual, and stood before the Sultan, who when he saw her ordered his Wezir, saying: "This is the woman I spake of to thee yesterday; bring her instantly before me that I may inquire into her suit and decide her business." And straightway the Wezir arose and brought 'Ala-ed-Din's mother to the Sultan. And when she found herself in the presence, she performed the obeisance and invoked glory upon him, and long life and perpetual prosperity; and she kissed the ground before him. And the Sultan said to her: "O woman, for some days have I seen thee at the levée, and thou hast not addressed a word to me; tell me if thou hast a want, that I may grant it." So she kissed the ground again and invoked blessings upon him, and said: "Yea, by the life of thy head, O King of the Age, verily have I a suit. But, first of all grant me immunity, if I can present my suit to the hearing of our lord the Sultan, for perhaps thy Felicity may find my petition strange." So the Sultan, wishing to know what was her petition, and being endowed with much mildness, promised her immunity, and at once ordered all who were there to depart, and remained alone, he and the Wezir.

Then the Sultan, turning to her, said: "Explain thy suit, and the protection of God Most High be on thee." But she answered: "O King of the Age, I shall need thy pardon also." And he replied, "God pardon thee." Then she said: "O our lord the Sultan, verily I have a son whose name is 'Ala-ed-Din. One day of the days he heard the herald proclaiming that none should open his shop or appear in the streets of the city, because the Lady Bedr-el-Budur, the daughter of our lord the Sultan, was going to the bath. And when my son heard that, he longed to see her, and hid himself in a place where he would be able to

look upon her closely, and that was behind the gate of the
Hammam. So when she drew near, he looked upon her
and gazed full upon her as much as he liked; and from the
moment he saw her, O King of the Age, to this instant,
life hath been intolerable to him; and he hath desired me
to ask her of thy Felicity that he may wed her. I have
not been able to banish this fancy from his mind, for the
love of her hath taken possession of his heart, so that he
told me: 'Be assured, O my mother, that if I do not
obtain my desire, without doubt I shall die.' So I trust for
clemency and pardon from thy Felicity for this hardihood of
mine and my son's, and punish us not for it."

When the King had heard her story, looking kindly at
her, he fell a-laughing, and asked her: "What is it thou
hast with thee, and what is this bundle?" Then the mother
of 'Ala-ed-Din, perceiving that the Sultan was not wroth at
her speech, but rather laughing, forthwith opened the cloth
and set before him the bowl of jewels. And when the
Sultan saw the stones, after the cloth was taken off, and
how the hall was lighted up, as it were, by chandeliers and
lustres, he was dazed and amazed at their sparkling, and
wondered at their size and splendour and beauty, saying:
—"To this day have I never seen the like of these jewels for
beauty and size and loveliness, nor do I believe that there
is in my treasury a single one equal to them." Then
turning to his Wezir, he said: "What sayest thou, O Wezir,
hast thou seen, thou in thy time, the like of these splendid
jewels?"

And the Wezir answered: "Never have I seen such, O
our lord the Sultan, and I do not think that the smallest of them is to be found in the treasuries of my
lord the King." And the King said to him: "Verily he
who hath presented me with these jewels is worthy to be
the bridegroom of my daughter Bedr-el-Budur, for, methinks, as far as I can see, none is worthier of her than he."
When the Wezir heard this speech of the Sultan, his tongue
became tied with vexation, and he grieved with sore
grieving, because the King had promised to marry the
Princess to his son. So after a little he said to him: "O
King of the Age, thy Felicity was graciously pleased to

promise the Lady Bedr-el-Budur to my son: it is therefore incumbent on thy Highness to graciously allow three months, when, please God, there shall be a present from my son more splendid even than this." So the King, though he knew that this thing could not be accomplished either by the Wezir or by any of the grandees, yet of his kindness and generosity granted a delay of three months, as he had asked. And turning to the old woman, 'Ala-ed-Din's mother, he said: "Go back to thy son, and tell him I have given my royal word that my daughter shall bear his name, but it is necessary to prepare her wardrobe and requisites, and so he will have to wait three months."

'Ala-ed-Din's mother accepted this answer, and thanked the Sultan and blessed him, and hastened forth, and almost flew with delight till she came home and entered. And 'Ala-ed-Din her son saw how her face was smiling; so he was cheered by the hope of good news; moreover, she had come back without loitering as heretofore, and had returned without the bowl. So he asked her, saying: "If it please God, my mother, thou bringest me good news, and perhaps the jewels and their rarity have had their effect, and the Sultan hath welcomed thee and been gracious to thee and hearkened to thy request?" And she related it all to him —how the Sultan had received her and marvelled at the multitude of the jewels and their size; and the Wezir also; and how he had promised that "his daughter shall bear thy name; only, O my son, the Wezir spake to him a private word before he promised me, and after the Wezir had spoken he covenanted for a delay of three months; and I am afraid the Wezir will be hostile to thee and try to change the mind of the King."

When 'Ala-ed-Din heard the words of his mother and how the Sultan had promised him after three months, his soul was relieved and he rejoiced exceedingly, and said: "Since the Sultan hath promised for three months, though it is indeed a long time, on all accounts my joy is immense." Then he thanked his parent and magnified her success above her toil, and said: "By Allah, O my mother, just now I was, as it were, in the grave, and thou hast pulled me out; and I praise God Most High that I am now sure that there liveth none richer or happier than I." Then he waited in patience till two months of the three were gone.

One day of the days the mother of 'Ala-ed-Din went forth about sunset to the market to buy oil and beheld all the bazars closed, and the whole city deserted, and the people were putting candles and flowers in their windows; and she saw troops and guards and cavalcades of aghas, and lamps and lustres flaming. And wonder gat hold of her at this marvel and gala, and she went to an oilman's shop which was still open, and having bought the oil, said to the dealer: "O Uncle, inform me what is the occasion to-day in the city, that the people make such adornment and the markets and houses are all closed and the troops paraded?" And the oilman answered: "O woman, I suppose thou art a stranger, not of this city." But she said, "Nay, I am of this city." So he cried: "Art thou of this city, and hast not heard that the son of the chief Wezir this night is to unite himself to the Lady Bedr-el-Budur, the daughter of the Sultan, and he is now at the bath; and these officers and soldiers are drawn up waiting to see him come forth from the bath and accompany him to the palace into the presence of the daughter of the Sultan!"

When the mother of 'Ala-ed-Din heard his words she was sad and perplexed in her mind how she should contrive to break this dismal news to her son, for her unhappy boy was counting hour by hour till the three months should be over. So she returned home after a little, and when she had come and entered to her son she said: "O my son, I would fain tell thee certain tidings, though thy grief thereat will cost me dear." And he answered, "Tell me, what is this news." And she said: "Verily the Sultan hath violated his covenant to thee in the matter of his daughter the Lady Bedr-el-Budur, and this night the Wezir's son goeth in to her. And O my child, I have long suspected that the Wezir would change the Sultan's mind, as I told thee how he spake privily to him before me." Then 'Ala-ed-Din asked her: "How knowest thou that the Wezir's son is going in this night to the Lady Bedr-el-Budur, the daughter of the Sultan?" So she told him about all the decorations she had noticed in the town when she went to buy oil, and how the aghas and grandees of the state were drawn up waiting for the Wezir's son to come forth from the bath, and how this was his nuptial night. When he learnt this, 'Ala-ed-Din was seized with a fever of grief, till after a while he bethought him of the Lamp. Then he cheered up, and said: "By thy life, O my mother, suppose the Wezir's son should not enjoy her, as thou thinkest. But now let us cease this talk, and arise; bring our supper, that we may eat, and after I have retired awhile within my chamber all will be well."

So after supper 'Ala-ed-Din withdrew to his chamber and fastened the door and took out the Lamp and rubbed it, and immediately the Slave came and said: "Ask what thou wilt, for I am thy slave, the slave of him who hath the Lamp, I and all the servants of the Lamp." And 'Ala-ed-Din said: "Listen. I asked the Sultan that I might marry his daughter, and he promised me, in three months; but he hath not kept his word, but hath given her to the son of the Wezir, and this very night it is his intention to go in to her. But I command thee, if thou be a true servant of the Lamp, that when thou seest the bride and bridegroom together this night thou bring them in the bed to this place. This is what I require of thee." And the Marid answered: "I hear and obey; and if thou hast any other behest, besides this, command me in all thou desirest." But 'Ala-ed-Din said: "I have no other command save that which I have told thee." So the Slave vanished, and 'Ala-ed-Din returned to finish the evening with his mother. But when the time came when he expected the Slave's return, he arose and entered his chamber, and soon after beheld the Slave with the bridal pair on their bed. And when 'Ala-ed-Din saw them he rejoiced with great joy. Then said he to the Slave: "Take away yonder gallows-bird and lay him in a closet." And immediately the Slave bore the Wezir's son and stretched him in a closet, and before leaving him he blew a cold blast on him, and the state of the Wezir's son became miserable. Then the Slave returned to 'Ala-ed-Din and said: "If thou needest aught else, tell me." And 'Ala-ed-Din answered, "Return in the morning to restore them to their place." So he said, "I hear and obey," and vanished.

Then 'Ala-ed-Din arose, and could hardly believe that this affair had prospered with him. But when he looked at the Lady Bedr-el-Budur in his own house, although he had long been consumed with love of her, yet he maintained an honourable respect towards her, and said: "O Lady of Loveliness, think not that I brought thee here to harm thine honour; nay, but only that none other should be privileged to enjoy thee, since thy father the Sultan gave me his word that I should have thee. So rest in peace." But when Bedr-el-Budur found herself in this poor and dark house, and heard the words of 'Ala-ed-Din, fear and shuddering took hold of her, and she was dazed, and could not make him any reply. Then 'Ala-ed-Din arose and stripped off his robe, and laying a sword between himself and her, slept beside her in the bed, without doing her wrong, for he wished only to prevent the nuptials of the Wezir's son with her. But the Lady Bedr-el-Budur passed the worst of nights; she had not passed a worse in all her life; and the Wezir's son, who slept in the closet, dared not move from his fear of the Slave which possessed him.

When it was morning, without any rubbing of the Lamp, the Slave appeared to 'Ala-ed-Din, and said: "O my master, if thou desirest anything, command me, that I may perform it on the head and the eye." So 'Ala-ed-Din said: "Go bear the bride and bridegroom to their place." And in the twinkling of an eye the Slave did as 'Ala-ed-Din bade him, and took the Wezir's son and the Lady Bedr-el-Budur and carried them and restored them to their place in the palace, as they had been, without seeing any one, though they almost died of fear when they found themselves being carried from place to place. Hardly had the Slave put them back again and departed, when the Sultan came to visit his daughter. And when the Wezir's son heard the door open, he forthwith leaped from the bed, for he knew that none but the Sultan could come in at that time; but it was exceedingly disagreeable to him, for he wished to warm himself a little, since he had not long left the [cold] closet; however, he arose and put on his clothes.

The Sultan came in unto his daughter the Lady Bedr-el-Budur, and kissed her between the eyes and wished her good-morning, and asked her concerning her bridegroom, and whether she was content with him. But she made him never an answer, but looked at him with an eye of anger; and he asked her again, and she remained silent and said not a word to him. So the Sultan went his way and departed from her house, and went to the Queen, and told her what had befallen him with the Lady Bedr-el-Budur. Then the Queen, loth to have him vexed with the Princess, said to him: "O King of the Age, this is the way with most brides in their honeymoon; they are shy, and a trifle whimsical. So chide her not, and soon she will return to herself and converse with people; for now it is her modesty, O King of the Age, that preventeth her speaking. However, it is my intention to go and visit her."

So the Queen arose and put on her robes and went to her daughter the Lady Bedr-ed-Budur, and approached her and gave her good-day, and kissed her betwixt the eyes. And the Princess answered her never a word. So the Queen said to herself: "Some strange thing must have happened to her to disquiet her thus." So she asked her: "O my daughter, what is the cause of the state thou art in? Tell me what hath come to thee, that when I visit thee and bid thee good-day, thou answerest me not." Then Bedr-el-Budur turned her head and said to her: "Chide me not, O my mother; it was indeed my duty to meet thee with all regard and reverence, since thou hast honoured me by this visit. However, I beg thee to hear the reason of this my behaviour, and see how this night which I have passed hath been the worst of nights for me. Hardly had we gone to bed, O mother, when one whose shape I know not lifted up the bed and bore us to a dark, loathly, vile place." And she related to her mother the Queen all that had happened to her that night, and how they had taken away her bridegroom and she had been left alone, till presently another youth came and slept, instead of her husband, and placed a sword betwixt them. "And in the morning he who took us returned to carry us back, and came with us to this our abode. Hardly had he restored us to it and left us, when my father the Sultan entered at the very hour of our return, and I had not heart or tongue to speak to him from the greatness of the fear and trembling which had come over me. And perhaps it may have vexed my father; so I pray thee, O my mother, tell him the reason for my condition, that he may not blame me for my lack of reply to him, but instead of censure, excuse me."

When the Queen heard the words of her daughter the Lady Bedr-el-Budur, she said to her: "O my child, calm thyself. If thou wert to tell this story to any one, it might be said that the daughter of the Sultan had lost her wits, and thou hast well done in not telling thy father this tale; and beware, my daughter, beware of telling him thereof." But the Princess answered her: "Mother, I have spoken to thee sensibly, and I have not lost my wits, but this is what hath happened to me; and if thou dost not believe it when I say it, ask my bridegroom." Then the Queen said to her: "Arise, now, my daughter, and away with such fancies from thy mind; put on thy robes and view the bridal fête which is going on in the city in thy honour and the rejoicings that are taking place all over the realm for thy marriage; and listen to the drums and songs, and look at these decorations, all done for the sake of pleasing thee, my daughter." Thereupon the Queen summoned the tirewomen, and they robed the Lady Bedr-el-Budur and straightened her up. And the Queen arose and went to the Sultan and told him that the Princess had been troubled that night with dreams and nightmare, and added: "Chide her not for her lack of answer to thee." Then she summoned the Wezir's son secretly, and asked him concerning the matter, and whether the story of the Princess were true or not; but he, in his fear of losing his bride from out his hand, answered: "O my sovereign lady, I know nothing of what thou sayest." So the Queen was sure that her daughter had been distraught by nightmare and dreams. The festivities lasted all day, with 'Almehs and singers and the beating of all sorts of instruments, and the Queen and the Wezir and the Wezir's son did their utmost to keep up the rejoicing, so that the Lady Bedr-el-Budur might be happy and forget her trouble; and all day they left nothing that incited to enjoyment undone before her, that she might forget what was in her mind and be content. But all this had no influence upon her; she remained silent and sad and bewildered at what had befallen her that night. Worse indeed had happened to the Wezir's son than to her, since he passed the night in a closet; but he had denied the fact and banished this calamity from his mind, because of his fear of losing his bride and his distinction, especially as all men envied him the connection and the exceeding honour thereof; and, moreover, because of the splendour of the bride's loveliness and her excessive beauty.

'Ala-ed-Din too went out that day to see the festivities which were going on in the city and the palace, and he began to laugh, above all when he heard people talking of the honour which had fallen to the Wezir's son and his good-fortune in becoming the son-in-law of the Sultan, and the great distinction shewn in his rejoicings and wedding festivities. And 'Ala-ed-Din said to himself: "Ye know not, ye rabble, what happened to him last night, that ye envy him!" And when night fell and it was bedtime, 'Ala-ed-Din arose and went to his chamber and rubbed the Lamp, and immediately the Slave presented himself. And he ordered him to bring the Sultan's daughter and her bridegroom as on the past night, before the Wezir's son had taken her to him. And the Slave waited not an instant, but vanished awhile, till he reappeared, bringing the bed in which was the Lady Bedr-el-Budur and the son of the Wezir. And he did with the latter as on the preceding night,—took and put him to sleep in a closet, and there left him bleached with excessive trembling and fear. And 'Ala-ed-Din arose and placed the sword betwixt himself and the Princess, and went to sleep. And when it was morning the Slave appeared and restored the pair to their own place; and 'Ala-ed-Din was filled with delight at the misadventure of the Wezir's son.

Now when the Sultan arose in the morning he desired to go to his daughter, Bedr-el-Budur, to see whether she would behave to him as on the preceding day. So, after he had shaken off his drowsiness, he arose and dressed himself and went to his daughter's palace and opened the door. Then the Wezir's son hastily got up and rose from the bed and began to put on his clothes, though his ribs almost split with cold; for when the Sultan came in the Slave had only just brought them back. So the Sultan entered, and approached his daughter Bedr-el-Budur, who was in bed; and drawing aside the curtain, he wished her good-morning, and kissed her betwixt the eyes, and inquired after her state. But he saw she was sad, and she answered him never a word, but looked at him angrily; and her state was wretched. Then the Sultan was wroth with her, since she replied not, and he fancied that something was wrong with her. So he drew his sword and said to her: "What hath come to thee? Tell me what hath happened to thee, or I will take thy life this very hour. Is this the honour and reverence thou shewest me, that I speak and thou repliest not a word?" And when the Lady Bedr-el-Budur saw how angry her father the Sultan was, and that his sword was drawn in his hand, she was released from her stupor of fear, and turned her head and said to him: "O my honoured father, be not wroth with me, nor be hasty in thy passion, for I am excusable, as thou shalt see. Listen to what hath befallen me, and I am persuaded that when thou hast heard my account of what happened to me these two nights, thou wilt excuse me, and thy Felicity will become pitiful toward me, even as I claim thy love." Then the Lady Bedr-el-Budur related to her father the Sultan all that had happened to her, adding: "O my father, if thou dost not believe me, ask the bridegroom, and he will tell thy Felicity the whole matter; though I knew not what they did with him when they took him away from me, nor did I imagine where they had put him."

When the Sultan heard the speech of his daughter, grief took hold of him and his eyes ran over with tears. And he sheathed the sword, and came and kissed her, saying: "O my daughter, why didst thou not tell me last night, that I might have averted this torment and fear which have fallen upon thee this night? However, it signifieth nothing. Arise and drive away from thee this fancy, and next night I will set a watch to guard thee, and no such unhappiness shall again make thee sad." And the Sultan returned to his palace, and straightway ordered the presence of the Wezir. And when he came and stood before him, he asked him: "O Wezir, what thinkest thou of this affair? Perchance thy son hath informed thee of what occurred to him and my daughter?" But the Wezir made answer: "O King of the Age, I have not seen my son, neither yesterday nor to-day." Then the Sultan told him all that his daughter the Princess Bedr-el-Budur had related, adding: "It is my desire now that thou find out from thy son the truth of the matter; for it may be that my daughter, from terror, did not understand what befell her, though I believe her story to be all true."

So the Wezir arose and sent for his son and asked him concerning all that the Sultan had told him, whether it were true or not. And the youth replied: "O my father the Wezir, God forbid that the Lady Bedr-el-Budur should tell lies! Nay, all she said is true, and these two nights that have passed were the worst of nights, instead of being nights of pleasure and joy to us both. But what befell me was the greater evil, for, instead of sleeping with my bride in the bed, I was put to sleep in a closet, a cursed, dark, and loathsome place smelling horribly, and my ribs almost split with the cold." And the young man told his father all that had happened to him, and added. "O honoured parent, I entreat thee, speak to the Sultan that he release me from this marriage. Truly it is a great honour to me to be the son-in-law of the Sultan, and most of all since the love of the Lady Bedr-el-Budur hath taken possession of my being; but I have not strength to endure another night like the two which are over."

When the Wezir heard his son's words he was exceeding sad and sorry, for he hoped to exalt and magnify his son by making him son-in-law to the Sultan; therefore he considered and pondered over this case, how to remedy it. It was a great hardship to him to break off the marriage, for he had been much congratulated on his success in so high a matter. So he said to his son: "Take patience, my child, till we see what may betide this night, when we set warders to watch over you; and do not reject this great honour, which hath been granted to none save thee alone."

Then the Wezir left him and returned to the Sultan and told him that what the Lady Bedr-el-Budur had said was true. Therefore the Sultan said: "If it be so, we must not delay." And he straightway ordered the rejoicings to cease

and the marriage to be annulled. And the people and folk
of the city wondered at this strange affair, and the more so
when they saw the Wezir and his son coming forth from the
palace in a state of grief and excess of rage; and men
began asking what had happened and what the cause might
be for annulling the marriage and terminating the espousals.
And none knew how it was save 'Ala-ed-Din, the lord of
the invocation, who laughed in secret. So the marriage
was dissolved, and still the Sultan forgot and recalled not
the promise he had made to the mother of 'Ala-ed-Din, nor
the Wezir either, and they knew not whence came that
which had come.

'Ala-ed-din waited in patience until the three months
were over, after which the Sultan had covenanted to wed
him to his daughter, the Lady Bedr-el-Budur. Then he
instantly despatched his mother to the Sultan to demand of
him the fulfilment of his promise. So the mother of 'Ala-
ed-Din went to the palace; and when the Sultan came to
the hall of audience and saw her standing before him, he
remembered his promise—that after three months he would
marry his daughter to her son. And turning to the Wezir,
he said: "O Wezir, this is the woman who gave us the
jewels, and to whom we did pledge our word for three
months. Bring her to me before anything else." So the
Wezir went and brought 'Ala-ed-Din's mother before the
Sultan; and when she came up to him she saluted him and
prayed for his glory and lasting prosperity. Then the Sultan
asked her if she had any suit. Whereto she answered: "O
King of the Age, verily the three months are over, for which
thou didst covenant with me, after which to marry my son
'Ala-ed-Din to thy daughter the Lady Bedr-el-Budur."

The King was perplexed at this demand, the more when
he observed her poor condition and that she was of the
meanest of the people. Yet the present she had given him
was exceedingly splendid, beyond his power to purchase.
Then turning to the Wezir, he said: "What stratagem hast
thou? Of a truth I pledged my word; yet it is evident to
me that they are poor people, and not of high degree."
And the Wezir, since envy was devouring him, and he was
beyond everything grieved at what had befallen his son,

said within himself: "How shall one like this wed the daughter of the Sultan and my son lose this honour?" So he answered the Sultan: "O my lord, it is an easy thing to be rid of this stranger, for it is not fit that thy Felicity should give thy daughter to a man like this,—one knoweth not who he is." The Sultan replied: "In what way shall we ward off this man from us, when I have pledged my word, and the word of Kings is sacred?" The Wezir answered: "O my lord, my advice is that thou demand of him forty bowls of pure gold full of jewels, such as this woman brought thee that day, and forty maids to carry the bowls, and forty black slaves." And the Sultan said: "By Allah, O Wezir, thou hast said well, for he cannot compass this thing, and thus we shall be freed from him." Then he said to the mother of 'Ala-ed-Din: "Go, tell thy son that I hold to the promise which I made to him, provided he be able to furnish my daughter's dowry, for which I require of him forty bowls of pure gold, each full of jewels, such as thou didst bring me, and forty maids to carry them, and forty black slaves to attend and escort them. If thy son can do this I will marry him to my daughter."

So the mother of 'Ala-ed-Din returned to her house shaking her head and saying: "Whence shall my poor son procure these bowls of jewels? Suppose he return to the Treasury and gather these jewels and bowls from the trees, yet with all this,—and I do not think he can, but say that he acquire them,—whence will he get the maids and slaves?" And she ceased not to commune with herself until she arrived at her house, where 'Ala-ed-Din was expecting her. And when she came in, she said: "O my son, did I not tell thee not to think that thou couldst attain to the Lady Bedr-el-Budur, and that such a thing was not possible for people like us?" And he said to her: "Explain to me what tidings there be." And she said: "O my son, verily the Sultan received me with all honour, as is his wont, and it is evident to me that his intentions towards us are benevolent. But thy enemy is the accursed Wezir; for after I had spoken to the Sultan, according to thy tongue (as thou saidst, 'Verily the time is come for which thou didst covenant'), and after I had said to him, 'Verily it behoves

thy Felicity to order the wedding of thy daughter the Lady
Bedr-el-Budur to my son 'Ala-ed-Din,' he turned to the
Wezir and spake to him; and he answered him secretly;
and afterward the Sultan gave me his answer." Then she
told 'Ala-ed-Din what the Sultan required, and said to him:
" O my son, verily he requireth of thee an immediate reply,
and methinks we have no answer for him."

When 'Ala-ed-Din heard the words of his mother, he
laughed and said: " O my mother, thou sayest that we have
no answer for him, and considerest the affair exceeding
hard; but compose thy mind, and arise, bring me something
to eat, and after we have eaten, if the Compassionate please,
thou shalt see my answer. And the Sultan like thee, think-
eth he hath required an enormous thing, in order to keep
me from the Lady Bedr-el-Budur; though really he hath
asked a smaller thing than I expected. But do thou arise,
and fetch me somewhat to eat, and trust me to provide
the answer for thee." So his mother arose and went forth
to fetch what was needed from the market to prepare dinner. And 'Ala-ed-Din went into his chamber, and took
the Lamp and rubbed it, and immediately there appeared
to him the Slave, who said: " O my master, ask what thou
desirest." And 'Ala-ed-Din answered: "I have demanded
the daughter of the Sultan in marriage, and the Sultan hath
required of me forty bowls of pure gold, each weighing ten
pounds, and they must be full of the jewels which are in the
garden of the Treasury; and to carry them there must be
forty maids, and to each maid a slave, forty slaves in all.
So I desire of thee that thou bring me all these." And the
Jinni said: "I hear and obey, O my master," and vanished
for the space of an hour, when he brought forty maids, and
with each maid a eunuch, and on each maid's head a bowl
of fine gold full of precious stones. And he set them before
'Ala-ed-Din, saying: "Here is thy wish: tell me then if
thou hast need of any affair or service beside this." But
'Ala-ed-Din answered: "I need nothing else; but if I require anything I will summon thee and inform thee thereof." So the Slave vanished. And presently 'Ala-ed-Din's
mother appeared and entered the house, and perceived the
slaves and maids. And she marvelled, saying: "All this

is from the Lamp. God preserve it for my son!" And as she was about to raise her veil, 'Ala-ed-Din said to her: " O my mother, this is the moment for thee, before the Sultan goes in to his seraglio, to his family. Take thou to him that which he demanded, and go to him forthwith, that he may know that I am able to do what he required, and more also. Verily he is deceived by the Wezir, and they both think to foil me." Thereupon 'Ala-ed-Din arose and opened the door of the house, and the maids and the slaves came forth side by side, each maid with a eunuch beside her, till they filled the street. And 'Ala-ed-Din's mother went before them. And the people flocked to the street when they saw this mighty, wonderful sight, and stood diverting themselves and marvelling and observing the forms of the damsels and their beauty and loveliness; for they all wore dresses embroidered with gold and trimmed with jewels, none worth less than a thousand dinars. And the folks gazed upon the bowls, and saw that the lustre transcended the light of the sun. Over each was a piece of brocade embroidered with gold and studded with precious stones. And the people of the quarter stood wondering at this strange spectacle. But 'Ala-ed-Din's mother walked on, and the damsels and slaves marched behind her, in all order and precision, and the people stopped to examine the beauty of the damsels, and glorified God the great Creator; and so they arrived and entered with 'Ala-ed-Din's mother, the palace of the Sultan. And when the aghas and chamberlains and officers of the army saw them, wonder gat hold of them and they were amazed at this sight, the like of which they had never witnessed in all their born days, above all, such damsels, every one of whom would turn the head of an anchorite. And although the chamberlain and officers of the Sultan's troops were all sons of grandees and nobles, yet they were astonished beyond measure at the costly dresses which the damsels wore, and the bowls upon their heads, which they could not gaze full upon by reason of their excessive flashing and dazzle.

Then the guard went in and informed the Sultan, and he at once ordered that they should be brought before him in the Hall of Audience. So 'Ala-ed-Din's mother came in with them; and when they appeared before the Sultan, they all saluted him with due reverence and worship, and they invoked blessings on his glory and good-fortune. Then they took the bowls from their heads and set them before him, and removed their coverings, and then stood respectfully. The Sultan marvelled with great admiration, and was bewildered at the splendour of the jewels and their loveliness, which transcended praise; and his wits were turned when he looked at the golden bowls full of precious stones, which captivated the sight; and he was confounded at this marvel till he became as the dumb, and could not say a word from excess of wonder. And his mind was the more perplexed how all this could have come about in the space of an hour. Then he gave commandment that the damsels with the bowls should enter the palace of the Lady Bedr-el-Budur; so they took up their loads and went in.

After that, the mother of 'Ala-ed-Din came and said to the Sultan: "O my lord, this is not a great thing wherewith to do honour to the Lady Bedr-el-Budur, for she merits the double of this [dower]." Then the Sultan turned to the Wezir and said: "What sayest thou, O Wezir? He who can procure such riches as these in so short a time, is he not worthy to be the Sultan's son-in-law and the daughter of the Sultan his bride?" But the Wezir, although he marvelled at the vastness of these riches, more even than the Sultan, yet, being devoured by envy, which grew stronger and stronger when he saw how content the Sultan was with the dower and riches, and though he could not disguise the truth, answered: "It is not worthy of her." And he was devising a plan for the Sultan, that he might not give his daughter the Lady Bedr-el-Budur to 'Ala-ed-Din, and accordingly he went on: "O my lord, all the treasures of the universe are not equal to the little finger of thy daughter. Thy Highness hath overvalued these presents as against her." When the Sultan heard these words of the Wezir, he perceived that they arose from excess of envy. So turning to 'Ala-ed-Din's mother, he said: "O woman, go to thy son, and tell him that I have accepted the dowry and I stand by my promise. My daughter is his bride and he my son-in-law; and bid him come hither, in order that I may know him. He shall have naught but honour and esteem from me. And this night shall begin the wedding; only, as I said, let him come to me without delay."

Then 'Ala-ed-Din's mother returned home with the speed of the wind, and abated not the quickness of her pace, in order to congratulate her son. She flew with joy at thinking that her child was going to become the son-in-law of the Sultan. After she had gone, the Sultan dismissed the audience and entered the apartments of the Lady Bedr-el-Budur, and bade them bring the damsels and the bowls before her that she might look at them. And when they brought them and the Princess examined the jewels, she was amazed and said: "Methinks there is not found in the treasuries of the universe a single gem like these!" Then she gazed upon the damsels and marvelled at their beauty and grace. And she knew that all this was from her new bridegroom, who had sent it in her service. So she rejoiced, though she had been sorrowful and sad on account of her bridegroom the son of the Wezir. Yet she rejoiced with great joy when she looked upon the jewels and the beauty of the damsels; and she made merry, and her father was greatly delighted at her cheerfulness, because he saw that her sadness and grief had departed from her. Then he asked her, saying: "O my daughter, Lady Bedr-el-Budur, does this astonish thee? Methinks this bridegroom of thine is goodlier than the Wezir's son; and presently, please God, O my daughter, thou shalt enjoy supreme delight with him." Thus was it with the Sultan.

As for 'Ala-ed-Din, when his mother returned and entered the house, laughing in the excess of her joy, and he saw her so, he scented good news, and said: "To God be praise everlasting! My desire is now accomplished." And his mother said: "Good news for thee, O my child! Cheer thy heart, and refresh thine eye for the fulfilment of thy wish. The Sultan hath accepted thy present, the riches and portion and dowry of the Lady Bedr-el-Budur; and she is thy bride, and this night, O my son, is the wedding and thy union with the Princess. To assure me of his promise the Sultan hath proclaimed thee before the world as his son-in-law, and saith that to-night is the consummation. More-over, he said to me: ' Let thy son come to me, that I may become acquainted with him and welcome him with all honour and regard.' And here am I, my son; my task is over; happen what may, it is now thy own affair."

Then 'Ala-ed-Din arose and kissed his mother's hand and thanked her, and magnified her goodness to him, and went and entered his chamber and took the Lamp and rubbed it, and behold, the Slave appeared, saying, "At thy service! Ask what thou desirest." So 'Ala-ed-Din answered: "I desire thee to take me to a bath the equal of which existeth not in the universe; and bring me there a dress so royal and exceeding costly that Kings possess not its match." And the Marid replied, "I hear and obey." And he lifted him and took him into a bath such as Kings and Emperors never saw, all of marble and carnelian, with wonderful pictures which captivated the eye; and not a soul was there. In it was a hall studded over with splendid jewels, which when 'Ala-ed-Din entered, there came to him one of the Jann in human shape, who washed and kneaded him to the top of his bent. After which 'Ala-ed-Din went from the bath into the spacious hall, and found his old clothes gone and in their place a suit of royal robes. Then there was brought to him sherbet and coffee flavoured with ambergris. And he drank and arose, and a number of slaves appeared before him, and clad him in resplendent clothes, and he was dressed and perfumed and scented. Though 'Ala-ed-Din was, in fact, a poor tailor's son, none would have supposed it, but rather would say: "This is the greatest of the sons of the Kings. Extolled be he who changeth others but himself changeth not!" Then the Jinni came and lifted him and returned him to his house, and said: "O my master, hast thou further need?" And 'Ala-ed-Din replied: "Yes, I want thee to bring me forty-eight memluks, twenty-four to go before me and twenty-four to follow me, with their chargers and habiliments and arms; and everything on them and their horses must be of the very costliest, such as is not in the treasuries of Kings. Then bring me a stallion fit for the Cæsars, and let his housings be of gold studded over with magnificent jewels;

and bring me forty-eight thousand dinars, to each memluk a thousand. For I wish to go to the Sultan's presence. So delay not, since without all these things of which I have told thee I cannot visit him. Bring me also twelve damsels; they must be of peerless beauty, and clad in the most sumptuous raiment, that they may accompany my mother to the palace of the Sultan. And let each damsel be attired like the King's ladies." And the Slave answered, "I hear and obey." And vanishing awhile, he brought him in the twinkling of an eye, all that he had commanded; and he led a steed the fellow of which did not exist among the horses of the Arabs, and his housings were of gorgeous cloth of gold.

'Ala-ed-Din sent for his mother at once, and delivered to her the twelve maidens, and gave her robes that she might be robed, when the damsels would escort her to the palace of the Sultan. And he sent one of the memluks which the Jinni had brought him to the Sultan, to ascertain whether he had come forth from his harem or not. So the memluk went quicker than lightning, and returned to him speedily, saying: "O my master, the Sultan expecteth thee." Then 'Ala-ed-Din arose and mounted and the memluks rode before him and behind him. And they were such as to make all men cry: "Extolled be the Lord who created them in such perfection of beauty and grace!" And they scattered gold among the people before their master 'Ala-ed-Din, who excelled them in beauty and comeliness,—and make no mention of the sons of Kings! Extolled be the Bountiful, the Eternal! And all this came by virtue of the Wonderful Lamp, which whoso possessed, it brought him beauty and loveliness and wealth and wisdom. And the people were astonished at the generosity of 'Ala-ed-Din and his excessive bounty, and were distraught as they gazed upon his beauty and comeliness and grace and courtliness. And they extolled the Compassionate for this his noble creation; and all blessed him, though they knew he was the son of Such-an-one the tailor; and none was envious of him, but all pronounced him worthy of his luck.

Thus was the crowd dazzled by 'Ala-ed-Din and his bounty and generosity, as he was going to the palace, scattering gold. And they blessed him, great and small, till he reached the palace, with the memluks before and behind him distributing largesse to the people. Now the Sultan had assembled the grandees of the state, and informed them that he had given his word for the marriage of his daughter to 'Ala-ed-Din. And he bade them await his coming, and then go forth, one and all, and receive him. And he sent for the emirs and the wezirs and chamberlains and gentlemen of the guard and officers of the army, and they were all in waiting for 'Ala-ed-Din at the gate of the palace. Now when 'Ala-ed-Din arrived he would have dismounted at the gate, but one of the emirs whom the Sultan had appointed for the office approached and said: "O my master, the order is that thou enter and remain mounted on thy charger till thou comest to the gate of the Hall of Audience." And they all marched before him and escorted him to the gate of the Divan, when some of them approached and held his stirrup, and others supported him on each side or took him by the hand, and the emirs and officers of state went before him and led him into the Hall of Audience close to the royal throne. Then the Sultan descended at once from his throne, and clasped him to his breast, and forbidding him to kiss the ground, kissed him and seated him beside him on his right. And 'Ala-ed-Din did as was proper towards Kings, in giving salutations and benedictions, saying: "O our lord the Sultan, verily the generosity of thy Felicity caused thee to vouchsafe me the Lady Bedr-el-Budur thy daughter, although I am not worthy of so great an honour, since I am of the meanest of thy slaves. And I beg God to prolong thy life perpetually. But in truth, O King, my tongue is powerless to thank thee for the greatness of the surpassing favours with which thou hast overwhelmed me. And I beg of thy Felicity that thou give me a piece of land where I may build a palace suitable for the Lady Bedr-el-Budur." And the Sultan was bewildered as he gazed upon 'Ala-ed-Din in his princely robes, and looked upon him and considered his beauty and comeliness, and saw the memluks arrayed for his service and their handsome apparel. And his wonder increased when 'Ala-ed-Din's mother approached in her costly attire, sumptuous as though

she had been a Queen; and when he perceived the twelve
damsels attending her standing before her in all respect and
worship. Further, the Sultan considered the eloquence of
'Ala-ed-Din, and the refinement of his language, and was
astounded at it, he and all those who were with him at the
levée. And fire was kindled in the heart of the Wezir for
envy of 'Ala-ed-Din, till he almost died. Then the Sultan,
after hearing 'Ala-ed-Din's benedictions, and perceiving the
loftiness of his bearing and his deference and eloquence,
pressed him to his bosom and kissed him, saying: "Alas
for me, my son, that I have not enjoyed thy company till
this day!"

When the Sultan saw 'Ala-ed-Din in this respect he rejoiced with great joy, and immediately ordered the music
and band to play. And he arose and took 'Ala-ed-Din and
led him into the palace, where supper was made ready and
the servants had laid the tables. So the Sultan sat down
and seated 'Ala-ed-Din on his right; and the wezirs also
sat, and the grandees of the state and lords of the realm, all
of them in their degree; and the band played, and they
made very merry in the palace. And the Sultan waxed
friendly with 'Ala-ed-Din and conversed with him, and he
answered with all courtliness and eloquence, as though he
had been brought up in the palaces of Kings and had been
their familiar. And the longer the conversation lasted between them the greater became the Sultan's joy and satisfaction, as he listened to his graceful replies and the charm of
his eloquence.

After they had eaten and drunk and removed the tables,
the Sultan commanded to bring the Kadis and witnesses,
and they came and tied the knot and wrote the contract of
marriage between 'Ala-ed-Din and the Lady Bedr-el-Budur.
After this 'Ala-ed-Din arose and would have gone out, but
the Sultan stopped him, saying: "Whither, O my son?
The festivities are beginning and the wedding is ready, and
the knot is tied and the contract written." But he answered:
"O my lord the King, it is my intention to build a palace
for the Lady Bedr-el-Budur befitting her rank and station;
and it is impossible that I should enter in to her before this
is done. But, please God, the building shall be finished in

the briefest space by the energy of thy servant and the countenance of thy Felicity. And for me, much as I long for union now with the Lady Bedr-el-Budur, yet it behoveth me to serve her and to do so first." So the Sultan said to him: "O my son, choose the land which thou deemest fit for thy project; take it altogether into thy hands; but the best place would be here in front of my palace on the open plain; then if thou so fanciest build the palace there." "This," said 'Ala-ed-Din, "is the height of my desire, to be near thy Felicity."

Therefore 'Ala-ed-Din took leave of the Sultan and went forth riding with his memluks before and behind him. And all the world blessed him and said, "By Allah, he is worthy!" till he reached his house. There he alighted from his horse and entered his chamber and rubbed the Lamp, and, behold, the Slave appeared before him and said: "Ask what thou wilt, O my master." So 'Ala-ed-Din said: "I require thee to do me an important service, which is to build me with all speed a palace in front of the Sultan's Serai; and let it be marvellous in its construction, such as Kings have not seen, and perfect in its fittings of stately furniture fit for princes; and so forth." And the Slave replied, "I hear and obey," and vanished. But before the break of dawn he came to 'Ala-ed-Din and said: "O my master, the palace is finished to the utmost of thy desire, and if thou wish to see it, arise at once and look at it." So 'Ala-ed-Din arose, and the Slave bore him in the twinkling of an eye to the palace. And when he saw it, he was astounded at its construction, for all its stones were of jasper and alabaster and porphyry and mosaics. Then the Slave took him into a treasury full of all sorts of gold and silver and precious stones, not to be numbered or estimated or appraised or valued. And again, he took him into another room, where he saw all the table equipments, plates and dishes, ewers and basins, of gold and silver, and likewise flagons and goblets; and he led him to the kitchen, where he saw the scullions with all their requisites and cooking utensils, all of gold and silver; and next to a chamber full of chests packed with royal raiment, such as captivated the reason, brocades from India and China, and embroideries. Again he led him to numerous rooms all full of what defieth description; and then to the stables, where he found horses the like of which were not found among the Kings in all the world; and from there he took him to the saddle-room, which was full of costly harness and saddles, studded with pearls and fine stones and the like. And all this was done in a single night. 'Ala-ed-Din was astounded and distraught at the vastness of these riches, which the mightiest sovereign on earth could not compass. And the palace was full of servants and maïdens whose loveliness would tempt a saint. But the most wonderful of all the things to be seen in the palace was a pavilion or kiosk with twenty-four bays, all of emeralds and diamonds and other jewels; and one bay was not finished by 'Ala-ed-Din's wish, in order that the Sultan might be unequal to completing it.

When 'Ala-ed-Din had surveyed the palace in every part, he rejoiced and was greatly delighted. Then turning to the Slave, he said: "I desire one thing of thee, which is still lacking, and of which I forgot to tell thee." And the Slave said: "Ask on, O my master, whatsoever thou wishest." So he said: "I desire of thee a carpet of splendid brocade, and let it be all worked with gold, and such that when spread it shall reach from my palace to that of the Sultan, so that the Lady Bedr-el-Budur when she cometh hither may walk upon it and not tread upon the bare ground." So the Slave went away for a while, and on his return said: "O my master, what thou didst ask of me is done." And he took and shewed him a carpet which captivated the reason, and it stretched from palace to palace. Then the Slave carried 'Ala-ed-Din back to his house.

At this moment it was already dawn, and the Sultan arose from sleep and opened the window of his chamber and looked out, and in front of his palace he perceived a building; so he began to rub his eyes, and opened them wide to observe it. And he saw a great palace, bewildering the wits; and he gazed upon the carpet laid down from his own palace to that other. And in like manner the door-keepers and all the royal household were perplexed in their minds at this thing. Just then the Wezir came in, and as he came he perceived the new palace and the carpet, and he too marvelled. And when the Sultan entered, the two began talking of this strange spectacle, and wondering at the sight of this thing, which dazzled the sight and delighted the heart, saying: "Of a truth, the like of this palace could not, we imagine, be built by Kings." And the Sultan turned to the Wezir and said: "Dost thou see now that 'Ala-ed-Din is worthy to mate my daughter the Lady Bedr-el-Budur, after seeing and considering this royal edifice and these riches which the mind of man could not conceive?" But the Wezir, on account of his envy of 'Ala-ed-Din, answered: "O King of the Age, verily this building and this edifice and these riches could not exist save by means of magic, for no man alive, be he the chiefest in authority or the greatest in wealth, could complete this edifice in a single night." Then answered the Sultan: "It is a wonder to me how thou art always imputing evil to 'Ala-ed-Din; meseems, however, that it proceedeth from thy envy of him; for thou wast present thyself when I gave him this land, when he asked me for a site to build a palace on for my daughter, and I granted him this piece of land for his palace before thine eyes. But shall he who bringeth such a dowry of jewels for my daughter as Kings possess not even a few thereof, shall he be unequal to building a palace like this?"

When the Wezir heard the Sultan's words, and perceived that he loved 'Ala-ed-Din greatly, his jealousy increased; only, as he could not do anything to avert it, he watched and could not answer the Sultan a word. But as to 'Ala-ed-Din, when he saw that it was morning, and the time had come for him to go to the palace, because his wedding fête was going on, and the emirs and wezirs and grandees of state had collected about the Sultan in order to be present at the wedding, he arose and rubbed the Lamp and the Slave appeared to him and said: "O my master, ask what thou desirest, for I am here at thy service." So 'Ala-ed-Din answered: "I intend to go now to the Sultan's palace, as this is my wedding-day, and I need ten thousand dinars which I wish thee to bring me." Then the Slave vanished for the twinkling of an eye and returned with the ten thousand dinars. Then 'Ala-ed-Din arose and mounted, and there rode with him his memluks, before and behind. And he proceeded to the palace, scattering gold to the crowd as he went, so that they were filled with affection for him, and his dignity was enhanced thereby. And when he arrived at the palace, and the emirs and aghas and guards who were drawn up in waiting saw him, they hastened immediately to the Sultan and apprised him. Then the Sultan arose and met him and embraced and kissed him, and holding him by the hand led him into the palace and sat down and seated him at his side on the right; while the whole town was decorated, and the musical instruments resounded in the palace, and the singers sang. Then the Sultan commanded that the banquet should be served, and the eunuchs and memluks hastened to lay the tables, which were such as befit Kings. And 'Ala-ed-Din and the Sultan and the grandees of the realm and the chief officers of state sat down and ate and drank till they were satisfied. And there were great rejoicings in the palace and the city; and all the nobles were delighted, and the people in all the kingdom rejoiced; and the rulers of provinces and chiefs of departments from distant regions came to see the wedding of 'Ala-ed-Din and the festivities. And the Sultan wondered in his mind at 'Ala-ed-Din's mother—how she used to come to him in shabby clothes when her son possessed such vast wealth. And the people who came to the Sultan's palace to witness the fêtes of 'Ala-ed-Din, when they saw his new palace and the beauty of the building, marvelled greatly how a splendid palace like that could be finished in a single night. And they fell to blessing 'Ala-ed-Din, and saying: "God give him enjoyment! By Allah, verily he deserveth it! God bless his days!"

When 'Ala-ed-Din had finished the banquet he arose and took leave of the Sultan, and mounting, he and his memluks proceeded to his palace, to prepare for the reception of his bride the Lady Bedr-el-Budur. And all the people cheered him with one shout as he went: "God give thee enjoyment! God increase thy glory! God prolong thy life!" And a vast concourse accompanied him as far as his home, while he scattered gold amongst them. When he was come to his palace, he dismounted and entered it and seated himself on the divan, and the memluks stood attentive before him; and presently they brought him sherbets. After which he gave command to his memluks and maidens, eunuchs and all his household, to prepare for the reception of the Lady Bedr-el-Budur his bride. Now when it was afternoon and the air had become cool and the heat of the sun had abated, the Sultan ordered the troops and emirs of the state and wezirs to descend into the Meydan or riding-ground; so they all went down, and the Sultan with them. And 'Ala-ed-Din arose, and mounted with his memluks, and went down also to the Meydan. And he displayed his horsemanship, playing with the Jerid[2] in the Meydan, so that none could stand against him. He was riding a stallion the like of which did not exist among the horses of the purest Arabs. And his bride the Lady Bedr-el-Budur watched him from a window of her apartments, and seeing his grace and horsemanship, she fell violently in love with him, and almost flew with joy. When they had jousted round the Meydan and had each shewn what horsemanship he possessed, and 'Ala-ed-Din the best of them all, the Sultan proceeded to his palace, and 'Ala-ed-Din returned to his own.

And when it was evening, the nobles and wezirs came and took 'Ala-ed-Din and conducted him in procession to the bath called Imperial, which he entered, and was bathed and perfumed, and coming forth put on a dress more gorgeous than before. Then he mounted, and the guards and emirs rode before him, and escorted him in stately progress, while four of the wezirs surrounded him with drawn swords. And all the people, natives and strangers alike, and all the troops, marched before him in procession, bearing candles and drums and pipes and instruments of joy and revel, till they arrived at his palace, where he dismounted, and entering, seated himself. And the wezirs and emirs who were with him sat also; and the memluks brought sherbets and sweet drinks, and served all the crowd who had come with him in procession—a multitude past numbering. And 'Ala-ed-Din ordered his memluks to go forth from the palace gate and scatter gold among the crowd. When the Sultan returned from the Meydan and entered his palace, he forthwith ordered them to form a procession for his daughter the Lady Bedr-el-Budur, to escort her to her bridegroom's

[2] Javelin of palm.

palace. Thereupon the guards and officers of state who had taken part in 'Ala-ed-Din's progress, mounted, and the handmaids and eunuchs brought forth tapers and escorted the Lady Bedr-el-Budur in a stately procession till they brought her to her bridegroom's palace. 'Ala-ed-Din's mother walked beside her; and in front were the wives of the wezirs and the emirs and grandees and chief officers; and along with her were the eight-and-forty damsels which 'Ala-ed-Din had given her, each carrying in her hand a tall taper of camphor and ambergris set in a candlestick of gold inlaid with jewels. And they all went forth with her from the seraglio, men and women, and marched before her till they came to her groom's palace, when they took her to her apartments, and changed her dress and displayed her. And when the displaying was over they led her to the chamber of her bridegroom 'Ala-ed-Din, and he went in to her.

Now his mother was with the bride, and when he came to unveil her, his mother began to observe the beauty of the bride and her loveliness. And she looked at the chamber she was in, all sparkling with gold and jewels; and there were lustres of gold all set with emeralds and rubies. And she said within herself: " I used to think the Sultan's palace magnificent, but this chamber is unique. Methinks not one of the greatest of Emperors and Kings ever attained to its like, and I do not believe that all the world could make a chamber like this." And the Lady Bedr-el-Budur also began to look and wonder at this palace and its splendour. Then the tables were laid, and they all ate and drank and made merry; after which eighty handmaidens came before them, each with an instrument of joy and revel in her hand; and they stretched their fingers and touched the strings and evolved harmonious modulations till they rent the hearts of the hearers. And the Lady Bedr-el-Budur wondered the more, and said within herself: " Never in my life have I heard songs like these," till she left off eating and gave herself up to listening. And 'Ala-ed-Din poured out wine for her and gave it her with his own hand. And content and great rejoicing fell upon them, and it was a glorious night, such as Alexander, Lord of the two Horns, never spent in his time. And when they had done eating and drinking and the tables were taken away, 'Ala-ed-Din arose and went in to his bride.

And when it was morning 'Ala-ed-Din arose, and the treasurer brought him a splendid costly suit of the richest of the robes of Kings. And he dressed, and they brought him coffee with ambergris, and he drank; and then ordered the horses to be saddled, and mounted, and his memluks rode before and behind him. And he proceeded to the palace of the Sultan, and as soon as he had arrived and entered, the servants went and informed the Sultan of his arrival; who, when he heard of it, arose straightway to meet him, and embraced and kissed him as though he were his son, and seated him on his right. And the wezirs and emirs and officers of state and nobles of the realm blessed him, and the Sultan blessed and congratulated him. And he ordered breakfast to be brought, and they all breakfasted. And when they had eaten and drunk their fill, and the servants had removed the tables from before them, 'Ala-ed-Din turned to the Sultan and said: "O my lord, will thy Felicity deign to honour me this day to dinner with the Lady Bedr-el-Budur, thy well-beloved daughter, accompanied by all the wezirs and nobles of thy realm?" And the Sultan, being charmed with him, answered: "Thou art too hospitable, O my son." And forthwith he ordered the wezirs and officers of state and grandees of the realm, and arose and took horses, and they likewise, and 'Ala-ed-Din rode with them till they came to the new palace. And when the Sultan had entered and considered the building and its construction and masonry, which was of jasper and carnelian, his reason was confounded and distraught at this splendour and wealth and magnificence. And turning to the Wezir, he asked: "What sayest thou, O Wezir? Hast thou seen in all thy time a thing like this, or is there to be found among the Kings of the world such wealth and gold and jewels as we see here in this palace?" And the Wezir replied: "O my lord the King, this is a thing that is not within the reach of any King of the sons of Adam, and all the people of the world could not have built a palace like this, nor could masons construct such a work, except, as I said to thy Felicity, by the power of magic." But the Sultan

knew that the Wezir could never speak without envy of
'Ala-ed-Din, and wished to prove to the Sultan that all this
was not done by strength of man, but wholly by force of
magic. So the Sultan answered him: "Enough, O Wezir;
thou hast no more to say; and I know the reason of thy
speaking thus."

Then 'Ala-ed-Din walked before the Sultan till they came
to the upper kiosk, where he looked at the ceiling and
windows and lattices all set with emeralds and rubies and
other precious stones, and he was astonished and astounded
and his wits were confounded, and he was distraught in his
mind. Then the Sultan began to wander about the kiosk
and look at things which captivated the reason. And he
perceived the bay which 'Ala-ed-Din had purposely left
unfinished. And when the Sultan had examined it and
saw that it was not complete, he cried: "Woe to thee, O
bay, that thou art not perfect!" And turning to the Wezir,
he said: "Knowest thou the cause of the unfinished state of
this bay and its lattices?" And he replied: "O my lord, I
think this window is left unfinished on account of thy
Felicity hastening the wedding of 'Ala-ed-Din, so that he
had not time to finish it." At that moment 'Ala-ed-Din
had gone to his bride, the Lady Bedr-el-Budur, to apprise
her of the visit of her father the Sultan. But when he
returned, the latter asked him: "O my son 'Ala-ed-Din,
what is the reason that this bay of the kiosk is not complete?" And 'Ala-ed-Din replied: "O King of the Age, in
consequence of the hurry of the wedding I could not get
workmen to finish it." Then said the Sultan: "It is a
fancy of mine to complete it myself." "God continue thy
glory, O King," answered 'Ala-ed-Din. "So shall thy
memory be perpetuated in thy daughter's palace." Then
the Sultan ordered them to bring the jewellers and goldsmiths, and commanded that they should be furnished
from the treasury with all they wanted of gold and jewels
and minerals; and when they were assembled he bade them
complete what was lacking in the lattice of the kiosk.

Meanwhile the Lady Bedr-el-Budur came to meet her
father the Sultan, and as she drew near he noticed her face
was smiling; so he embraced and kissed her, and led her

into the kiosk, where all entered together. It was the time of the noon meal, and one table was prepared for the Sultan and the Lady Bedr-el-Budur and 'Ala-ed-Din, and a second for the Wezirs and lords of state and grandees of the realm and officers of the army and chamberlains and gentlemen of the guard.

Then the Sultan seated himself between his daughter and his son-in-law. And when he stretched forth his hand to the food and tasted it, he was filled with surprise at the viands and the admirable and savoury cookery. And before him stood eighty damsels, each of whom might say to the full moon: "Get up, that I may seat myself in thy stead!" And they all held instruments of joy and revel in their hands, and tuned them, and stretched out their fingers and touched the strings, and drew forth melodious strains, which would expand the heart of the sorrowful. And the Sultan was delighted. The moment was agreeable, and he was happy, and said: "Verily this thing transcendeth the power of Emperors and Kings." So they fell to eating and drinking, and the cup went round among them till they were satisfied; then fruits and sweetmeats and the like were brought and served in another apartment, whither they repaired and took their fill of these delights. Then the Sultan arose to look at the work of the jewellers and goldsmiths, and see if it resembled that of the palace. So he ascended to them and inspected their work and how they had progressed; but he perceived a strong contrast, and that they were unable to produce such work as the palace of 'Ala-ed-Din. They told him that they had brought all the jewels they could find in the [ordinary] treasury, but it was not enough. Upon this he ordered the Great Treasury to be opened, and gave them what they wanted; and [said that] if that were still insufficient, they might take the present which 'Ala-ed-Din had given him. So the jewellers took all the precious stones which the Sultan allowed, and they worked with them and again found that they had not enough, and were unable to complete half what remained unfinished of the lattices of the kiosk. Thereupon the Sultan commanded them to seize all the jewels which they might find among the wezirs and grandees of the state. So the jewellers took them all and continued their task, and even so there was not enough.

When morning came, 'Ala-ed-Din ascended to see how the jewellers had worked, and perceived that they had not completed half the deficient bay. So he immediately ordered them to take down all that they had done and return the jewels to their owners. So they undid it all, and sent to the Sultan what was his, and to the wezirs what was theirs. Then the jewellers went to the Sultan and told them that 'Ala-ed-Din had ordered them thus. And he asked them: "What did he say? What was his reason, and why was he not pleased that the bay should be finished, and why did he demolish what ye had done?" They answered: "O our lord, we have no knowledge at all, but he bade us demolish all we had done." Thereupon the Sultan called for his horses and mounted and went to 'Ala-ed-Din's palace.

Now 'Ala-ed-Din, after dismissing the goldsmiths and jewellers retired into his closet, and rubbed the Lamp, when the Slave instantly appeared, saying: "Ask whatsoever thou desirest, for thy Slave is in thy hands." And 'Ala-ed-Din said: "I wish thee to finish the bay that was left incomplete." "On the head and also the eye," answered the Slave, and vanished, but shortly returned, saying: "O my lord, that which thou didst command me to do is finished." So 'Ala-ed-Din mounted to the kiosk and saw all the bays were perfect. And whilst he was inspecting them, lo, a eunuch came and said: "O my master, the Sultan cometh to thee, and entereth the palace gate." So 'Ala-ed-Din went down at once to meet him. When the Sultan saw him he cried: "O my son, wherefore hast thou done thus, and wouldest not let the jewellers finish the lattice of the kiosk, so that an unfinished spot remaineth in thy palace?" And 'Ala-ed-Din replied: "O King of the Age, I left it imperfect only for a purpose; for I was not unequal to finishing it, nor could I wish thy Felicity to honour me at a palace wherein anything was imperfect. But that thou mayest know that I am not incapable of perfecting it, I beg of thy Felicity to inspect the bays of the kiosk, and see if there be aught unfinished there." So the King ascended to the apartments and entered the kiosk and began to look over it to the right and the left, but he found nothing whatever incomplete, but found all the bays perfect. And seeing this he was astonished, and embraced 'Ala-ed-Din and fell to kissing him, saying: "O my son, what strange doing is this! In a single night thou canst accomplish a work which the jewellers would fail to do in months! By Allah, I do not think thou hast a fellow or peer in the world." And 'Ala-ed-Din replied: "God prolong thy life and continue thy length of days forever! Thy servant is not worthy of such praise." But the King said, "O my son, verily thou art worthy of all praise, since thou hast accomplished a thing which all the workmen in the universe could not do." Then the Sultan descended and went to the apartments of his daughter the Lady Bedr-el-Budur to rest with her; and he saw that she was very happy at the state and magnificence that surrounded her, and after resting awhile he returned to his palace.

Every day 'Ala-ed-Din used to ride through the city with his memluks before and behind, scattering gold right and left among the people, and all the world, foreigners and neighbours, the far and the near, were alike drawn with love to him by reason of his excessive generosity and bounty. And he increased the provision for the poor and indigent, and himself gave them alms with his own hand; for which deeds he acquired great renown throughout the realm; and many of the grandees of the state and the emirs ate at his table, and men swore only "by his precious life!" And he went frequently to the chase and the Meydan and horse exercises and javelin jousts in the presence of the Sultan. And whenever the Lady Bedr-el-Budur saw him performing on the backs of horses, her love for him waxed stronger, and she thought within herself that God had been very gracious to her in causing to happen that which happened with the son of the Wezir, so that she was reserved to be the virgin bride of 'Ala-ed-Din.

Thus 'Ala-ed-Din daily increased in fair fame and renown, and the love of him grew stronger in the hearts of all the subjects, and he was magnified in the eyes of the people. At this time, moreover, certain of the Sultan's enemies rode down against him, and the Sultan equipped the troops to resist them, and made 'Ala-ed-Din leader of the army. So 'Ala-ed-Din went with the troops, till he drew near to the enemy, whose armies were very strong. And he drew his sword, and rushed upon the enemy, and the battle and slaughter began, and the conflict was sturdy. But 'Ala-ed-Din broke them and dispersed them, killing the greater part, and looting their goods and provisions and cattle beyond number. Then he returned triumphant after a glorious victory, and made his entry into his city, who had adorned herself for him in her rejoicing over him. And the Sultan went forth to meet him and congratulated him and embraced and kissed him, and there was a magnificent fête and great rejoicings. And the Sultan and 'Ala-ed-Din entered the palace, where there met him his bride, the Lady Bedr-el-Budur, who was rejoicing over him, and kissed him between the eyes. And they went into her palace, and presently the Sultan and all sat down, and the damsels brought sherbets. So they drank; and the Sultan ordered throughout the kingdom that they should illuminate for the victory of 'Ala-ed-Din over the enemy. And the chiefs and the soldiers and the crowd turned [their prayers] only to God in Heaven and 'Ala-ed-Din on earth, for they loved him exceedingly, because of the excess of his bounty and generosity and his fighting for his country, and his charge, and his rout of the foe. And thus was it with 'Ala-ed-Din.

But as to the Moorish sorcerer, when he had returned to his country, he spent all this time in lamenting the labour and trouble he had taken in his quest of the Lamp, and the more because his labour was fruitless; and the morsel had fallen from his hand just as it was touching his lips. And he fell to thinking over all this, and lamented, and cursed 'Ala-ed-Din in his exceeding rage, and at times he would mutter: " That this misbegotten boy is dead below ground I am satisfied, and I hope yet to get the Lamp, since it is still safe."

One day of the days he drew a table in sand and put the figures down and examined them carefully and verified them, that he might perceive and be certified of the death of

'Ala-ed-Din and the preservation of the Lamp, beneath the ground; and he looked into the figures, both "mothers" and "daughters," intently, but he saw not the Lamp. At this, anger overcame him, and he drew the figure again, to be certain of 'Ala-ed-Din's death; but he saw him not in the Treasury. So his rage increased and the more so when he ascertained that the boy was alive on the surface of the earth. And when he knew that he had come forth from underground and was possessed of the Lamp for which he himself had endured privations and labour such as man can hardly bear, then he said within himself: "I have borne many pains and suffered torments which no one else would have endured for the sake of the Lamp, and this cursed boy has taken it without an effort; and if this accursed knoweth the virtues of the Lamp, no one in the world should be richer than he." And he added: "There is nothing for it but that I compass his destruction." So he drew a second table, and inspecting the figures, discovered that 'Ala-ed-Din had acquired immense wealth and had married the daughter of the Sultan. So he was consumed with the flame of anger begotten of envy.

He arose that very hour, and equipped himself, and journeyed to the land of China, and when he arrived at the metropolis wherein dwelt 'Ala-ed-Din, he entered and alighted at one of the Khans. And he heard the people talking of nothing but the splendour of 'Ala-ed-Din's palace. After he had rested from his journey, he dressed himself and went down to perambulate the streets of the city. And he never met any people but they were admiring this palace and its splendour, and talking together of the beauty of 'Ala-ed-Din and his grace and dignity and generosity and the charm of his manners. And the Moor approached one of those who were depicting 'Ala-ed-Din with these encomiums, and said to him: "O gentle youth, who may this be whom ye praise and commend?" And the other replied: "It is evident that thou, O man, art a stranger and comest from distant parts; but be thou from ever so distant a land, how hast thou not heard of the Emir 'Ala-ed-Din whose fame, methinks, hath filled the world and whose palace one of the Wonders of the World hath been heard of far

and near? And how hast thou not heard anything of this
or of the name of 'Ala-ed-Din, our Lord increase his glory
and give him joy?" But the Moor answered: "Verily it
is the height of my desire to see the palace, and if thou wilt
do me the favour, direct me to it, since I am a stranger."
Then the man said, "I hear and obey," and proceeded
before him and guided him to the palace of 'Ala-ed-Din.
And the Moor began to examine it, and knew that it was
all the doing of the Lamp, and cried: "Ah! There is
nothing for it but that I dig a pit for this cursed son of
a tailor, who could not even earn a supper. And if the
fates aid me I will undoubtedly send his mother back to
her spinning, as she was before; and as for him, I will take
his life."

He returned to the Khan in this state of grief and
regret and sadness for envy of 'Ala-ed-Din. When he
arrived at the Khan he took his instruments of divination
and drew a table to discover where the Lamp was; and he
found it was in the palace, and not on 'Ala-ed-Din himself.
Whereat he rejoiced mightily, and said: "The task remaineth
easy, to destroy the life of this accursed; and I have a way
to obtain the Lamp." Then he went to a coppersmith and
said: "Make me a number of lamps, and take their price,
and more; only I wish thee to hasten to finish them." And
the coppersmith answered, "I hear and obey." And he set
to work at them and completed them; and when they were
done the Moor paid him the price he asked for them, and
took them and departed and went to the Khan, where he
put them in a basket. Then he went about the streets
and bazars of the city, crying: "O who will exchange old
lamps for new?" And when the people heard him crying
thus, they laughed at him, saying: "No doubt this man is
mad, since he goeth about to exchange old lamps for new."
And all the world followed him, and the street boys pursued
him from place to place and mocked at him; but he gain-
said them not nor cared for that, but did not cease perambu-
lating the city till he came under 'Ala-ed-Din's palace, when
he began to cry in a louder voice, while the boys shouted
at him, "Madman! Madman!"

Now by the decrees of destiny the Lady Bedr-el-Budur

was in the kiosk, and hearing some one crying and the boys shouting at him, and not understanding what it was all about, she ordered one of her handmaids, saying: "Go and find out who it is that crieth and what he is crying." So the damsel went to look, and perceived a man crying: "O who will exchange old lamps for new?" and the boys around him making sport of him. And she returned and told her mistress Bedr-el-Budur, saying: "O my lady, this man is crying: 'O who will exchange old lamps for new?' and the urchins are following him and laughing at him." So the Lady Bedr-el-Budur laughed too at this oddity. Now 'Ala-ed-Din had left the Lamp in his apartment, instead of replacing it in the Treasury and locking it up, and one of the maids had seen it. So she said: "O my mistress, methinks I have seen in my master's room an old lamp; let us exchange it with this man for a new one, to find out if his cry be true or false." And the Lady Bedr-el-Budur said to her: "Bring the Lamp which thou sayest thou didst see in thy master's room." For the Lady Bedr-el-Budur had no knowledge of the Lamp and its qualities, and that it was this which had brought 'Ala-ed-Din her husband to his present high station; and her chief desire was to try and discover the object of this man who exchanged new lamps for old. So the damsel went and ascended to the apartment of 'Ala-ed-Din and brought the Lamp to her mistress, and none of them suspected the guile of the Moorish wizard and his cunning. Then the Lady Bedr-el-Budur ordered an agha of the eunuchs to go down and exchange the Lamp for a new one. So he took the Lamp and gave it to the Moor and received from him a new lamp, and returned to the Princess and gave her the exchange; and she, after examining it, saw it was really new, and fell a-laughing at the folly of the Moor.

But he, when he got the Lamp and knew it was the Lamp of the Treasure, instantly put it in his bosom and abandoned the rest of the lamps to the people who were chaffering with him, and went running till he came to the outskirts of the city, when he walked on over the plains and waited patiently till night had fallen, and he saw that he was alone in the desert, and none there but he. Then he took forth the Lamp from his bosom and rubbed it, and immediately the Marid appeared to him, and said: "At thy service, I am thy slave in thy hands; ask of me what thou desirest." So the Moor replied: "I require thee to remove the palace of 'Ala-ed-Din from its site, with its inmates and all that is in it, and myself also, and set it in my country, the land of Africa. Thou knowest my town, and I wish this palace to be in my town, among the gardens." And the Marid slave replied, "I hear and obey. Shut thine eye and open it, and thou wilt find thyself in thy country along with the palace." And in a moment this was done, and the Moor and the palace of 'Ala-ed-Din and all in it were removed to the land of Africa. Thus it was with the Moorish sorcerer.

To return to the Sultan and 'Ala-ed-Din. When the Sultan arose in the morning from his sleep, in his affection and love for his daughter the Lady Bedr-el-Budur, he was wont every day when he was aroused from sleep to open the window and look out towards her. So he arose that day, as usual, and opened the window to look upon his daughter. But when he approached the window and looked towards the palace of 'Ala-ed-Din, he beheld nothing—nay, the place was as bare as it was of yore, and he saw neither palace nor any other building. And he was wrapped in amazement and distraught in mind; and he rubbed his eyes, in case they were dimmed or darkened, and returned to his observation, till at last he was sure that no trace or vestige of the palace remained; and he knew not how or why it had disappeared. So his wonder increased, and he smote his hands together, and the tears trickled down over his beard, because he knew not what had become of his daughter.

Then he sent at once and had the Wezir fetched. And he stood before him, and as soon as he came in he noticed the sorrowful state of his sovereign, and said to him: "Pardon, O King of the Age. God defend thee from calamity. Wherefore dost thou grieve?" The Sultan replied: "Perhaps thou dost not know my trouble?" And the Wezir said: "Not a whit, O my lord. By Allah, I have no knowledge of it whatever." Then said the Sultan: "It is evident thou hast not looked towards the palace of

'Ala-ed-Din." "True, O my master," replied the Wezir, "it must now be still closed." Then said the King: "Since thou hast no knowledge of anything, arise and look out of the window and see where 'Ala-ed-Din's palace is which thou sayest is shut up." So the Wezir arose and looked out of the window towards the palace of 'Ala-ed-Din, and could espy nothing, neither palace nor anything else. So his reason was amazed and he was astounded, and returned to the Sultan, who said: "Dost thou know now the reason of my grief, and hast thou observed the palace of 'Ala-ed-Din which thou saidst was shut?" The Wezir answered: "O King of the Age, I informed thy Felicity before that this palace and all these doings were magic." Then the Sultan was inflamed with wrath, and cried out: "Where is 'Ala-ed-Din?" He answered: "Gone to the chase." Thereupon the Sultan instantly ordered some of his aghas and soldiers to go and fetch 'Ala-ed-Din, pinioned and shackled. So the aghas and soldiers proceeded till they came upon 'Ala-ed-Din, whom they thus addressed: "Chastise us not, O our master 'Ala-ed-Din, for the Sultan hath commanded us to take thee chained and pinioned. So we beg thy pardon, for we are acting under the royal mandate, which we cannot oppose." When 'Ala-ed-Din heard the words of the aghas and soldiers, wonder took hold of him, and his tongue became tied, for he understood not the cause of this. Then turning to them, he said: "O company, have ye no knowledge of the cause of this order of the Sultan? I know myself to be innocent, and to have committed no sin against the Sultan or against the kingdom." They answered: "O our master, we know no cause at all." Then 'Ala-ed-Din dismounted and said to them: "Do with me what the Sultan ordered, for the command of the Sultan must be on the head and the eye." Then the aghas chained 'Ala-ed-Din and manacled him and bound him with irons and led him to the city. And when the citizens saw him bound and chained with iron, they knew that the Sultan would cut off his head; and since he was exceedingly beloved of them all, the lieges assembled together and brought their weapons and went forth from their houses and followed the soldiers to see what would be the event.

When the troops with 'Ala-ed-Din reached the palace, they entered and told the Sultan; whereupon he straightway commanded the executioner to come and cut off his head. But when the citizens knew this, they barred the gates and shut the doors of the palace, and sent a message to the Sultan. saying: "We will instantly pull down thy house over thy head and all others in it, if any mischief or harm come to 'Ala-ed-Din." So the Wezir went in and informed the Sultan, saying: "O King of the Age, thy command is about to seal the book of our lives. It were better to pardon 'Ala-ed-Din lest there come upon us the calamity of calamities; for the lieges love him more than us." Now the executioner had already spread the carpet of death, and seated 'Ala-ed-Din thereon, and bandaged his eyes, and had walked round him thrice, waiting for the King's command, when the Sultan looking out of the window, beheld his subjects attacking him and scaling the walls with intent to pull them down. So he immediately ordered the executioner to stay his hand, and bade the herald go out to the crowd and proclaim that he had pardoned 'Ala-ed-Din and granted him grace. When 'Ala-ed-Din saw he was free, and espied the Sultan seated on his throne, he drew near and said to him: "O my lord, since thy Felicity hath been gracious to me all my life, vouchsafe to tell me what is my offence." Then the Sultan said: "O traitor, hitherto I knew of no offence in thee." And turning to the Wezir, he said: "Take him and shew him from the windows where his palace is." And when the Wezir had led him and he had looked out of the window in the direction of his palace, he found the site bare as it was before he built his palace thereon; and he saw never a vestige of the palace at all. So he was amazed and bewildered and knew not what had happened. And when he returned, the King asked him: "What hast thou seen? Where is thy palace, and where is my daughter, the kernel of my heart, my only child, than whom I have none other?" And 'Ala-ed-Din answered: "O King of the Age, I know not at all, nor what this is that hath occurred." Then said the Sultan: "Know, O 'Ala-ed-Din, that I have pardoned thee in order that thou mayest go and look into this matter and search for my daughter for me; and do not present thyself without her; for if thou bringest her not, by my life I will cut off thy head." And 'Ala-ed-Din replied: "I hear and obey, O King of the Age. Only grant me a delay of forty days, and then if I do not bring her, cut off my head and do what thou wilt." And the Sultan answered: "I grant thee a delay of forty days, as thou askest, but think not to escape from my hand, for I would bring thee back even if thou wert up in the clouds instead of on the face of the earth." "O my lord the Sultan," said 'Ala-ed-Din, "as I told thy Felicity, if I fail to bring her at the appointed time, I will come and have my head cut off."

Now when all the people and citizens saw that 'Ala-ed-Din was released, they rejoiced with exceeding joy and were glad at his escape; but the shame of what had befallen him, and bashfulness, and the jealous satisfaction [of his enemies] caused 'Ala-ed-Din's head to droop. So he went wandering about the city, and was bewildered at the case and knew not what had happened to him. For two days he remained in the city, in a sorrowful state, knowing not how to find his wife and palace, while some of the people brought him food and drink. After the two days he left the city, and wandered about the desert in an aimless manner, and walked on without stopping till the road led him beside a river, where, in the heaviness of the grief that oppressed him he gave up hope, and longed to throw himself into the river. But being a Muslim, and professing the Unity of God, he feared God in his soul, and he stood at the river's bank to perform the religious ablutions. Now as he was taking the water in his hands, he began to rub his fingers together, and, so doing, he chanced to rub the Ring. Thereupon the Marid [of the Ring] appeared and said: "At thy service! Thy slave is in thy hands. Ask of me what thou desirest." And when he saw the Marid, 'Ala-ed-Din rejoiced with great joy, and said: "O Slave, I desire thee to bring me my palace and my wife, the Lady Bedr-el-Budur, in it, and all else that it containeth." But the Marid answered: "O my master thou askest a hard matter which I cannot do. This thing pertaineth to the Slave of the Lamp, and I am not able to attempt it." So 'Ala-ed-Din replied: "Since this thing is beyond thy power, take me only and place me beside my palace wherever it may be on the earth." And the Slave answered: "I hear and obey, O my master." So the Marid bore him away, and in the twinkling of an eye set him down beside his palace in the land of Africa, in front of the apartment of his wife. It was then nightfall, yet he espied the palace and knew it to be his. And his grief vanished, and he hoped in God, after hope had been cut off, that he should see his wife once more. And he began to consider the mysterious workings of God (glory to his omnipotence!), and how the Ring had cheered him, when all hope would have died had not God aided him with the Slave of the Ring. So he rejoiced, and all his tribulation left him. And as he had gone four days without sleep, from the heaviness of his grief and anxiety and excess of pondering, he went beside the palace and slept under a tree; for, as hath been said, the palace was amid the gardens of Africa outside the city.

That night he slept beside the palace under a tree in perfect repose, though he whose head belongeth to the headsman sleepeth not of nights save when drowsiness compelleth him. But for the space of four days sleep had deserted him. So he slept till broad day, when he was awakened by the warbling of birds, and arose and went to the river there, which flowed to the city, and washed his hands and face, and performed the ablutions, and said the morning-prayer. And when he had done praying he returned and sat under the window of the apartment of the Lady Bedr-el-Budur. Now she, in the excess of her grief at her separation from her husband and from the Sultan, her father, and the horror of what had befallen her from the accursed Moorish wizard, was wont to arise every day at the streak of dawn, and to sit weeping; for she slept not at all of nights, and avoided food and drink. And her handmaiden would come to her at prayer-time to dress her, and as fate had decreed, the girl had opened the window at that instant in order for her to look upon the trees and the streams and console herself. And the maid looked out of the window and discovered 'Ala-ed-Din, her master, sitting beneath the apartment, and she said to the Lady Bedr-el-Budur: "O my mistress, O my mistress! Here is my master 'Ala-ed-Din sitting under the window." So the Lady Bedr-el-Budur arose in haste and looked out of the window and saw him, and 'Ala-ed-Din turned his head and saw her, and she greeted him and he greeted her, and they were both like to fly with joy. And she said to him: "Arise and come in to me by the secret door, now that the accursed is away." And she bade the girl descend and open the secret door for him. And 'Ala-ed-Din arose and entered thereby, and his wife, the Lady Bedr-el-Budur, met him at the door, and they embraced and kissed one another in perfect bliss till they began to weep from excess of happiness. And when they were seated 'Ala-ed-Din said to her: "O Lady Bedr-el-Budur, before anything it is my wish to ask thee somewhat. It was my habit to put an old copper lamp in my apartment in a certain place. . . ." When the Lady Bedr-el-Budur heard this, she sighed and said: "Alas, my beloved, it was that Lamp that was the cause of our falling into this misfortune." And 'Ala-ed-Din asked her, "How did this affair happen?" And she told him the whole story from first to last, and how they had exchanged the old lamp for a new one. And she added: "The next day we hardly saw one another in the morning before we found ourselves in this country; and he who cozened us and exchanged the Lamp told me that he had done this by force of magic by the aid of the Lamp, and that he is a Moor of Africa, and we are in his town."

When the Lady Bedr-el-Budur had done speaking, 'Ala-ed-Din said to her: "Tell me what this accursed is going to do with thee, and what and how he speaketh to thee, and what is his will of thee." She answered: "He cometh to see me every day only once, and he would win me to love him, and marry him instead of thee, and forget thee and be consoled for thee. And he saith that the Sultan, my father, hath cut off thy head, and telleth me that thou art of poor people, and that he is the cause of thy wealth. And he blandisheth me with his words, but he never seeth in me anything but tears and weeping, and he hath not heard a kind word from me." Then 'Ala-ed-Din said: "Tell me, if thou knowest, where he keepeth the Lamp." But she replied: "He carryeth it always with him, and it is not possible to part him from it for a single instant. But once, when he told me what I had related to thee, he took it from his bosom and shewed it to me." So when 'Ala-ed-Din heard these words he rejoiced greatly, and said: "O Lady Bedr-el-Budur, listen. I propose to go out now and return after changing my dress. So be not surprised at it; but instruct one of thy maidens to stand by the private door till she see me, and then open it at once. And now I will plot how to slay this Accursed."

Therefore 'Ala-ed-Din arose and went forth from the palace gate, and proceeded till he met by the way a peasant, to whom he said: "O man, take my clothes and give me thine." But the peasant would not do so. So 'Ala-ed-Din compelled him and took his clothes from him and put them on, and gave him his own costly robes. Then he went along the road till he reached the city. And he went to the bazar of the perfumers and bought of them some potent benj, the son of an instant,[3] buying two drachms of it for two dinars. Then he returned along the road till he came to the palace; and when the slave-girl saw him she opened the private door. And he entered to the Lady Bedr-el-Budur, and said to her: "Listen! I wish thee to dress and adorn thyself and dismiss grief; and when this damned Moor cometh, do thou receive him with a pleasant welcome, and meet him with a smiling face, and bid him come and sup with thee; and shew him that thou hast forgotten thy beloved 'Ala-ed-Din and thy father, and that thou lovest him with vehement love. Then ask him for a drink, and let it be red wine; and, shewing all the tokens of joy and happiness, drink to his secret; and when thou hast served him with three cups of wine, so as to make him careless, put this powder in the cup and crown it with wine; and as soon as he drinketh this cup wherein thou hast put this powder, he shall instantly fall, like a dead man, on his back." And when the Lady Bedr-el-Budur heard these words of 'Ala-ed-Din she said: "This is an exceedingly difficult thing for me to do; but to escape from the profanation of this accursed, who hath afflicted me with separation from thee and from thy father, it is lawful to kill the

---

[3] I. e., which took effect in a moment.

wretch." Then, after 'Ala-ed-Din had eaten and drunk with his wife and appeased his hunger, he arose without delay or hindrance and went forth from the palace.

Then the Lady Bedr-el-Budur sent for her tirewoman, who attired her and adorned her and put on her handsomest dress and perfumed her. And whilst she was doing so, behold, the cursed Moor appeared. And when he looked at her in this array, he rejoiced greatly, and all the more when she received him with a smiling face, contrary to her habit; and his love for her increased, and he desired her passionately. Then she took him by her side and seated him, saying: "O my beloved, if thou wilt, come to me this night and let us sup together. Enough of sorrow have I had, and were I to sit mourning for a thousand years or two, 'Ala-ed-Din would not come back to me from the grave. And I rely upon what thou saidst yesterday, that my father slew him in his sorrow at my absence. Do not wonder that I am changed since yesterday; it is because I have resolved to take thee as my lover and intimate instead of 'Ala-ed-Din, for I have no other man than thee. So I look for thy coming to me to-night, that we may sup together and drink a little wine with one another. And it is my desire that thou give me to taste of the wine of thy native Africa; perhaps it is better than ours. I have with me some wine of our country, but I desire greatly to taste the wine of thine."

When the Moor saw the love which the Lady Bedr-el-Budur displayed towards him, and how she was changed from her former melancholy, he believed she had given up hope of 'Ala-ed-Din, and he rejoiced greatly, and said, "O my soul, I hear and obey whatever thou desirest and biddest me. I have in my house a jar of wine of my country, which I have kept laid up underground for eight years; and now I am going to draw sufficient for us, and will return to thee speedily." But the Lady Bedr-el-Budur, in order to coax him more and more, said: "O my dearest, do not go thyself, and leave me; but send one of the servants to fill for us from it, and remain here sitting by me that I may console myself with thee." But he said: "O my mistress, none knoweth but I where the jar is, and I will not tarry long away from thee." So the Moor went out, and after a little time returned with as much wine as they needed. Then the Lady Bedr-el-Budur said to him: "Thou hast taken pains for me, and I have suffered for thy sake, O beloved." And he answered: "Not so, O my eye; I am honoured in serving thee." Then the Lady Bedr-el-Budur sat with him at the table, and they ate, and presently the lady asked him for drink; and immediately the handmaid filled for her a goblet, and then filled another for the Moor. So she drank to his long life and his secret, and he to her life; and she made a boon-fellow of him. Now the Lady Bedr-el-Budur was accomplished in eloquence and refinement of speech, and she bewitched him by addressing him in a delicious way, so that he might become more in love with her. But the Moor thought this was sincere, and did not imagine that her love was feigned, a snare to kill him. And his infatuation for her increased, and he almost died of love when he saw her shew him such sweetness of word and thought; and his head swam, and the world seemed nothing in his eye.

When they came to the end of the supper and the wine had already mastered his brain, and the Lady Bedr-el-Budur observed it, she said: "We have a custom in our country, but I know not if ye have it here. Tell me if ye have or not." And the Moor asked, "What is this custom?" "At the end of supper," she replied, "for every one to take the cup of his beloved and drink it." And she forthwith took his cup and filled it with wine for herself, and bade the handmaid give him her cup, wherein was wine mixed with the benj. Now the maid knew what to do, for all the maids and eunuchs in the palace wished for his death, and sympathised with the Lady Bedr-el-Budur. So the girl gave him the cup, and he, when he heard her words and saw her drinking out of his cup and giving him hers to drink, thought himself Alexander the Great, Lord of the two Horns, as he gazed upon all these tokens of love. Then she said to him, undulating her sides, and putting her hand in his: "O my soul, here is thy cup in my hand, and my cup in thine; thus do lovers drink from one another's cups." Then she kissed his cup and drank it and put it down and came to him and kissed him on the lips. And he flew with delight, and resolved to do as she did, and raised the cup to his mouth and drank it off, without thinking if there were anything in it or not. And instantly, in a moment, he fell on his back, like a corpse, and the cup fell from his hand.

Then the Lady Bedr-el-Budur rejoiced, and the maidens ran and opened the door to 'Ala-ed-Din, their master, who came in, and went up to his wife's room, and found her sitting at the table, with the Moor lying in front of her like a dead man. And he drew near and kissed her and thanked her. Then rejoicing with excessive joy, he turned to her and said: " Do thou and thy slave-girls retire to thy apartment and leave me alone now, that I may arrange my plan." And the Lady Bedr-el-Budur delayed not, but went, she and her maidens. Then 'Ala-ed-Din arose, and locking the door after them, went up to the Moor and put his hand into his bosom and took forth the Lamp; after which he drew his sword and cut off his head. Then he rubbed the Lamp, and there appeared the Marid slave, who said: " At thy service, O my master. What wilt thou? " And 'Ala-ed-Din answered: " I desire thee to lift this palace from this country and bear it to the land of China, and set it down in the place where it was, opposite the Sultan's palace." And the Marid replied, " I hear and obey, O my master." Then 'Ala-ed-Din went and sat with the Lady Bedr-el-Budur, his wife, and embraced and kissed her, and she him. And they sat in company while the Marid carried the palace and set it in its place opposite the palace of the Sultan.

And 'Ala-ed-Din ordered the maids to bring a table before him, and seated himself, he and the Lady Bedr-el-Budur, his wife; and they fell to eating and drinking in all joy and happiness till they were satisfied. Then withdrawing to the hall of carousal, they sat and drank and caroused and kissed each other in perfect bliss. For the time had been long since they had enjoyed themselves together. So they ceased not till the sun of wine shone in their heads, and drowsiness overcame them. Then they arose and went to bed in all contentment. Next morning 'Ala-ed-Din arose and awoke his wife, the Lady Bedr-el-Budur; and the slave-girls came and dressed and arrayed and adorned her, while 'Ala-ed-Din put on his handsomest dress, and both were like

to fly for joy at their re-union after separation. And the
Lady Bedr-el-Budur was the more happy that day, because
she was going to see her father. Thus was it with 'Ala-ed-
Din and the Lady Bedr-el-Budur.

But as for the Sultan, after he had banished 'Ala-ed-Din,
he never ceased grieving for his daughter; and every hour
of every day he would sit and weep for her like a woman,
for she was his only child and he had none other. And as
he shook off his slumber, morning after morning, he would
go in haste to the window and open it and look where
'Ala-ed-Din's palace once stood, and his tears would flow
till his eyes were dry and his eyelids sore. Now that day
he arose at daybreak and looked out as usual, when, lo, he
espied before him a building; so he rubbed his eyes and
considered it attentively till he was sure it was 'Ala-ed-Din's
palace. So he ordered his horse instantly on the spot, and
when it was saddled he went down and mounted and went
to 'Ala-ed-Din's palace. And when his son-in-law saw him
coming, he went down to meet him half-way, and took him
by the hand and led him to the apartments of the Lady
Bedr-el-Budur, his daughter. And she, being very anxious
to see her father, came down and met him at the door of
the staircase in front of the hall on the ground floor. So
her father embraced her and kissed her, and wept, and she
likewise. Then 'Ala-ed-Din led him to the upper rooms,
and they sat; and the Sultan asked her of her state and
what had befallen her. And the Lady Bedr-el-Budur told
him all that had happened to her, and said: " O my father,
I did not arrive till yesterday, when I saw my husband.
And it was he who delivered me from the power of that
man, the Moor, the wizard, the accursed. Methinks on the
earth's face there is none viler than he. And but for 'Ala-
ed-Din, my beloved, I had not escaped from him, nor hadst
thou seen me again all my days. But heavy grief and sorrow
took possession of me, O my father, not only for my separation from thee, but also for the parting from my husband,
in whose debt I shall be all the days of my life, seeing he
delivered me from that accursed wizard." Then she began
to relate to her father all that had befallen her, and how the
Moor had cheated her in the shape of a seller of lamps,

exchanging new for old, and how she had thought this his folly and laughed at him, and being deceived, had taken the old lamp that was in her husband's room and sent it by a eunuch and exchanged it for a new lamp. "And the next day, O my father, we found ourselves, with the palace and all besides, in the land of Africa. And I knew not the virtue of the Lamp which I exchanged till my husband came and plotted a stratagem by which we escaped. And had he not helped us, the accursed would have possessed himself of me by force. But 'Ala-ed-Din, my husband, gave me a potion and I put it into his wine-cup, and I gave it him, and he drank and fell down like a corpse. Thereupon my husband, 'Ala-ed-Din, came in, and I know not how it was done, but we were carried from Africa to our place here." And 'Ala-ed-Din said: "O my lord, when I ascended and saw him like the dead, drunk and drowsy with benj, I told the Lady Bedr-el-Budur to go, she and her maids, to the inner apartments, and she arose and went, she and her maids, from that polluted place. Then I drew near to that accursed Moor and put my hand into his bosom, and drew out the Lamp (for the Lady Bedr-el-Budur had informed me that he always kept it there), and when I had taken it, I bared my sword and cut off his damnable head. Then I worked the Lamp and ordered its Slave to bear the palace and all therein and set it down in this spot. And if thy Felicity doubt my words, arise with me and look upon this cursed Moor." So the King arose and went with 'Ala-ed-Din to the apartment and saw the Moor, and immediately commanded that they should take the carcase away and burn it and scatter the ashes to the winds.

Then the Sultan embraced 'Ala-ed-Din and fell a-kissing him, saying: "Forgive me, O my son, that I was going to take thy life, through the wickedness of this cursed sorcerer, who threw thee into this calamity; but I may be excused, my son, for what I did to thee, since I saw myself deprived of my daughter, the only child I have, dearer to me than my kingdom. Thou knowest how the hearts of parents yearn over their children, and the more when they are like me, who have only the Lady Bedr-el-Budur." Thus the Sultan began excusing himself to 'Ala-ed-Din and kissing him. But 'Ala-ed-Din replied: "O King of the Age, thou didst nothing to me contrary to law, nor did I sin against thee; but all this arose from the Moor, that filthy wizard." Then the Sultan ordered that the city should be decorated, and they adorned it, and the rejoicings and festivities were held. And he ordered the herald to proclaim through the streets: "This day is a high festival, and let rejoicings be held throughout the kingdom for a whole month of thirty days, for the return of the Lady Bedr-el-Budur and her husband." Thus was it with 'Ala-ed-Din and the Moor.

Yet 'Ala-ed-Din was not wholly quit of that accursed Moor, although his body had been burnt and its ashes scattered to the winds. For this miscreant had a brother viler than himself, and even more skilled in necromancy and geomancy and astrology,—"two beans split," as the proverb saith. Each dwelt in his own region of the world, to fill it with his spells, his deceit, and his wickedness. Now it chanced one day that this brother wished to know how it was with the Moor; and he brought out his table and marked the figures, and carefully inspecting them, discovered that his brother was in the abode of the tomb. So he mourned, being assured of his death. Then he tried a second time, to see how he died and the place of his death; and he found that he died in China and had perished by the vilest of slaughter, and that his destroyer was a youth named 'Ala-ed-Din. So he forthwith arose and prepared for a journey, and travelled over plains and wastes and mountains a number of months, till he came to the land of China and the metropolis wherein 'Ala-ed-Din dwelt. And he went to the foreigners' Khan and hired a room and rested there awhile. Then he arose to wander about the streets of the city to find a way for the accomplishment of his fell design, of wreaking vengeance upon 'Ala-ed-Din for his brother.

Presently he entered a coffee-house in the bazar. It was a large place, and many people had gathered together there to play, some at Mankala, and others at backgammon, or at chess, and so forth. And he sat down there and listened to the people who sat beside him talking about a pious woman called Fatimeh, who was always at her devotions in a cell outside the town, and never came into the city except twice a month, and how she had worked a number of miracles. And when the Moorish sorcerer heard this, he said within himself: "Now I have found what I wanted. If it please God, by means of this woman I shall accomplish my purpose." Then he drew near to the people who were talking of the miracles of this old ascetic, and he said to one of them: "O Uncle, I heard you discussing the miracles of some saint named Fatimeh. Who is she, and where doth she dwell?" And the man answered: "Wonderful! how art thou in our town and hast not heard of the miracles of our Lady Fatimeh? It is plain that thou, my poor friend, art a stranger, since thou hast not heard of the fasts of this holy woman and her abstraction from the world and the perfection of her piety." And the Moor rejoined: "Yes, O my master, I am a foreigner, and only yesternight came I to your city; and I hope thou wilt inform me concerning the miracles of this good woman and where she hath her dwelling, for I have fallen into trouble, and my intention is to go to her, and ask for her prayers. So that perhaps God (honour and glory to him!) may deliver me from my trouble by means of her prayers." So the man told him about the miracles of holy Fatimeh, and her piety and the excellence of her devotions. And he took him by the hand and led him forth outside the city, and shewed him the way to her dwelling in a cave on the top of a little hill. So the Moor magnified his favour and thanked him for his goodness and returned to his place in the Khan.

As destiny had decreed, the next day Fatimeh descended to the town, and the Moorish wizard went forth in the morning from the Khan and watched the people thronging, and he drew nigh to see what was the news. So he saw Fatimeh standing, and all who had any sickness came to her, and were blessed by her, and asked for her prayers; those whom she touched recovered from whatever disease they had. The Moorish wizard followed her about till she returned to her cave. Then he waited till the evening had fallen, when he went to the shop of a wine-seller and drank a cup of wine. Then he went forth in search of the cave of Fatimeh the ascetic, and, arriving there, entered and saw her lying on her back upon a piece of matting. So he

approached, and sat upon her, and drew his hanger and
shouted at her; whereupon she awoke and opened her
eyes, and saw a man of Morocco with a drawn dagger
sitting upon her breast as though with intent to kill her. So
she was afraid and startled. Then he said to her: "Listen!
if thou utter a syllable or scream, I will kill thee outright
that very minute. Get up, now, and do all that I tell thee."
And he swore to her an oath that if she did what he told
her, he would not slay her. Then he got up from her, and
Fatimeh arose, and he said to her: "Give me thy clothes
and take mine." So she gave him her clothes and head-
bands and veil and cloak; and he said: "Thou must also
anoint me with what shall stain the colour of my face like
thy colour." So Fatimeh went inside the cave and brought
a pot of ointment, and took some of it in her palm, and
rubbed it on his face, till it became of the same colour as
hers. And she gave him her staff, and taught him how to
walk and what to do when he went down into the city; and
she put her rosary round his neck. Finally she gave him a
mirror, saying: "Look, now, thou art not different from me
a whit." And he saw himself as it were Fatimeh in very
deed, there as she was. But when he had attained his wish,
he broke his oath, and asking for a rope, which she brought
him, he seized her and strangled her with it in the cave;
and when she was dead he dragged her out and cast her
into a pit which was there outside the cave. After which he
returned to her cave and went to sleep till day broke.

Then he arose and went down to the city and stationed
himself beneath the apartment of 'Ala-ed-Din, while the
people gathered around him, for they were sure he was
Fatimeh the ascetic. And he began to do as she did, and
laid his hands on the suffering, and recited for these the
opening chapter of the Kur'an, and for those another
chapter, and prayed for others. And the crowding of the
people upon him and their clamour reached the ears of
the Lady Bedr-el-Budur, and she said to her maidens:
"See what is the news and what is the cause of the uproar."
So an agha of the eunuchs went to see what was the
matter, and returned, saying: "O my mistress, this noise
is on account of the Seyyideh Fatimeh, and if thou wilt so

order, I will bring her before thee that thou mayest be blessed by her." And the Lady Bedr-el-Budur replied: "Go and bring her to me, for I have long heard continually of her miracles and her merits, and I yearn to see her and be blessed by her; for people in trouble profit greatly by her virtues." So the agha went and fetched the Moorish sorcerer, disguised in Fatimeh's clothes. And when he came before the Lady Bedr-el-Budur, and looked upon her, he began saying his beads, and none there doubted that he was the saint herself. Then the Lady Bedr-el-Budur arose and saluted him and seated him beside her, and said: "O my mistress Fatimeh, I wish thee to stay with me always, that I be blessed by thee and learn of thee the paths of piety and devotion, and be thy disciple." Now this was a trick of this accursed magician, and he resolved to complete his treachery further. So he said: "O my lady, I am a poor woman, dwelling in the desert, and the like of me is not worthy to stay in the palaces of Kings." But the Lady Bedr-el-Budur answered: "Have no anxiety at all, O mistress Fatimeh. I will give thee a place in my house, where thou shalt worship and none ever disturb thee, and thou shalt serve God here better than thou couldst in thy cave." So the Moor replied: "I hear and obey, O my lady. I will not gainsay thy words, for the word of the children of Kings cannot be contradicted or disobeyed. Only I beg that my eating and drinking and sitting may be in my own room alone, where none may enter; and I do not require dainties, but each day vouchsafe to send me by thy handmaid to my chamber a piece of bread and a drink of water; and when I desire to eat let me eat in my room alone." The wretch resolved thus for fear lest he should lift his veil, when his affair might be foiled and he be proved a man by his beard and mustache. "O my mistress Fatimeh," replied the Princess, "be of good cheer; nothing shall be but as thou desirest. Arise now with me that I may shew thee the chamber which I mean to make ready for thy stay with us." So the Lady Bedr-el-Budur arose and took the wizard, who was disguised as Fatimeh the ascetic, and led him to the place which she had promised him to stay in, saying: "O my mistress Fatimeh, here

shalt thou live and this chamber is for thyself, where thou
shalt dwell in all ease and comfort and privacy." So the
Moor thanked her for her goodness and blessed her. Then
the Lady Bedr-el-Budur took him and shewed him the
lattices and the kiosk of jewels with its twenty-four windows,
and said: "What thinkest thou, O my mistress Fatimeh, of
this wonderful kiosk?" The Moor answered: "By Allah,
my daughter, it is wonderful and splendid, and methinks
there is none like it in the world. But alas! for one thing
which is wanting to its beauty and adornment." "What is
that, O my mistress Fatimeh," Lady Bedr-el-Budur asked,
"which is lacking, and what is this thing which would adorn
it?" And the sorcerer replied: "O my lady, all it lacketh
is that there should hang from the dome an egg of the bird
called the rukh; and were this hung, the kiosk would not
be equalled in the world." Then the Lady Bedr-el-Budur
said: "What is this bird, and where is its egg to be found?"
And the Moor said: "O my lady, the rukh is a huge bird
that lifteth camels and elephants in its claws and flieth off
with them, so vast is its strength. And this bird is found
chiefly in the mountains of Kaf; and he who built this kiosk
can bring thee one of its eggs." Then they ceased talking,
as it was the dinner hour; and when the maidens had laid
the table the Lady Bedr-el-Budur seated herself and invited
the accursed Moor to eat with her. But he refused and
retired to his own room, and there the slave-girls brought
him his food.

When it was evening 'Ala-ed-Din returned from hunting,
and his wife met him and saluted him, and he embraced and
kissed her. Then looking in her face he perceived a trace
of melancholy, and, unlike her habit, she was not smiling.
So he asked her: "What hath come over thee, O my beloved?
Tell me hath anything disturbed thy mind?" And she said:
"Nothing at all; but, O my beloved, I fancied that there was
nothing wanting to our kiosk; yet, O my eyes, if an egg of
the rukh were hung from the dome there would not be its
equal in the universe." And 'Ala-ed-Din said: "And for this
thou art sad! when it is as easy as possible to me. So be of
good cheer, and whatsoever thou dost want, only inform me
of it, and I will bring it from the bowels of the earth in an

instant." Then, after cheering her, he retired to his chamber and took the Lamp and rubbed it, and immediately the Marid appeared and said: "Ask what thou desirest." And 'Ala-ed-Din replied: "I wish thee to bring me an egg of the rukh to hang from the dome of the kiosk." But when the Marid heard these words his face became terrible, and he was wroth, and shouted with a tremendous voice: "O hinderer of good deeds, is it not enough for thee that I and all the slaves of the Lamp are at thy service, but thou wishest, moreover, that I bring thee our Lady for thy amusement, to hang her up in the dome of thy kiosk to please thee and thy wife? By God, ye both deserve to be burnt to ashes this instant and scattered to the winds; but as ye were ignorant of this, not knowing its meaning, I pardon you, since ye are innocent. The insult cometh from the accursed magician, brother of the Moorish sorcerer, who pretendeth to be Fatimeh the ascetic, after putting on her dress and slaying her in her cave. And he is come to kill thee in revenge for his brother; and he it was who made thy wife demand this thing of me." Then the Marid vanished. But when 'Ala-ed-Din heard his words his faculties departed and his limbs shook at the Marid's fearful shout. But he plucked up resolution, and went forth from his chamber to his wife's apartments, where he pretended that his head ached, for he knew that Fatimeh was renowned for the mystery of curing all aches. When the Lady Bedr-el-Budur saw him putting his hand to his head and complaining of pain, she asked him the cause, and he answered: "I know not, except that my head aches badly." So she instantly sent for Fatimeh, that she might lay her hand upon his head. And 'Ala-ed-Din said, "Who is Fatimeh?" And she told him how she had established Fatimeh the ascetic in the palace. So the slave-girls went and brought the accursed Moor. And 'Ala-ed-Din rose to him; and, shewing that he knew nothing of the trick, saluted him as though he were saluting Fatimeh the ascetic, and kissed the hem of his gown, and welcomed him, and said, "O my mistress Fatimeh, I hope thou wilt do me a favour, since I have heard of thy success in curing sickness; and I have a violent pain in my head." Then the accursed Moor hardly believed these words, for it was just what he wanted;

but he approached 'Ala-ed-Din to lay his hand on his head and cure his pain. And he laid one hand on him, and putting the other under his dress drew forth a dagger to kill him. But 'Ala-ed-Din was watching him, and waited till he had bared the dagger, when he seized him and took the dagger and plunged it into his heart.

When the Lady Bedr-el-Budur saw him, she screamed and said: "What hath Fatimeh the ascetic done that thou shouldst place this awful burden of her blood upon thy soul? Dost thou not fear God, that thou slayest Fatimeh, a holy woman, whose miracles are famous?" And 'Ala-ed-Din said: "I have not killed Fatimeh, but he whom I killed first killed Fatimeh, and this is the brother of the cursed Moorish sorcerer who seized thee and removed thy palace to Africa by his spells. And this accursed brother of his came to this country, and contrived this trick, and slew Fatimeh and assumed her dress, only to wreak vengeance upon me for his brother's blood. And he it was who made thee ask for the rukh's egg, that it might cause my destruction. And if thou doubtest me, come and look at him I slew." Then 'Ala-ed-Din lifted the veil of the Moor, and the Lady Bedr-el-Budur looked and saw a man with a beard all over his face. Then she understood the truth, and said to 'Ala-ed-Din: "O my beloved, twice have I brought thee in peril of death!" But he replied: "No harm is done, O Lady Bedr-el-Budur. Blessing on thine eyes! I accept all that cometh from thee with perfect delight." And the Lady Bedr-el-Budur, when she heard these words, hastened and embraced and kissed him, saying: "O my beloved, all this is my love for thee, and I knew nothing; and I treasure thy love." And he kissed her and pressed her to his bosom, and their love grew stronger.

Now at that moment the Sultan appeared, and they told him all that had befallen from the brother of the Moorish sorcerer. And they looked at him, and he was dead. So the Sultan ordered that he should be burnt and his ashes scattered to the winds, like his brother's. But 'Ala-ed-Din abode with his wife, the Lady Bedr-el-Budur, in all content and happiness and escaped all danger. And after a time the Sultan died, and 'Ala-ed-Din sat on the royal throne and ruled and administered justice to the subjects, and all the people loved him, and he lived with his wife, the Lady Bedr-el-Budur, in perfect peace and happiness, till they were visited by the terminator of delights and the separator of companions.

THE STORY OF 'ALI BABA AND THE FORTY THIEVES

IN former days there lived in a town of Persia two brothers, one named Kasim, and the other 'Ali Baba. Their father divided a small inheritance equally between them. Kasim married a rich wife, and became a wealthy merchant. 'Ali Baba married a woman as poor as himself, and lived by cutting wood and bringing it upon three asses into the town to sell.

One day, when 'Ali Baba was in the forest, and had just cut wood enough to load his asses, he saw at a distance a great cloud of dust approaching him. He observed it with attention, and distinguished soon after a body of horsemen, whom he suspected to be robbers. He determined to leave his asses in order to save himself; so climbed up a large tree, planted on a high rock, the branches of which were thick enough to conceal him, and yet enabled him to see all that passed without being discovered.

The troop, to the number of forty, well mounted and armed, came to the foot of the rock on which the tree stood, and there dismounted. Every man unbridled his horse, tied him to some shrub, and hung about his neck a bag of corn which they carried behind them. Then each took off his saddle-bag, which from its weight seemed to 'Ali Baba to be full of gold and silver. One, whom he took to be their captain, came under the tree in which he was concealed, and making his way through some shrubs, pronounced the words: "Open, Simsim!"[4] A door opened in the rock; and after he had made all his troop enter before him, he followed them, when the door shut again of itself.

The robbers stayed some time within the rock, during

[4] This talismanic word, though it is the Arabic name of sesamè (*Sesamum orientale*, a plant producing oil-grain much used in the East), must have some other meaning. A German folk-tale, "Simeliberg," beginning in something of the same way with the magical opening of a rock, has the phrase "Open *Simsi*," which the Grimms explain as an old German word for "mountain" (Hartland, Inst. Folklore Congress, 1891). There is nothing to prove that 'Ali Baba is not a European folk-tale turned into Arabic by Galland's Syrian munshi.

which 'Ali Baba, fearful of being caught, remained in the tree.

At last the door opened again, and as the captain went in last, so he came out first, and stood to see them all pass by him; when 'Ali Baba heard him make the door close by pronouncing the words: "Shut, Simsim!" Every man at once went and bridled his horse, fastened his wallet, and mounted again; and when the captain saw them all ready, he put himself at their head, and returned the way they had come.

'Ali Baba followed them with his eyes as far as he could see them, and afterward waited a long time before he descended. Remembering the words the captain of the robbers used to cause the door to open and shut, he wished to try if his pronouncing them would have the same effect. Accordingly he went among the shrubs, and, perceiving the door concealed behind them, stood before it, and said, "Open, Simsim!" Whereupon the door instantly flew wide open.

Now 'Ali Baba expected a dark, dismal cavern, but was surprised to see a well-lighted and spacious chamber, lighted from an opening at the top of the rock, and filled with all sorts of provisions, rich bales of silk, embroideries, and valuable tissues, piled upon one another, gold and silver ingots in great heaps, and money in bags. The sight of all these riches made him suppose that this cave must have been occupied for ages by robbers, who had succeeded one another.

'Ali Baba went boldly into the cave, and collected as much of the gold coin, which was in bags, as his three asses could carry. When he had loaded them with the bags, he laid wood over them so that they could not be seen. Then he stood before the door, and pronouncing the words, "Shut, Simsim!" the door closed of itself; and he made the best of his way to the town.

When he got home, he drove his asses into a little yard, shut the gates carefully, threw off the wood that covered the panniers, carried the bags into his house, and ranged them in order before his wife. He then emptied the bags, which raised such a heap of gold as dazzled his wife's eyes, and then he told her the whole adventure from beginning to end, and, above all, recommended her to keep it secret.

The wife rejoiced greatly at their good fortune, and would count all the gold piece by piece. "Wifey," replied 'Ali Baba, "you do not know what you undertake, when you pretend to count the money; you will never have done. I will dig a hole, and bury it. There is no time to be lost." "You are in the right, husband," replied she, "but let us know, as nigh as possible, how much we have. I will borrow a small measure, and measure it, while you dig the hole."

So the wife ran to her brother-in-law Kasim, who lived hard by, and addressing herself to his wife, desired her to lend her a measure for a little while. The sister-in-law did so, but as she knew 'Ali Baba's poverty, she was curious to know what sort of grain his wife wanted to measure, and artfully put some suet at the bottom of the measure.

'Ali Baba's wife went home, set the measure upon the heap of gold, filled it, and emptied it often upon the divan, till she had done, when she was very well satisfied to find the number of measures amounted to so many as they did, and went to tell her husband, who had almost finished digging the hole. While 'Ali Baba was burying the gold, his wife carried the measure back again to her sister-in-law, but without taking notice that a piece of gold had stuck to the bottom. "Sister," said she, giving it to her again, "you see that I have not kept your measure long. I am obliged to you for it, and return it with thanks."

As soon as she was gone, Kasim's wife looked at the bottom of the measure, and was amazed to find a piece of gold sticking to it. Envy immediately possessed her breast. "What!" said she, "has 'Ali Baba gold so plentiful as to measure it? Whence has he all this wealth?"

Kasim, her husband, was at his shop. When he came home, his wife said to him: "Kasim, I know you think yourself rich, but 'Ali Baba is infinitely richer than you. He does not count his money, he measures it." Then she told him the stratagem she had used to make the discovery, and shewed him the piece of money, which was so old that they could not tell in what prince's reign it was coined.

Now Kasim, after he had married the rich widow, had never treated 'Ali Baba as a brother, but neglected him;

and now, instead of being pleased, he conceived a base envy at his brother's prosperity. He could not sleep all that night, and went to him in the morning before sunrise. " 'Ali Baba," said he, "I am surprised at you; you pretend to be miserably poor, and yet you measure gold. My wife found this at the bottom of the measure you borrowed yesterday."

By this discourse, 'Ali Baba perceived that Kasim and his wife, through his own wife's folly, knew what they had so much reason to conceal; but what was done could not be undone. Therefore, without showing the least surprise or trouble, he confessed all, and offered his brother part of his treasure to keep the secret.

Kasim rose the next morning long before the sun, and set out for the forest with ten mules bearing great chests, which he intended to fill, and followed the road which 'Ali Baba had indicated. He was not long before he reached the rock, and found the place, by the tree and other marks which his brother had given him. When he reached the entrance of the cavern, he pronounced the words, "Open Simsim!" The door immediately opened, and when he was in, closed upon him. In examining the cave, he was rejoiced to find much more riches than he had expected. He quickly laid as many bags of gold as he could carry at the door of the cavern; but his thoughts were so full of the great riches he should possess, that he could not think of the word to make it open, but instead of "Simsim," said, "Open, Barley!" and was much amazed to find that the door remained fast shut. He named several sorts of grain, but still the door would not open, and the more he endeavoured to remember the word "Simsim," the more his memory was confounded, and he had as much forgotten it as if he had never heard it mentioned. He threw down the bags he had loaded himself with, and walked distractedly up and down the cave, without having any regard to the riches around him.

About noon the robbers visited their cave. At some distance they saw Kasim's mules straggling about the rock, with great chests on their backs. Alarmed at this, they galloped full speed to the cave. They drove away the mules, who strayed through the forest so far, that they were soon out of sight, and then, with naked sabres in their hands,

Baba Mustafa went with Marjaneh, who, after she had bound his eyes with a handkerchief at the place she had mentioned, conveyed him to her deceased master's house, and never uncovered his eyes till he had entered the room where she had put the corpse together. "Baba Mustafa," said she, "you must make haste and sew the parts of this body together; and when you have done, I will give you another piece of gold."

After Baba Mustafa had finished his task, she blindfolded him again, gave him the third piece of gold as she had promised, and recommending secrecy to him, carried him back to the place where she first bound his eyes, pulled off the bandage, and let him go home, but watched him that he returned towards his stall, till he was quite out of sight, for fear he should have the curiosity to return and follow her. She then went home, and, on her return, warmed some water to wash the body, and at the same time 'Ali Baba perfumed it with incense, and wrapped it in the grave-clothes with the accustomed ceremonies. Not long after, they brought the bier, and the Imam and the other ministers of the mosque arrived. Four neighbours carried the corpse to the burying-ground, following the Imam, who recited the prayers. 'Ali Baba came after, and Marjaneh followed in the procession, weeping, beating her breast, and tearing her hair. Kasim's wife stayed at home mourning, uttering lamentable cries with the women of the neighbourhood, who came, according to custom, during the funeral, and, joining their lamentations with hers, filled the quarter far and near with sounds of grief.

Three or four days after the funeral, 'Ali Baba removed his few goods openly to his sister-in-law's house, in which he would in future live; but the money he had taken from the robbers he conveyed thither by night. As for Kasim's shop, he intrusted it entirely to the management of his eldest son.

While these things were being done, the forty robbers again visited their retreat in the forest. Great, then, was their surprise to find Kasim's body taken away, with some of their bags of gold. "We are certainly discovered," said the captain. "The removal of the body, and the loss of some of the money, plainly shews that the man whom we killed had an accomplice; and for our own lives' sake we must try and find him. What say you, my sons?"

All the robbers unanimously approved of the captain's proposal.

"Well," said the captain, "one of you, the boldest and most skilful among you, must go into the town, disguised as a traveller and a stranger, to try if he can hear any talk of the man whom we have killed, and endeavour to find out who he was, and where he lived. This is a matter of the first importance, and for fear of any treachery, I propose that whoever undertakes this business without success, even though the failure arises only from an error of judgment, shall suffer death."

Without waiting for the sentiments of his companions, one of the robbers started up, and said: "I submit to this condition, and deem it an honour to expose my life to serve the troop." He then disguised himself and went into the town just at daybreak, and walked up and down, till accidentally he came to Baba Mustafa's stall, which was always open before any of the shops. Baba Mustafa was seated with an awl in his hand, just going to work. The robber gave him good-morrow, and perceiving that he was old, said: "O Uncle, you begin to work very early. Is it possible that one of your age can see so well? I question, even if it were somewhat lighter, whether you could see to stitch."

"You do not know me," replied Baba Mustafa; "for old as I am, I have extraordinary good eyes; and you will not doubt it when I tell you that I sewed the body of a dead man together in a place where I had not so much light as I have now."

"A dead body!" exclaimed the robber, with affected amazement. "Yes, yes," answered Baba Mustafa, "I see you want to have me speak out, but you shall know no more."

The robber felt sure that he had discovered what he sought. He pulled out a piece of gold, and putting it into Baba Mustafa's hand, said to him: "I do not want to learn your secret, though you might safely trust me with it. The only thing I desire of you is to shew me the house where you stitched up the dead body."

"If I were disposed to do you that favour," replied Baba Mustafa, "I could not. I was taken to a certain place, whence I was led blindfold to the house, and afterwards brought back again in the same manner; it is therefore impossible for me again to do what you wish."

"Perhaps," said the robber, "you may remember a little of the way that you were led blindfold. Come, let me blind your eyes at the same place. We will walk together; perhaps you may recognize some part; and as everybody ought to be paid for their trouble, there is another piece of gold for you; gratify me in what I ask you." So saying, he put another piece of gold into his hand.

"I cannot promise," said Baba Mustafa, "that I can remember the way exactly; but since you wish it, I will try what I can do." At these words he arose, to the great joy of the robber, and led him to the place where Marjaneh had bound his eyes. "It was here," said Baba Mustafa, "I was blindfolded; and I turned this way." The robber tied his handkerchief over his eyes, and walked by him till he stopped at Kasim's house, where 'Ali Baba then lived. The thief, before he pulled off the band, marked the door with a piece of chalk which he had ready in his hand, and then asked him if he knew whose house that was; to which Baba Mustafa replied, that as he did not live in that neighbourhood, he could not tell. The robber thanked him for the trouble he had taken, and left him to go back to his stall, while he returned to the forest.

A little after the robber and Baba Mustafa had parted, Marjaneh went out of 'Ali Baba's house upon an errand, and upon her return, seeing the mark the robber had made, stopped to observe it. "What can be the meaning of this mark?" she said to herself; "somebody intends my master no good; however, with whatever intention it was done, it is advisable to guard against the worst." Accordingly, she fetched a piece of chalk, and marked two or three doors on each side, in the same manner, without saying a word to her master or mistress.

In the meantime, the robber rejoined his troop in the forest, and recounted to them his success; expatiating upon his good fortune in meeting so soon with the only person who could inform him of what he wanted to know. All the robbers listened to him with the utmost satisfaction, when the captain, after commending his diligence, addressing himself to them all, said : " Comrades, we have no time to lose ; let us set off well armed, without its appearing who we are ; but that we may not excite any suspicion, let only one or two go into the town together, and join at our rendezvous, which shall be the great square. In the meantime, our comrade who brought us the good news and I will go and find out the house, that we may consult what had best be done."

This was approved by all, and they filed off in parties of two each, after some interval of time, and got into the town without being suspected. The captain and he who had visited the town in the morning as spy came in the last. He led the captain into the street where he had marked 'Ali Baba's residence ; and when they came to the first of the houses which Marjaneh had marked, he pointed it out. But the Captain observed that the next door was chalked in the same manner, and in the same place ; and shewing it to his guide, asked him what house it was, that, or the first. The guide was so confounded, that he knew not what answer to make, but still more puzzled, when he and the captain saw five or six houses similarly marked. He assured the captain, with an oath, that he had marked but one, and could not tell who had chalked the rest, so that he could not distinguish the house which the cobbler had stopped at.

The captain, finding that their design had proved abortive, went directly to the place of rendezvous, and told his followers that they had lost their labour and must return to the cave. So they all returned as they had come.

When the troop was all got together, the captain told them the reason of their returning ; and presently the conductor was declared by all worthy of death. But as the safety of the troop required the discovery of the second intruder into the cave, another of the gang, who promised himself that he should succeed better, came forward, and his offer being accepted, he went and corrupted Baba Mustafa, as the other had done ; and being shewn the house, marked it in a place more remote from sight, with red chalk. Not long after, Marjaneh, whose eyes nothing could escape, went out, and seeing the red chalk, and arguing with herself as she had done before, marked the other neighbours' houses in the same place and manner. Accordingly, when the robber and his captain came to the street, they found the same difficulty; at which the captain was enraged, and the robber in as great confusion as his predecessor. Thus the captain and his troop were forced to retire a second time, and much more dissatisfied; while the robber, who had been the author of the mistake, underwent the same punishment.

The captain, having lost two brave fellows of his troop, was afraid of diminishing it too much by pursuing this plan to get information of the residence of their plunderer; and therefore resolved to take upon himself the important commission. Accordingly, he addressed himself to Baba Mustafa, who did him the same service he had done to the other robbers. He had not set any particular mark on the house, but examined and observed it so carefully, by passing often by it, that it was impossible for him to mistake it. Well satisfied with his attempt, and informed of what he wanted to know, he returned to the forest; and when he came into the cave, where the troop waited for him, said: "Now, comrades, nothing can prevent our full revenge, as I am certain of the house; and in my way hither I have thought how to put it into execution; but if any one can form a better expedient, let him communicate it." He then told them his contrivance; and as they approved of it, ordered them to go into the villages about, and buy nineteen mules, with thirty-eight large leather jars, one full of oil, and the others empty.

In two or three days' time the robbers had purchased the mules and jars, and as the mouths of the jars were rather too narrow for his purpose, the captain caused them to be widened; and after having put one of his men into each, with the weapons which he thought fit, leaving open the seam which had been undone to leave them room to breathe, he rubbed the jars on the outside with oil from the full vessel.

When the nineteen mules were loaded with thirty-seven robbers in jars, and the jar of oil, the captain set out with them, and reached the town by the dusk of the evening. He led them through the streets till he came to 'Ali Baba's door where he was sitting after supper to take the air. He stopped his mules, addressed himself to him, and said: "I have brought some oil a great way, to sell at to-morrow's market; and it is now so late that I do not know where to lodge. If I should not be troublesome to you, do me the favour to let me pass the night with you."

Though 'Ali Baba had seen the captain of the robbers in the forest, and had heard him speak, it was impossible to know him in the disguise of an oil-merchant. He told him he should be welcome, and immediately opened his gates for the mules to go into the yard. At the same time he called to a slave, and ordered him, when the mules were unloaded, to put them into the stable, and to feed them; and then went to Marjaneh, to bid her make a good supper for his guest. After they had finished supper, 'Ali Baba, charging Marjaneh afresh to take care of his guest, said to her: "To-morrow morning I am going to the bath before daybreak; take care my bathing linen be ready, give them to 'Abd-Allah, and make me some good broth against I return."

After this he went to bed.

In the meantime the captain of the robbers went into the yard, and took off the lid of each jar, and gave his people orders what to do. Beginning at the first jar, and so on to the last, he said to each man: "As soon as I throw some stones out of the chamber window where I sleep, do not fail to come out, and I will immediately join you." After this he returned into the house, when Marjaneh, taking up a light, conducted him to his chamber.

Marjaneh, remembering 'Ali Baba's orders, got his bathing linen ready, and ordered 'Abd-Allah to set on the pot for the broth; but while it was preparing the lamp went out, and there was no more oil in the house. So she took the oil-pot, and went into the yard; when as she came nigh the first jar, the robber within said softly, "Is it time?" Without showing her amazement, she answered, "Not yet, but presently." She went quietly in this manner to all the jars, giving the same answer, till she came to the jar of oil.

By this means Marjaneh found that her master 'Ali Baba had admitted thirty-eight robbers into his house, and that this pretended oil-merchant was their captain. She made what haste she could to fill her oil-pot, and returned into her kitchen, where, as soon as she had lighted her lamp, she took a great kettle, went again to the oil-jar, filled the kettle, set it on a large wood fire, and as soon as it boiled, went and poured enough into every jar to stifle and destroy the robber within. When she had done this, she returned into the kitchen; and having put out the great fire she had made to boil the oil, and leaving just enough to make the broth, put out the lamp also, and remained silent, resolving not to go to rest till she had observed what might follow through a window of the kitchen, which opened into the yard. She had not waited long before the captain of the robbers got up, opened the window, and finding no light, and hearing no noise, or anyone stirring in the house, gave the appointed signal, by throwing little stones at the jars. He then listened, but not hearing or perceiving anything, he began to grow uneasy, threw stones again a second and also a third time, and could not comprehend the reason that none of them should answer his signal. Much alarmed, he went softly down into the yard, and going to the first jar, whilst asking the robber, whom he thought alive, if he was in readiness, smelt the hot boiled oil, which sent forth a steam out of the jar. Hence he suspected that his plot to murder 'Ali Baba, and plunder his house, was discovered. Examining all the jars, one after another, he found that all his gang were dead; and, enraged to despair at having failed in his design, he forced the lock of a door that led from the yard to the garden, and climbing over the walls, made his escape.

When Marjaneh saw him depart, she went to bed, satisfied and pleased to have succeeded so well in saving her master and family.

'Ali Baba rose before day, and, followed by his slave, went to the bath, entirely ignorant of the important event which had happened at home. When he returned he was much surprised to see the oil-jars, and that the merchant was not gone with the mules, and asked Marjaneh the reason of it. "O my master," answered she, "God preserve you and your family. You will be better informed of what you wish to know when you have seen what I have to shew you, if you will follow me." Then she bade him look into the first jar, and see if there was any oil. 'Ali Baba did so, and seeing a man, started back in alarm, and cried out, "Be not afraid," said Marjaneh, "the man you see there can neither do you nor any one else any harm. He is dead." "O Marjaneh," said 'Ali Baba, "what is it you shew me?" "Moderate your astonishment," replied Marjaneh, "and do not excite the curiosity of the neighbours; for it is of great importance to keep this affair secret. Look into all the other jars."

'Ali Baba examined all the other jars, one after another; and when he came to that which had the oil in, found it prodigiously sunk, and stood for some time motionless, sometimes looking at the jars, and sometimes at Marjaneh, without saying a word, so great was his surprise. Marjaneh then told him all she had done, from the first observing the mark upon the house, to the destruction of the robbers, and the flight of their captain.

On hearing of these brave deeds from the lips of Marjaneh, 'Ali Baba said to her: "God, by your means, has delivered me from the snares these robbers laid for my destruction. I owe my life to you; and, for the first token of my acknowledgment, give you your liberty from this moment, till I can complete your recompense as I intend."

'Ali Baba's garden was very long, and shaded at the further end by a great number of large trees. Near these he and the slave 'Abd-Allah dug a trench, long and wide enough to hold the bodies of the robbers; and as the earth was light, they were not long in doing it. When this was done, 'Ali Baba hid the jars and weapons; and as he had no occasion for the mules, he sent them at different times to be sold in the market by his slave.

Meanwhile the captain returned to the forest with inconceivable mortification. He did not stay long; the loneliness of the gloomy cavern became frightful to him. He determined, however, to avenge the fate of his companions, and to accomplish the death of 'Ali Baba. For this purpose he returned to the town, and took a lodging in a Khan, and disguised himself as a merchant in silks. Under this assumed character he gradually conveyed a great many sorts of rich stuffs and fine linen to his lodging from the cavern, with all necessary precaution to conceal the place whence he brought them. In order to dispose of the merchandise, when he had thus amassed them together, he took a warehouse, which happened to be opposite to Kasim's, which 'Ali Baba's son had occupied since the death of his uncle.

He took the name of Khoja Hoseyn, and, as a new-comer, was, according to custom, extremely civil and complaisant to all the merchants his neighbours. 'Ali Baba's son was, from his vicinity, one of the first to converse with Khoja Hoseyn, who strove to cultivate his friendship more particularly. Two or three days after he was settled, 'Ali Baba came to see his son, and the captain of the robbers recognised him at once, and soon learned from his son who he was. After this he increased his assiduities, caressed him in the most engaging manner, made him some small presents, and often asked him to dine and sup with him.

One day 'Ali Baba's son and Khoja Hoseyn met by appointment, took their walk, and as they returned, 'Ali Baba's son led Khoja Hoseyn through the street where his father lived, and when they came to the house, stopped and knocked at the door. "This," said he, "is my father's house, who, from the account I have given him of your friendship, charged me to procure him the honour of your acquaintance; and I desire you to add this pleasure to those for which I am already indebted to you."

Though it was the sole aim of Khoja Hoseyn to introduce himself into 'Ali Baba's house, that he might kill him, yet he excused himself, and offered to take his leave; but a slave having opened the door, 'Ali Baba's son took him by the hand and led him in. 'Ali Baba received Khoja Hoseyn with a smiling countenance, and in the most obliging manner he could wish. He thanked him for all the favours he had done his son; adding withal, the obligation was the greater as he was a young man, not much acquainted with the world, and that he might contribute to his information. After a little more conversation, he offered again to take his leave, when 'Ali Baba, stopping him, said: "Where are you going in so much haste? I beg you would do me the honour to sup with me; though my entertainment may not be worthy your acceptance, such as it is, I heartily offer it." "O my master," replied Khoja Hoseyn, "I am thoroughly persuaded of your good-will; but the truth is, I can eat no victuals that have any salt in them; therefore judge how I should feel at your table." "If that is the only reason," said 'Ali Baba, "it ought not to deprive me of the honour of your company; for there is no salt ever put into my bread, and as to the meat we shall have to-night, I promise you there shall be none in that. Therefore do me the favour to stay."

Then 'Ali Baba went into the kitchen, and ordered Marjaneh to put no salt to the meat that was to be dressed that night; and to make quickly two or three dishes besides what he had ordered, but to be sure to put no salt in them. Now Marjaneh, who was always ready to obey her master, could not help being surprised at this order. "Who is this strange man," said she, "who eats no salt with his meat? Your supper will be spoiled if I keep it back so long." "Do not be angry, Marjaneh," replied 'Ali Baba. "He is an honest man; therefore do as I bid you."

Marjaneh obeyed, though with no little reluctance, and had a curiosity to see this man who ate no salt. To this end, when she had finished what she had to do in the kitchen, she helped 'Abd-Allah to carry up the dishes; and, looking at Khoja Hoseyn, knew him at first sight, notwithstanding his disguise, to be the captain of the robbers, and examining him very carefully, perceived that he had a dagger under his garment. "I am not in the least amazed," said she to herself, "that this wicked man, who is my master's greatest enemy, would eat no salt with him, since he intends to assassinate him; but I will prevent him."

When 'Abd-Allah had put the service of fruit with the wine before 'Ali Baba, Marjaneh retired, dressed herself neatly, with a suitable head-dress, like a dancer, girded her waist with a silver-gilt girdle, to which were hung a poniard with a hilt and guard of the same metal, and put a handsome veil on her face. When she had thus attired herself, she said to 'Abd-Allah: " Take your tabor, and let us go and divert our master and his son's friend, as we do sometimes when he is alone."

'Abd-Allah took his tabor and played all the way into the hall before Marjaneh, who, when she came to the door, made a low obeisance by way of asking leave to exhibit her skill. " Come in, Marjaneh," said 'Ali Baba, " and let Khoja Hoseyn see what you can do, that he may tell us what he thinks of your performance."

After she had danced several dances with much grace, she drew the poniard and, holding it in her hand, began a dance, in which she outdid herself, by the many different figures, light movements, and the surprising leaps and wonderful exertions with which she accompanied it. Sometimes she presented the poniard to one breast, sometimes to another, and oftentimes seemed to strike her own. At last, she snatched the tabor from 'Abd-Allah with her left hand, and holding the dagger in her right, presented the other side of the tabor, after the manner of those who get a livelihood by dancing, and solicit the liberality of the spectators.

'Ali Baba put a piece of gold into the tabor, as did also his son; and Khoja Hoseyn, seeing that she was coming to him, had pulled his purse out of his bosom to make her a present; but while he was putting his hand into it, Marjaneh plunged the poniard into his heart.

'Ali Baba and his son, shocked at this action, cried out aloud. " Ill-omened woman!" exclaimed 'Ali Baba, " what have you done to ruin me and my family?" " It was to preserve, not to ruin you," answered Marjaneh; " for see here," continued she, opening the pretended Khoja Hoseyn's garment, and shewing the dagger, " what an enemy you had entertained! Look well at him, and you will find him to be both the pretended oil-merchant and the captain of the gang of forty robbers. Remember, too, that he would eat no salt with you; and what would you have more to persuade you of his wicked design? Before I saw him, I suspected him as soon as you told me you had such a guest. I knew him, and you now find that my suspicion was not groundless."

Then 'Ali Baba, seeing that Marjaneh had saved his life a second time, embraced her. "O Marjaneh," said he, "I gave you your liberty, and then promised you that my gratitude should not stop there, but that I would soon give you higher proofs of its sincerity; which I now do by making you my daughter-in-law." Then addressing himself to his son, he said: "I believe you, son, to be so dutiful a child, that you will not refuse Marjaneh for your wife. You see that Khoja Hoseyn sought your friendship with a treacherous design to take away my life: and if he had succeeded, there is no doubt but he would have sacrificed you also to his revenge. Consider that by marrying Marjaneh you marry the preserver of our family."

A few days afterwards, 'Ali Baba celebrated the nuptials of his son and Marjaneh with great solemnity, a sumptuous feast, and the usual dancing and spectacles; and had the satisfaction to see that his friends and neighbours, whom he invited, had no knowledge of the true motives of the marriage; but that those who were not unacquainted with Marjaneh's good qualities commended his generosity and goodness of heart. 'Ali Baba did not visit the robber's cave for a whole year, as he supposed the other two, whom he could get no account of, might be alive.

At the year's end, when he found they had not made any attempt to disturb him, he resolved to make another journey. He mounted his horse, and when he came to the cave he alighted, tied his horse to a tree, then approaching the entrance, pronounced the words, "Open, Simsim!" whereupon the door opened. He entered the cavern, and by the condition he found things in, judged that nobody had been there since the captain had fetched the goods for his shop. From this time he believed he was the only person in the world who had the secret of opening the cave, and that all the treasure was at his sole disposal. He put as much gold into his saddle-bags as his horses would carry, and returned to the town. Some years later he carried his son to the cave and taught him the secret, which he handed down to his posterity, who, using their good fortune with moderation, lived in great honour and splendour till they were visited by the terminator of delights and the separator of companions.